Abraham Lincoln, President-Elect

Abraham Lincoln, President-Elect

The Four Critical Months from Election to Inauguration

LARRY D. MANSCH

McFarland & Company, Inc., Publishers

Jefferson, North Carolina, and London

LIBRARY OF CONGRESS CATALOGUING-IN-PUBLICATION DATA

Mansch, Larry D., 1958–
Abraham Lincoln, president-elect : the four critical months
from election to inauguration / Larry D. Mansch.
p.   cm.
Includes bibliographical references and index.

ISBN 0-7864-2026-X (illustrated case binding : 50# alkaline paper) ∞

1. United States— Politics and government —1857–1861.   2. Presidents—
United States— Election —1860.   3. Lincoln, Abraham, 1809–1865.   I. Title.
E440.5.M355   2005   973.7'092 — dc22   2004025790

British Library cataloguing data are available

On the cover: Lincoln on November 25, 1860, against
a background of inauguration day, March 4, 1861
(*Lincoln Museum, Fort Wayne, Indiana, # 0-40 and # 0-54*)

Manufactured in the United States of America

*McFarland & Company, Inc., Publishers
Box 611, Jefferson, North Carolina 28640
www.mcfarlandpub.com*

For Lincoln Joseph Mansch

Acknowledgments

Many people offered advice, encouragement and good humor, all of which I needed at various points along the way. For their efforts I gratefully acknowledge Tanya Bain; Patricia Carlson; Donna and Max Daniels; Kelvin Dodge; Bruce and Bridget Fuglei; Nik and Kate Geranios; Ann C. Kitchel, associate director of the Klutznick Law Library at Creighton University; Bill and Lynn Lamberty; Jean Luckowski; Scott and Liz Mansch; Phyllis Mansch; Mark and Julie McLaverty; Becky Mosbacher; Roger Norton; Joe and Elaine Novak; Fred Schuld; Velvet Stough; Betty Tanck; and Perry Tschida.

I am particularly grateful to Kim Bauer of the Abraham Lincoln Presidential Library; Tim Mosbacher, who prepared the maps and graphs; Timothy P. Townsend, historian of the Lincoln Home National Historic Site; Nicky Stratton of the Springfield Convention and Visitors Bureau; and Cindy VanHorn of the Lincoln Museum.

Most of all, I give my love and thanks to Kim, Bethany, Lincoln, Abigail and Madison, without whose encouragement I might not have begun this project, and without whose support I never would have finished.

Contents

States!
Were you looking to be held together by the lawyers?
By an agreement on a paper? Or by arms?

Away!
I arrive, bringing these, beyond all the forces of courts and arms,
These! to hold you together as firmly as the earth itself is held together.

Walt Whitman
Leaves of Grass
1860

Preface

Immediately after Abraham Lincoln was elected president, the nation began to fall apart. From his election in November 1860 until his inauguration four months later Lincoln was pushed, pulled, blamed and praised by all people, from all sides, as the country began its inevitable slide toward war. Southerners refused to see him as anything but a "Black Republican," an abolitionist poorly disguised as a moderate who was committed only to destroying their beloved slave system, and with it, their entire way of life. They found in Lincoln an excuse to carry out what they had long threatened: secession from the Union, proclaiming for themselves a sort of Declaration of Independence, Dixie-style. Northerners, meanwhile, frustrated by lame-duck president Buchanan's refusal to act in any meaningful way to avert the crisis, pleaded with Lincoln to speak out and reassure the country that his election, and his policies, brought not separation, but harmony. This he refused to do, insisting that the Republican platform set forth his position more clearly than he ever could. Politicians from both political parties worked feverishly to forge a compromise measure that might somehow satisfy everyone, but Lincoln all but dismissed their efforts. And many in Lincoln's own Republican party doubted that he could effectively lead the country through its time of crisis. Strangely, Lincoln chose for his cabinet the very men who had been his chief rivals for the nomination for president, giving them the chance to closely observe his style (which they deplored) and criticize his shortcomings (they found many).

Against this backdrop of turmoil Lincoln sought support from those he best understood: the common people who had elected him. Since he had not campaigned (acting upon the advice of his political managers, who correctly predicted that he could gain the presidency if he stayed home and allowed others to do the talking for him), Lincoln decided to travel to Washington indirectly and gauge the mood of the country, as best he could, from the back of a railroad car. And so in mid–February 1861, Lincoln and his entourage, which at various times included family, friends, advisors, politicians, newsmen and security guards, began a circuitous cross-country trip that would last 12 days, meander through eight states and over 1,500 miles, and most important, allow the president-elect to be seen for the first time by hundreds of thousands of people. Men and women, farmers and shopkeepers, mayors and governors, even a former president, all turned out to take a look at the man who had been selected to preside over a country that seemed bent on destroying itself.

Ignoring the formation of the new Confederate nation in the South, and traveling in the midst of repeated assassination threats, Lincoln would shake hands, deliver speeches, tell jokes— he would, in essence, campaign *after* his election — and attempt to convince those who saw and heard him that, if they would only stay the course, "all would yet be well." All would not be well, of course, but the generally positive reaction Lincoln received on his journey — there were notable exceptions—cheered him, at least temporarily. His appearances also undoubtedly helped persuade many young men to respond to his forthcoming call for volunteers to put down the insurrection, and to inspire the families who would sacrifice their sons in the name of the Union.

In examining the people and events that surrounded Lincoln as he prepared to become president I have utilized, in addition to better-known works, sources that are sometimes overlooked or underappreciated: newspaper accounts from across America (particularly from the cities Lincoln passed through on his journey to Washington); journals and diaries of his contemporaries (including his private secretary, John Hay); and correspondence (as contained in *The Lincoln Papers*, compiled by David C. Mearns in 1948). Lincoln's speeches are found in *The Collected Works of Abraham Lincoln*, edited by Roy P. Basler in 1953, and more recently available online through the Abraham Lincoln Association. These speeches appear here as they did in newspapers in 1860 and 1861; crowd reactions and Lincoln's occasional banter with individuals who called out to him are faithfully reproduced as well.

For all the momentous challenges that greeted Lincoln the president-elect — his burdens were "greater than those which rested upon Washington," he said — he never forgot that he was simply a lawyer from the prairies of Illinois. His heart was there. He was happiest there. Had he lived, he would have returned there. The relatively unadorned lifestyle that he forged for himself in Springfield would not change much after he moved into the White House, even as the complexities of the issues that he faced increased a hundredfold. In their wonderful biography of Lincoln the Kunhardts suggest that we "remember also that he was plain, funny, kind, withdrawn.... Everything about him was real." I have done my best to follow that advice.

Larry D. Mansch
Missoula, Montana
December 2004

Prologue

"Honest Old Abe of the West"

In the hot afternoon hours of Friday, August 3, 1860, dark masses of storm clouds began to build up in the western Illinois skies. By early evening the clouds had become a tornado, gaining in size and gathering momentum, rolling eastward toward Sangamon County and sending ominous lightning-flash warnings to all who watched it approach. At just past seven o'clock the tornado touched down on the capital city of Springfield, unleashing torrents of rain, raging winds and ear-splitting thunder — "heaven's heaviest artillery," said the Illinois *State Journal*— and in its fury "canopying the whole earth with gloomy blackness."[1]

The storm subsided within the hour, but the damage left in its wake was severe. Trees were uprooted, windows shattered, roofs of houses lifted and blown away. A good portion of Springfield's sidewalk system, a source of considerable pride to city officials who had worked for 10 years to implement the project, was wrecked. Some buildings were destroyed, including the three-story Withey's carriage manufacturing plant, where nearly 50 carriages and buggies were buried by collapsing brick walls, leaving some $15,000 in damages. William Crowder's stable on Washington Street was struck by lightning and burned to the ground, and workers scrambled in the midst of the deluge to put out the fire before it spread to other structures. The chimney of the Corneau & Diller Drug Store collapsed through the roof and into the store, demolishing the upper works inside. A good part of the roof of the Chenery House, one of Springfield's finest hotels, blew away, leaving at least some of the 200 or so guests unprotected from the elements. And the canvas-peaked roof of the massive "Wigwam," the brand new showcase of the local Republican Party, was carried away and lost.[2]

Any damage to the Wigwam was a serious matter to Republicans, for the structure held symbolic, as well as practical, significance to the party. It had been hastily constructed that summer on a vacant lot at the corner of Sixth and Monroe streets, and was intended to host Republican social events and political rallies in preparation for the election in November. It was modeled, on a slightly smaller scale, after its namesake, Chicago's Great Wigwam. That gigantic wooden two-story structure, designed to hold 10,000 delegates, spectators, and press representatives, had hosted the National Republican Convention in May, and there, after several ballots and three days of bickering, posturing, and empty promises of patronage, Springfield's Abraham Lincoln had been nominated for president.

Despite the havoc wreaked by the tornado, Springfield's Wigwam was formally dedicated the following night, August 4. Republicans gathered for a "Grand City Mass Meeting" to "hear speeches, inaugurate the new head-quarters and just see how it would look."[3] The monstrous "Lincoln cannon," specially cast at the foundry of A.S. Booth and designed to summon Republicans to the Wigwam for political events, rested near the entrance to the building. Next to the cannon stood a pole rising 120 feet in the air; at its top was attached a broom, symbolizing Lincoln's determination to sweep clean the corruption of President Buchanan's Democratic administration. Below the broom was a weathervane shaped like an axe, placed there to remind voters of Lincoln's rural background and his identification with the common man.

The Wigwam was circular in frame, 90 feet in diameter. Although its main section and upper level seating galleries were designed to hold 3,000 people, on this special occasion nearly twice that number packed inside. The interior was festively decorated with flags, banners and lights, the handiwork of "patriotic Republican ladies of the city," and it looked, opined the *State Journal,* "more charming than anything else except the ladies themselves."[4] Marble busts of George Washington, the Marquis de Lafayette, Henry Clay and Daniel Webster were displayed, although most of the crowd was more interested in viewing the flattering likeness of Lincoln. On the wall above Lincoln's bust a large banner quoted him: "We shall not fail; sooner or later the victory is sure to come."[5]

Enthusiasm mounted as the Young America Silver Band played rousing renditions of "Campaign Quick Step" and "The Railsplitter's Polka," and the local Glee Club harmonized:

> Then we'll up with our banners and shout, boys.
> And the principle boldly contest,
> And the foe we will gallantly rout, boys,
> With honest old Abe of the West.
> Then hurrah! For honest old Abe, boys
> For honest old Abe of the West.
> He will wind up the race in a hurry,
> And distance their bravest and best.[6]

From the podium at the front of the hall — carved roughly out of logs in honor of Lincoln, the Railsplitter candidate — local Republican Party president J.M. Allen introduced the main speakers for the evening. First came United States Senator Lyman Trumbull, perhaps the most influential figure in Illinois politics. A former Illinois secretary of state and supreme court justice, Trumbull was a moderate Republican who shared Lincoln's views on slavery: leave it alone in the South, but do not allow it to spread to the western territories. Trumbull's relationship with Lincoln went back 20 years. They had routinely been on opposite sides of many political issues of the day, arguing over the establishment of state banks, improvement of the internal canal and river systems, even American entry into the Mexican War. Still, the two men had managed to maintain a genuine, if distanced, friendship, as well as a mutual professional respect: when Trumbull was sued over financial irregularities while secretary of state, he retained Lincoln to defend him. Although Trumbull had initially backed William Seward and then John McLean for the 1860 Republican presidential nomination, he came to realize that Lincoln stood the best chance of winning the election. Since the convention he had wholeheartedly supported Lincoln.

Gaunt and serious, Trumbull looked older than his 47 years. Peering out from behind gold-rimmed glasses, he urged the Wigwam crowd to "stand by the old principles and practices under which this Republic flourished ... free institutions, free speech, free press, and freedom generally." Trumbull attacked Democratic presidential candidate Steven A. Douglas as "an imposter and a cheat." Douglas' campaign was based upon "popular sovereignty," the proposition that the people of new territories could determine for themselves whether to allow slavery, and Trumbull blasted the notion as "humbug." Does Douglas, asked Trumbull, "advocate the right of the people of Utah to introduce the abomination of Polygamy into a civilized community, the right of the people of Kansas to revive the African slave trade, or the right of some other Territory or country or town to license theft or murder?" Popular sovereignty could appeal only to the "unthinking," said Trumbull, "like the Irishman, who, when landed in this country, knocked down the first man he met, exclaiming, 'Be jabbers, I'm in a free country now, and have the right to do as I please.'" The Wigwam crowd roared in delight.[7]

The next speaker was Norman Judd, like Trumbull a former Democrat and now chairman of the Illinois Republican Party. Judd had few passions in life, chief among them development of the railroad system, the improvement of race relations in America, and the success of the Republican Party. He was one of the first prominent party officials to recognize Lincoln's enormous political potential, and was instrumental in organizing the Lincoln-Douglas debates of 1858, the events that thrust Lincoln into the national spotlight. Judd's history, however, of alienating members of his own party cost him the nomination for governor in 1860. Still, by virtue of his position on the national committee he had brought the Republican convention to Chicago, and was given the honor of placing Lincoln's name into nomination.

Short and stout, full-bearded and raspy, Judd waved an unlit cigar in the air as he played to the charged atmosphere at the Wigwam. He heatedly criticized the United States Supreme Court for holding, in the 1857 *Dred Scott* case, that Negroes were not to be considered full citizens under the Constitution. That decision had fueled the Lincoln-Douglas debates and remained a controversial and emotional issue across the country. The Supreme Court, said Judd, had demonstrated that it was "wholly devoted to the interests of the slave power." He knew that Illinois was particularly negrophobic; though the state was officially antislavery, most of its citizens believed that the black race was genetically inferior to the white. While blacks were not legally entitled to citizenship, they reasoned, neither did they deserve to be slaves. Many Republicans, Lincoln and Judd among them, positioned themselves on this high moral ground. They believed that the "servile race" ought to be colonized, or removed from American soil. This proposition made perfect sense to those present in the Wigwam, who believed it far more logical to remove the source of the national agitation than go to war over it.[8]

While both Trumbull and Judd admired Lincoln's dedication to party principles and appreciated his political appeal, they shared a disapproval for another speaker that evening—Lincoln's law partner, William Herndon. Herndon was a bit of an eccentric, the former mayor of Springfield, a self-proclaimed intellectual, and, for a time, a zealous temperance leader. Nine years Lincoln's junior at age 42, Herndon's skills as an attorney were in research, not in advocacy. He managed the law office and championed various social causes while Lincoln traveled the judicial circuit and tried cases. Most people, Herndon included, were mystified why the ambitious and charismatic Lincoln had selected him for a partner, but the partnership—and friendship—had lasted 16 years.

Herndon was a radical Republican whose strict abolitionist views placed him well outside the mainstream. When, for example, the deranged John Brown had led a raid on the federal arsenal at Harpers Ferry, Virginia, in 1859, with the hope of freeing legions of slaves and creating for them a safe haven, most observers saw the act as lunacy and felt justice was served when Brown was hanged. Herndon, however, predicted Brown would "live amidst the world's gods and heroes through all the infinite ages."[9] Herndon had long thought that the only way for North and South to resolve the slavery issue was through "bloody Revolution." Such reckless talk of war was at odds with the more conservative—and voter friendly—position of the Republican Party, and a source of embarrassment to men like Trumbull and Judd, and, to a slightly lesser degree, Lincoln himself. While he had once valued Herndon's political counsel, Lincoln ignored him as the summer of 1860 wore on. Stung by the secondary role he was forced to play in his partner's campaign, Herndon had responded by accusing Judd of using party funds for personal business, a charge that outraged Judd and drew Lincoln's stern admonition.

On this night and in front of many of his friends, however, Herndon's muzzle was off, and he took full advantage of the few minutes allotted him. He harshly criticized Stephen Douglas: "Let public indignation rest heavily upon his shoulders," he shouted. "Let public scorn burn to ashes what it lights to death." He compared slavery to Europe's old feudal system and to the Spanish Inquisition, and seeing civil war as inevitable asked, "why all men are not gods enough to embark in the eternal conflict between right and wrong?" Benjamin S. Edwards, a wealthy Springfield lawyer who was active in Douglas' campaign, also drew Herndon's wrath. The criticism was noteworthy: rarely did one member of the bar publicly chastise another in the name of politics. Herndon concluded with passionate praise of Lincoln. It was here in Springfield, he noted, where Lincoln had matured as a man and as a leader, and the city was to be congratulated for producing him. The partisan crowd stood and cheered in approval. If nothing else, agreed the Republicans of Springfield, Herndon knew how to give a speech.[10]

More speeches by party dignitaries followed, interspersed with the music of brass bands, rallying cries, and repeated cheers for Lincoln. It was past midnight when the Wigwam finally cleared and the satisfied throng dispersed. In all, the evening was judged a resounding success. "Nothing," it was said, "could exceed the enthusiasm and hilarity displayed throughout."[11]

Nothing, that is, except for another display of Republican fervor. For the following Wednesday, August 8, Springfield hosted an enormous political rally that drew national attention and served to eclipse all other events of its kind ever held.

The idea behind the extravaganza came from the leadership of the Illinois Republican Party. The party had restrained itself since Lincoln's nomination in May. In fact, most party leaders saw no need for Lincoln personally to campaign; that work would not appear dignified or presidential. Besides, any comments he made might easily be misconstrued by unfriendly press and contribute to the restlessness of southern states. Since May, Lincoln had only rarely left Springfield, and had not even bothered to meet his running mate for vice president, Senator Hannibal Hamlin of Maine.

This cautious approach appeared to be paying off. Recently the Democratic Party had hopelessly split—some of its delegates supporting Douglas; others supporting Buchanan's vice president, John C. Breckinridge of Kentucky; still others John Bell of Tennessee—and a Lincoln victory in November seemed reasonably certain. Now was the time, felt the Republicans, to show the rest of the country that their candidate was strong and that the enthusiasm of his supporters was unmatched. Here, in Springfield, was the opportunity to flex some political muscle and announce that the Republican Party, barely six years old in 1860, had arrived.

The "Great Lincoln Rally" was months in planning and heavily advertised in sympathetic newspapers across the northern United States; all "friends of freedom" were invited to attend and "give honest Old Abe a shake of the hand at his own home."[12] "No place is more appropriate for the assemblage of the hosts of freedom than at the home of one of her noblest sons," declared the Chicago *Journal.* "By all means let us meet and counsel together at the home of Abraham Lincoln."[13] An illustration of an elephant with marching boots on its feet appeared in the Springfield paper. "Clear the Track!" read the banners the animal carried, "We Are Coming!" It was the first use of an elephant as the symbol of the Republican Party.[14]

The advertisements worked: an estimated 50,000 people (some sources reported 90,000) descended on Springfield for the event. For three days prior to the rally all roads leading into the city were choked with carriages and buggies, and surrounding fields were dotted with campsites. The Great Western Railroad dispatched an extra 120 cars from all points east and west, and the St. Louis, Alton and Chicago brought in 60 more from north and south. At an average of 80 persons per car, these two lines alone carried some 14,500 Republican revelers into Springfield. City hotels took in twice their capacity in customers, and many homeowners offered spare rooms for rent. Restaurants scrambled to procure enough food for hungry travelers. Anyone who could not secure a room or a meal simply presented themselves at the Wigwam and their needs were met, courtesy of the Republican Party. In view of the staggering crowd, Springfield was determined that no mischief would undermine the celebration. The police department assigned an extra 50 officers for duty, a fact, warned the *Journal,* that "swindlers, pick-pockets and bacchanalians were advised to remember."[15] (Normally the force numbered just six, and those officers had to purchase their own uniforms; the city could not afford such an extravagance.)

The day's events began at nine o'clock, when an immense procession began to form at the Wigwam under the direction of Chief Marshal John Williams. A telegraph was established in the cupola of the statehouse, connected to 25 managers on the ground who positioned arriving delegations, bands, displays and floats. At 10 o'clock the Lincoln cannon boomed and the march began, following a winding route through the residential streets of Springfield to the fairgrounds west of town. Throngs of people lined sidewalks and assembled on porches and rooftops. Others viewed the procession from tops of telegraph poles or tree branches. Steamers, flags and banners "flung to the breeze in all directions, and the city assumed a holiday appearance."[16]

Leading the parade was a silver ball eight feet in diameter, rolled by four men and signifying the onward march of Republican principles. "The Republican ball is in motion," read the rotating banner. "Lincoln, Hamlin and the whole state ticket." Another banner followed which read, "The people mourn insulted laws, and curse Steve Douglas as the cause"; and "Westward the Star of Empire takes its way, We link on to Lincoln — our fathers were for Clay."[17]

The Springfield Wide-Awakes, a loosely organized but enthusiastic group of nearly 400 Lincoln supporters, had the honor of being the first delegation in the parade. Composed of young men between the ages of 14 and 22, Wide-Awake clubs had sprung up all over the northern United States in 1860; naturally, the Springfield contingent was particularly eager to show its zeal for Lincoln. Smartly outfitted in white pants, black hats and capes, the members carried oil-burning tin torches fastened atop poles (or "rails") and stepped lively, marching and countermarching in precision as the crowd whistled and shouted hurrahs. Every few blocks the Wide-Awakes marked time and sang a favorite theme song:

> Forward! forward! Is the word,
> The time is near at hand,
> When each stout heart must take his post
> Throughout this mighty land!
> The foe is strong, yet he must fall,
> If we united are,
> And boldly arrive to do our part
> In this most glorious war.
>
> Forward! forward! take no rest,
> Till the great struggle's o'er,
> Till freedom's foes their colors strike,
> And struck-be raised no more.
> Let freedom still maintain its own,
> And, rightly, conquer more,
> To spread the blessings of its sway
> From center, to the shore.
>
> Forward! forward! till the end,
> A glorious triumph gives!
> For this, we keep our courage up,
> For this, each freeman lives!
> Then now unsheathe the freeman's sword,
> Nor let your arm be still.

Till slavery knows a freeman's power!
Obeys a freeman's will![18]

The German Wide-Awake club followed, smaller in number but equal in enthusiasm. Placement of the group near the start of the parade was no accident, for Republicans were mindful of the importance of the foreign-born vote. They were followed by 39 other clubs and accompanying brass bands, many from Illinois and some from as far away as Milwaukee, Cleveland, St. Louis, and Hannibal, Missouri. In all nearly 15,000 Wide-Awake members tramped through the streets of Springfield.

The crowd took particular delight in the precision drill-steps of the U.S. Zouave Cadets of Chicago, a paramilitary group dressed in exotic costumes complete with feathered plumage. The Zouaves were led by 23-year-old Elmer Ellsworth, who was supposed to be working as law clerk for Lincoln and Herndon. This exciting summer, however, Ellsworth spent most of his time organizing and drilling the Zouaves, exhibiting their skills at parades and rallies in 20 cities throughout the North, and dreaming of battlefield glory.

Over 1,000 wagons and floats, pulled by horses, oxen and men, and representing dozens of Illinois counties, cities and towns joined the procession. The Republican Party wagon took the form of a full-rigged schooner, complete with prairie farmers dressed as sailors. The Springfield Woolen Mill decorated its wagon like a giant power loom, workers busily stitching an oversized pair of pantaloons for presentation to Mr. Lincoln. A banner on the side of the wagon read, "Protection to Home Industry." This entry was pulled not by horses or oxen, but by steam engine, a novelty that impressed the crowd. The Williamsville County delegation numbered over 500 people in 96 wagons. One immense wagon, drawn by 25 yoke of oxen, carried blacksmiths, shoemakers, wheelwrights, carpenters, tinners and railsplitters, all busily plying their crafts and showing support for the worker's candidate.

Forty-three men from Mechanicsburg County dressed as Indians and enacted the famed Boston Tea Party of old. "They acted their part well," said the *State Journal*, "and the deception was complete, many persons thinking they were the genuine Aborigines of the plains on a visit to their lost prairie homes. Their horsemanship was superb, and their conduct and general appearance gave universal pleasure."[19] The Cotton Hill entry was one of many that featured a log cabin on wheels. An old settler tirelessly split rails in front of the cabin, reminding the cheering crowd of Lincoln's humble backwoods heritage. Christian County sent 103 wagons, Scott County 200, Spring Creek 170 more. Once fully commenced the procession stretched an amazing eight miles in length.

One wagon from Chatham County carried 33 young ladies surrounded by 33 horsemen, representing each state of the Union. A smaller wagon representing the territory of Kansas followed closely behind, its banner asking, "Won't you let me in?" This particular delegation reached Lincoln's home at Eighth and Jackson streets at about one o'clock in the afternoon, and here the parade halted. A photographer had climbed to the top of Harriet Dean's house across the street and set up his equipment. Told this, Lincoln was obliged to step out onto his front porch and strike a pose in his white linen suit, surrounded by a throng of nameless admirers. Though

The Great Lincoln Rally, August 8, 1860 (the Lincoln Museum, Fort Wayne, Indiana # 0-34).

the six-foot four-inch Lincoln hardly needed it, he stood on a crate to tower even further above the crowd, and the moment was recorded for posterity.

By midafternoon the procession's last entry had arrived at the fairgrounds. Wagons and carriages were packed tightly at neighboring Tainter's Grove, and teams of stock were watered and rested at surrounding fields and pastures. Local confectioners Henry C. Myers and J.C. Hall, among others, served hundreds of sandwiches to hungry, and hot, parade participants. Whole steers and pigs roasted over open pits, and tubs of lemonade and ice water were scattered about the grounds. Vendors sold Lincoln-Hamlin buttons, ribbons, pendants and other souvenirs. Miniature log rails were a popular item, as were copies of Lincoln's official campaign biography, which sold for 50 cents.

Brass bands roamed the grounds, followed by hundreds of revelers. One song in particular was requested over and over, and to the tune of "The Old Grey Mare" the crowd sang:

> Ain't you glad you joined the Republicans
> Joined the Republicans
> Joined the Republicans
> Ain't you glad you joined the Republicans
> Down in Illinois.[20]

The party lasted all afternoon and into the early evening. Nearly 40 speakers, including Senators James Doolittle from Wisconsin and Schuyler Colfax from Indiana, U.S. Land Office commissioner John Wilson, and many other state and national politicians, filled the air with Republican rhetoric from five stands (there were so many speakers, and so many listeners, that speeches had to be given simultaneously.) Suddenly, while party dignitary Charles L. Wilson of Cook County was exhorting the crowd from the first podium, a tremendous cheer went up. Lincoln himself had been persuaded to make an appearance. Thousands of supporters rushed to his carriage, and a path for his exit had to be forcibly cleared. He was lifted on shoulders and carried to the speaker's stand, and after a deafening 10-minute ovation he began to speak:

> My fellow citizens: I appear among you upon this occasion with no intention of making a speech.
>
> It has been my purpose, since I have been placed in my present position, to make no speeches. This assemblage having been drawn together at the place of my residence, it appeared to be the wish of those constituting this vast assembly to see me; and it is certainly my wish to see all of you. I appear upon the ground here at this time only for the purpose of affording myself the best opportunity of seeing you, and enabling you to see me.
>
> I confess with gratitude, be it understood, that I did not suppose my appearance among you would create the tumult which I now witness. I am profoundly gratified for this manifestation of your feelings. I am gratified, because it is a tribute such as can be paid to no man as a man. It is the evidence that four years from this time you will give a like manifestation for the next man who is the representative of the truth on the questions that now agitate the public. And it is because you will then fight for this cause as you do now, or with even greater ardor than now, though I be dead and gone, that I most profoundly and sincerely thank you.
>
> Having said this much, allow me now to say that it is my wish that you will hear this public discussion by others of our friends who are present for the purpose of addressing you, and that you will kindly let me be silent.[21]

Though he had said almost nothing of substance the adoring crowd roared with approval, and once again it descended on Lincoln as he made his way back to the carriage. As he took his seat, however, some overzealous supporters climbed to the top of the carriage and fell through, nearly crushing him. Finally a friend maneuvered his horse next to the carriage and "slipped him over the horse's tail onto the saddle," and Lincoln was carried away from the bedlam to the relative safety of his home.[22]

By nightfall most of the crowd had drifted out of the fairgrounds and gathered again on the sidewalks of Springfield. The Wide-Awakes launched another march from the Wigwam, this one a magnificent torchlight procession that wound over a length of two miles to the public square. Many homes and buildings along the route were also lit brilliantly with candles and lanterns. All observers marveled at the spectacle; it was known ever after as the "grand rally of the banners of light." One correspondent wrote that the parade seemed, "in its blazing lights and glittering uniforms, like a beautiful serpent of fire."[23] As the Springfield Wide-Awakes reached the corner of Fifth and Adams they marched in place and again began to sing:

> O, what is all this noise about,
> This midnight confusion?
> 'Tis the Wide-Awakes have all turned out,
> and made this grand intrusion![24]

To the wild cheer of the crowd dozens of Roman candles were ignited into the air, and the "hissing and bursting blaze of fiery splendor … cast a lurid glare on the upturned faces of the excited thousands."[25] The scene, said the *State Journal*, "gave to the vicinity an emphatic title to the appellation of *terra del fuego*."[26]

Later that night the Wigwam was again jammed to capacity and beyond, hundreds of celebrants milling about outside in hopes of catching a part of the many speeches and songs that came from within. The celebration at the Wigwam, and in the streets and saloons of Springfield, lasted until dawn.

It seemed to take a day or two for Springfield to catch its breath. Never before, said the *State Journal*, had Springfield "been so completely surcharged with an electric current…. Hearts beating to the cadence of freedom for the oppressed, backed by tongues and lungs that made the very heavens echo with the glad acclaims of victory, rendered the scene one sublime, magnificent spectacle of triumph and joy." The Great Lincoln Rally was nothing short of a "political earthquake…. The numbers present and the spirit displayed, gave us convincing evidence of the ruling of a spirit which will insure us a glorious victory in November."[27] Most observers agreed that the celebration even outranked the legendary William Henry Harrison celebration

Abraham Lincoln, Republican candidate for president, and admirers (the Lincoln Museum, Fort Wayne, Indiana, # 0-34).

of 1840, famous for its "Tippecanoe and Tyler, too," and "Log Cabin and Hard Cider" slogans that caught the nation's fancy and propelled a most unremarkable man into the White House. Even haughty journalists from the metropolises of the East, who had grumbled about their dispatch to the western frontier outpost of Illinois, had to admit that Springfield put on quite a show.

Illinois Republicans were thrilled with the success of the rally and pleased with the favorable press coverage it received. Lincoln's secretary, John Hay, wrote that "superlatives grow tame and insipid in view of the facts," and was left only to quote the poet Walt Whitman: "I will not say it was this, I will not allege it was that—I will swear it was glorious."[28] The *State Journal* put it another way. "The prairies," it concluded, "were on fire for Lincoln."[29]

1

Sangamon

Abraham Lincoln lived in Springfield for nearly 25 years. Thus he was a bit dismayed to learn that only three of Springfield's 11 clergymen voted for him for president in 1860. It was not that he was a particularly religious man; indeed, while he held vague beliefs about the existence of God and the relationship between deity and man, and had often contemplated an afterlife, Lincoln claimed no organized denomination for his own and only rented a pew at the First Presbyterian Church to appease his wife. Rather, the ministerial vote disappointed him on a more practical, and political, level. If ordained servants of God were indifferent to the issue of slavery's expansion, he believed, they were hypocrites. "God cares and humanity cares," Lincoln complained, "and if (Springfield's ministers) do not they surely have not read their Bible aright."[1] The clergy's vote also showed that Lincoln was far from an overwhelming political favorite in his own hometown. He barely carried Springfield with 1,395 votes, only 69 more than Stephen Douglas. He did not carry Sangamon County, however, losing to Douglas by a tally of 3,598 votes to 3,556. It was small solace that, in this strangest of elections, only one of the four presidential candidates managed to carry his home county: Bell won his own Davidson County, Tennessee (county seat, Nashville); but Breckenridge's Fayette County, Kentucky (Lexington) also went for Bell; and Lincoln easily carried Douglas's Cook County (Chicago).

Despite the mixed results of the election, Lincoln was proud of his hometown, and of Illinois. His first view of Springfield and the Sangamon valley came in March 1831, just after his 22nd birthday. He had quarreled with his father, Thomas, perhaps over the amount of time he spent reading and writing instead of assisting with the farmwork, and left the Coles County homestead his family called Goosenest Prairie. With his cousin Dennis Hanks, Lincoln traveled by canoe down the Sangamon River to Judy's Ferry, and met up with his stepbrother John Johnston. From here the young men walked five miles to Springfield, where they stepped into the Buckhorn Tavern and entered into a conversation with an aspiring entrepreneur named Denton Offutt. Offutt was "wild, noisy and reckless, windy, rattle-brained, unsteady, and improvident."[2] He was also absolutely unafraid to take risks in financial matters, and in these three strangers he saw an opportunity. Offutt hired them at 50 cents per day to build a crude flatboat measuring 80 by 18 feet. When the boat was completed a month later Offutt loaded it with pork barrels, corn and hogs, and Lincoln,

Hanks and Johnston set out for the markets of New Orleans. They would be paid $60 apiece for successful delivery of the goods.[3]

Trouble came some 20 miles upriver. On April 19 the flatboat became lodged on a flooded milldam near the tiny village of New Salem. Most of the town's residents walked to the bluff overlooking the river and watched as Lincoln and his companions worked tirelessly to free the boat before rushing waters filled it and the cargo perished. When manual efforts failed, Lincoln bored a hole in the boat's bow, then directed that most of the cargo be unloaded onto another boat, while some of the barrels were rolled forward. Water poured quickly through the hole as the stern rose, and as the crowd cheered the boat floated safely over the dam. Offutt was so impressed with Lincoln's ingenuity that he promised him employment in New Salem as manager of the general store he planned to build.

But when Lincoln returned from New Orleans later that summer he found that while Offutt had ordered merchandise to sell, he had no building from which to operate the enterprise. Unwilling to return to his father's home and to the farmwork he despised, Lincoln decided to stay in New Salem. There he found about 100 people clustered in 12 or 15 log houses and stores. The town boasted a blacksmith, tanner, wheelwright, cooper, hatter, tavern and several shopkeepers. It had no church, although occasionally services were held in private homes, but it did have a "blab school" where students of all ages learned through continuous recitation of their lessons, at a cost to their parents of 50 cents per month. The town's first physician, Dr. James Allen of Vermont, arrived a few months after Lincoln. In 1832 another doctor, Francis Reginer, came from Ohio. Those who had founded New Salem, and those who later settled there, had a particular dream in common: they believed that the Sangamon River might prove navigable by steamboat and thus ensure commercial success to its inhabitants. Unless and until that day arrived, however, New Salem struggled along as an unofficial business and trade center for the surrounding rural areas.

Lincoln later recalled that he spent a fair amount of time in his new hometown "stumbling about."[4] He did not lack in ambition, but he had only the vaguest ideas of what profession might suit him, and he was, he thought, nothing more than "a piece of floating driftwood."[5] His first job was as clerk of an election board; throughout the day, as votes came slowly in, Lincoln kept the crowd at the polls entertained with jokes and outlandish stories. He managed to find steady, if temporary, employment as a manual laborer, clearing fields, gathering hay, splitting rails for fences. He made very little money but was content to board at the homes of those who employed him. Once he piloted a family down the Sangamon to Beardstown on a raft, then happily walked back to New Salem with a few dollars in his pocket. His willingness to work from dawn to dusk was impressive, but it was his natural charm and his sense of humor (self-deprecating around the women, raunchy and earthy around the men) that made him the most popular figure in the village.

Lincoln's new friends and neighbors soon noticed that there was something different, something admirable, about him. He was, despite having almost no formal education, exceedingly bright, inquisitive and dedicated to learning. His intellect quickly set him above and apart from the rest of the "suckers" (slang for Illinoisans).

One of New Salem's founders, James Rutledge, had a small library of 25 or 30 volumes, and to the wonder of most Lincoln read each book. He memorized the rules set forth in *Kirkhams' Grammar* and recited them aloud to himself or whoever would listen. When Rutledge formed a debating society, Lincoln eagerly joined. His mannerisms were unpolished and awkward, but his extraordinary grasp of logic overshadowed his stylistic faults. "He pursued the question with reason and argument so pithy and forcibly," a fellow debater said, "that all were amazed."[6]

Lincoln's talents were not limited to matters of intellect. His physical prowess earned him acclaim and a certain degree of notoriety, as well. At six feet four inches and 214 sinewy pounds, Lincoln was taller, stronger and more athletic than anyone in the region. He astonished everyone with his ability to swing an axe, throw a ball, and ride a horse. He could out-wrestle any and all challengers, although privately he admitted that he did not much care for the "wooling and pulling" of the sport.[7] One wrestling match, promoted by the bombastic Offutt, came against a young tough named Duff Armstrong, who acted as town constable when he wasn't carousing with a group of rowdies known as the Clary's Grove boys. Most of the town turned out for the event, and there was much wagering of "money, whiskey and knives" on the outcome. Armstrong was 10 inches shorter and 40 pounds lighter than Lincoln, but had earned his reputation as a relentless competitor. No one could agree who won the match — most of those who witnessed it reported that neither man could throw the other, while others claimed that Armstrong used an illegal move to take Lincoln down — but Lincoln's performance was noteworthy. Lincoln "took the matter in such good part, and laughed the matter off so pleasantly that he gained the good will of the roughs and was never disturbed by them."[8] Lincoln had not only won himself a loyal new friend — he became a regular houseguest of Armstrong and his wife Hannah — but also most assuredly established himself as a community icon.

In the fall of 1832 Lincoln helped Offutt finally build his general store and began to manage it, assisted by a man named William Greene. Lincoln also worked at Offutt's gristmill and sawmill, sleeping in one of the buildings at night. Townspeople would regularly stop by and discuss politics or current events, tell stories, and exchange gossip with Lincoln. "He was among the best clerks I ever saw," said Mentor Graham, New Salem's schoolteacher. "He was attentive to his business, was kind and considerate to his customers and friends, always treated them with great tenderness — kindness and honesty."[9] During his short tenure at the soon-to-fail store, Lincoln built a reputation for integrity. On one occasion, as legend has it, Lincoln walked six miles to return a small amount of money to a woman he had overcharged. On another he walked nearly as far to deliver to another customer the correct amount of tea.

The respect that Lincoln commanded among the townspeople brought him his first legal experience. New Salem justice of the peace Bowling Green, who was Jack Armstrong's half-brother and unofficial town political leader, loaned Lincoln his tattered copy of the *Revised Laws of Illinois*, which Lincoln appreciatively studied at every available moment. Green allowed Lincoln to sit in on informal court sessions and make known his opinions concerning the cases to be called. Soon Lincoln was performing basic legal tasks for villagers. He drafted pleadings, simple wills, deeds and receipts, refusing pay but happy for the experience ("pettyfogging," Lincoln called it).[10]

Lincoln came to realize that the law might be the vocation he had been searching for, and he made sincere, if erratic, strides toward achieving his goal. He paid a traveler 50 cents for a barrel of junk that happened to contain a volume of *Blackstone's Commentaries*, the most widely used lawbook of the day. He traveled to Boonville, Indiana, for the chance to hear the noted attorney and orator John A. Brackenridge defend a client charged with murder. When Brackenridge concluded his final remarks, Lincoln charged through the crowd and shook the lawyer's hand. "I felt that if I could ever make as good a speech as that my soul would be satisfied," he said later.[11]

Lincoln was also drawn to politics, and the most important local political issue involved the Sangamon River. New Salem's leading citizens had long believed that if the river was improved it could be made navigable, and commercial success would come to the cental Illinois region. A strong voice was needed in the state legislature; someone intelligent enough to grasp the issues and savvy enough to maneuver politically, and, ideally, someone who was an experienced and knowledgeable river man. Lincoln seemed the logical choice. He needed little persuasion to plunge into political waters, and in March 1832, a full five months before the election, Lincoln announced his candidacy by publishing a letter in Springfield's *Sangamo Journal*, later distributed through handbills posted throughout the county. In it he maintained that he supported internal improvements to ensure the region's economic well-being. But a railroad system would be too expensive; rather, Lincoln advocated the utilization of state dollars to improve the river. He was well qualified to state his positions and bring them to the legislature. His experience on the water, he exaggerated, was as great as "any other person in the country."[12]

Lincoln knew that his local appeal rested as much on his folksy charm as on his political viewpoints. "I am young and unknown to many of you," he wrote. "I was born and have ever remained in the most humble walks of life. I have no wealthy or popular relatives or friends to recommend me. My case is thrown exclusively upon the independent voters of the county; and if elected they will have conferred a favor upon me for which I shall be unremitting in my labors to compensate. But if the good people in their wisdom shall see fit to keep me in the background, I have been too familiar with disappointments to be very much chagrined."[13]

Just days after his announcement the region had its most exciting news in years. A Springfield man named Vincent Bogue had purchased a steamboat in Cincinnati and announced his plan to prove the navigability of the Sangamon River. The "splendid, upper cabin steamer *Talisman* was to travel to Portland Landing, just six miles from New Salem and Springfield, via the Ohio, Mississippi, Illinois and Sangamon rivers."[14] While local merchants advised their customers that the vessel would be stocked with goods and took subscriptions, or advance orders, for their sales, Lincoln and a few friends worked for days on the river, clearing overhanging brush from its banks and removing any other physical obstructions. Lincoln's efforts, and his respected knowledge of the river, were rewarded; he was chosen to pilot the *Talisman* from Beardstown to Portland Landing on March 24, and was a guest of honor at the festivities that evening in Springfield. One week later the Sangamon's water level had badly receded, and Lincoln, along with Billy Herndon's cousin Rowan, took the ship back to Beardstown. He was paid $40 for his work, and proudly walked back home.

But Offutt's store soon failed, and with the election still months away Lincoln was once again unemployed. His next job came unexpectedly. Black Hawk, the 67-year-old chief of the Sauk Indians, had violated a 10-month-old treaty by crossing the Mississippi River into Illinois. With his band of 500 braves, plus 700 more women and children, Black Hawk proceeded into the Rock River Valley in search not of battle, but land on which he could plant corn for his starving band. Illinois governor John Reynolds called for 1,000 volunteers to put down the "insurrection," and Lincoln, along with most of New Salem's young men, quickly responded. They formed up at nearby Richland where, to his delight, Lincoln was elected captain of a small company. Jack Armstrong was named first sergeant, and a good number of Clary's Grove boys were also placed under Lincoln's command.

Lincoln's company saw no action in the war, but muddled their way through a series of minor misadventures. The outfit lacked discipline, and Lincoln's orders were just as likely to be met with the response "Go to the devil, sir," as they were to be carried out.[15] Lincoln attempted to put the men through basic drilling and military tactics, but his complete lack of military experience made for awkward moments. Once, when the company marched to a fence, he could not remember the order to allow the men to pass through the gate. He improvised and ordered the company to fall out, then reform again on the fence's other side. On another occasion some of the men stole a good supply of liquor from the officers' quarters, and the next day were too hungover to march. Lincoln took the blame for his men and as punishment relinquished his sword for two days. The closest the company came to combat was when an elderly and confused Indian stumbled into the camp. The men wanted to execute the Indian for spying, but Lincoln realized the man posed no danger to anyone, and ordered that he be allowed to leave in peace.

After his 30 days of service were over, Lincoln reenlisted for another 20 days, serving this time as a private with the Independent Rangers under Capt. Elijah Iles, an old-time settler and one of Springfield's founders. Lincoln's decision to extend his military service was more a product of economic necessity than of patriotism. "I was out of work," he later wrote, "and there being no danger of more fighting, I could do nothing better than enlist again."[16]

On June 16 Lincoln enlisted yet again, this time for 30 days. His commanding officer was Jacob Early, a Springfield physician who doubled as a Methodist minister. Early had organized the "Independent Spy Corps" which served at the pleasure of Gen. Henry Atkinson, commander in chief of the 450-member Army of the Illinois Frontier. The Spy Corps tramped through the marshes, thickets and forests of Illinois and Wisconsin, but could not find the elusive Black Hawk. Again Lincoln saw no action, although he did serve on a burial contingent for five soldiers who had been killed and scalped. All told Lincoln served some 80 days in the four-month-long war. He finally mustered out on July 10, 1832, at Black River, Wisconsin, receiving an honorable discharge, a stipend of $124, and some tracts of Iowa farmland as payment for his service. His horse was promptly stolen and he had to ride with a friend, travel by canoe, and walk back to New Salem. This embarrassment did not dampen the pride he forever felt for his brief military service, however, and he often spoke fondly of the experience.[17]

Lincoln arrived home just two weeks before the state legislative election. He toured the county, giving a standard speech:

> Fellow citizens, I presume you all know who I am. I am humble Abraham Lincoln. I have been solicited by many friends to become a candidate for the Legislature. My politics are short and sweet, like the old woman's dance. I am in favor of a national bank. I am in favor of the internal improvement system and a high protective tariff. These are my sentiments and political principles. If elected I shall be thankful; if not it will be all the same.[18]

Lincoln finished eighth of 13 candidates, with the top four going to the legislature. He later wrote that his very first election campaign was "the only time I was ever beaten on a direct vote of the people."[19] His immense popularity in New Salem, however, shone through clearly. In that precinct he received all but three of 300 votes cast.

Lincoln was again left with little to do. He considered becoming a blacksmith, but had wearied of physical labor and decided against it. He wanted to study law, but felt his education was inadequate. Instead, he invested his military pay in another general store enterprise, this time with a partner named William Berry. But Lincoln's heart was not in business. He preferred to spend his time reading, talking, and philosophizing, and he did not seem to care much that his partner drank away what little money was taken in. This store, too, soon "winked out," as Lincoln later put it, and when Berry died two years later Lincoln was left owing some $1,100 — the "national debt," he called it.[20]

Fortunately, Lincoln soon fell into a couple of political appointments, first as postmaster for New Salem, then as deputy county surveyor, positions which managed to occupy his time and pay off some of his bills. He was good at both jobs, but he knew, and those around him knew, that he was destined for greater things. His mind never drifted far from politics and the law. He spent every spare minute reading; he most enjoyed *The Congressional Globe*, Chitty's *Pleadings*, Greenleaf's *Evidence*, Story's *Equity* and *Equity Pleadings*, and Thomas Paine's *The Age of Reason*, among others.

On August 4, 1834, Lincoln was elected to the House of Representatives for the Ninth General Assembly, finishing second in a field of 13 candidates from Sangamon County. The victory was the first of Lincoln's four successive elections to the Illinois legislature. He borrowed $200 from a friend, bought a new suit of clothes, and in November made the two-day trip by stagecoach to Vandalia, the Illinois state capitol. There he roomed with a Springfield lawyer named John T. Stuart, who had served with Lincoln in the Black Hawk War. Though Stuart had been a legislator only since 1832, his cunning had earned him the nickname "Jerry Sly" in Vandalia. A strong Whig, Stuart became Lincoln's political mentor, and Stuart had Lincoln draft legislative proposals for him. As had many others, Stuart quickly took notice of Lincoln's immense potential. More importantly, he loaned Lincoln some law books and encouraged him to continue his self-education when he wasn't attending to politics.

The House met on the first floor of the statehouse, in what had formerly been a bank building. Legislators sat three to a table, the room warmed by a fireplace and stove and illuminated by candlelight, the proceedings occasionally interrupted by falling plaster from the ceiling. Most of the 54-member Illinois legislature were Jackson Democrats; as Whigs, Lincoln and Stuart found themselves on the losing side of many issues. Still, Lincoln proved to be a hard-working, mildly effective freshman. He cast his vote on issues concerning public roads, canals, regulation of gambling, debt collection practices and salaries for public officials. He introduced several bills of his own, one having to do with the jurisdiction of justice of the peace courts, which failed, and another authorizing the building of a toll bridge across Salt Creek in Sangamon County, which was passed into law. His sense of humor was greatly appreciated by his fellow legislators. Early in the session the House nominated a man named Samuel McHatton to fill a vacancy for Schuyler County surveyor. It was then discovered that no vacancy in fact existed, because the incumbent was still alive. McHatton could not legally remove the incumbent, stated Lincoln, "if the incumbent persisted in not dying." The matter should be tabled, he thought. Later, "if the old surveyor should hereafter conclude to die, there would be a new one ready without troubling the legislature." Lincoln was thought to be "raw-boned, angular, features deeply furrowed, ungraceful, almost uncouth ... and yet there was a magnetism and dash about the man that made him a universal favorite."[21] In February the session ended. Lincoln collected $358 for his salary and expenses, and went back to New Salem to resume his study of the law.

And now Lincoln threw himself into his studies as never before. He became "wholly engrossed, and began for the first time to avoid the society of men, in order that he might have more time for study."[22] He continued to serve as part-time postmaster, and still dabbled in surveying, but by all accounts his focus, and his future, now appeared certain. He "studied with nobody," and "still mixed in the surveying to pay board and clothing bills. When the legislature met, the law books were dropped but were taken up again at the end of the session."[23] One friend recalled, "So intense was his application and so absorbed was he in his study that he would often pass his best friends without observing them." No bar examinations were required in mid-19th century Illinois, but in March 1836 the Sangamon Circuit Court issued Lincoln a certificate of good character. Six months later he was licenced to practice law.

The legislative session of 1836-37 had a dramatic impact on Lincoln's life. Lincoln was then a member of "The Long Nine," a group of seven Sangamon representatives and two senators who all surpassed six feet in height. The Long Nine strongly advocated two things: statewide internal improvements and removal of the capital from Vandalia to Springfield. The improvements legislation sailed through the legislature (a key supporter was young Senator Stephen Douglas), but the financial panic of 1837 negated the action. Railroad construction was left uncompleted, road improvement projects were abandoned, and canals were left only partially dug. The state would long feel the effects of the economic collapse.

But there were fewer problems surrounding the capital relocation. Vandalia was considered too small and inaccessible, and its southern location was also seen as inappropriate for a state whose main growth was in the north and central regions. Lincoln and his fellow Sangamon delegates lobbied long and hard for passage of a bill moving the capital to Springfield, and on February 28, 1837, the measure was approved. That night a victory celebrations was held at Cipp's Tavern, and all members of the legislature attended, whether they had voted for the bill or not, to partake in a feast of oysters, almonds, raisins, fine cigars and champagne. More celebrations were subsequently held all over Sangamon County, and Lincoln, now dubbed "one of Nature's Noblemen" attended each one with the rest of the Long Nine contingent.[24] Lincoln had "fulfilled the expectations of his friends and disappointed the hopes of his enemies," said the Sangamon *Journal*.[25] He had become a frontier celebrity of sorts. His "driftwood" days seemed a distant memory.

Once the parties were over, Lincoln returned to New Salem, now for the last time. His home of six years was dying. Despite his efforts, all legislative attempts to improve the Sangamon River and make it navigable had failed. The New Salem post office had been relocated two miles away, to Petersburg. There was talk that a new county, to be called Menard, would soon be created, and that Petersburg, not New Salem, would become the county seat (this prediction came true in 1839). Lincoln would be leaving close friends behind, but he knew that his hopes for a legal career must take him elsewhere. John Stuart's partner had left to start his own practice in Beardstown, and Stuart asked Lincoln to replace him. Like the Illinois capital itself, Lincoln was moving to Springfield.

When Illinois became a state in 1818 about 40,000 people lived there. But only one man, a horse trader named Robert Pulliam, resided in the fertile valley of the Sangamon River, his log cabin located about 12 miles south of what was to become the town of Calhoun, later renamed Springfield. Within a year over 200 families had settled in the area, and by 1824 the Illinois legislature appointed five commissioners to choose a county seat for Sangamon County on the basis of "the geographical situation of said county, its present and the future population and permanent interest."[26] Lots were sold, crude streets were laid out, and permanent buildings were constructed. On Christmas Eve 1830 a heavy snowstorm began that continued for nearly a week, leaving behind drifts five feet deep. The "Deep Snow" marked a transition for Springfield, for when it finally melted civic leaders commenced an ambitious building project that included a courthouse, market house, and rows of brick stores, along with houses, grocery and dry goods stores, hotels, restaurants, drug and clothing stores, and craftsman establishments of all variety. In 10 years Springfield, with a population of about 1,400 people, was the largest city in Illinois.

On April 15, 1837, Lincoln rode into Springfield on a horse he had borrowed from Bowling Green, everything he owned stuffed into his saddlebags. He had $7 in his pockets, the proceeds of the sale of his surveying equipment. He first stopped at Joshua Speed's general store and asked if he could acquire a bed, mattress and bedclothes on credit, the price of $17 far more than he could afford. He told Speed he might be able to pay him back by Christmas, "if my experiment here as a lawyer is a success." Lincoln looked so melancholy that Speed felt sorry for him, and offered to let him share his double bed in the room over the store. Lincoln wasted no time. He took his saddlebags upstairs and threw them down, then returned in a happy mood. "Well, Speed," he said, grinning, "I am moved."[27]

Lincoln joined Stuart in the practice of law in a coarse office above the county courthouse on Hoffman's Row, on the north side of the public square in downtown Springfield. The office held only a table, chair and bench, a shaky bookshelf and a small bed covered with a buffalo robe. Stuart was away from the office much of the time — he had campaigned unsuccessfully for Congress in 1836, but would win the seat in 1838, defeating Stephen Douglas — and Lincoln was often left alone to finish up Stuart's business and greet potential clients who walked through the door. His very first case was *Hawthorne v. Wooldridge*; an argument over the use of oxen and the breaking of prairie sod had escalated into assault and battery allegations. Lincoln settled the matter just as it was to go to trial.

In August Lincoln took on a case that caught his interest and gained the firm some positive publicity as well. A widow named Mary Anderson believed that her husband had left her 10 acres of land, and she sought Lincoln's help in recovering the property. A search of the title record, however, showed that the land had been deeded to a man named James Adams, who claimed to be an army general and was running for probate justice of the peace. Lincoln believed that Adams had forged the document, and a few days before the election he wrote as much in an anonymous letter published in the *Journal* and in handbills posted in public places. Adams denied the charge, and after he won the election he angrily claimed that Lincoln had authored the materials in a poor attempt to defame him. Lincoln and Adams traded public allegations for the next several weeks. In his final letter Lincoln wrote, "Farewell, General. I will see you again in court if not before — when and where we will settle the question whether you or the widow shall have the land." Miraculously, news surfaced that a criminal indictment against Adams for forgery had been brought in New York 20 years earlier, throwing Adams' credibility into question. But Adams died soon thereafter and the case did not go to trial. Lincoln's client was granted clear title to the land, and the people of Springfield took notice of Lincoln as an aggressive and effective attorney.

Lincoln worked with Stuart for the next four years. The practice of law was often routine. Lincoln prepared wills, drafted contractual agreements and sought to enforce debts. He defended many people charged with petty crimes and other minor offenses. He lost his first major criminal trial when his client, William Fraim, was convicted of murder and hanged. Slowly Lincoln honed his skills and began to earn the respect of his peers. While the firm never made a lot of money — its average income was about $1,600 a year, and the partners often took vegetables, produce or poultry in exchange for their services — a solid, busy practice was built. From 1837 to 1841 Stuart and Lincoln handled more cases in the Circuit Court of Illinois than any other firm.

The Eighth Judicial Circuit was the heart of Lincoln's legal practice. At its largest the circuit covered 17 counties, approximately 110 by 140 miles, or more than 15,000 square miles, roughly one-fifth of the entire area of Illinois.[28] Twice each year for three months, once in the spring and again in the fall, the circuit court was in session. From county seat to county seat a regular group of lawyers including Lincoln, Douglas, Edward Baker, John J. Hardin and James Shields, among others, rode the circuit, "bringing justice to the people." Samuel H. Treat, and later David Davis, presided as judge, and they traveled with the lawyers, on horseback in the early days and later in buggies. Life on the circuit was notorious for inclement weather, poor lodging and wretched food. The legal caravan stayed at inns or taverns, sleeping two to a bed, rising early and heading to the courthouse in search of legal business. After a full day of wrangling and arguing over the cases—trespass, divorce, assault, theft; whatever the clients brought in—the contingent gathered around a fire at the tavern, telling jokes, swapping stories, and playing cards. The next morning the group either headed back to court or packed their saddlebags and headed for the next town.

When he wasn't on the road Lincoln found a spot in Springfield—specifically, Speed's general store—where he regularly met with a fast-growing group of male friends, many of them merchants and businessmen and other lawyers. On most evenings after work Lincoln and his friends would meet and discuss current events, politics and business, enjoying a closeness and camaraderie that Lincoln craved. And

as in New Salem, Lincoln's charisma was the magnet that drew admiring men to him. "Mr. Lincoln was a social man, though he did not seek company; it sought him," Speed later said. "After he made his home with me, on every winter's night at my store, by a big wood fire, no matter how inclement the weather, eight or ten choice spirits assembled, without distinction of party. It was a sort of a social club without organization. They came there because they were sure to find Lincoln."[29]

Lincoln and Speed soon became the closest of friends. Also from Kentucky, Speed was five years younger than Lincoln. He was a Whig, as well, but it was more than politics and age that drew the two men together. Speed was, like Lincoln, a young man who wanted desperately to fall in love but lacked the self-confidence to do so. Lincoln found in Speed a sort of kindred soul and the two men confided in each other in matters intensely

Judge David Davis, Lincoln's friend from his circuit-riding days and campaign manager in the election of 1860 (the Lincoln Museum, Fort Wayne, Indiana, # 3810).

personal. Together the two would share confidences, fears, joy and heartbreak for as long as their friendship lasted. Lincoln valued Speed's opinions and trusted his advice. He once wrote to Speed, "You know my desire to befriend you is everlasting—that I will never cease, while I know how to do anything."[30]

At age 28 when he came to Springfield, Lincoln certainly had some experience with the opposite sex. In New Salem he had known the town's most sought-after young lady, James Rutledge's pretty daughter Ann. In 1832 Ann became engaged to a merchant named John McNamar who also owned 40 acres of land and whose prospects for commercial success outweighed Lincoln's. But McNamar was called to New York, supposedly to care for ill relatives. Inexplicably McNamar did not correspond with Ann during his absence, which stretched into three years, a fact that led to much gossip in New Salem and extreme embarrassment for Ann. It was during this time, the Rutledge family later claimed, that Ann and Lincoln began a secret courtship, and Ann agreed to marry Lincoln if and when she could honorably break off her engagement to McNamar. But Ann died of typhoid fever in August 1835, and while Lincoln surely grieved her loss, the exact nature of their relationship has never been made clear.

A year later Lincoln renewed an acquaintance with a young woman from Green County, Kentucky, named Mary Owens. Sophisticated and highly educated, Mary had come to New Salem in 1833 to visit her older sister, Mrs. Bennett Abell, and met Lincoln. Three years later (perhaps in the wake of Ann Rutledge's death) Mrs. Abell told Lincoln she could convince Mary to move to New Salem permanently if Lincoln would marry her. Cavalierly Lincoln agreed, and Mary returned to New Salem. But the courtship was a troubled one; while the couple shared somewhat similar intellectual pursuits it appears that no physical attraction existed. Lincoln later claimed that when he saw Mary again her appearance disappointed him. While she had once been pleasingly plump, now "she was a fair match for Falstaff." Further, there was a "weather-beaten" look about her, and she had lost some teeth, criticisms that seem unfair coming from a man who was usually described as homely.[31]

While Lincoln felt obligated to fulfill his promise and wed Mary, he maneuvered as best he could to get out of it. If the couple corresponded while Lincoln attended legislative sessions in Vandalia the letters have not survived. He moved to Springfield without her and his letters from there were thinly veiled attempts to persuade her to release him. Alluding to his near-poverty, he wrote, "I am afraid you would not be satisfied. There is a great deal of flourishing about in carriages here, which it would be your doom to be without shareing in it. You would have to be poor without the means of hiding your poverty.... My opinion is that you had better not do it. You have not been accustomed to hardship, and it may be more serious than you now imagine. I know you are capable of thinking correctly on any subject, and if you deliberate maturely upon this before you decide, then I am willing to abide your decision." If Mary wished to release him, he wrote, "it is my sincere wish that you should."[32]

Mary did not do so immediately, and for a while the two continued their uneasy relationship. Finally in the fall of 1837 Lincoln proposed marriage. Mary listened—and then turned him down. Lincoln had badly miscalculated her; it was not his economic standing that concerned her, but his inability to exercise common courtesy around her (and perhaps all women). On one occasion Lincoln had failed to offer to carry her sister's baby; on another he did not assist her in crossing a deep stream on horseback. These episodes, and others, had put her off. "Mr. Lincoln was deficient in those little links which make up the chain of woman's happiness," she later wrote.[33] She returned to Kentucky where she married and raised six children, never regretting that she had refused a man who would become famous. As for Lincoln, his pride was most assuredly wounded. He claimed later that he would "never again think of marrying; and for this reason; I can never be satisfied with any one who would be blockhead enough to have me." He had managed to make a fool of himself, and perhaps all along, he now sheepishly admitted, he was "really a little in love with her."[34]

With this unfortunate background in romance Lincoln's prospects seemed bleak in Springfield, where eligible bachelors outnumbered single young women by nearly 10 to one. He was no doubt lonely for female companionship. After a month in town he wrote, "I have been spoken to but by one woman since I've been here, and should not have been by her, if she could have avoided it." His lack of confidence in these matters continued to plague him. "I can't even go to church for fear I don't know how to behave."[35] He knew that he should pay more attention to his appearance, but was simply uninterested in any form of fashion. William Butler was clerk of the circuit court and allowed Lincoln to take his meals and occasionally spend the night with his family for five years. "You know he was always careless about his clothes," Butler said. "In all the time he stayed at my house, he never bought a hat or a pair of socks, or a coat, whenever he needed them, my wife went out and bought them for him, and put them in the drawer where he could find them."[36]

His fairly prominent professional standing, however, opened some avenues for him. Through his association with Stuart and his acquaintance with Speed and others, Lincoln gained a gradual acceptance into Springfield social society. He attended banquets and cotillions, where eventually he drew at least a little notice from the ladies. "We liked Lincoln though he was not gay," commented one young woman. "He rarely danced, he was never very attentive to ladies, but he was always a welcome guest everywhere, and the center of a circle of animated talkers. Indeed, I think the only thing we girls had against Lincoln was that he always attracted all the men around him."[37]

Most significantly Lincoln renewed his acquaintance with Ninian Wirt Edwards, the son of Illinois' first governor and a Whig legislator who had served with Lincoln in Vandalia. Edwards was married to Elizabeth Todd (a cousin of John Stuart), and their beautiful two-story brick home on a hilltop called Aristocracy Hill was the elite center of the Springfield social scene. Lincoln attended many parties, teas and dances in the parlor of the Edwards home, and it was there that he first met Elizabeth's younger sister Mary, who would, eventually, become his wife.[38]

Mary Ann Todd was born on December 13, 1818, in Lexington, Kentucky, the fourth of six children of Robert Smith Todd and Eliza Parker. Todd was a prominent lawyer and banker who strongly supported the politics of Henry Clay and particularly hated slavery. His wife died when Mary was only six, and Todd quickly remarried. His new wife, Elizabeth Humphreys, bore him eight more children. But

Mary grew to detest her stepmother. Though she enjoyed a childhood of privilege, including sessions at Dr. John Ward's Academy and the finishing school of Madame Victorie Mentelle, she later called her childhood "desolate."

In 1837 the 19-year-old Mary traveled to Springfield to visit her sister Elizabeth. She returned to Lexington, but after two more years of studies at Dr. Ward's it became clear to her that she would be unhappy in Kentucky, perhaps because she was too near her stepmother, and she returned to Springfield for good in 1839. Undoubtedly matrimony was very much on her mind, and Elizabeth was an accomplished match-maker, particularly within the family. She had introduced older sister Frances to William Wallace, a pharmacist originally from Pennsylvania, and younger sister Ann Maria to Clark M. Smith, one of Springfield's leading merchants; both matches resulted in marriage. Now, perhaps, it was Mary's turn.

And with or without her sister's help, Mary quickly became Springfield's most desirable belle. Just five feet two inches tall, she was pretty if not beautiful, with blue eyes, auburn hair and an engaging smile. Mary was witty, cultured, always exquisitely dressed, and at ease in polite society. She could be alternatively flirtatious and demanding, charming and sarcastic. One young Springfield attorney, James C. Conkling, spoke for all of the city's eligible bachelors when he called her "the very creature of excitement."[39] Her brother-in-law Ninian Edwards said that Mary could "make a bishop forget his prayers."[40] Even Billy Herndon, who would eventually come to dislike her (the feeling would be mutual) described Mary as "young, dashing, handsome — witty…, cultured — graceful and dignified" who led "the young men of the town on a merry dance." She was courted by Stephen Douglas and though she "liked him well enough" she ultimately rejected him.[41] Edwin B. Webb, yet another Springfield attorney, also pursued her, but he was a widower with two small children, and these "sweet little objections" posed an insurmountable problem for Mary.[42] Joshua Speed was perhaps for a time a candidate for her affections, but he seemed to be gravitating toward another young lady named Fanny Henning. Instead, it was Speed's roommate and confidante Lincoln who would win Mary's heart.

Legend has it that Lincoln was mesmerized at his first sight of Mary. He approached her and said he wanted to dance with her "in the worst way," and after a clumsy whirl around the floor she said that "he certainly did."[43] This story may or may not be true, but undoubtedly Lincoln was immediately attracted to Mary, and she was certainly charmed by him. They developed a kinship, a bond of affection bound together by an intense mutual interest in each other. He found her beautiful, fascinating, intriguing. He was impressed by her education — particularly her ability to speak French — and her ability to hold a conversation on topics ranging from Whig politics to Shakespeare to national social issues. He seemed at times to be almost spellbound by her charms. "He would listen and gaze on her as if drawn by some superior power," said Elizabeth Edwards.[44] Mary was drawn to Lincoln's natural, if roughly hewn, intelligence, his gentle manner, and his sense of humor. She easily overlooked his lack of social graces and preferred to concentrate on his potential, which seemed limitless. The two spent hours together on the horsehair sofa in the parlor of the Edwards' home on the hill. Even though Elizabeth did not fully approve of Mary's choice among all her beaux, the relationship steadily grew. Within

the year rumors of an impending marriage were flying around Springfield, and neither Lincoln nor Molly, as he called her, attempted to quell them.

But the winter of 1840 brought troubles to the couple. Lincoln began to experience self-doubt, probably reflecting on his failed relationships with other women
in recent years. He did not know if he could truly make a woman happy. Perhaps,
too, he was still unsure of his financial standing and his ability to provide for a wife
and, someday, a family. Some historians believe that Lincoln became upset over
Mary's flirtations with other men, including Stephen Douglas. Others suggest that
he was actually in love with an 18-year-old woman named Matilda Edwards, Ninian's cousin, who did not return similar feelings to him. Certainly Ninian and Elizabeth were less than thrilled with Lincoln as a prospective match for Mary, who could
choose from among every bachelor in Springfield. Mary's own family in Kentucky,
who did not even know Lincoln, also may have voiced their concerns over the engagement. Lincoln was not impressed with the Todd family's sense of social standing:
One *d* was enough for God, he remarked, but it took two *d*'s to spell Todd.[45]

Whatever the reason, the new year brought an end to the engagement. On "that
fatal first of Jany," as he put it, Lincoln asked Mary to release him from his obligation, and she graciously did so. He immediately fell into a deep depression, exhibiting symptoms both mental and physical. His state of mind was "deplorable," he
wrote, and he had "been making a most discreditable exhibition of myself in the way
of hypochondrianism." Springfield physician Anson G. Henry diagnosed anxiety and
exhaustion, and Lincoln began to rely so heavily on Henry that the doctor became
"necessary to my existence." Lincoln took to his bed for a week, then dragged himself back to the legislature, where he was listless and ineffective. This would be his
last term as a state politician and he felt, not incorrectly, that his once-promising
career had faded to mediocrity. His partner, Stuart, was more interested in his congressional career than in building their law practice, and while Lincoln could hardly
blame Stuart for his political ambitions, he could see that their partnership was in
its final days. Even worse, his best friend Joshua Speed had sold his store and moved
back to Kentucky. Lincoln was now "the most miserable man living…. Whether I
shall ever be better I can not tell; I awfully forbode I shall not. To remain as I am is
impossible. I must die or be better."[46]

Lincoln did get better, but it was a slow process. When the legislative session
ended he returned to the spring court circuit, and while he enjoyed the traveling he
kept to himself as never before. His mood seemed darker, more serious, and to his
friends it was obvious that he was attempting to "drown his cares among the intri-
cacies and perplexities of the law."[47] In August Dr. Henry suggested that Lincoln
leave Springfield, at least for a while. Lincoln agreed that a change of scenery might
be beneficial and traveled to Speed's home in Louisville. He stayed with Speed's family at their plantation for several weeks, relaxing in the spacious home, romping in
the fields, enjoying being waited on by a personal servant. He observed the happiness that a close family felt, and he no doubt resolved to one day obtain the same
sort of contentment. Speed introduced Lincoln to Fanny Henning, a lovely young
girl with whom he was falling in love, and Lincoln referred to her as "one of the
sweetest girls in the world," taking special notice of her "heavenly black eyes."[48] When

he left Speed's mother presented him with an Oxford Bible, the "best cure for the Blues," a gift he cherished for many years. [49] He left feeling refreshed, and a bit like his old self.

For her part, Mary handled the breakup with dignity, but sadness. She did not see Lincoln for many months, but clearly he was on her mind. "The last two or three months have been of *interminable* length," she wrote in June. She was "left in the solitude of my own thoughts, and some *lingering regrets* over the past, which time can alone overshadow with its healing balm, thus has my *spring time* been passed...." She presumed that Lincoln "deems me unworthy of notice, as I have not seen *him* in the *gay* world for months ... yet I would that the case were different, that he would once again resume his Station in Society, that 'Richard should be himself again,' much, much happiness would it afford me."[50] Mary had other suitors during her separation from Lincoln, but none who particularly impressed her as he had.

Despite some misgivings of his own, and after some unlikely encouragement from Lincoln, Speed proposed to Fanny and they were married in February 1842. After Speed, in turn, assured Lincoln that the union made him happier than he had imagined, Lincoln reexamined his own self-doubts and seemed to resolve them. While he had regained his confidence he was still tormented by Mary's despair. "There is *one* still unhappy whom I have contributed to make so, he confided. "That still kills my soul. I can not but reproach myself, for even wishing to be happy while she is otherwise."[51]

Neither party was willing to approach the other. Sometime in the summer of 1842 Mrs. Simeon Francis, wife of the editor of the *Sangamo Journal*, took the matter into her own hands and invited Lincoln and Mary to a party. "Be friends again," she insisted, and they listened. Lincoln and Mary began to meet discreetly, usually at the Francis home, and the romance was quickly rekindled. Then one of the stranger incidents of Lincoln's life cemented the relationship for good.

Sometime that August, Mary and her friend Julia Jayne wrote an anonymous letter to the *Journal*, poking fun at James Shields, the state auditor and staunch Democrat (and, like so many others, a rejected suitor of Mary's). On the 27th Lincoln joined in the fun, lampooning Shields with own lengthy, and more or less tasteless, annonymous letter to the paper. Shields fumed and demanded that the identity of the writer be disclosed. To protect Mary's honor Lincoln came forward and took full responsibility for both letters, and to his astonishment Shields challenged him to a duel. The event very nearly came off before representatives of the two men agreed to settlement terms, under which Lincoln apologized. While the incident embarrassed Lincoln, and he seldom spoke of it again, his chivalry impressed Mary. They began to make private plans to wed.

On Thursday morning, November 2, Lincoln contacted Noah Matheny, clerk of the Sangamon County court, and applied for a marriage license. With Speed unavailable Lincoln needed a best man, and Matheny's son James agreed to stand in. The two men tracked down the Rev. Charles Dresser of St. Paul's Episcopal Church, and Lincoln told him, "I want to get hitched tonight."[52] The Reverend Dresser was happy to comply on short notice, but not at his church; instead, he offered to perform the ceremony at his own home. Lincoln then luckily ran into Ninian Edwards on the street, who was not surprised at Lincoln's announcement, only that it came so suddenly. Edwards considered himself to be Mary's guardian, however, and insisted that the wedding take place at his home, if his wife would agree.

Elizabeth was angry when Mary told her the news that morning. She had never been able to persuade Mary that Lincoln was not a suitable match for her; now her sister wanted to marry him with no advance notice. The local sewing society was scheduled to meet that evening at her home; how could she alter the plans of the ladies? Besides, she could not possibly prepare an appropriate meal for a wedding party in just a few hours. "Mary Todd," she scolded her sister, "even a free Negro would give her family time to bake a ginger cake."[53] But Elizabeth at last relented when the wedding was switched to Friday night. She enlisted the help of her sister Frances Wallace and sister-in-law Mrs. Ben Edwards, who worked nearly nonstop to prepare the home, and the food, for the wedding. The local bakery did not have time to prepare a proper wedding cake, so Mrs. Edwards suggested an unorthodox alternative: she baked the cake herself, and the proprietor of Old Dickey's tavern supplied a sufficient quantity of bread and beer for the 30 invited guests.

For a man who had so much trepidation about love and marriage, Lincoln was surprisingly calm about his decision to take a wife. He dressed at the Butler home, and as Mrs. Butler straightened his necktie her young son asked, "Where are you going, Mr. Lincoln?" "To hell, I reckon," he joked.[54] Lincoln remained cheerful at the wedding and reception that evening. "He acted just as he always acted in company," recalled Mrs. Wallace.

Mary chose Julia Jayne (who would marry Lyman Trumbull a year later), Anna Rodney and her 17-year-old cousin Elizabeth as bridesmaids. Mary dressed simply but elegantly in a white Swiss muslin dress. She wore no veil but a single strand of pearls adorned her neck, and everyone agreed that she had never looked lovelier. As a hard rain fell outside, she and Lincoln exchanged vows by the light of astral lamps that had been placed on the fireplace's mantel in the parlor of the Edwards home, the same parlor where they had spent countless hours laughing and talking when first they met. Lincoln placed a small gold wedding band on his bride's finger, purchased just a few days before at Chatterton's jewelry store. Inscribed on the inside of the ring were the words "Love is Eternal." He was 33 years old, Mary 10 years younger.

Lincoln and Mary took no honeymoon. Lincoln returned to work the Monday following the wedding, representing a full load of clients in nearby Christian County. Mary set up house, as it were, at a boisterous, second-rate boarding house called the Globe Tavern. The Lincolns were familiar with the place; formerly known as the Spottswood Rural Hotel, the Globe had also been the home to Mary's sister Frances and her husband, William Wallace. In fact, the Lincolns now occupied the same eight by 14 room as the Wallaces had, and for which they paid $4 per week. The Globe advertised itself as under the "prudent management of Mrs. Beck, eight pleasant and comfortable rooms for boarders as well as convenient resting places for the weary."[55]

It was a loud establishment, catering to stagecoach travelers who rang the bell clapper when the stage pulled in. Next door was a busy blacksmith's shop, and all boarders took their meals in the common dining room. Although it was a significant step downward for Mary, it was perhaps a step up for Lincoln. They lived here for a full year, and if Mary complained about her living conditions no record of it has survived.

Lincoln continued to improve his skills as a lawyer. He had been affiliated with Stephen T. Logan since the spring of 1841, and the firm prospered. Nine years Lincoln's senior, Logan was also a Kentuckian and a Whig. He had served as circuit judge for two years, and while he enjoyed the position he found the salary of $750 per year insufficient, and established his own practice, quickly earning the reputation as the finest attorney in Springfield, if not all of Illinois. Logan was physically unimpressive, short, unkempt, with an immense head of hair and a grating, shrill voice. But he demanded much of himself, was superbly organized and possessed a brilliant legal mind. He challenged Lincoln to strive for this same excellence in his work, and while Lincoln would never completely overcome his sloppiness he did acquire a certain discipline that had previously been lacking. In many ways Logan became Lincoln's legal mentor, a fact reflected by the fee structure: as the firm's senior partner Logan took a higher percentage of fees than did Lincoln. With Logan managing the day-to-day business affairs of the office, and Lincoln traveling the circuit twice each year, the pair fairly dominated the Illinois legal landscape for the next three years.

On August 1, 1843, just three days less than nine months from her wedding, Mary delivered her first child, a baby boy named Robert Todd after her father. There were no midwives in Springfield, and Mary was likely attended in childbirth by either her uncle, Dr. John Todd, or her husband's physician, Dr. Anson Henry (who charged $5 for an "accouchement.") Though Mary described her labor as "a suffering time" she was comforted by her "darling husband bending over me."[56] Lincoln had joked that he was afraid his firstborn would have one long leg, after his father, and one short one, after his mother, but save for being slightly cross-eyed Robert was a relatively healthy baby. But Mary had no nurse to assist her, and the noisy, drafty room at the Globe Tavern proved less than ideal. Soon Robert developed expansive lungs, and in the fall, as cooler weather arrived, the Lincolns moved into a four-room cottage on South Fourth Street at a rent of $100 per year.

Mary's father, Robert Smith Todd, may not have been overjoyed at his daughter's choice for a husband, but he was certainly pleased to have a namesake. Todd had 15 children, his last born just two years earlier in 1841, but two of his sons, both named Robert Smith Todd, had died. In December 1843 he traveled to Springfield, where four of his daughters now lived, and paid special attention on this trip to the Lincolns. With a surprising display of affection for Mary "without remark he dropped a $25 gold piece in her hand."[57] He then deeded to the Lincolns 80 acres of land in Illinois, and promised them a stipend of $200 per year for the rest of his life, a period that lasted six years. He apparently was won over by his son-in-law's charms, for he hired Lincoln to pursue a debt collection suit against a business creditor, and allowed him to keep the monies he recovered.

Seven years after he moved to Springfield, Lincoln finally managed to pay off his "national debt." Buoyed by the gift from his father-in-law, and now making a solid living as an attorney, Lincoln was ready to purchase a home. The Reverend Charles Dresser, the same man who had performed Lincoln's wedding ceremony, had a house for sale, and Lincoln bought it for $1,500. The five-room, one-and-one-half story frame cottage, built in 1839, rested on a one-eighth acre lot at the corner of Eighth and Jackson Streets. At the rear of the lot, next to the privy, well, pump and cistern was a small barn where Lincoln stored his buggy and kept his horse, "Old Bob," along with a cow he milked twice a day. Enlarged to a full two stories in 1856, the house was painted Quaker brown, accented by deep green shutters. By no means situated in Springfield's finest residential section — it stood only a few blocks from open fields— the home was nonetheless a source of pride to Lincoln, and was the only home he ever owned.

Here the family lived for 17 years. Three more children were born, all boys: Edward in 1846, William in 1850, and Thomas in 1853. The Lincolns settled into a comfortable routine. While her husband traveled the circuit — sometimes as many as 20 or 25 weeks per year — and busied himself in the affairs of his law office, Mary cooked, cleaned, sewed and raised her children, usually with the help of a teenage girl she hired. The Lincolns secured a place in Springfield's respectable society. They often entertained — a favorite event was to invite friends over on warm summer evenings for fresh strawberries, white cakes and iced teas— and just as often were invited to balls and receptions thrown by others. Together they attended performances of the Illinois Theatrical Company. Musical groups and chorales gave concerts and recitals, and while Lincoln was no great fan of music he gladly escorted Mary to these events. Traveling circuses, including the great P.T. Barnum's collection of oddities, came to Springfield two or three times per year, and Lincoln took not just his own children but the neighborhood kids, as well. Sometimes distinguished orators or statesmen like Martin Van Buren or Daniel Webster came to town, and as one of Springfield's leading citizens Lincoln often was a member of the delegation that greeted them. On such formal occasions the Lincolns hosted receptions at their home, the highlight of which was an elegant meal prepared by Mary and her domestic helper. "In her modest and simple home, " recalled one Springfield resident, "everything orderly and refined, there was always, on the part of both host and hostess, a cordial and hearty Western welcome, which put every guest perfectly at ease. Mrs. Lincoln's table was famed for the excellence of many rare Kentucky dishes, and in season, it was loaded with venison, wild turkeys, prairie chickens, quail and other game, which was then abundant. Yet it was her genial manners, and ever-kind welcome, and Mr. Lincoln's wit and humor, anecdote, and unrivaled conversation, which formed the chief attraction."[58]

The Lincolns shared a strong commitment to their family and placed the happiness of their children above all else. Both parents were lenient with the boys. When he was home Lincoln played with them, pulled their carts, carried them on his shoulders, and to the consternation of his partners let them run unmolested in his office. Mary was just as indulgent in her "little darlings." She allowed them to keep stray kittens and puppies (when they moved into the White House the troupe came to include turkeys, goats and ponies). She could easily overlook whatever mischief they created, for in her view their worst fault was that they were simply noisy or rambunctious. She hosted grand birthday parties for them, inviting as many as 50 or 60 of Springfield's youngsters to the events. Lincoln admitted that he and his wife "never controlled our children much."[59] Mary believed that the leniency she granted her boys would pay dividends in her later years. "When my children are grown up," she wrote to a friend, "I hope to have great comfort in them, for I have certainly been a slave for their interest the best part of my life."[60]

But for their contentment things did not always run smoothly at the Lin-

Mary Lincoln with Willie and Tad in November 1860 (the Lincoln Museum, Fort Wayne, Indiana, # 3155).

coln house. As Lincoln was gone from Springfield more frequently, and for longer periods of time, Mary sometimes felt overwhelmed with housework and the responsibilities of raising her boys alone. She often felt afraid when he was on the circuit, and hired neighborhood boys to sleep in her house and protect her from imagined intruders. She constantly fretted that the teenaged girls she hired might entertain their boyfriends under her roof. Lightning storms frightened her. She frequently suffered from migraine headaches. When Lincoln was home he could be sullen and contemplative, and sometimes she took his long periods of silence for a lack of caring. She was impatient with her husband's indifference to cleanliness, proper manners and decorum. It annoyed her when he lounged around the parlor of her carefully cleaned home, reading or roughhousing with the boys, answering the door in his shirt sleeves and socks. She could not understand his long periods of silence and contemplation. Sometimes her temper erupted, and Lincoln felt her wrath both at home and in public. But he accepted her angry displays with characteristic calm. A tantrum "does her lots of good and it doesn't hurt me a bit," he explained.[61] Mary sometimes convinced herself that the family was nearly destitute, and she worried excessively how the bills would be paid. When her husband reassured her that they were on solid financial ground, she would spend excessively for items she did not need, such as clothes for herself, a pattern that she kept up her entire life.

In late 1843 Lincoln tired of his junior partner status, and with Logan desiring to enter practice with his son, the two men terminated their relationship. Lincoln surprised everyone by selecting as a new partner William Herndon, a young man just 25 years of age and with almost no legal experience. Lincoln had first met Herndon in 1832, when Herndon's cousin had piloted the *Talisman* up the Sangamon River, assisted by Lincoln. Later Herndon worked at Joshua Speed's store, where Lincoln regarded him as a younger brother. Herndon, in turn, fairly worshiped Lincoln. Herndon completed his studies at Illinois College in Jacksonville, then studied to become a lawyer. He was thrilled when Lincoln asked him to join his practice, and the friendship between the two men cemented their informal partnership agreement: "Bill," said Lincoln, "I can trust you, if you can trust me."[62]

Lincoln did not forget politics or his Whig principles. At Mary's urging he had long set his sights on a congressional career. "Now if you should hear anyone say that Lincoln don't want to go to Congress, I wish you as a personal friend of mine, would tell him you have reason to believe he is mistaken," he wrote in 1843.[63] But others had their eyes on the same Seventh Congressional District seat, most notably his good friends John J. Hardin, who happened to be Mary's cousin, and Edward Baker, who was a respected lawyer and for whom Lincoln's son was named. The three men reached an agreement: each would take his turn, if elected, and then step aside for the successor. Hardin served from 1842 to 1844, and Baker was elected as designed. But Hardin surfaced again in 1846, informing Lincoln that he intended to run in spite of the agreement. Lincoln stumped hard in the primary to earn the nomination, employing none of the dirty tricks or slanderous accusations of his early days in the Illinois legislature; instead, he simply reminded the voters that "turn about is fair play." Hardin was an honorable man and a fine Whig, but he had his chance in Washington and must live up to his part of the bargain. With area Whigs behind Lincoln, and the Whig press supporting him, Hardin had no choice but to withdraw from the race. Lincoln then turned his attention to the general election, running against an unlikely Democratic opponent named Peter Cartwright.

Cartwright was a 61-year-old Methodist preacher who seemed to hold no particular political principles. Rather, he was a fire-and-brimstone evangelist who was interested only in exposing Lincoln as an infidel. Lincoln defended himself by circulating handbills throughout the district. "That I am not a member of any Christian Church, is true," he wrote, "but I have never denied the truth of the Scriptures; and I have never spoken with intentional disrespect of religion in general, or of any denomination of Christians in particular."[64] Cartwright's unorthodox campaign strategy backfired, and on August 3, 1846, Lincoln won a landslide victory, carrying eight of 11 counties and nearly two-thirds of the vote. But the excitement of his election quickly faded, for Lincoln's congressional experience proved to be a disappointment.

By the time Lincoln and his family arrived in Washington, D.C., in December

1847 the country was at war with Mexico. While he had been silent on the issue during the campaign, Lincoln now adopted the official Whig position and opposed the war, partly because he viewed it as an attempt to conquer Mexico and thus expand slavery, and partly because Democratic president James K. Polk supported it. Two weeks after his arrival Lincoln spoke out on the House floor, demanding to learn the exact "spot" where any American had lost his life; it could then be discerned what country had started the war. If, as he suspected, the war had begun on peaceful Mexican soil, Polk, "a bewildered, confounded, and miserably perplexed man," had provoked an unjust war.[65] The war soon died down, but the criticism Lincoln received for his position did not. He was castigated in Washington and back home in Illinois, where even Herndon thought Lincoln's remarks were inappropriate and perhaps unpatriotic.

The mild furor that Lincoln's "spot" remarks proved to be the only noteworthy event of Lincoln's first term in Congress. Mary left to visit her family in Kentucky, and Lincoln soon felt lonely and mildly depressed without her and the boys. He busied himself with Whig party politicking of little real consequence, and to his surprise found himself bored and disillusioned with his work in Washington. He spent the fall stumping for presidential candidate Zachary Taylor, a contest "Old Rough and Ready" won by a healthy margin, and returned wearily to Springfield.

Lincoln's second term was even less impressive than his first. Congress was gridlocked on every major issue, almost always because of sectional differences over slavery. Lincoln offered no bills, although he drafted a bill authorizing gradual emancipation of Washington's slaves, provided the electorate approved it and slave owners were compensated. He could not garner much support for the measure, however, and never offered it. In the last days of the session he tried to secure for himself the commissionership of the General Land Office, figuring the position should go to one of Taylor's most tireless workers—but to his disappointment the job went to another. He was offered first the secretaryship, then the governorship, of the Oregon Territory, but was not inclined to accept either post. Lincoln slouched back home to Springfield, certain his political career was over for good. He wrote glumly to a friend, "I neither seek, expect, or deserve" to ever return to Washington.[66]

2

Moving Heaven and Earth

Mary Lincoln had no desire to move her family to the unsettled wilds of the far-off Oregon Territory. Neither did the $3,000 per year salary the governorship position offered particularly impress her. Lincoln, dissatisfied with the workings of national politics and an unfair patronage system, agreed with his wife. He also turned down an opportunity closer to home. A prominent Chicago attorney named Grant Goodrich invited Lincoln to join in his practice there, but after some consideration Lincoln decided against it. Another reason, more personal and painful, necessitated the family's return to Springfield. In December 1849 the Lincolns' second son, Eddie, developed a chronic cough and fever—symptoms of what was then deemed consumption, later known to be pulmonary tuberculosis—and the Lincolns wanted to care for him back in the familiar house at Eighth and Jackson streets. Eddie was attended to by Mary's brother-in-law Dr. William Wallace, but there was no known cure or effective treatment for the disease. The Lincolns could only keep an anxious vigil as Eddie's condition steadily deteriorated, and as they watched helplessly he died on February 1, 1850, shortly before his fourth birthday.

The funeral took place at the Lincoln home, and the body was buried just a few blocks away at Hutchinson's Cemetery. Already grieving the recent loss of both her father and grandmother, Mary was devastated by Eddie's death. She stayed in her bedroom for days, curtains drawn, and refused to eat. But Lincoln patiently consoled her, and she eventually found refuge in the comforting words of James Smith, pastor of Springfield's Second Presbyterian Church. Though she had previously been affiliated with the Episcopalians, Mary now joined Pastor Smith's church just a few blocks from home and began to regularly worship there. At Mary's insistence Lincoln rented a family pew, and although he occasionally attended services and regularly welcomed Pastor Smith to his home for dinner, he never joined this or any other church. Smith's friendship with Lincoln paid an unusual dividend; in 1863 Lincoln named him United States consul to his native Scotland at Dundee.[1]

Mary became pregnant within just a few weeks of Eddie's death, but the joy of a new child could not replace the heartache of her loss—and never would. Three years later she wrote that "our second boy, a promising bright creature of four years we were called upon to part with several years ago and I grieve to say that even at this day I do not feel sufficiently submissive to our loss."[2]

Lincoln internalized his grief and rarely ever again mentioned Eddie or his heart-breaking death. Certain that his career in politics was over, he devoted himself to his law practice. The legal profession, he wrote, "superceded the thought of politics in his mind."[3] He and Herndon soon moved to a second-floor office on the west side of the public square, and this dingy and unkempt room, equipped only with two tables, a desk, couch and some bookshelves, became Lincoln's center of operations for the next 10 years.

Lincoln's early career as a lawyer had earned him the reputation as being honest, capable, quirky but effective. He now sought to attain a higher level of respect among clients and associates alike. He studied harder, read less for pleasure and more for professional advantage, and injected a more serious tone to his courtroom appearances. The circuit remained at the heart of his practice, and he faithfully traveled it twice per year, every year (the only other attorney who made both circuit trips was the prosecutor), even though it kept him from home for up to six months out of the year. Lincoln continued to enjoy the company of his fellow lawyers. Often he associated in cases with men like Ward Hill Lamon of Danville, Leonard Swett of Bloomington, and Orville H. Browning of Quincy, men who would eventually play instrumental roles in his rise to the presidency. He greatly appreciated the warm receptions the lawyers received in the numerous small towns they visited. He never complained about the bad food, uncomfortable lodging, or the unpredictable weather that often hampered his travel, for he sincerely loved to be out among the common people of his state, and he never stopped considering himself one of them. He took his clients as he found them. For modest fees— often only $5 or $10 dollars per case — Lincoln handled matters in divorce, probate, foreclosure and trespass. He drafted deeds, mortgages and simple contracts. He represented creditors in collections, and while there was money to be made in this kind of work, Lincoln did not prefer it: he was usually too busy to track down debtors and investigate their assets, and he had to get moving to the next town on the circuit. When Lincoln was traveling across the prairie he was, according to Judge Davis, "as happy as he could be."[4]

In addition to his varied civil practice, Lincoln began to earn a reputation as a skilled criminal defense attorney. He defended clients charged with crimes ranging from gambling, public drunkenness and disorderly conduct to larceny, assault and murder. Sometimes Lincoln's clients were acquitted and sometimes they were convicted, but the juries that delivered verdicts on his cases came away with an admiration for his energy and devotion to his cause. His mastery of logic, attention to detail and advocacy skills became so well respected that on at least one occasion he was called in to act as a special prosecutor. He gained a conviction in a rape case, and the guilty man was sent to prison.

Lincoln's dedication to his clients rose above personal feelings. In 1859 he successfully defended "Peachy" Harrison on a murder charge. Harrison was the grandson of preacher David Cartwright who had run a bitter campaign against Lincoln for Congress in 1846. Lincoln once represented a woman in a collection suit against old Mentor Graham, the man who was greatly responsible for Lincoln's informal education, not because he could earn a fee but because he knew the woman was in the right. He represented runaway slaves who sued for their freedom, and he worked just as diligently for slaveowners who sought to reclaim their human property.

In 1858 Lincoln participated in what was to become his most famous case, the defense of William "Duff" Armstrong against murder charges. Duff was the son of Lincoln's old friend Jack Armstrong, who had died a year earlier, and his widow, Hannah, could not control her 24-year-old son. Like his father, Duff had a wild streak, and one drunken evening he brawled with other men outside of town. A man named James Metzker was killed, and when Duff was indicted for the crime Hannah turned to Lincoln, who readily agreed to take the case for no fee.

Some 25 witnesses testified at the trial, but the case turned on Lincoln's ingenious cross-examination of an eyewitness named Charles Allen, who claimed to have seen Duff strike the victim in the eye with a slingshot, killing him. Allen saw the incident, he said, from a distance of 150 feet by the light of a full moon, at about 11 o'clock. Lincoln produced an almanac and proved that on the night in question the moon was barely past its first quarter, and in fact had disappeared by 11 o'clock. The witness was lying and could not be believed.

But Lincoln could not resist playing an emotional card. He told the jury how he had once been a penniless stranger in New Salem, and Jack and Hannah Armstrong had mercifully taken him in. They had fed him, provided a warm bed for him, and allowed him to rock their baby — none other than this defendant, Duff — in his cradle. Deep in his heart, said Lincoln, he knew that Duff was innocent of this horrible charge. By convincing the jury of that fact, he would, in small part, be able to repay a debt he owed to the Armstrong family for their kindness of many years ago. When the jury went to deliberate Lincoln comforted his friend Hannah. "They'll clear Duff before dark," he predicted, and he was right.[5]

The decade of the 1850s saw the growth of state and national railroad networks, and as Lincoln's reputation grew the railroads sought him out to represent their interests. He advised the Alton & Sangamon, the Chicago, Rock Island & Pacific, and the mighty Illinois Central Railroad, among others, on issues involving organization and charter, merger, acquisition, taxation, right of way and regulations. In one major case Lincoln's successful argument before the Illinois Supreme Court on behalf of the Alton & Sangamon was cited as precedent in 25 other jurisdictions.[6] In another case Lincoln argued that the state legislature had acted constitutionally when it exempted the Illinois Central from local taxation. The court was persuaded by Lincoln's argument and ruled for the railroad. Lincoln presented his client with a bill of $2,000, pointing out that if the railroad had lost the case it would have been liable for millions in taxes. The railroad balked, claiming, "This is as much as Daniel Webster himself would have charged." Lincoln brought suit for collection in the upgraded amount of $5,000, and was eventually awarded this amount, the largest fee of his career.

In 1855 the Federal District of Illinois was divided into two, one division in Chicago and one in Springfield. Lincoln enjoyed an extensive and successful practice in both of these courts, handling cases in interstate commerce and admiralty, constitutional law, and his particular favorite, patent law. His reputation grew from local to regional to statewide attorney, and he became one of the mainstays, if not the outright leader, of the Illinois bar. Older attorneys respected his dedication to his clients and his ability to persuade juries. Younger attorneys admired his wit and appreciated his willingness to share his knowledge. Lincoln's reputation for honesty, integrity and intellect was so impeccable that Judge Davis sometimes asked him to serve as acting judge, an unparalleled honor. Lincoln was admitted to practice before the United States Supreme Court in 1849, and he appeared before the nation's highest Court three times in his career, the last of which came in 1853.

The attorneys around him could not help but notice that he was changing. He began to spend more and more time alone. For every hour spent telling stories and joking with his friends, he spent twice as much time in silent contemplation. When on the circuit he lay awake at the end of his bed reading by candlelight, long after the other lawyers had retired. He was always the first to awaken, and he went for long walks along a river or out in the prairie fields, or simply sat by the fire and waited for the day to begin. Some speculated that family troubles were to blame for Lincoln's moodiness. Perhaps his frustration with an increasingly temperamental wife might explain why he stayed away from home for such long stretches, and why he was so often filled with melancholy. But in reality Lincoln was simply coming to terms with himself, for he knew that unlocked within him was a vast potential. He did not communicate any ambitions or aspirations, even to his closest friends, but he sensed that he was destined for something greater for his life's work.

Although it seemed likely that Lincoln's political career was over he remained active within the Whig Party, where his role was limited to advisor and not candidate. He supported Winfield Scott for president in 1852, although he gloomily (and correctly) predicted that Scott would be easily defeated by Democrat Franklin Pierce. Most significantly Lincoln kept a watchful eye on the slavery issue that surfaced, subsided and resurfaced again, dividing the people and threatening the very Union itself.

While the slavery issue had always interested Lincoln, he had never any reason to confront it directly. His Baptist parents would not live in a slave state and had left Kentucky for free-soil Indiana and Illinois. Lincoln, then, believed himself to be "naturally anti-slavery." He could not remember, he later said, "when I did not so think, and feel."[7] Lincoln's first view of slaves had been in 1831, when he had encountered a group in New Orleans while on his raft trip. He was haunted by a scene he had witnessed in 1841, the selling of a dozen slaves shackled in leg-irons. As an Illinois legislator he was one of only a handful to vote against resolutions condemning abolitionism and declaring that the Constitution contemplated that slaves were to be treated as property. The institution of slavery, Lincoln wrote as a protest against the resolutions, "is founded on both injustice and bad policy."[8] In the eulogy he delivered for his political idol Henry Clay in 1852, Lincoln was careful to note that his "beau ideal of a statesman" was "on principle and in feeling, opposed to slavery."[9] He admired his father-in-law for supporting a very unpopular cause, the gradual emancipation of slaves in Kentucky. Lincoln naively favored colonization, at least in the District of Columbia where Congress could not intervene, as the perfect compromise to the slavery issue: blacks would be freed on condition they relocate to Liberia, while their owners would be justly compensated. Lincoln held this view, which had almost no chance of becoming law, until well into his presidency.

While his personal experience with blacks was minimal (Springfield had only 171 blacks in 1850, although one man, William LeFleur, was Lincoln's barber), Lincoln knew that slavery was the single most important issue of the era. His philosophical opposition to slavery did not rise to the level of northern abolitionists, who in their fervor would do almost anything to eliminate slavery everywhere, and forever. While Lincoln recognized that many southerners supported slavery whether they held slaves or not, and understood that the institution was an important element in the southern lifestyle, he did not believe that slavery would endure forever. Rather, Lincoln hoped that eventually most or all Americans, including southerners, would come to realize that slavery was incompatible with the freedoms expressed in the Declaration of Independence, and he clung to the hope that slavery was on the course of ultimate extinction. And at least, until that day came, Lincoln could take comfort that slavery would not be extended westward into the territories by virtue of the famed Missouri Compromise.

For 35 years the Missouri Compromise had effectively balanced the slave and antislave interests in America. By that law Missouri had entered the Union as a slave state in 1821, and slavery was then forever banned in all other lands acquired through the Louisiana Purchase and north of the 36 percent 30' line. But by the early 1850s immigrants began to pour into the territories of Kansas and Nebraska, and Congress needed to act to organize governments there and pave the way for completion of a planned transcontinental railroad, which would be laid out directly through the region. In January 1854, Senator Stephen Douglas introduced his Kansas-Nebraska bill, which allowed for the peoples of those vast regions to determine for themselves whether to allow slavery or prohibit it. This concept of "popular sovereignty" would of course effectively repeal the key provisions of the Missouri Compromise. After a bitter congressional struggle the bill was signed into law by President Pierce on May 4, 1854, and Douglas correctly predicted that "a hell of a storm" would ensue.[10]

Lincoln was on the circuit in Urbana when news of the new law came over the telegraph wires. Though he knew the bill was pending, he was "thunderstruck and stunned" when it passed. He "reeled and fell in utter confusion," he later wrote, but soon "rose ... fighting."[11] Politicians from every state had something to say about the controversial new law; many in the North were particularly outraged. Douglas himself acknowledged that his popularity in the North plummeted. "I could travel from Chicago to Boston by the light of my own effigy," he said.[12] In August, Lincoln spoke out against the "Nebraska bill" at a campaign rally for Whig senatorial candidate Richard Tyler. Before a crowd of 150 people in Winchester, Lincoln characterized the Missouri Compromise as "something sacred," noting that it had been introduced in the Senate in 1820 by Jesse B. Thomas of Illinois. Stephen Douglas, under the guise of his popular sovereignty doctrine, was in reality aggressively pursuing a policy of slavery's extension. If the law stood unchecked, cautioned Lincoln, the country was on the path to disaster.

The Nebraska bill was the precursor to Lincoln's entry into politics, for it "aroused him as he had never been before."[13] He allowed his name to be placed into nomination for a seat in the Illinois legislature. He won the election easily, but then suddenly resigned his seat before the term began. By law a state legislator was prohibited from running for the U.S. Senate, and what Lincoln really wanted was to challenge his old adversary and the man behind all the furor, Stephen Douglas.

But Lincoln had known for some time that the popular appeal of the Whigs was fading, due in part to its members' split over the slavery issue, and he realized that he must break free from the constraints of his old party. He struggled with his political identity as he searched for a party he could embrace. He could never be a Democrat, of course. He could not identify with the radical abolitionists because he believed that the Constitution protected slavery in those states where it existed. A new party, the Know-Nothings, did not appeal to him. The group was comprised of Protestants who opposed further immigration and hated Catholics; when asked about their political affiliations, members claimed to "know nothing." How could Lincoln oppose the oppression of slavery, he wondered in a candid letter to Joshua Speed, if he supported the oppression of immigrants? Lincoln needed a party that promoted the political ideals he espoused and, just as important, could show real promise as a significant and prominent party of the future.

There were others in Illinois who felt the same way. Two years earlier, in 1854, a group of antislavery men (including Billy Herndon)—"free-soilers" or "anti-Nebraskans," they called themselves—met informally to organize what was to become the Republican Party. By May 1856 the group was gaining momentum and increasing in numbers. They gathered for a state convention at Bloomington, and Lincoln attended, for after much deliberation he had concluded that he must join the party or forever fade from view. The trick, as he saw it, was to appease the abolitionists while attracting as many former Whigs, liberal Democrats, free-soilers and antislavery Know-Nothings as possible. The party must bring together, in an improbable coalition, all those who saw the necessity of working toward a common goal: to keep slavery from spreading to the territories (and, incidentally, bring an end to the southern dominance of American political life). Lincoln felt that joining the new party might be a gamble, but it was one worth taking. "I have no objection to 'fuse' with anybody provided I can fuse on ground which I think is right," he said.[14]

Undoubtedly encouraged by Lincoln's endorsement, other important Illinois political leaders including Norman Judd, Lyman Trumbull, David Davis and Leonard Swett also attended the convention. Lincoln electrified his friends, and all those in attendance, with an inspired, rousing speech. Slavery was the cause of all the nation's woes, he claimed, and through the passage of the Nebraska bill its authors intended that the abomination be extended into the territories. He pledged to stand with anyone who opposed the slave power. A united North must be forceful and unwavering on the issue, even if it meant risking southern discontent. The glorious words of Daniel Webster, he shouted over the din of the roaring crowd, should be the standard of the Republican Party: "Liberty and Union, now and forever, one and inseparable."[15] Lincoln was, according to Herndon, "newly baptized and freshly born; he had the fervor of a new convert; the smothered flame broke out; enthusiasm unusual to him blazed up; his eyes were aglow with an inspiration; he felt justice; his heart was alive to the right; his sympathies, remarkably deep for him, burst forth, and he stood before the throne of the eternal Right."[16]

Opponents of the Nebraska bill found bloody ammunition for their cause in the West, where free-state men were engaged in a savage civil war with proslavery forces in Kansas and Missouri. Militia and "border-ruffians" conducted a reign of terror on free-state communities and families, robbing, burning and killing any who opposed them. In retaliation an antislavery zealot named John Brown, believing he was God's instrument, led a massacre of proslavery men at Pottawatomie Creek. If anyone wondered whether popular sovereignty would ever work, observed Lincoln, they need only look west to "Bleeding Kansas." The people of the territory could never decide for themselves whether to allow or disallow slavery, as the violence showed. Douglas's cursed law was "conceived in violence, passed in violence, and executed in violence."[17]

The Republican Party quickly gained strength throughout the North. It suffered a temporary setback in 1856, when Democrat James Buchanan defeated Republican John Fremont for president, but made a respectable showing at the polls. Lincoln had been considered as Fremont's running mate for vice president, but he was not discouraged when the nomination went to William Dayton of New Jersey. He was so dedicated to the Republican cause that he enthusiastically gave more than 50 speeches that summer in support of the Buchanan-Dayton ticket. Eventually, he believed, his new party would capture the White House. Still, he remained wary of the strength of the Democrats, and though there was a substantial antislavery element within that party, he was not sure that it could be defeated in 1860. But "the free-soil party is bound to win in the long run," he predicted to young newspaperman Noah Brooks. "It may not be in my day, but it will in yours, I really do believe."[18]

In March 1857 the Supreme Court gave antislavery advocates new fuel for debate when it issued its decision in the *Dred Scott* case. Chief Justice Roger B. Taney, himself a slaveholder, wrote for a divided Court that "Negroes were beings of an inferior order ... and altogether unfit to associate with the white race ... they possessed no rights which the white man was bound to respect."[19] Thus, Taney wrote, Negroes were not and never had been citizens under the Constitution, and the subject of the litigation, a slave named Dred Scott who had sued for his freedom when his master had taken him into a free territory, had no right to bring the action. Further, wrote Taney in dictum, the Missouri Compromise itself was unconstitutional in outlawing slavery from the territories.

Lincoln quickly condemned the Court's decision. When the country was formed, he said, "the Declaration of Independence was held sacred by all, and thought to include all. But now, to aid in making the bondage of the Negro universal and eternal, it is assailed, and sneered at, and construed, and hawked at, and torn, till, if its framers could rise from their graves, they could not at all recognize it." The Supreme Court had often overruled its own decisions, Lincoln noted, and "we shall do what we can to have it overrule this."[20]

In June, Illinois Republicans met in Springfield for their state convention and nominated Lincoln to run against Douglas in the upcoming senatorial campaign. The conclusion of the "grand affair," as Lincoln described it, was his acceptance speech, given at the statehouse on the evening of the 16th. Lincoln had spent weeks in preparing it. He applied biblical language to the crisis facing the country. "A house divided against itself cannot stand," he said. "I believe this government cannot endure, permanently half slave and half free. I do not expect the Union to be dissolved — I do not expect the house to fall — but I do expect it will cease to be divided. It will become all one thing, or all the other." Lincoln warned that the Democrats were working with the Supreme Court to establish a national slavery policy. "We shall lie down pleasantly dreaming that the people of Missouri are on the verge of making their State free; and we shall awake to the reality, instead, that the Supreme Court has make Illinois a slave State. To meet and overthrow the power of the dynasty, is the work now before all those who would prevent that consummation." The Republicans must now rally around their righteous cause. "The result is not doubtful," Lincoln concluded. "We shall not fail — if we stand firm, we shall not fail. Wise councils may accelerate or mistakes delay it, but, sooner or later the victory is sure to come."[21]

Some of Lincoln's supporters felt that his language was too radical; it seemed to predict, if not invite, civil war and might doom his prospects for election. But Lincoln did not have second thoughts. "You will see the day when you will consider it the wisest thing I ever said," he predicted.[22] Stephen Douglas was in Washington when he learned of Lincoln's nomination. "I'll have my hands full," he said. "He's the strong man of the party — full of wit, facts, dates — and he's the best stump speaker, with his droll way and dry jokes, in the West. He's as honest as he is shrewd, and if I beat him my victory will be hardly won."

Douglas came to Illinois in July to begin the campaign, and immediately embarked on a nonstop speaking tour, touting his popular sovereignty plan and defending the Nebraska bill. Lincoln began to follow Douglas around the state, listening carefully to his opponent's speeches, taking notes, and at larger venues like Chicago and Springfield offering rebuttal remarks of his own. Douglas at first mocked Lincoln's strategy. Lincoln could not draw crowds on his own, he sneered, so he had to trail Douglas in hopes of finding someone who might listen. But eventually Douglas sharpened his tone: Lincoln's shadow tactics were simply cowardly. Stung by criticism from Democratic newspapers, and at the urging of Judd and Davis, who were acting as his unofficial advisors, Lincoln finally issued a formal challenge: he wanted to debate Douglas, face to face, at 40 or 50 places around the state. Douglas had never been afraid of a fight, and he did not back down from this one. But he insisted on limits. He agreed to a series of seven debates, one in each of Illinois' districts less Chicago and Springfield. They would consist of a one-hour opening statement, an hour and a half reply, and half-hour rebuttal, with the speakers alternating opening and closing statements. The 1858 senatorial debates — Honest Abe vs. the Little Giant — became one of the most significant events in the history of American politics.

The debates drew immense crowds at every stop. On August 21, 12,000 people attended the first debate at Ottawa, and similar throngs also appeared in Freeport, Jonesboro, Charleston, Galesburg, Quincy and Alton. Douglas arrived at the cities via private railroad coach owned by George McClellan, vice president and chief engineer of the Illinois Central Railroad and strong Democrat (and who would become, in 1861, commanding general of the Union army and, in 1864, Lincoln's opponent in the presidential election). Douglas was accompanied by his beautiful wife, Adele. The couple took their lodging at the finest hotels and dined at the finest restaurants. Douglas was carried to the sites of the debates like a foreign dignitary, drawn by four-horse carriages to the roar of cannon blast, flags and streamers fluttering, military bands playing lively tunes. He dressed splendidly in a velvet blue coat and shiny gold buttons, a white ruffled shirt, polished shoes and a wide-brimmed hat placed on his oversized head. His stomped about the speakers' platform, shaking his fists, taunting his adversary, his voice booming in a magnificent baritone. He was in his glory and he reveled in it.

Lincoln put on no airs. He traveled alone by public railroad car, his frayed carpetbag resting on his lap. He cared little about fancy surroundings or expensive meals. He was carried from his hotel to the debate site by buggy; if it was close enough, he walked. Lincoln's appearance had not changed noticeably since his days as a young man in New Salem. He wore a stovepipe hat and his characteristic shabby overcoat. When the weather got too hot he removed it to reveal an equally shabby shirt and plain suspenders. His trousers were baggy and several inches too short, and his boots were unpolished. His voice was high-pitched with more than a trace of Kentucky drawl. He began his speeches haltingly, nervously, holding one hand behind his back as he spoke, then gradually becoming more animated as he warmed to the passion of his topic. Sometimes to emphasize a point he bent himself downwards, then thrust his lanky frame up to his tiptoes. His grey eyes darted from his notes to his audience and sometimes to his adversary Douglas, who sat confidently on the platform.

While the two speakers challenged and badgered each other, scoffing at the other's position and appealing to boisterous supporters, the main substance of their speeches remained constant. Douglas accused Lincoln and his supporters of a conspiracy meant to galvanize former Whigs, antislavery Democrats and disgruntled abolitionists into one sectional party aimed only toward the abolition of slavery, which was contrary to the views of most Americans. Douglas vigorously defended his popular sovereignty doctrine as a "great American principle," nothing less than a cornerstone of democracy that allowed the people to choose whether or not they wanted slavery.

Douglas denied the humanity of the black race and declared that blacks could not enjoy the freedoms of whites because of their inferior position. "I do not regard the Negro as my equal, and positively deny that he is my brother or any kin to me whatever," he said.[23] Lincoln was nothing but a Black Republican who favored amalgamation of the races, a wicked and unnatural practice that could never be tolerated. Further, Douglas argued, the nation's founders held the same opinions. They had established the government for the benefit of white men like themselves. Douglas ridiculed Lincoln's famous assertion that America could not endure half free and half slave. Why couldn't it exist forever divided on this issue? It had for over 80 years.

Lincoln tossed about a conspiracy charge of his own. Douglas, he charged, was working in tandem with no less than Chief Justice Taney himself. Taney's decision in *Dred Scott* had only set the stage for what was surely to come: a Supreme Court ruling that excluded states from prohibiting slavery. That was what Douglas and the

Democrats really wanted. Lincoln looked upon slavery as a great moral issue. He believed the words of the Declaration of Independence: all men, and not just white men, were created equal. The founding fathers never intended that slavery spread as the country expanded; rather, they meant to limit its growth, thereby setting it on the road to ultimate extinction.

Lincoln was careful to point out that he was not in favor of total equality between the races. He did not support black voting rights and did not want blacks to hold office. Just because he did not want a black woman for a slave, he said, did not necessarily mean that he wanted one for a wife. But he would never understand why blacks were not allowed the opportunity to toil for their own bread and then eat it as well. Slavery was wrong, and would always be wrong. "That is the issue," he said, "that will continue in this country when these poor tongues of Judge Douglas and myself shall be silent. It is the eternal struggle between … right and wrong — throughout the world."[24]

While the debates were the focal point of the campaign, they were not all of it. In between debates the candidates traveled relentlessly across the state, giving speeches once or twice per day. By November Douglas was physically exhausted, his face was puffy, his voice reduced to a rasp. Lincoln's simpler living style helped him make it through the campaign in better shape physically, but drained emotionally. When Mary finally joined him in Alton he was greatly relieved, and her soothing words comforted him.

Election day was November 2. Voters did not technically vote for either Lincoln or Douglas, but rather for legislative representatives who would decide which candidate captured the Senate seat. Although Republicans polled about 4,000 more votes than Democrats, political alignment and the apportionment of districts in Illinois gave the edge, and the victory, to Douglas. Lincoln was again for a time disappointed — he lamented that he "may now sink out of view, and be forgotten" — but he took solace in the fact that he had exposed Douglas as a fraud and "have made some marks which will tell for civil liberty long after I am gone."[25] He was proud of his performances against Douglas, and put together a scrapbook of newspaper accounts of the debates. He had received favorable coverage in the national press, and Republican leaders, particularly in the heavily populated Northeast, could not help but notice the unlikely figure from Illinois. Lincoln's name was now being mentioned as a potential presidential candidate in 1860, and although he wanted another run at Douglas in 1864, he told friends that he would serve at any position if it was in the best interests of the party.

Lincoln was now flooded with offers to speak. When he could find time between his busy court schedule, Lincoln toured extensively, addressing audiences in Wisconsin, Ohio and Indiana. The slavery issue did not quiet down. Senator William H. Seward of New York, thought by many to be the leading candidate for the Republican nomination for president, caused a mild sensation when he blamed slavery for the "irrepressible conflict" that was sure to come. Seward also believed that a "higher law than the Constitution" mandated the extermination of slavery; these phrases were praised by abolitionists but denounced by moderates as reckless and radical. In October 1859, John Brown and a group of fanatics seized a federal arsenal at Harper

Ferry, Virginia, in the deranged belief that a slave revolt would ensue. A detachment of soldiers headed by a Virginia commander named Robert E. Lee restored order only after 16 of Brown's 18 followers were killed. On December 2, the day Brown was hanged, Lincoln made a speech in Atchison, Kansas. While he knew that southern sentiment in favor of secession was rising, he hoped that the slavery issue would be dealt with at the ballot box and not on the battlefield. But if southern states meant to disrupt the Union, he warned, "it will be our duty to deal with you as old John Brown has been dealt with."[26]

In February 1860 Lincoln accepted an invitation from the famed preacher Henry Ward Beecher to speak at his Plymouth Church in Brooklyn. When Lincoln arrived, however, he learned that his appearance had been changed to the Cooper Institute in Manhattan, and his sponsor would not be the Reverend Beecher but the Young Men's Republican Club. The switch in plans was fortunate for Lincoln: on the club's board of advisors were influential New York *Tribune* editor Horace Greeley, poet and New York *Evening Post* editor William Cullen Bryant and jurist David Dudley Field, all important Republicans who did not necessarily favor Seward and who would be very interested in hearing what Lincoln might have to say. Lincoln knew how important the speech would be to his political future; not only was it his first opportunity to address a New York audience, but the building would be packed with press representatives. He worked long hours on his speech, bought a new suit for $100 (Mary would not have approved; it fit him poorly), and had a formal portrait taken at the studio of photographer Matthew Brady. On the night of the 27th he climbed into a buggy and was driven through the streets of New York in a raging snowstorm to the Cooper Institute. There, to his surprise, he learned that 1,500 people — "largest assemblage of intellect and culture of our city," said Greeley — had paid 25 cents to see and hear "the Westerner."[27]

Lincoln began his address as he had the debates with Douglas, slowly, nervously, self-conscious about his appearance and his accent. But soon his words began to flow easily with the passion of a man who truly believed in what he was saying. He attacked the "conspirators" Stephen Douglas and Roger Taney, and proclaimed that a majority of the founding fathers had, at some point in their careers, voted to let Congress alone determine if slavery was ever to extend to the territories. The founders had marked slavery as "an evil not to be extended, but to be tolerated and protected only because of and so far as its actual presence among us makes it a necessity." Lincoln attacked John Brown, who was seen by radicals as a martyr. Republicans denounced Brown as a madman whose raid on Harpers Ferry "was so absurd that the slaves ... saw plainly enough it could not succeed." And Lincoln belittled southern threats of secession as a "rule or ruin" philosophy. "You say you won't abide the election of a Republican President! In that supposed event, you say, you'll destroy the Union and then, you say, the great crime of having destroyed it will be upon us! That is cool. A highwayman holds a pistol to my ear, and mutters through his teeth, 'Stand and deliver, or I'll kill you, and then you'll be a murderer!'"

Lincoln closed with advice to his fellow Republicans. While the slavery issue was momentous, maintaining the Union was of greater import. Republicans must "do nothing through passion and ill temper," he said. Rather, they must convince their southern brothers that they had nothing to fear if and when Republicans won the White House. But while Republicans would leave slavery alone where it existed, and would fight against its expansion, they would never agree that it was *right*. "Their thinking it right, and our thinking it wrong, is the precise fact upon which depends the whole controversy," Lincoln said. "Thinking it wrong, as we do, can we yield to them? Can we cast our votes with their view, and against our own?" The Cooper crowd was on its feet now, clapping and whistling, and Lincoln's voice raised to another level. "Let us not be slandered from our duty by false accusations against us, nor frightened from it by menaces of destruction to the government nor of dungeons to ourselves." Lincoln shouted above wild cheering, "Let us have faith that right makes might, and in that faith, let us, to the end, dare to do our duty as we understand it."[28]

Lincoln's words boomed like a cannon shot across the Northeast. Greeley wrote that "no man ever before made such an impression on his first appeal to a New York audience."[29] Pamphlets of Lincoln's speech were quickly printed and distributed everywhere. Lincoln continued on an extended speaking tour of New England, delivering substantially the same speech to much acclaim at every venue. Hordes of people surrounded him at train depots, and brass bands greeted him with fanfare at his hotels. The governor of Rhode Island shared the podium with Lincoln at Providence, and in Manchester, New Hampshire, he was introduced as "the next President." At Hartford, when Lincoln learned that shoemakers were on strike, he emphasized his humble background while offering an implied criticism of the slave system. "I am glad to see that a system of labor prevails in New England under which laborers *can*

strike," he said. "I like a system which lets a man quit when he wants to, and wish it might prevail everywhere. I don't believe in a law to prevent a man from getting rich; it would do more harm than good."[30] Lincoln was a common man, with common values and common sense, just like the people he wished to represent.

Back in Illinois, Lincoln's advisors sensed that the momentum was theirs, and, with a little luck and skilled maneuvering, they believed could bring Lincoln the presidential nomination. When Norman Judd miraculously convinced the National Republican Committee that the convention should be held in Chicago, Lincoln's own back yard, even Lincoln began to feel that his time might finally have come. "The taste *is* in my mouth a little," he wrote to Lyman Trumbull.[31]

Norman Buel Judd, who brought the Republican convention to Chicago and placed Lincoln's name into nomination (the Lincoln Museum, Fort Wayne, Indiana, # 76).

In May, Illinois Republicans met in Decatur for their state convention. To the delight of several thousand delegates Lincoln's cousin John Hanks and another man marched in carrying two log rails and a banner that read:

> ABRAHAM LINCOLN The Rail Candidate For President in 1860 Two rails from a lot of 3,000 made in 1830 by John Hanks and Abe Lincoln, whose father was the first pioneer of Macon County.[32]

That the banner's accuracy was doubtful was of no consequence; Lincoln was known ever after as the Railsplitter candidate, and Hanks sold rails from his farm nationwide for a dollar apiece. The next day Illinois Republicans voted to officially endorse Lincoln's nomination at the national convention.

Chicago hosted that event just a few days later. The Great Wigwam nearly burst at its seams with 10,000 delegates, politicians and reporters, but Lincoln was not among them. He stayed home in Springfield while Davis, Judd, Swett, Logan and other cronies planned strategy from the nearby Tremont House and wired Lincoln as to their progress. These managers realized that Lincoln's greatest strength lay in the fact that each of his rivals had at least one glaring weakness. Seward was too radical, and while he had the backing of New York politico Thurlow Weed, he was despised by influential Horace Greeley (who, for unknown reasons, had managed to secure a position as delegate not from New York, but the Oregon Territory). Attorney Edward Bates of Missouri was tainted by a brief affiliation with the Know-Nothings and a too-recent endorsement of Republican principles. Former Ohio governor and senator Salmon Chase suffered from a puzzling lack of popularity even within his own state. Senator Simon Cameron of Pennsylvania came from a crucially important state, but a reputation for corruption — he had personally profited from a treaty he negotiated as a state commissioner with the Winnebago Indian tribe — had dogged

Leonard Swett, another of Lincoln's friends who helped him gain the Republican nomination for president (the Lincoln Museum, Fort Wayne, Indiana, # 1360).

him since 1838. Lincoln's own private choice for the nomination, Supreme Court justice John McLean, who had dissented in the *Dred Scott* decision, was simply too old at age 75. Lincoln's moderate positions appealed to many and displeased very few. "My name is new in the field; and I suppose I am not the first choice of a very great many," Lincoln wrote. "Our policy, then, is to give no offence to others—leave them in a mood to come to us, if they shall be impelled to give up their first love."[33]

While the Republican platform was formalized and adopted during the first days of the convention, Lincoln's managers worked tirelessly behind the scenes. Davis went almost without sleep for several days, trying to persuade uncommitted delegates that only Lincoln could carry the important states of the lower North, while at the same time urging Seward or Bates men to switch their votes to Lincoln on the second ballot. Lincoln's other lieutenants carried his message of Republican unity, emphasizing that his principles were unwavering, even in these uncertain times. Davis wired Lincoln: "We are quiet but moving heaven and earth. Nothing will beat us but old fogy politicians."[34] All this cajoling and persuasion took place in a "Lincoln atmosphere." Ward Hill Lamon distributed thousands of bogus tickets to raucous Lincoln men who arrived at the Wigwam hours before the doors opened and then filled the place, all to the disgust of Seward and Chase supporters, who were left to fume outside the building.

On Friday, May 18, the balloting began. After the first ballot Seward led with 173½ votes, with 233 needed to secure the nomination. Lincoln was second with 102, followed by Cameron, Chase and Bates. Though Lincoln had been clear that his managers were not to make deals in exchange for votes, they now did exactly that. "Lincoln ain't here and don't know what we have to meet," proclaimed Davis.[35] They negotiated with the Pennsylvania delegation by promising of a cabinet post, then did the same with Indiana and Ohio. On the second ballot these crucial states came through as promised. Lincoln waited anxiously in his law office in Springfield, sometimes stepping out into the alley and streets to play ball with neighborhood boys. Finally a messenger arrived from the *State Journal*. Lincoln opened the envelope and read it silently. He did not speak for three minutes. "Well," he finally said, "We've got it." Soon another telegram came from his managers in Chicago: "We did it Glory to God."[36]

In Chicago a cannon was fired from the roof of the Wigwam when the announcement was made. Men cheered wildly, tossed their hats and canes into the air, and danced in merriment. Boats passing down the Chicago River blew their whistles as they passed, and church bells rang throughout the city. Senator Hannibal Hamlin from Maine was selected as Lincoln's running mate. After Lincoln learned this he shook hands with his friends and then started for home. "There's a little woman down at our house would like to hear this," he said. "I'll go down and tell her."[37] That night he greeted hundreds of friends at his home, who found him pleasant and gracious, and Mary "the very creature of excitement."[38] A parade passed by and he acknowledged the participants from his doorway, telling them that he regretted his house was not big enough to invite them all inside. "We'll get you a larger house on the fourth of next March," a supporter shouted from the crowd.[39]

3

Election

In the pre-dawn darkness of Tuesday, November 6, 1860, a boisterous contingent of about 40 raw-boned young men, representing the finest of the Springfield Wide-Awakes, gathered on the front lawn of the Sangamon County Courthouse. The group, comprised mostly of farmers, shopkeepers and clerks, formed up under the command of their leader, a 26-year-old barber named David King. Some of the men carried drums or bugles, while others carried lit torches set atop poles designed to look like log rails. Oilcloth capes and glazed caps covered their uniforms, protecting them from sparks and dripping hot oil. On King's orders the strongest dozen of the group wheeled the massive Cerro Gordo cannon — affectionately called "El Cyclope"—from its resting place on the courthouse grounds to a bluff just outside the city called Menard Hill, the procession illuminated by columns of flaming torches held high. When the sun rose King gave the order to fire the ancient weapon over the prairie, shattering the tranquility of the morning and waking most of the locals, and setting off answering chains of church bells, firecrackers and brass bands from all across town. The blast was meant by the Wide-Awakes as a preemptive celebratory signal to Springfield, and all of Sangamon County, that on this day their champion, 51-year-old Abraham Lincoln, would be elected president of the United States.

Lincoln did not need a cannon salute to roust him from his bed, for he was by nature a restless sleeper and early riser. He looked into the mirror that rested above the bureau in his bedroom, and brushed his thick black hair that had only recently begun showing flecks of silver. His gray eyes were clear but tired, and still sparkled when he laughed, though in recent months his right eye had begun to droop slightly when he became tense. He put on a sweat-stained, crumpled white shirt and covered it with his only black suit coat, and carelessly adjusted his tie. His drab clothing hung loosely, almost comically, on his gaunt frame. He had lost some 20 pounds over the course of the summer and now weighed only 180 pounds. His weight loss was not because of illness or excessive physical exertion; rather, the campaign so distracted him that often he simply forgot to eat. Pulling on his worn black boots that were caked from the mud of Springfield streets, he made his way down the central stairway that divided his home and greeted an already bustling household.

Mary, his wife these last 18 years, was seated at the dining room table with sons Willie, age nine, and Tad, seven. The Lincolns' oldest boy, 17-year-old Robert, was away from home in his first year at Harvard University, but his place at the table was filled by 14-year-old Philip Dinkell, the son of a neighbor (it eased Mary's mind to have a teenage boy in the house to protect against intruders, real or imagined, when her husband was working late at the office or on business trips out of town.) Eighteen-year-old Emma Johnson, one of a long line of servant girls hired by Lincoln to assist his wife with the cooking and cleaning, served breakfast.[1]

Lincoln took only a cup of coffee before leaving the house, placing an apple in the pocket of his overcoat for lunch. He smiled at his boys and took his shawl and stovepipe hat from the rack in the hallway. Mary walked him to the door and wished him luck with a light kiss on the cheek, and then stood in the front doorway and watched him walk away. In the weeks preceding the election she had grown increasingly anxious. As her husband's career had forged and faltered, from state legislator to one-term congressman, from prominent attorney to unsuccessful candidate for the U.S. Senate, so too had her own aspirations risen and fallen. She had long felt her husband was qualified to be president; her confidence in his abilities sometimes surpassed his own. "He is to be President of the United States some day," she had said as early as 1847. "If I had not thought so I never would have married him, for you can see he is not pretty. But look at him! Doesn't he look as if he would make a magnificent President?"[2]

But it was her destiny as well, she believed, to live in the White House. She had been interested in politics since her privileged childhood in Kentucky, and she happily admitted that the mutual love of politics had brought her and Lincoln together. She was not afraid to express her opinion on any issue, no matter how sensitive or controversial, and in fact prided herself in the advisory role she had long played in her husband's career. But in the weeks prior to the election her insecurities, and her knowledge that in a political campaign nothing could be taken for granted, had shaken her. Should her husband lose the election the humiliation would be unbearable. "I scarcely know, how I would bear up under defeat," she had written to a friend. "You must think of us on election day. I trust we will not have the trial."[3] Perhaps, too, she felt anxious for another reason. One of her husband's opponents for the presidency, Senator Stephen Douglas of Illinois, had once courted her. Twenty years ago she insisted that she would marry the suitor who had the best chance of becoming president. Was it possible that she had chosen the wrong beau?

Lincoln began the six-block walk from his home to the Governor's Room at the statehouse, his temporary office since he had won the Republican nomination in May. While it was not yet eight o'clock, many people were already about on this calm, pleasant day. Immediately recognizable by his long, ambling gait, with his hands clasped behind his back, friends and neighbors called out and wished Lincoln well. Small groups of party faithful, gathered at street corners and waiting for the polls to open, cheered as he passed. Brass bands played patriotic songs, some musicians standing on street corners beneath red and white Lincoln and Hamlin banners, others perched in open buckboards and carriages, moving about Springfield in attempts to arouse voters. Hundreds of placards pasted on buildings and light poles challenged the citizenry to show their support at the polls: "Republicans of Springfield, the eyes of the nation are upon you!"[4]

Lincoln was quietly optimistic about the outcome of the election. He knew, of

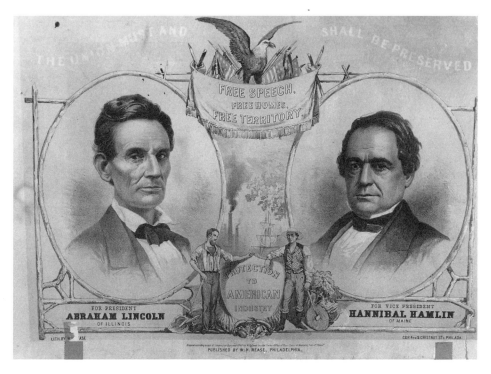

The Lincoln-Hamlin campaign banner touts freedom and industry, and proclaims that "The Union Must and Shall Be Preserved" (the Lincoln Museum, Fort Wayne, Indiana, # 3356).

course, that a presidential victory for his ticket seemed reasonably certain. The Republican Party consisted mainly of old Whigs and a smaller number of former Democrats and others who were committed to bringing about the end of slavery by political means. Unlike abolitionists, most Republicans believed that slavery—while a barbaric institution—was constitutionally protected. But while Congress had no authority to interfere with slavery, it could confine it to those southern states where it had long existed. If slavery was not allowed to spread to new western territories and states, ultimately, hoped Republicans, it would become extinct. To be sure, the Republican Party favored other causes, including higher tariffs and the building of a transcontinental railroad. But free soil, free labor, and upward social mobility were at the heart of the platform, all ideals Republicans considered essential in a true republic and very much at odds with the aristocracy and immorality of slavery.

Four years earlier, in 1856, the first Republican presidential candidate, John C. Fremont, had carried 11 states in a losing effort. Lincoln now hoped to build on that respectable showing. If the larger states of the Northeast came through as expected—October state elections in Pennsylvania, Indiana, and Ohio had been favorable, and New York seemed promising—the Republicans would carry the day. But Lincoln was careful not to appear overconfident, at least in public. "I hesitate to say it," he had written confidentially to a friend, "but it really appears now, as if success ... is inevitable. We have no reason to doubt any of the states which voted for Fremont.... Our friends are also confident in Indiana and Illinois.... Add to these Minnesota,

Pennsylvania, and New Jersey, and the thing is done."[5] In truth he was far more concerned about his party's chances for the Illinois governorship and legislative seats than his own opportunity to win the White House. In fact, it was not even certain that Republican candidates, including himself, would carry his own Sangamon County.

Lincoln's personal secretary greeted him at the statehouse office. John George Nicolay was born in Bavaria in 1832 but had lived in Illinois since the age of six. He worked his way up from printer's devil to owner of the Pittsfield *Free Press*, a Whig newspaper, and then in 1857 became a clerk in the office of Ozias Hatch, the Illinois secretary of state and Lincoln's good friend. During the summer of 1858 Nicolay played a role in Stephen Douglas' campaign against Lincoln for the U.S. Senate, and two years later, as a journalist for a Missouri newspaper, he attended the Chicago convention where Lincoln was nominated for president. Although Nicolay never lost his respect for Douglas, he quickly became an admirer of Lincoln's. He hoped to ghostwrite Lincoln's autobiography for the presidential campaign (out of over 50 applicants, the coveted job went to John Locke Scripps, editorial writer for the Chicago *Press and Tribune),* but Lincoln nonetheless hired Nicolay as his personal secretary.

The position suited Nicolay perfectly. He was quiet, thoughtful and studious, and was so dedicated to his position that he insisted on sleeping in a cot in the statehouse basement. (Nicolay's loyalty to Lincoln was perhaps exceeded only by his devotion to his fiancée, a lovely girl from Indiana named Therena Bates.) Nicolay laboriously reviewed the stacks of mail that poured in — sometimes hundreds of letters per day — bringing letters of political significance to Lincoln's attention first, followed by those of a purely personal nature. Newspaper correspondents and editors from across the country routinely requested clarification of Lincoln's position on the threat of southern secession, and Nicolay patiently answered them with Lincoln's standard line: it would be inappropriate to comment on issues, or potential issues, not yet before him; an analysis of the Republican platform sufficed to set forth Lincoln's guiding principles.

People wrote to Lincoln with requests for autographs, photographs, or locks of his hair. Libbie "Lincoln" and her sister Minnie wrote to "Dear brother Lincoln: I suppose you will be very much surprised to hear that you have two sisters ... your sentiments in regards to the slave system ... coincided so well with our own, that we determined to adopt you as our brother, and call ourselves by your name." A man named William Mathews wrote from Orange, New Jersey, advising that he had been injured while firing a cannon salute to Lincoln and Hamlin, and sent along a press account to prove it. Would Lincoln mind paying the hospital bills? Joseph Gerhard of Washington wanted permission to name his newborn son after Lincoln, and requested that the candidate serve as the boy's godfather. Oliver Parker, proprietor of the Franklin House hotel in Philadelphia, wrote and suggested that Lincoln disassociate himself from "Roman Catholics or Papists." It would be wiser, wrote Parker, to have "none but American born, black, and white, and have nothing but Protestants about you, and then I will feel as though you will be comparatively safe." Dozens of people requested positions in a new Republican administration (and there were a lot of patronage positions to go around; Lincoln would replace 1,195 Democrats with Republican political appointees in 1861).[6] J. H. Weed of New Lebanon, Illinois, bluntly asked for money. "With a little assistance from you, I can secure a number of votes to help you in getting a Home in the White House for the next 4 years.... I think if I had $50 or $100 or $200."[7]

Not all writers wanted something from Lincoln. A man from Kansas named R.S. Bassett advised Lincoln to "be Exceeding Careful What you Eat or Drink as you May be Poisoned by your Enemys." Men from Massachusetts and Kansas and Pennsylvania sent similar warnings. Z.C. Robbins of Washington, D.C., who described himself as "one of the oldest Republicans of this city" offered to make his house available to Lincoln and his family "on your arrival in this city, making it your home until the White House shall be made ready for your reception." And at least some members of the United States Army were also anticipating Lincoln's election. Maj. David Hunter of Fort Leavenworth wrote to Lincoln and advised him of suspected assassination attempts, and Capt. George Hazzard provided military intelligence on alarming buildups of southern arsenals in Georgia, Louisiana, Virginia and South Carolina, among other places.[8]

Lincoln's temporary office at the statehouse reflected his need for utility and indifference to style or pretense. The room was nearly square in shape and so small that barely a dozen people could fit into it at one time. It was furnished with six armchairs, one table covered with law books and another with newspapers and boxes of mail, and a desk for Nicolay. On the floor lay one of Lincoln's prized possessions: a scrapbook filled with news accounts of his 1858 debates with Douglas. On the far wall rested a sofa where Lincoln liked to stretch out, and above the sofa were three windows which provided a view of the public square and county courthouse to the east. Scattered about the room was an assortment of gifts and good-luck charms Lincoln had received from well-wishers, the items reflecting the oddities and peculiarities, perhaps, of those who had sent them, including axes, wedges, nails, wood carvings, even a barrel of flour. A chair made of 34 different kinds of wood stood untested in its crate. One admirer sent Lincoln a large salmon caught in the Mississippi River; he hoped that the fish would "grace the table of the next President."[9] Daniel Garner of Springfield sent Lincoln some homemade soap, a gift that merited a personal, and humorous, response. "Dear Sir," Lincoln wrote, "Some specimens of your Soap have been used at our house and Mrs. L. declares it is a superb article. She at the same time, protests that *I* have never given sufficient attention to the 'soap question' to be a competent judge."[10]

Nicolay began to scan the pile of letters that had arrived the night before, and laughed as Lincoln told him what had transpired at the post office. Lincoln stood in line waiting for the bundle to be set in his arms, when some acquaintances approached and asked, "How can you stand the pressure?" Lincoln replied that he could "sustain himself until Tuesday night, at least." One of the men inquired as to how he might vote the following day, and Lincoln told him he would vote for Yates, the Republican candidate for governor. But this was not what the group wanted to hear. What about the presidential contest? "How vote?" said Lincoln. "Well, I will tell you — by ballot." And he left the group convulsed in laughter.[11]

Lincoln began each day by studying numerous daily newspapers. He had been an avid reader virtually his entire adult life, and much of his literary appetite was satisfied through newspapers. One benefit of his first real job, postmaster of New Salem in 1833, was a free subscription to a daily paper, and he routinely read other papers before the intended recipients picked them up. Over the years he occasionally contributed articles and opinions to local papers. In addition to the local newspapers, Lincoln regularly read the Chicago *Press and Tribune*, Horace Greeley's New York *Tribune*, the Louisville *Journal*, the Cincinnati *Gazette*, and the St. Louis *Republican*, carefully underlining noteworthy political sentiments.

Lincoln understood the enormous political power held by newspapers. In early 1859 Theodore Canisius, editor of the *Illinois Staats-Anzeiger*, Springfield's German weekly, had asked Lincoln his position on a new statute that prohibited foreign-born naturalized citizens from holding office or voting until two years after their naturalization. Lincoln criticized the law in a letter printed in the paper, and a kinship with Canisius developed. In May Lincoln purchased the paper for $400, with the understanding that Canisius would stay on and produce pro-Republican editorials. The blatantly political ploy was kept a secret. Lincoln did not even tell Herndon of the transaction, and probably kept it from Mary, as well, who sometimes expressed her consternation that he subscribed to so many papers, much less actually own one. But in 1860 over one-quarter of the nation's foreign-born citizens, or 1.3 million people, were Germans, and Lincoln knew that the winning of the German vote would play a crucial role in his election.[12]

The Springfield *State Journal*, edited by Edward L. Baker, had long been pro-Whig, and was now pro-Republican, and its headlines on this important day shouted "Once More to the Breach! Strike for Freedom! Lincoln men of Old Sangamon, do not let it be said that you have failed to do your whole duty in this great crisis." Republicans were urged to vote early, for "nothing so cheers those at the polls as to see their friends prompt. The earlier you get the Republican vote in, the more time you will have for working among the doubtful." Voters were to be wary of any Democratic shenanigans. "Prevent frauds and ballot stuffing! Let us watch the ballot box and prevent illegal voting. Let us see the votes counted out of the ballot box and prevent fraudulent returns! Having done this, we can abide the result with a consciousness that we have done everything in our power to bury political corruptionists and disunionists in one common grave."[13]

As biased as the *State Journal* was, the other Springfield daily newspaper, the Illinois *State Register*, was just as zealous in its dislike of Lincoln and his party. "Black Republicans," cautioned the *Register*, only wished to place blacks on equal social and economic status with whites, allow them to vote, intermarry with whites, and take the place of whites in the labor forces of industry and commerce. And all these evils would take place not just in the South, but also here in Illinois. If Lincoln's concept of "equality" was realized, warned the *Register*, "free negroes from every quarter of the Union will be invited here to become citizens, and the equals of white men."[14] The *Register* predicted that "the election of Mr. Lincoln will be a national calamity, a calamity that will do more to destroy the comity that ought to exist between the states, and to destroy the affection that should be entertained by the people of all sections for their fellow countrymen." And while the *Register* did not necessarily support or condone secession of southern states from the Union, neither would it stand for an administration bent on tyranny. "We believe that in a clear case of the unconstitutional exercise of power by the president, the Senate would, upon a constitutional form of trial, convict Abraham Lincoln and dismiss him from office."[15]

Since his nomination in May, Lincoln had received visitors every morning through early afternoon. Nicolay now suggested that it might be more appropriate to keep the office doors closed, so that Lincoln would not be bothered by the usual rush of visitors that had taken so much of his time for many months. But Lincoln rejected the idea. If the people wanted to see him, even on this day, he would not refuse them.

Soon the crowd began to file in, many just returning from the polls and wanting to get a good look at the man they had, or had not, just voted for. Nicolay made no attempt to screen Lincoln's visitors, for he knew Lincoln would receive everyone. Some had known Lincoln for 20 years or more, others had only heard about him. In came farmers, shopkeepers, businessmen — "Muddy boots and hickory shirts are just as frequent as broadcloth and fine linen," as one correspondent described the visitors — all wanting to shake Lincoln's hand. Some "rough-jacketed constituents" arrived, and embarrassed by their coarse exterior, could not bring themselves to speak, only stare dumbly at Lincoln. Young Springfield dandies brought in their sweethearts, dressed in their finest crinolines and bonnets, to be introduced to the candidate. Several men came in and advised that they were from New York, to which Lincoln suggested that they "ought better to be at home voting." Many noticed the pair of steel wedges, used to separate logs, stacked in a corner of the room; were those the actual wedges Lincoln had used as a youth? Lincoln had a favorite answer: "These are the identical wedges — that were sent to me a week ago," he joked.[16]

In the early afternoon, after a short rest, Lincoln was visited by his inner circle of political confidants. Ward Hill Lamon was a near-constant companion of Lincoln, so much so that Lincoln referred to him as "his particular friend." Lamon was a lawyer who had ridden the circuit with Lincoln in the 1850s and associated with him on many cases, but his real value was in his imposing physical presence. Over six feet tall and at least 250 pounds, and adorned with a thick, drooping mustache, "Hill" was a bear of a man who could intimidate others with just a surly look. Despite his menacing demeanor, Lincoln appreciated Lamon's coarse sense of humor and his musical abilities: his talents with his voice and ever-present banjo brought entertainment to many lonely nights on the circuit and campaign trails. He had been an organizer and unofficial sergeant-at-arms in Lincoln's Senate campaigns of 1854 and 1858, and planned on accompanying Lincoln to Washington if he won the presidency.

Ozias Hatch had been elected secretary of state in 1856 and was now up for reelection. He had been friends with Lincoln since the 1840s, when he had been clerk of the Pike County circuit court. Hatch had served a term in the Illinois House of Representatives as a Whig, and was now a Republican, although he disagreed with Lincoln on a number of issues. For example, he was outspoken in his nativist, or anti-immigrant, views, something Lincoln could not understand or tolerate. Hatch's political ambitions were not as lofty as Lincoln's, but he always kept an eye out for personal advantage to be gained through friendship: he was already lobbying Lincoln for a job in the hoped-for Republican administration.

Zouave leader Elmer Ellsworth also spent most of election day at the statehouse with Lincoln. Just 23 years old, Ellsworth was an uncommonly ambitious young man. He had taken his colorful and crowd-pleasing Zouaves on a tour of 20 cities that summer, impressing onlookers with the group's marching precision and apparent readiness for a fight. Ellsworth had written a book entitled *A Manual of Arms for Light Infantry,* and Lincoln was convinced he had "a real genius for war."[17] Officially Ellsworth was working as Lincoln's law clerk in 1860, but spent most of his time drilling the Zouaves and had even given a few fiery political speeches on Lincoln's behalf. Lincoln and his wife were both impressed with Ellsworth, and though Lincoln never dared say it to Mary, he saw in Ellsworth some of the drive that seemed lacking in his own eldest son Robert. He already had a position in mind for Ellsworth in Washington: he was to establish a Bureau of Militia in the War Department.[18] But Ellsworth wanted action, not a bureaucratic post. When Virginia seceded in May, Ellsworth rushed to take Alexandria, just across the Potomac from Washington. A rebel flag was flying from the top of the Marshall House hotel, visible from the White House. Ellsworth removed the flag but was shot and killed by the hotel proprietor. He became the first hero for the Union cause, and his body lay in state in the East Room of the White House. "Our affliction here, is scarcely less than your own," Lincoln wrote to Ellsworth's parents. The lad was "my young friend, and your brave and early fallen child."[19]

Now these men gathered around Lincoln and discussed, as they had countless times, his Democratic opponents and their prospects on this election day. The most dangerous candidate, of course, was Senator Stephen Douglas. Standing just five feet four inches tall, the "Little Giant" had long been a vital force in the state and national political scene. A Democrat because of his admiration for Andrew Jackson, Douglas was elected state's attorney at age 22 and legislator at 23. He went on to become secretary of state, and then justice on the Illinois Supreme Court. He became a congressman in 1843, and three years later won the first of three successive terms in the U.S. Senate, where he earned his reputation as a visionary, tirelessly advocating for statehood for western territories.

Douglas was also a racist who believed that blacks were inferior to whites and incapable of self-government. For those reasons he supported the *Dred Scott* decision, and argued that anyone who objected to the decision must necessarily stand for equality among the races. The American form of government, Douglas asserted, was "established on the white basis. It was made by white men for the benefit of white men."[20] Douglas was inflexible in his popular sovereignty position. He believed that the country could exist half-slave and half-free because the founding fathers had envisioned such a scheme. To Democrats of the North, Douglas's arguments made perfect sense, and he won the nomination of his party at the convention held in Baltimore in June.

But Douglas's views did not sit well with the southern wing of the Democratic Party. Representatives from Alabama, South Carolina, Georgia, Florida, Mississippi, Virginia and Texas stormed out of Baltimore and held their own convention a few days later in Richmond. There they nominated John C. Breckenridge of Kentucky for president. Breckenridge was serving as James Buchanan's vice president (at age 35 he was the youngest ever to hold that office), and believed that the federal government was obligated to protect slaveholders' rights in the western territories. Thus, he advocated a federal "slave code," believing that if Congress did not so act, the territories were certain to enter the Union as free states, leading to the ultimate demise of slavery. Breckinridge's support in the election would come from the Deep South. After the election Breckenridge would become a major general in the Confederate Army, and would eventually serve as Jefferson Davis' secretary of war.

The third Democratic candidate was John Bell of Tennessee. A wealthy mine and mill owner and former U.S. senator, Bell's Constitutional Union Party held itself as a populist party, denouncing the others for sectionalism and divisiveness. Its platform, it claimed, was simply the United States Constitution; if that document was adhered to, the Union would be preserved. The party employed a bizarre strategy: its aim was to win enough electoral votes to send the election into the House of Representative, where, it believed, Bell might well prevail. Lincoln knew that Bell's support would come from the border states of Tennessee, Kentucky, Virginia, and Missouri.

William Herndon arrived at the statehouse in midafternoon. He later claimed that he was surprised to learn that his partner did not intend to vote. He convinced Lincoln, he said, to do so, though it seems more likely that Lincoln was merely waiting for some of the lines at the polling place to diminish. Regardless, at about 3 P.M., Lincoln declared that it was time to cast his vote. He grabbed a Republican ballot and carefully cut off the top, where his own name was located. It would be inappropriate, thought Lincoln, to vote for himself, but he intended to vote for every other nominee on the ticket. Accompanied by Hatch, Lamon, and Ellsworth, and an elderly gentleman who decided that it would be an honor to accompany Lincoln on this historic moment, the group made its way down the staircase. But the man grew tired and said he'd rather watch from the window. Lincoln dutifully escorted his friend back to the office and helped him to the sofa, and then started off again.

Lincoln was not noticed until he got to the sidewalk just outside the courthouse. There a dense crowd of voters cheered him heartily and cleared a path for him into the building. Many followed him inside and up the stairs, where Lincoln met another round of cheers inside the voting room. Seemingly oblivious to the commotion surrounding him, Lincoln removed his hat and calmly dropped his ballot in the Republican box as his name was recorded by the clerks. Outside once again, the crowd pressed toward him to shake his hand, slap him on the back, wish him well. Journalists noted that people of all political persuasions joined in the expression of good will. One "spry old party, with his hand full of Democratic documents, forgot his special function so far as to prance upon a railing, and to take the lead in an infinite series of Lincoln cheers."[21] At the urging of his companions Lincoln returned again to the Governor's Room, where he "turned to the entertainment of his visitors as unconcernedly as if he had not just received a demonstration which anybody might well take a little time to think of and be proud over."[22] He had barely been gone five minutes, yet his brief appearance at the polls was recorded by journalists and transmitted as important news to eager Americans across the North.

At sunset the polls closed. Nicolay shooed the remaining visitors out of the office, and Lincoln returned home. Normally this was his favorite time of the day, for he could play with his boys, talk with Mary, and forget about his troubles. But tonight he was tired and anxious and wished to be alone. He went upstairs to his bedroom and tried to rest. He later told Herndon that he was unable to sleep, and glancing over from his bed to the mirror, he noticed not one, but two images staring back. He rose for a closer look and the second image vanished. Back on his bed, however, it returned. Later he told Mary about the strange episode. It was certainly a sign, she said. The double images meant that he would twice be elected president, but would not live out the second term.

By early evening Lincoln was off again, now to wait for the returns to announce his fate. A day earlier C.F. McIntire, manager of Springfield's Illinois & Mississippi Telegraph Company, had wired Lincoln: "If convenient for you, we would be happy to have you and any friends you may wish to bring, spend tomorrow night with us, where you can receive the good news without delay. Not wishing to have a noisy crowd inside, the doors will be closed at 9 o'clock P.M."[23] So Lincoln joined his advisors there, nonchalantly reclining on a shabby sofa while the rest stood nervously, listening to the clicking of the telegraph machines. The first returns of the day arrived from Decatur, in nearby Macon County, showing solid Republican gains as compared to the 1856 election, a good sign indeed. Soon Lyman Trumbull arrived, just in time to hear that his seat in the Senate was safe, a result that pleased everyone. Now the important returns from the Northeast trickled in, McIntire deciphering the code and reading the results aloud. Ten o'clock brought a dispatch from Indianapolis: Indiana was secure. A message from wealthy Republican activist — and former presidential nomination contender — Simon Cameron relayed that Lincoln had carried Pittsburgh and all of Allegheny County; Pennsylvania had been won by 70,000 votes. Reports of solid Republican victories came in from Massachusetts, Maine and Ohio. Each bit of positive information brought cheers from everyone in the room except Lincoln, who remained curiously silent.

At midnight returns from southern states began to arrive. The first came from Missouri, and Lincoln raised himself up from the sofa to declare that "we should now get a few licks back."[24] And he was correct, although the news from the South did not overwhelm anyone in the office, who were aware that Lincoln's name had not even appeared on the ballot in 10 states. Other states reported as expected. Bell took early leads in Tennessee and Kentucky, Breckenridge was winning in Texas, Mississippi and Georgia. Douglas looked solid in New Jersey and was neck-and-neck with Bell in Missouri. But still no word from New York.

By 12:30 the group needed some air and walked to Watson's Saloon at the far side of the square. Here the Republican ladies of Springfield had prepared an enormous supply of sandwiches and cakes to sustain their men on this long night. When Lincoln walked into the hall a group of 100 women called to him, "How do you do, Mr. President!" and as he ate they surrounded and serenaded him with the familiar "Old Abe Lincoln came out of the wilderness, down in Illinois!" He acknowledged them with an embarrassed smile. A newspaper correspondent wondered at the display the women put on: "It is difficult to express the utter abandonment of hospitality with which these ladies honored all, even the least of their guests; but how can I attempt to describe the manner in which they surrounded, and took possession of, and clung to Mr. Lincoln, when he appeared among them? I can only say that that rare possibility — the last extremity of feminine enthusiasm — was here overwhelmingly illustrated."[25]

But Lincoln did not get swept up in this show of devotion. He found a corner of the hall and sat next to Mary, who had consented to enter such an establishment only because of the extraordinary circumstances of the evening. Lincoln stayed with her for half an hour as they sipped coffee, then promised to meet her later at home with the news.

As he was leaving the saloon a messenger rushed up, breathless, with a critical "'spatch." The returns from New York were arriving, and the outlook was promising. Lincoln hurried back to the telegraph office with his friends. New York political organizer Thurlow Weed first wired Lincoln, "All safe in this State."[26] Within the hour official word arrived that Lincoln had carried New York by 50,000 votes; now his election was all but guaranteed. Immediately the streets of Springfield exploded in joyous bedlam. Everywhere Republicans of all ages raced around like madmen, linking arms, dancing, shouting, and singing, "Ain't you glad you joined the Republicans?" Some rolled on the ground in delight, others tossed their hats in the air. The news was shouted from rooftops and open windows, and a celebration of music and fireworks began in earnest. One Springfield woman later wrote to a friend: "Father was out till half past two. He describes the scene as perfectly *wild*. While the votes were being counted the republicans were *singing, yelling! Shouting!!* The boys *(not children) dancing*. Old men, young, middle aged, clergymen and *all!*"[27]

Lincoln was not yet ready to celebrate. He stayed at the telegraph office a while longer, waiting for results from the local elections. Many races were close, and Lincoln admitted that he "did not feel quite easy" about the situation. But he felt good enough to give out a little laugh, his first show of any real emotion this night. "I guess I'll go down and tell Mary about it," he finally said to Trumbull before he walked out the door.[28]

Lincoln made his way through the wild crowd that, strangely, seemed too caught up in the moment to notice him. He walked home in silence, alone. He made his way through the dark house and climbed the stairs to Mary's bedroom, where he was surprised to find her asleep. "Mary," he said, gently shaking her. "Mary, we are elected."[29] He lay down and tried to rest, but could not. "I then felt as I never felt before," he said later, "the responsibility that was upon me."[30] At 4 A.M. the telegraph wires at last officially confirmed his victory, and the roar of cannon fire once again shook the citizens of Springfield.

4

Reaction

In 1860 more Americans voted for president than in any other election in the country's history. Over 81 percent of all white males over the age of 21 cast their ballots in what had essentially become two sectional contests: Lincoln vs. Douglas in the North, and Bell vs. Breckinridge in the South. Lincoln received 1,865,593 votes, or 39.82 percent of the popular vote. He won 17 states, including all of the North and California and Oregon in the West. His dominance in the North was reflected by the fact that he won every single county in New England, 109 of 147 counties in the Mid-Atlantic states, and 252 of 392 counties in the Midwestern states of Illinois, Indiana, Michigan and Ohio. Douglas's Herculean campaign efforts gained him little. Despite an exhausting and unprecedented schedule in which he visited 23 states, giving two or three lengthy speeches per day, Douglas managed to carry only two states, Missouri and New Jersey, and received 1,382,713 votes, or 29.46 percent of the popular vote. Lincoln's plurality vote in the North gave him 180 electoral votes, to only 12 for Douglas.

But the results in the South showed how fractured the country had become. While Lincoln received some support in several slaveholding states—just over 17,000 votes in Missouri, where he carried St. Louis, 3,800 in Delaware, 2,300 in Maryland, 1,900 in Virginia, and 1,300 in Kentucky—his name did not appear on the ballot in any other southern state. Lincoln won only two of 996 counties in the South. As expected, Breckinridge carried almost every southern state and earned 72 electoral votes, while Bell took Kentucky, Tennessee and Virginia and their 39 electoral votes. While Lincoln was literally ignored in most of the South, however, his election had legitimacy: even if the Democratic voters had united behind one candidate, Lincoln would still have won the electoral college and the presidency.[1]

The country that elected Lincoln was prospering like never before. Population had increased from 23.3 million people in 1850 to 31.5 million 10 years later. Nearly 3 million immigrants had arrived in America since 1850, most of them German and Irish who settled in the northern states of New York, Pennsylvania and Ohio. Immigrants contributed mightily to the industrial and agricultural labor base, and emerged as a force at the voting booth that could not be ignored. (Realistic political observers noted that this massive influx of healthy young men provided a huge pool of potential soldiers, as well.) Virtually every economic indicator skyrocketed in the middle years of the 19th century. The growth of per capita wealth placed the United States

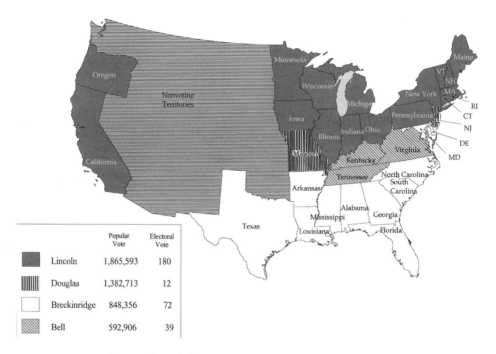

		Popular Vote	Electoral Vote
	Lincoln	1,865,593	180
	Douglas	1,382,713	12
	Breckinridge	848,356	72
	Bell	592,906	39

The presidential election of 1860 (map by Tim Mosbacher).

on the same level as world leaders Britain and France. Real wages had increased year by year, decade by decade since 1810. Manufacturing showed remarkable gains, as production of machinery, clothing, furniture, jewelry, chemicals, lumber, iron, petroleum and a host of other commodities increased in northern factories. Home, business and transportation construction was booming. Agriculture, which commanded 59 percent of the labor force, reflected this prodigious industrial growth: the utilization of new inventions, equipment, machinery and education brought about impressive gains in wheat, corn, hay, dairy, meat and fruit production.[2]

The North, with its prosperous diversity and integrated economy, necessarily had an interest in maintaining this miraculous national growth. The secession of southern states would bring about serious economic damage. Nearly one-fifth of the country's population, along with almost half of its territory, would be lost. The prosperous Ohio and Mississippi valleys would lose New Orleans as their primary cash crop port. And northern banks would face forfeiture on nearly $300 million loaned to southern plantation owners and farmers if secession occurred.[3] Thus the populace of the North supported Lincoln and the Republicans, the candidate and the party who were most committed to the preservation of the Union and the constitutional, economic and political institutions that would allow the country to move toward even loftier heights.

It helped the Republican cause that discontent with the corrupt Democratic Buchanan administration was widespread. In June 1860, a House investigating committee reported that officials in the War and Navy departments had awarded government contracts without requiring competitive bidding in exchange for contributions to the

Democratic Party. Postmasters in New York and Chicago were caught siphoning thousands of dollars of public funds into party coffers. Democratic officials had bribed judges from Pennsylvania and Indiana into prematurely naturalizing Irish immigrants, who then voted for Buchanan in the 1856 election. Buchanan representatives had even paid off United States congressmen in exchange for favorable votes on Democratic legislative proposals. The Buchanan administration was seen as the most corrupt in American history, and voters would make the Democrats pay at the ballot box.[4]

Many northern newspapers reacted favorably to Lincoln's election. "Enforce the laws," said editorial after editorial, as if such a simple concept was the solution to complex sociological problems. The Chicago *Tribune* assured its readers that "Lincoln and the Republican Party will not interfere with the rights of the South.... Southern states would not be so foolish as to go off and organize a Confederacy.... When eighteen millions of freemen speak as they spoke on Tuesday, they make a noise that even the most stupid secessionist cannot fail to hear."[5]

In Pennsylvania, the post-election headline of the Harrisburg *Telegraph* shouted, "The Union Saved! Freedom and Free Labor Gloriously Triumphant!" Its editor called the election a "sublime spectacle which the people of the Old World do not understand ... for liberty the Republican party struggled as men struggle for life and religion. And the result, Abraham Lincoln's triumphant election, proves that the sentiment of the American people is in favor not of the name of liberty alone, but of its practical operation among all men.... His election settles all the issues that have entered into the contest, slavery extension, secession, and what just now is probably still more vital, the equal right of the free with the slave States to share in the administration of the Federal Government."[6]

Lincoln's victory was called a "glorious event" by the St. Louis *Democrat*. "Let a choral shout of exultation rise from the soul of the people, at this, their great victory, over the enemies of freedom and the upholders and champions of wrong. The joy is too great for verbal expansions; the vista opened is too radiant and boundless for description.... Peace will follow our victory. The President-elect is a wise, temperate, conservative, patriotic statesman, whose noble ambition it will be to demean himself in his high office for the good of all.... He is the nation's choice, and no anointed king since the days of David could claim a diviner right to rule than he."[7]

In New York, however, the reaction to Lincoln's election was difficult to gauge, at least as evidenced by the varied opinions of the most influential newspapers. Horace Greeley was the editor of the powerful New York *Tribune*. He had only indirectly contributed to Lincoln's nomination for president; because of a personal grudge he held against the favored William H. Seward, he initially supported Edward Bates, who stood little chance of winning. Greeley eventually supported Lincoln in the campaign, but his editorials throughout the summer were lukewarm at best. Now his writing took a strange, indecisive tone: "It is not to be supposed that the election of Abraham Lincoln as President of these United States—conspicuous and glorious triumph as it is— will at once restore the country to political harmony and quiet, though we are convinced that the agitation raised in the South will gradually and surely subside into peace." At least for a short time, Greeley advocated a go-in-peace policy toward unhappy southern states. While secession might be nothing short of revolutionary, perhaps the right of individual states to leave the Union did in fact exist. "We hope never to live in a republic whereof one section is pinned to the residue by bayonets," Greeley wrote. "But we must insist that the step be taken, if ever it shall be, with the deliberation and gravity befitting so momentous an issue. Let ample time be given for reflection; let the subject be fully canvassed before the people; and let a popular vote be taken in every case before secession is decreed."[8]

Greeley repeated his comments in a post-election speech at Stuyvesant Hall in lower Manhattan, where a large crowd gathered to celebrate Lincoln's victory at a Jubilee meeting. He was joined at the podium by William Cullen Bryant of the New York *Evening Post*. After Lincoln's triumph at Cooper Union, Bryant appointed himself Lincoln's chief unofficial campaign advisor — he had written Lincoln a long letter in June, urging him to make no speeches or write no letters over the summer, and although Lincoln never had any other intentions, Bryant took full credit for the strategy — and now felt it was time to gloat. "We stand upon the battlefield of the great contest," he said, "while around us and before us lie the carcasses of the slain. At our feet, conquered, lies that great oligarchy which has so long held the South through submission and fear, and has ruled the North through the treachery of northern men. A new era in now inaugurated, the old order of things has passed away, never, we hope to return."[9]

James Gordon Bennett was editor of the New York *Herald*, one of the city's most influential, if not unconventional, newspapers. Bennett, 65 years old in 1860, was a native of Scotland and a Roman Catholic who had renounced the church. He had been in the newspaper business as correspondent, freelance writer and editor for nearly 40 years. His *Herald* combined political and public interest stories with sensational reports of crime, scandal and natural disaster. (In 1836, for example, he shocked his readers with detailed front-page reports of the murder of a Manhattan prostitute.) Above all else, Bennett was an innovator. He was one of the first to sell papers for a penny, utilizing newsboys on street corners instead of customer subscription. He transmitted his papers across the country via railroad, Pony Express, telegraph and even carrier pigeon. He revolutionized newspaper advertising by initiating a cash-in-advance policy, a practice all others quickly followed. Bennett also was eager to viciously attack editors of other papers who disagreed with his politics. His unorthodox styles worked; in 1860 the *Herald* boasted the highest circulation of any newspaper in the country.

Early in the campaign Bennett had called Lincoln a "third-rate country lawyer" who told "coarse and clumsy jokes" and "could not speak good grammar."[10] But Lincoln knew that Bennett's views reached thousands of voters, and he needed, and sought, Bennett's support. He sent Joseph Medill of the Chicago *Tribune* to visit Bennett in June, in an attempt to "sound out" Bennett and ascertain how his endorsement might be gained. Medill was no fan of Bennett — he called him "his Satanic Majesty" — but he knew that Bennett could cause the Republicans "much harm if hostile. If neutralized a point is gained." Medill surmised that Bennett was "too rich to want money. Social position we suspect is what he wants. He wants to be in a position to be invited with his wife and son to dinner or tea at the White House, occasionally, and to be 'made of' by the big men of the party. I think we can afford to agree to that much."[11]

Bennett, however, was not much impressed with the visit of Medill, who left New York without an endorsement for Lincoln. In 1860 Bennett first backed Breckenridge, then Bell, for president. His refusal to support Lincoln's candidacy was odd, for Bennett opposed the expansion of slavery into the territories. (It was also short-lived; Bennett backed the Union cause throughout the war and promoted the image of Lincoln as martyr after his assassination). But Bennett's knack for the uncommon approach sold papers, and perhaps explains the post-election coverage he provided his readers. He sent reporters out to the streets of the city to monitor reaction to Lincoln's election, and if their comments could be believed, New Yorkers were indifferent to the result:

> As far as New York was concerned, the business people had resumed their occupation; carts and stands, ready to take up — and take in — a fare if they had the chance; workmen and mechanics pursued their daily business, at least such as had not received too many wounds in the head by means of the political pocket pistol, the whiskey bottle. In fact, everything had resumed its wonted appearance.... The City Hall was deserted. The few democrats who made their appearance walked in with a long but resigned countenance. Whey they spoke they did so good humouredly, and expressed their conviction that "the best man was elected." Some seemed to think that "if any trouble broke out in the South it would be principally of a commercial character and not warlike." The courts may be said to have been idle; and, as regarded election day, the persons around the Hall asserted that they never had seen such a quiet Presidential election. One respectable gentleman, who had witnessed six of them, besides all the minor ones, said the "quietness of the thing was unprecedented."... Along Broadway business went on as usual.... Political medals and photographs were much reduced in price — the unsuccessful candidates selling only for two cents, while Lincoln was worth six cents.... Some observers noted that as Congress was "composed mainly of democrats, old Uncle Abe, honest or not, would not have much power to act or veto."... The only real excitement occurred when a pedestrian thought he had been insulted by an Irish policeman, and he loudly proclaimed that he was glad Lincoln was elected, as he would soon remove every Irishman from the force.[12]

German-born Carl Schurz was one of Lincoln's most passionate and tireless supporters. He was an active revolutionary in Germany in 1849; when the revolution failed, he fled to America, where his strong antislavery sentiments led him to the Republican Party. His vociferous criticisms of Stephen Douglas's popular sovereignty proposal quickly earned Lincoln's respect and friendship. As head of the "foreign department" of the Republican Committee in 1860, Schurz galvanized German, Norwegian, and Dutch voters and gained a reputation as a solid and effective public speaker. "I began speaking the day after the convention," Schurz later reminisced, "and continued until the day of the election, making from one to three speeches, with the exception of about ten days in September when I was so fatigued that I had to stop for a little while. I spoke in both English and German, under the auspices of the National Committee, and not only in the larger towns, but frequently also in country districts." Schurz certainly earned the respect of the New York *Evening Post*. He was "young, ardent, aspiring," said the *Post*. "The romances connected with his life and escape from his fatherland, his scholarly attainments, and, above all, his devotion to the principles which cast him an exile on our shores, have all combined to

The Mohawk, New York, Wide Awakes celebrate Lincoln's victory (the Lincoln Museum, Fort Wayne, Indiana, # 2383).

render him dear to the hearts of his countrymen and to place him in the foremost rank of their leaders."[13] After the election Schurz spoke for hundreds of thousand of voters: "The election is over, the battle is fought, the victory is won.... I am happy in the thought of the future. We are to be one again, and unless I am greatly deceived we shall bring back a part of the old idyllic life." Schurz wrote to Lincoln: "Yours, dear Sir, is the greatest mission that ever fell to the lot of mortal man: the restoration of original principles in the model Republic of the world."[14]

In Iowa, Senator James Harlan, a free-soil Republican (and future father-in-law of Robert Lincoln) was reelected in 1860. He calmly reassured his nervous constituents that the new president would be ruled by reason and intellect, not inflamed passions. "Mr. Lincoln will administer the government fairly and justly to all parts of the Union," said Harlan, expressing confidence in a man he had never met. "His inauguration will be a new era in the public affairs of this country."[15]

Long-time slavery opponent and unsuccessful presidential aspirant Salmon Chase mistakenly thought that Lincoln would use his executive powers to immediately do away with slavery. The day after the election he wrote, "You are President elect. I congratulate you and thank God. The great object of my wishes & labors for nineteen years is accomplished in the overthrow of the Slave Power. The space is now clear for the establishment of the policy of Freedom on safe & firm ground. The lead is yours. The responsibility is vast. May God strengthen you for your great duties."[16] As a future member of Lincoln's cabinet Chase would have many opportunities to impress upon Lincoln his views.

Praise of Lincoln was not limited to political commentators and politicians. Acclaimed poet and educator Henry Wadsworth Longfellow called Lincoln's election "a great victory. One can hardly overrate its importance. It is the redemption of the country. Freedom is triumphant."[17] Longfellow's contemporary John Greenleaf Whittier seemed to sense the burden that rested upon the new administration, and the country. "Well God has laid the great responsibility upon us," he wrote. "We must take it up and bear it."[18] In Brooklyn, a 41-year-old poet and newspaper reporter named Walt Whitman pondered the fate of the Union. Just five years earlier Whitman's *Leaves of Grass* had caused a mild sensation with its transcendental portrayal of freedom, which he recognized as America's beauty and spiritual strength. Whitman could now see that the very diversity he had celebrated in his poetry was literally dividing the country he adored. Lincoln, hoped Whitman, could be the "Redeemer President" he had written about, one who could keep his country together by convincing the various states that their dissatisfaction with each other could be resolved through overarching affection.[19]

In the South, slavery was at the very heart of society—a society, southerners earnestly believed, that was honorable and aristocratic, and one that the North could never hope to comprehend. In 1860 nearly 4 million of 4.5 million black Americans were slaves. Fully one in four southern families held slaves. Cotton production, of course, depended upon slave labor, and capital investment in the institution totaled some $4 billion. Southerners proudly noted that the region furnished three-fourths of the world's supply of cotton: over 4 million bales annually. The average southern white male was nearly twice as wealthy as the average northern white male, and most of this wealth was concentrated on land and slavery.[20]

As important as economics were, it was the connection to the land itself that southerners loved most. Rural life "promotes a generous hospitality, a high and perfect courtesy, a lofty spirit of independence ... and all the nobler virtues and heroic traits," said a South Carolinian. The North was welcome to its congested cities, factories and trade markets. "Ours is an agricultural people, and God grant that we should continue so," wrote one Alabama plantation owner. "It is the freest, happiest, most independent, and with us, the most powerful condition on earth."[21]

But northerners saw no romantic elements in a system built on slavery. The most popular book of the age, Harriet Beecher Stowe's *Uncle Tom's Cabin*, published to incredible acclaim in 1852, had graphically made clear to northern—and worldwide—readers that slaves were property, or mere chattel, to be bought, sold, traded, branded, whipped or even killed if discipline dictated. Human bondage was repugnant to the ideals of the republic, argued northern constitutionalists, while fanatical abolitionists claimed that slavery violated the higher law of God himself. As if any proof of the immorality of slavery was needed, one need only look to southern laws: in most southern states blacks were prohibited from testifying against whites in court; thus rape, murder and other crimes against blacks were commonplace and went unpunished.

But southern defenders of slavery were quick to counter attacks on the morality of slavery. The founding fathers, they argued, had explicitly recognized and authorized the institution. George Washington himself, as well as Thomas Jefferson, had owned slaves. A strange sort of benevolent justification was imbedded in the southern psyche. Blacks were, believed southerners, better off as American slaves than African heathens. After all, slavery had lifted ignorant blacks from barbarity, clothed them, housed them, fed them. Slavery had given blacks a station in life fitting to their abilities. It had brought them Christianity. Southerners argued that their slaves enjoyed better living conditions than did free blacks and factory workers in the sanctimonious North.

And, wondered southerners, what if slavery were to be abolished, as (they insisted) Lincoln wished? Who would feed and clothe millions of suddenly free black men, women and children? Where and how would they live? With their limited skills, where would black workers find employment save for the cotton fields from which they came? Far from an evil institution, slavery was the very salvation of the black race, and the basis of prosperity for slaves and slave owners alike. To many southerners who had developed a patriarchal affection for their slaves, upholding the institution of slavery was more than an economic necessity; it was also an expression of love and charitable kindness.

To most southerners, Lincoln was the candidate who most threatened their beloved slave system. Throughout the campaign he had been relentlessly portrayed as an abolitionist, or "Black Republican." Lincoln had repeatedly insisted that he had no inclination or constitutional authority to disturb slavery where it existed. Rather, by insuring that slavery not be allowed to expand to the territories, Lincoln believed that slavery would die a slow but steady death. He did not believe that the black race was the intellectual or social equal of the white race, and he consistently maintained that he would deny blacks the right to vote, serve on juries or hold office. But his personal sense of justice held that "no man is good enough to govern another man, without that other's consent." Further, the sacred Declaration that "all men are created equal" meant that the government itself must rest on the consent of the governed. Self-government, then, was but a reflection of equality, and self-government depended upon a fair and orderly process. Expanded slavery threatened the very ideal upon which the country was founded and had prospered. Further, Lincoln believed, equality was nothing if not rooted in economic opportunity. Every man had the right to advancement based upon his own labor, or "the right to eat the bread, without leave of anybody else, which his own hand earns."[22]

But these positions were lost on southerners, who only knew that any attack on the institution of slavery was nothing less than an attack on the very fabric of the southern lifestyle. Lincoln was viewed as a "nigger lover," an "ape," a "baboon." Born in Kentucky, his migration to Indiana and Illinois and subsequent adoption of anti-slavery principles was seen as treasonable actions against his homeland. Lincoln was nothing more than a "relentless, dogged, free-soil border ruffian ... a vulgar mobocrat and a southern hater ... an illiterate partisan ... possessed only of his inveterate hatred of slavery and his openly avowed predilections of Negro equality."[23] Even Lincoln's choice for a running mate, Hannibal Hamlin, was rumored to be of African ancestry. "Hamlin is what we call a mulatto," said Robert Barnwell Rhett, editor of the Charleston *Mercury* and the South's most outspoken proponent of secession. "He has black blood in him, and let me tell you that it is his nomination that has a remarkable peculiarity. [The Republicans] design to place over the South a man who has Negro blood in his veins."[24]

According to the southern press, Lincoln's Black Republicans were behind all manner of hideous and incendiary plots to overthrow the southern way of life. It was widely believed that Lincoln's election would act as a trigger signal, and slaves throughout the region would riot and rebel against their owners. Northern abolition agents were said to be conducting secret night meetings, urging blacks to arm themselves and prepare for revolution. Slaveowners and their families were to be murdered in their beds, dwellings and towns were to be torched, water wells poisoned. The plan of the Black Republicans, according to Alabama congressman Jabez L.M. Curry, was to invade the South with an army of half a million abolitionists, free its slaves and lay waste its fields, and "amalgamate the poor man's daughter and the rich man's buck-nigger."[25] Mississippi senator Albert G. Brown warned that Lincoln's election would create chaos in the southern social order. "The Negro will insist on being treated as an equal," he wrote. "That he shall go to the white man's table, and the white man to his—that he shall share the white man's bed, and the white man his—that his son shall marry the white man's daughter, and the white man's daughter his son. In short, they shall live on terms of perfect social equality.... Then will commence a war of races."[26] A North Carolina newspaper cautioned its readers that "if we submit now to Lincoln's election, before his term of office expires, your home will be visited by one of the most fearful and horrible butcheries that has cursed the fate of the globe."[27] These reckless rumors were unsubstantiated, but secessionist advocates had no interest in checking the accuracy of the stories; what mattered most was that the stories were believed, and the cause of disunion advanced.

For decades southern states had protected the institution of slavery from national interference by controlling Washington, D.C. The southern region exerted tremendous influence over the office of the president. Democratic presidents Pierce and now Buchanan were weak puppets of the Democratic Party, willing to veto any legislation that might adversely impact the South and its slavery society. (Buchanan's proclivities to coddle to southern interests were so well-known that he had earned the sarcastic nickname "dough face.") Southern congressmen and judges opposed any measures that might adversely impact slavery, from federal control over interstate commerce to increased tariffs, river and harbor improvement, homestead encouragement, establishment of an intercontinental railroad, and even federal support for higher education. Any measure designed to promote development on a national scale, through national control, was seen as a threat to slavery and therefore to the southern way of life. But now, with northern (Republican) power growing, the possibilities of presidential vetoes and Republican legislative proposals with anti-South ramifications seemed all too real and all too threatening. If, as Lincoln hoped, slavery was barred from the new western territories, southerners feared that the resulting new states would drive the southern states deeper into a minority position. Eventually free states would have the necessary three-to-one majority that would authorize a constitutional amendment abolishing slavery forever.

Frederick Douglass, former slave and abolitionist journalist, was not initially impressed with Lincoln, whom he saw as far too moderate and conciliatory. He did see, however, that the South's hold on the machinery of national government had now been weakened. "For fifty years the country has taken the law from the lips of exacting, haughty and imperious slave oligarchy," he wrote. "The masters of slaves have been masters of the Republic. Their authority was almost undisputed, and their power irresistible. They were the President makers of the Republic, and no aspirant dared to hope for success against their frown. Lincoln's election has vitiated their authority, and broken their power. It has taught the North its strength, and shown the South its weakness. More important still, it has demonstrated the possibility of electing, if not an Abolitionist, an *anti-slavery reputation* to the Presidency."[28]

For Lincoln, Washington, D.C., presented a special set of postelection problems. Although it was the capitol of the entire nation, Washington was clearly a southern city both in culture (slavery was legal there), and in political persuasion. Thirty years of Democratic dominance had resulted in a settled arrogance among the thousands of southern men who filled patronage positions throughout the bureaucracy. On a rainy election day many of these men ventured from their offices to polling places to cast their votes for Breckinridge or Bell, not bothering to return to work, instead opting to commiserate with friends at local saloons. At Washington theaters that evening performances were regularly interrupted with news of election returns; reports of Democratic gains brought cheers, while any mention of Lincoln's progress drew angry hisses. The hostility against him, Lincoln could only hope, would decrease by the time he was inaugurated in March.

Southern newspapers overwhelmingly condemned Lincoln's election, but in differing degrees of hostility. Many newspapers offered a word of warning to the president-elect. The Richmond *Dispatch* stated that "the election of Abraham Lincoln has indeed put the country in peril." The Raleigh *Standard* proclaimed, "We will never permit Mr. Lincoln or his party to touch the institution of domestic Slavery." The New Orleans *Crescent* said, "The Northern people, in electing Mr. Lincoln, have perpetrated a deliberate, cold-blooded insult and outrage on the people of the slaveholding states." Wrote the New Bern (N.C.) *Progress*, "If Lincoln violates his oath, let us dethrone him."[29] Lincoln's election was the "last straw," wrote the Dallas *Herald*. Now would an "outraged and forbearing people stand up in their majesty and say '*thus far and no farther....* The evil days are upon us."[30]

Many southern newspapers urged their readers to support secession from the Union. "Secession becomes the glory and prosperity of the South," stated the Atlanta *Intelligencer*. The Oxford *Mercury* said, "Devotion to the Union is treason to the South." The Atlanta *Confederacy* wrote, "Every member of Congress representing a southern constituency should resign at once." "You men of the South are the greatest power on earth, and you can dictate to Christendom as a separate Confederacy," wrote the Montgomery *Advertiser*. "You can only sink to the condition of Ireland as members of this Union."[31]

In the opinion of some papers secession could not occur peacefully. Said the Atlanta *Southern Confederacy*, "Let the consequences be what they may — whether the Potomac is crimsoned in human gore, and Pennsylvania Avenue is paved ten fathoms deep with mangled bodies, the South, the loyal South, the constitutional South, will never submit to such humiliation and degradation as the inauguration of Abraham Lincoln." The Augusta *Constitutionalist* advised, "The South should arm at once." The Richmond *Enquirer* wrote, "The Northern people, by a sectional vote, have elected a President for the avowed purpose of aggression on southern rights. The purpose of aggression has been declared. This is a *declaration of war.*"[32]

The Charleston *Mercury*, headed by the bombastic Rhett, led the way with its fiery rhetoric against Lincoln and its call for violent breakaway from the Union. The 59-year-old Rhett (who had changed his name from Smith; Rhett sounded more aristocratic), referred to himself as the "Father of the Confederacy." He had advocated secession from the Union for nearly 30 years, and believed that Lincoln's election would garner enough support among South Carolinians that finally his dream would be realized. Before the election he advocated for "the separation of South Carolina, whether alone or with others, from the Union which can only be a badge of infamy to her!" Now that Lincoln had been elected, he rejoiced. "The tea has been thrown overboard," he wrote. "The revolution of 1860 has been initiated."[33] Outside the office of his Charleston *Mercury* he ordered that the South Carolina flag — blue with a white crescent and palmetto tree — be unfurled. He hoped the flag would become the symbol of a new nation: a confederacy of Southern states.

Some border state newspapers, however, cautiously advised against secession. The Memphis *Enquirer* stated, "Let every man put his foot down on disunion; it is no remedy for southern wrongs; it is only the mad man's remedy." The Louisville *Journal* stated that the Congress and Supreme Court would act as insurmountable checks on Lincoln's actions. "Patriots ought to stand loyally and patiently in the Union," it said. "(Lincoln) can do no harm…. The Union and the Constitution must be preserved." The Baltimore *Clipper* predicted that "Lincoln cannot do worse than the Democratic administration that is now drawing to an ignoble and despised conclusion." Said the Gallatin *Courier and Enquirer*, "We trust that the counsel of wiser and better men will prevail."[34]

How real was the threat of southern secession? Many northern observers were unsure. For decades southern states had regularly threatened to break from the Union. Every national tariff proposal, it seemed, led southern politicians and editorialists to claim that their state's sovereignty was imperiled; every non-Democratic presidential candidate's sole aim was to trample on the rights of the South; every election would determine the future, if not the very existence, of the southern lifestyle. In short, every issue was a "crisis" in the eyes of the South, and every crisis could only be solved by secession.

But not once had any southern state ever backed up its threat and seceded, and by 1860 such talk was treated in the North as a tired joke. Lincoln, along with many other Republicans, was not at all convinced that the crisis was real. He knew that southern states had threatened secession many times in the past — like "the ticking of a familiar clock" at nearly every national election since 1832 — and never once had they carried out their threats.[35] The Chicago *Tribune* advised its readers that Lincoln "does not believe that any of the States will go off and organize a Confederacy." Once his administration took power, and southern states realized that he had no intention of interfering with the South and its "peculiar institution" of slavery they would be content. In 1856 Lincoln had dismissed talk of disunion as "folly and humbug" and he saw no reason to change his mind now. "In no probable event will there be any formidable effort to break up the Union," he predicted. "The people of the South have too much of good sense and good temper to attempt the ruin of the government rather than see it administered by the men who made it. At least, so I hope and believe."[36]

Republicans had dismissed the notion of secession with varying degrees of scorn, ridicule and humor throughout the fall campaign. Williams Seward's remarks at a September rally in St. Paul were typical of the Republican attitude. "The slave power rails now with a feeble voice, instead of thundering as it did for twenty or thirty years past. With a feeble and muttering voice they cry out that, they will tear the Union to pieces. Who's afraid? Nobody."[37] To Thurlow Weed, strategist for Seward and the editor of the Albany *Evening Journal*, talk of disunion was "a game for the Presidency ... nothing but a game. That it will be played desperately we admit, because southern sportsmen play desperately."[38] Carl Schurz sneered that, at most, unhappy southern states would "secede, go out and take two drinks, and come back again.[39] U.S. Representative Schuyler Colfax of Indiana wrote a letter to his mother that summarized what many Republicans felt. "We (in the House) are still just where we started six months ago, except that our Southern friends have dissolved the Union forty or fifty times since then."[40]

But this time southern leaders seemed intent on carrying through with their promises. South Carolina senator James H. Hammond expressed confidence that the South would prosper in a new nation. "I firmly believe that the slave-holding South is now the controlling *power* of the world — that no other power would face us in hostility," Hammond said. "Cotton, rice, tobacco, and naval stores command the world; and we have sense to know it, and are sufficiently Teutonic to carry it out successfully. The North without us would be a motherless calf, bleating about, and die of mange and starvation."[41] A legislator from South Carolina told his colleagues that "the representative of one of the Imperial Powers of Europe" had given assurances that it would recognize a new southern nation for purposes of the cotton trade, "for the future as their increasing demand for that article will require."[42]

Governor William H. Gist of South Carolina knew his state played the leader's role in the secession movement, and his annual message to the legislature, just one day before the election, welcomed that responsibility with an accompanying call to arms. (This was to be Gist's last official act as governor; Francis W. Pickens, also a secessionist, took office in January.) The Republican Party, he warned, was committed to "reducing the Southern States to mere provinces of a consolidated despotism, to be governed by a fixed majority in Congress hostile to our institutions, and fatally bent upon our ruin." Gist therefore ordered the legislature to remain in session, for the only alternative was "the secession of South Carolina from the Federal Union. The indications from many of the Southern States justify the conclusion that the secession of South Carolina will be immediately followed, if not adopted simultaneously, by them, and ultimately by the entire South.... The State has, with great unanimity, declared that she has the right peaceably to secede, and no power on earth can rightfully prevent it.... If, in the exercise of arbitrary power, and forgetful of the lessons of history, the Government of the United States should attempt coercion, it will become our solemn duty to meet force by force.... I would also respectfully recommend a thorough reorganization of the Militia, so as to place the whole military force of the State in a position to be used at the shortest notice, and with the greatest efficiency. Every man in the State, between the ages of eighteen and forty-five, should be well armed with the most efficient weapons of modern warfare…. I would recommend that the services of ten thousand volunteers be immediately accepted…. With this preparation for defense, and with all the hallowed memories of past achievements, with our love of liberty, and hatred of tyranny, and with the knowledge that we are contending for the safety of our homes and firesides, we can confidently appeal to the Disposer of all human events, and safely trust our cause in His keeping."[43]

The South Carolina legislature dutifully remained in session and discussed its options in the wake of Lincoln's election. After three days of fiery speeches, the legislature by unanimous vote decided to call for the election of delegates to consider relations "with the Northern States and the Government of the United States." A citywide celebration erupted at the news, complete with parades, fireworks and music. Secession seemed so certain, and public sentiment so much in favor of it, that Robert Barnwell Rhett, editor of the Charleston *Mercury*, wrote to President Buchanan: "The crowds that thronged the streets of Charleston on the morning of November 7th were of one mind. From their point of view they had an undoubted grievance; consequently their complaint was just. With one accord they invoked Secession as the remedy. At noon the palmetto and lone star flag was stretched across the street from an upper window of the Charleston *Mercury* office, and was hailed with cheers and expressions of passionate attachment."[44] The South Carolina convention was called for December 17th. As expected Alabama, Georgia, Florida and Louisiana rallied behind South Carolina and called for state conventions of their own, while only North Carolina seemed reluctant. Mississippi also seemed poised to secede, although one of its heroes, former senator and secretary of war Jefferson Davis, continued to speak of possible reunification.

South Carolina's postelection response was not limited to state officials. James Chestnut resigned his seat in the United States Senate, followed by James H. Hammond. The day after Lincoln's election the United States District Court for South Carolina was in session, the Honorable Judge Caleb Magrath presiding. But the grand jury did not go about its usual course of business that day. Instead, it delivered a message to the court: "The verdict of the Northern section of the confederacy, solemnly announced to the country, through the ballot-box on yesterday, having swept away the last hope for the permanence, for the stability of the Federal Government of these sovereign States; and the public mind is constrained to lift itself above the consideration of details in the administration of Law and Justice, up to the vast and solemn issues which have been forced upon us. These issues involve the existence of the Government of which this Court is the organ and minister. In these extraordinary circumstances, the Grand Jury respectfully decline to proceed with their presentments. They deem this explanation due to the Court and to themselves."[45]

Judge Magrath promptly resigned his office. Normally, he stated, he would simply thank the jury for its service and dismiss its members. "But now I have something more to do, the omission of which would not be consistent with propriety. In the political history of the United States, an event has happened of ominous import to fifteen slaveholding States. The State of which we are citizens has been always understood to have deliberately fixed its purpose whenever that event should happen. Feeling an assurance of what will be the action of the State, I consider it my duty, without delay, to prepare to obey its wishes. That preparation is made by the resignation of the office I have held. For the last time, I have, as a Judge of the United States, administered the laws of the United States within the limits of the State of South Carolina.... So far as I am concerned, the Temple of Justice, raised under the Constitution of the United States, is now closed. If it shall never be again opened, I thank God that its doors have been closed before its altar has been desecrated with the sacrifices to tyranny."[46]

With Congress not scheduled to reconvene until December, suggested some in the border states, perhaps ideas for compromise might be considered now. State senator John Tyler of Virginia called for a peace conference of southern politicians, who might discuss their fears and present them to their northern counterparts. Perhaps, thought Tyler, if the fiery rhetoric of the campaign were toned down, governmental leaders could find a solution to the "vexing problem" the country now faced. But even though President Buchanan favored Tyler's idea in principle, it was quickly branded as nothing but an "Old Ladies Convention" by secessionists and the radical wing of the Republican Party, and nothing came of it.

Many other proposals were also made, then ignored. Let both North and South each have a president, it was suggested, to succeed each other in alternating terms. No laws would be valid unless signed by both presidents, and secession could only be accomplished if a majority of states in a section approved it. Another proposal called for the election of a president from the free states, and a vice president from the slave states; the practice could be alternated every four years. It was suggested that Arizona and New Mexico be admitted as slave states; from then on, the acquisition of any additional territories would be prohibited. Let all territory north of 36 percent 30' be forever free, and south of that line forever slave. Gen. Winfield Scott, general in chief of the United States Army, suggested that four unions, not one or two, be established, so that the wishes of all the country's citizens could be accommodated in one way or another.

But to southern secessionists the prospect of Lincoln as president was so daunting that the Union could not and would not be preserved. Howell Cobb of Georgia served as secretary of the treasury under Buchanan. "An intense mutual hatred," he said, made separation of the Union "a necessity which could not be avoided."[47] When the postelection edition of *Harper's Weekly*, adorned with an illustration of the president-elect on the cover, arrived in New Orleans, thousands of copies were shipped back to the publisher as a show of contempt. Lincoln was hanged in effigy in Pensacola, Florida, an event that was transmitted throughout the country on the telegraph wires, and the news of which reached Lincoln himself.

Despite the sensational and wildly varied reactions to his election, Lincoln stubbornly refused to comment publicly on the crisis that imperiled the country. Perhaps, though, a casual comment he made to a group of supporters who had gathered at his home to congratulate him revealed what he surely knew. "Well, boys, your troubles are over now," he said, "but mine have just begun."[48]

5

"No Sign Shall Be Given Them"

By seven o'clock on the morning following Lincoln's election, several hundred people had gathered outside his home. Within the hour, after breakfast was served to her family, Mary allowed her husband to receive his callers. The admirers and well-wishers proceeded through Lincoln's front door, into the parlor, and out again — one newspaper reported that the "entire community" turned out — and Lincoln greeted each person with a handshake and a smile.

Later Lincoln went to his office at the statehouse, but found it even more crowded than his house. He stood at the doorway and shook hands with a steady stream of callers, many of whom then stood around the office, some settling on chairs or the sofa. Some wanted to meet Lincoln, or simply get a good look at him, while others wanted jobs: they had helped elect him, they claimed, and now wanted to be rewarded with a postmastership, customs position, or Federal clerkships. Lincoln tried to be polite, but in private complained about office seekers and called them "vultures." Soon the room was jammed beyond capacity and Lincoln was, in his words, "driven to the wall."[1] At five o'clock Lincoln returned home for supper, but found yet another throng of people crowded around his home, standing in his yard and on the steps leading to his front door. At 7:30 that evening local Republicans assembled at the statehouse for speeches, but Lincoln was too tired to speak, preferring instead to listen to Secretary of State Ozias Hatch and other party officials address the gathering. Later that night Lincoln went home, and finding his family asleep, finally had some time alone to collect his thoughts.

No man elected president had ever been in a stranger position. Lincoln knew his rise to the presidency had come not because of any demonstrated leadership abilities or administrative expertise — in fact, his experience in those areas was almost nonexistent. Neither could Lincoln point to a distinguished military career that had prepared him to assume the duties of commander in chief. While Lincoln had been a respected state legislator, save for one unremarkable term in Congress he had no national political experience. Rather, his rise to national prominence had come from a series of debates with Stephen Douglas (that precluded an election he lost) and one well-received speech in front of a New York audience at Cooper Union. He had not even been the front-runner for his party's nomination. Because Lincoln was the second choice of a great many Republicans he represented, instead, simply a workable compromise. And now as the nominal head of the party, Lincoln had to act to unify diverse interests and satisfy the many groups that had contributed to his election, including conservative Republicans, former Whigs, free-soil Democrats, and elements of radical abolitionists and Know-Nothings. Lincoln knew he could never satisfy all these groups on the slavery question, and had no intention of altering his no-expansion policy in any event. His immediate challenge was to bring together his party with a careful selection of a cabinet that would help him govern. Lincoln's managers had ostensibly bound him by their promises of patronage at the convention in May. He did not feel personally obligated by those promises, yet had to be sensitive to the wishes of those who had relied upon them. In selecting his cabinet Lincoln had to appease the very rivals he had defeated for the nomination of his party.

Sitting at his bedroom desk Lincoln took out a blank card and wrote on the left-hand side these names, next to his own: Seward, Bates, Dayton. On the right he wrote: Judd, Chase, M. Blair, Welles. All these men were prominent Republicans who represented different constituencies, different states, different regions of the country. The names represented, as well, the diverse factions within the party itself. The first group of names had ties, in one form or another, to the old Whig Party. William Seward of New York, who had unsuccessfully sought the presidential nomination, seemed a logical choice for a top cabinet post, most likely secretary of state. Edward Bates of Missouri was a former Know-Nothing who had the support of powerful newspaperman Horace Greeley. William L. Dayton of New Jersey had been the Republican vice-presidential candidate in 1856, and should perhaps now be rewarded for his allegiance to the party.

The names on the right side of Lincoln's card were all former Democrats who had become Republicans and helped raise the new party to prominence. Norman Judd had worked hard to bring the convention to Chicago, had been given the honor of placing Lincoln's name into nomination and had seated delegates to Lincoln's advantage. Although Lincoln's managers David Davis and Leonard Swett advised against it, it seemed natural now that Lincoln would consider rewarding Judd with a cabinet position. Senator Salmon Chase of Ohio had twice been a Republican hopeful for the presidential nomination, and while his inability to control the Ohio delegation had twice defeated him, Chase remained a powerful voice in Washington. Montgomery Blair of Maryland had been a free-soiler since 1848 and was, like Lincoln, an advocate for colonialism. And Gideon Welles of Connecticut was said to be Hannibal Hamlin's personal choice for a cabinet position. Lincoln put the card in his coat pocket as a reminder; he would contact Hamlin and ask for his opinions of these men, among others.

On a larger scale, of course, Lincoln's task was not only to satisfy the various factions of his party but placate the South that despised him. The country itself was supposed to be falling apart because of his election. Journalists and politicians were beginning their descent on Springfield, intent on learning what Lincoln's strategy would be, insisting that their readers and constituents demanded answers and explanations. How did he respond to southerners who insisted that his goal was to destroy their lifestyle? What concessions was he willing to make to keep southern states in the Union? Would he deviate from the Republican platform in order to do so? With his inauguration four months away, how effective could he be *now* to thwart secession?

Lincoln was determined not to answer these questions. He was, after all, not the president but merely president-elect, and he could not speak for a government he did not yet control.[2] He felt a personal commitment to remain true to his political principles. "I know the justness of my intentions," he wrote, "and the utter groundlessness of the pretended fears of the men who are filling the country with their clamor. If I go into the presidency, they will find me as I am on record, nothing less, nothing more. My declarations have been made to the world without reservation. They have been often repeated, and now self-respect demands of me and of the party which has elected me that, when threatened, I should be silent."[3] Lincoln believed that the official platform of his party sufficiently set forth his views. "What is it I could say which would quiet alarm?" he wondered. "Is it that no interference by the government, with slaves or slavery within the states, intended? I have said this so often already, that a repetition of it is but mockery, bearing an appearance of weakness, and cowardice, which perhaps should be avoided. Why do not uneasy men *read* what I have already said? and what our *platform* says? If they will not read, or heed, then would they read, or heed a repetition of them?"[4]

But the pressure on Lincoln to speak out was relentless. Truman Smith was a former representative and senator from Connecticut who had served with Lincoln in Washington. He wrote to Lincoln the day after the election and urged him to make a public statement "to disarm mischief makers, to allay causeless anxiety, to compose the public mind and to induce all good citizens to 'judge the tree by its fruits.'"[5] Lincoln responded to Smith's plea with a letter marked "private and confidential." He wrote, "It is with the most profound appreciation of your motive, and highest respect for your judgment too, that I feel constrained, for the present, at least, to make no declaration for the public.... First, I could say nothing which I have not already said, and which is in print, and open for the inspection of all. To press a repetition of this upon whose who *have* listened, is useless; to press it upon those who have *refused* to listen, and still refuse, would be wanting in self-respect, and would have an appearance of sycophancy and timidity, which would excite the contempt of good men, and encourage bad ones to clamor the more loudly."[6]

Because of the threat of disunion, business slowed to a crawl after Lincoln's election, particularly in the North. The stock market in New York staggered. Northern banks contracted their credit, and some banks in the South and West folded altogether. Most northern financiers watched and waited anxiously, expecting bad news. They had extended hundreds of thousands of dollars in loans to southern cotton and tobacco growers. Now that the harvest was completed, debtors in the South were holding onto their crop in anticipation of secession; many had begun negotiations with European exporters for purchase and direct trade, rather than through northern factories and mills. The Federal Treasury weakened as revenues decreased, and it was expected that when Congress reconvened in December it would be unable to pay congressional salaries. "It is an awful time for merchants," wrote businessman George Livermore. "If there is not some speedy relief, more than half the best concerns in the country will be ruined."[7] Many thought that a statement from Lincoln could smooth turbulent economic waters brought about by widespread anticipation of civil war. But Lincoln scoffed at the notion that the country's economic woes might be blamed on his silence. "I am not insensible to any commercial or financial depression that may exist," he wrote. "But nothing is to be gained by fawning around the *respectable scoundrels* who got it up. Let them go to work and repair the mischief of their own making; and then perhaps they will be less greedy to do the like again."[8]

Nathaniel P. Paschall was editor of the *Missouri Republican*, a pro-Union newspaper. He advised Lincoln that if Missouri was to be kept in the Union reassurances from Lincoln were needed. If he would not speak, suggested Paschall, perhaps some of his speeches could be consolidated for publication. Lincoln turned down the offer. "I am not at liberty to shift my ground — that is out of the question," he wrote. "If a thought a *repetition* would do any good I would make it. But my judgment is it would do positive harm. The secessionists, *per se* believing they had alarmed me, would clamor all the louder."[9]

Those who wanted answers to their questions about the future of the country, thought Lincoln, would be better off to direct those questions to President Buchanan, who was in a position to do something about the so-called "crisis." That Buchanan seemed content to ride out his term without taking action of any sort was maddening to everyone, and Lincoln could only hope that the president would change his mind and do something — anything — to calm the country before he left office. Perhaps Buchanan would say something of substance in his annual message on December 3, when Congress reconvened.

Southern states began to move boldly toward secession. It was widely reported that various southern militia groups were organizing and stockpiling arms and ammunition in anticipation of civil war. Georgia's legislature appropriated $1 million for arsenal purchase, and it was rumored that soon it would seize Forts Pulaski and Jackson. Louisiana was said to be considering the seizure of all federal property within its borders, as were Florida, Alabama and Mississippi. All southern eyes, it seemed, were on South Carolina to take the first formal steps toward disunion, at its convention on December 17.

Gen. Winfield Scott directly advised Lincoln of the Southern dangers he saw and recommended that Lincoln take action. One week before the election Scott wrote a memorandum entitled "Views suggested by the imminent danger of a disruption of the Union by the secession of one or more Southern States," predicting that secession might lead to as many as four confederacies. Now that he was elected, suggested Scott, Lincoln should make clear that slavery would be unprofitable in the western territories. He should seize southern federal forts as a show of strength; a policy of firmness would convince the seceding states that their course was unwise. While Lincoln thought Scott's views well-intentioned, he also believed them to be unrealistic. Still, he had no intention of alienating a highly respected military man and someone whose services might very well be needed. Lincoln sent Scott his "sincere thanks … and especially for this renewed manifestation of (your) patriotic purposes as a citizen, connected, as it is, with (your) high official position, and most distinguished character, as a military captain."[10]

Lincoln naively thought that the armament of the South could actually be beneficial, if it motivated true Unionists there. "I am rather glad of this military preparation in the South," he wrote. "It will enable the people the more easily to suppress any uprisings there, which their misrepresentations of purposes may have encouraged."[11] Privately, however, Lincoln had doubts "as to the practicability of holding the Slave States in the Union by main force, if they were all determined to break it up." Never had he dreamed that, as president, "his principal duty would be to raise great armies and fleets for the suppression of the rebellion."[12]

Unwilling to change his position, Lincoln remained steady in his silence. A Republican rally was held in Springfield on November 20, and many national journalists attended, hoping that Lincoln would take this opportunity to address the nation's concerns. That afternoon a group of supporters gathered at Lincoln's home and called for him so boisterously that he finally appeared. But even among his friends and neighbors Lincoln would not speak of policy:

> Friends and fellow citizens: Please excuse me, on this occasion, from making a speech. I thank you for the kindness and compliment of this call. I thank you, in common with all others, who have thought fit, by their votes, to endorse the Republican cause. I rejoice with you in the success which has, so far, attended that cause. Yet in all our rejoicing let us neither express, nor cherish, any harsh feeling towards any citizen who by his vote, has differed with us. Let us at all times remember that all American citizens are brothers of a common country, and should dwell together in the bonds of fraternal feeling. Let me again beg you to accept my thanks, and to excuse me from further speaking at this time.[13]

While he would not appear at the rally, however, Lincoln came up with a way to express his views in a limited manner and perhaps quiet some of the clamor. He wrote out a short passage and allowed Trumbull to deliver the message on his behalf, his managers making sure that the press credit these particular words and thoughts to Lincoln:

> I have labored in, and for, the Republican organization with entire confidence that whenever it shall be in power each and all of the States will be left in as complete control of their own affairs respectively, and at as perfect liberty to choose, and employ, their own means of protecting property, and preserving peace and order within their respective limits, as they have ever been under any administration. Those who have voted for Mr. Lincoln, have expected, and still expect this; and they would not have voted for him had they expected otherwise. I regard it as extremely fortunate for the peace of the whole country, that this point, upon which the Republicans have been so long, and so persistently misrepresented, is now to be brought to a practical test, and placed beyond the possibility of doubt. Disunionists *per se*, are now in hot haste to get out of the Union, precisely because they perceive they can not, much longer, maintain apprehension among the Southern people that their homes, and firesides, and lives, are to be endangered by the action of the Federal Government. With such *"Now, or never"* is the maxim.

But these remarks, delivered through a third party, did not satisfy anyone, and Lincoln was annoyed at the coverage they received. He wrote: "Has a single newspaper, heretofore against us, urged that speech (upon its readers) with a purpose to quiet public anxiety? Not one, so far as I know. On the contrary the Boston *Courier*, and its' [sic] class, hold me responsible for the speech, and endeavor to inflame the North with the belief that it foreshadows an abandonment of Republican ground by the incoming administration; while the Washington *Constitution*, and its' class hold the same speech up to the South as an open declaration of war against them.... This is just as I expected, and just what would happen with any declaration I could make. These political fiends are not half sick enough yet. 'Party malice' and not 'public good' possesses them entirely. 'They seek a sign, and no sign shall be given them.' At least such is my present feeling and purpose."[14]

But Lincoln took solace from a speech delivered by his old congressional friend Alexander H. Stephens of Georgia. Stephens shared Lincoln's birthday, February 12, and both men had been Whigs in Congress. Frail and sickly most of his life, never weighing more than 90 pounds, Stephens was nonetheless a man of great intellect and admired by all who knew him, including Lincoln. After Lincoln's election, Governor Joe Brown had called the Georgia legislature into special session to consider calling a secession convention. Among many calls for action, Stephens called for patience. "Shall the people of Georgia secede from the Union in consequence of the election of Mr. Lincoln to the Presidency of the United States?" he said. "My countrymen, I tell you frankly, candidly, and earnestly, that I do not think that they ought." Stephens noted that Lincoln would face a majority against him in both the House and Senate. The president is "no Emperor, no Dictator — he is clothed with no absolute power.... If Lincoln violates the Constitution, then will come our time to act.... I do not anticipate that Mr. Lincoln will do anything, to jeopardize our safety or security, whatever may be his spirit to do it;.... I am for exhausting all that patriotism demands, before taking the last step.... If the evil has got beyond our control ..., we can appeal to the God of Battles, if it comes to that, to aid us in our cause."[15]

Lincoln read excerpts of the speech in the newspaper and was so impressed that he wrote to Stephens and asked for a copy. When it arrived Lincoln was cheered by its cautionary tone, yet concerned that the South truly feared northern hostility. He wrote to Stephens, "Do the people of the South really entertain fears that a Republican administration would, *directly*, or *indirectly*, interfere with their slaves, or with them, about their slaves? If they do, I wish to assure you, as once a friend, and still, I hope, not an enemy, that there is no cause for such fears.... You think slavery is *right* and ought to be extended; while we think it is *wrong* and ought to be restricted. That I suppose is the rub. It certainly is the only substantial difference between us."[16]

Stephens replied to Lincoln's short note with a lengthy and reasoned statement. He most certainly was not Lincoln's enemy, he wrote. He shared Lincoln's desire to preserve and maintain the Union if it could be done peacefully. But southerners were concerned that the Republican administration was bound to "put the institution of (African slavery) under the ban of public opinion and national condemnation." Suppose the North decided to condemn a southern religion, Stephens asked hypothetically, formed a political party to extinguish it, and attempted to prevent the spread of the religion to the western territories. "Is it not apparent that a general feeling of resistance to the success, aims, and objects of such a party would necessarily and rightfully ensue?" People in the South, wrote Stephens, believed that slavery was morally right because of "the inferiority of the black race." Of course the South was now aroused, when an antislavery attitude prevailed in the North, when an antislavery administration was about to assume office, and when no voice in the North even bothered to speak out against "the madness of the John Brown raid in Virginia."[17]

The Union was formed by the consent of independent, sovereign states, concluded Stephens. It could not be maintained by force. Now, like everyone else, Stephens advised Lincoln to speak out. "A word 'fitly spoken by you,'" he urged, "would indeed be like 'apples of gold in pictures of silver.' I entreat you be not deceived as to the nature and extent of the danger, nor as to the remedy."[18] While Lincoln did not respond to Stephens' letter, in just a few months Stephens' actions would again gain Lincoln's attention: in February Stephens would be sworn in as vice president of the newly formed Confederate States of America.

Lincoln wished to confer privately with his own vice president, Hannibal Hamlin. Already weary of ever-increasing crowds of journalists, politicos and curiosity-seekers, and frustrated by the public's inability to understand his silence, Lincoln sought to get out of Springfield, at least for a little while. Lincoln wanted Hamlin to have a voice in the cabinet selections, and wasted no time in arranging a meeting. "I am anxious for a personal interview with you at as early a day as possible," he wrote on November 9. "Can you, without much inconvenience, meet me at Chicago?"[19] Hamlin canceled plans to attend his son's wedding and immediately prepared to travel to Illinois at the end of the month.

Shortly after the election the New York *Herald* dispatched a 25-year-old reporter named Henry Villard to Springfield, instructing him to send daily dispatches as to the activities of the president-elect. Though the *Herald* had bitterly opposed Lincoln's candidacy, Lincoln welcomed Villard to town and into his home, authorizing Villard "to come to him at any time for any information I needed."[20] Although Lincoln undoubtedly wanted to court the favor of the *Herald*, he had another reason for extending such hospitality toward Villard: he had first met Villard, and become friends with him, two years earlier during his debates with Stephen Douglas.

In 1858 Villard, a native of Germany, covered the debates in German for the New York *Staats-Zeitung*. He came upon Lincoln accidentally at a railroad "station" outside of Petersburg — really nothing more than an uncovered platform and bench in the middle of the Illinois prairie. Lincoln had been driven in a buggy to the station, then left alone waiting for the train to arrive and take him home to Springfield. Villard sat with Lincoln for an hour and a half waiting for the overdue train, first in the sultry heat, then in an empty freight car when a thunderstorm struck. Despite the uncomfortable surroundings, Villard found Lincoln "most approachable, good natured and full of wit and humor" with "a lean, lank, indescribably gawky figure, an odd-featured, wrinkled, inexpressive, and altogether uncomely face." Lincoln confessed to Villard that he was not confident of his chances to defeat Douglas in the contest for U.S. Senate. Early in his career, he said, his highest ambition had been to serve in the state legislature. "Since then, of course, I have grown some," he laughed, "but my friends got me into *this* business. I did not consider myself qualified for the United States Senate, and it took me a long time to persuade myself that I was. Now, to be sure, I am convinced that I am good enough for it; but, in spite of it all, I am saying to myself every day: 'It is too big a thing for you; you will never get it.' Mary insists, however, that I am going to be Senator and President of the United States, too. Just think," Lincoln said with a hearty laugh, "of such a sucker as me as President!"[21] A year later Villard encountered Lincoln again, this time on a cold autumn day outside of St. Joseph, Missouri. Lincoln was on his way to Kansas on a speaking tour, and Villard was returning to the East from the gold camps of Colorado. The two men renewed their acquaintance, and noticing that Lincoln was shivering in the wind, Villard gave him a buffalo robe to cover his legs. Lincoln promised to return it soon, but Villard never saw it again.

But Lincoln did not forget the kindness of the journalist, and now as president-elect allowed Villard access to all but the most confidential of meetings and regularly invited him to his home. For the next four months, or until the inauguration in March, Villard was in almost daily contact with Lincoln. While Villard had always been attracted to Lincoln's earthy charm and sense of humor, it was his abilities as a conversationalist that Villard most appreciated. Lincoln was "the very embodiment of good humor," wrote Villard. "It seems as though from this fact, much that happens about him partakes of a comical character.... Although he is naturally more listened to than talked to, he does not allow a pause to become protracted. He is never at a loss as to the subjects that please the different classes of visitors and there is a certain quaintness and originality about all he has to say, so that one cannot help feeling interested. His 'talk' is not brilliant. His phrases are not ceremoniously set, but pervaded with a humorousness and, at times, with a grotesque joviality, that will always please. I think it would be hard to find one who tells better jokes, enjoys them better and laughs oftener than Abraham Lincoln."[22]

Despite the hospitality shown Villard by Lincoln and the personal feelings of friendship between the two men, Villard at first did not believe that Lincoln was capable, on an intellectual level, of carrying out the duties of his office in such turbulent times. "I doubt Mr. Lincoln's capacity for the task of bringing light and peace out of the chaos that will surround him," he wrote. "A man of good heart and good intention, he is not firm. The times demand a Jackson." Perhaps Villard was prejudiced by his personal feelings about slavery; in 1866 he would marry Fanny Garrison, the only daughter of famed abolitionist preacher William Lloyd Garrison. But Villard was impressed with Lincoln's resolve that the Union must and would be preserved. "No one who heard him talk upon the other question (secession)," wrote Villard, "could fail to discover his 'other side' and to be impressed with his deep earnestness, his anxious contemplation of public affairs, and his thorough sense of the extraordinary responsibilities that were coming upon him."[23]

Villard accompanied Lincoln on his trip to Chicago. On November 21 Lincoln and Mary drove their carriage to the Great Western Depot, just three blocks from their home, to board the train. A crowd had gathered at the station and cheered Lincoln as he climbed down from the carriage. Since Lincoln did not yet hold office he was afforded no security or travel arrangements at government expense. After purchasing their tickets, Lincoln and his party, which included Senator and Mrs. Trumbull along with Villard, were seated in a crowded passenger car. Although Lincoln did not seem to mind, Villard was offended when the Sangamon County sheriff, "a Douglas Democrat," allowed ironed convicts, including a murderer, to take seats between Lincoln and Trumbull. The railroad had certainly not shown such callous disrespect several months earlier, noted Villard, when the Prince of Wales, later to be crowned King Edward the VII, had been extended a private and secure luxury car while passing through Illinois.[24]

Also boarding the train that morning was Donn Piatt, a poet and journalist from West Liberty, Ohio. Piatt's name was being mentioned as a possible nominee for secretary of the treasury, should Salmon Chase decline the post, and Lincoln wanted Piatt along on this trip so that he could meet Illinois party officials in Chicago. Piatt was determined to join Lincoln's inner circle, but could not picture Lincoln as a statesman. "Mr. Lincoln was the homeliest man I ever saw," he had written that fall after attending a dinner at Lincoln's home. "His body seemed to me a huge skeleton in clothes. Tall as he was, his hands and feet looked out of proportion, so long and clumsy were they. Every movement was awkward in the extreme. He sat with one leg thrown over the other, and the pendant foot swung almost to the floor. And all the while two little boys, his sons, clambered over those legs, patted his cheeks, pulled his nose, and poked their fingers into his eyes without causing reprimand or even notice. He had a face that defied artistic skill to soften or idealize."[25] Now, as the train rolled along, Piatt attempted to convince Lincoln that civil war was inevitable, and that it would begin in the early spring. "Well," said Lincoln, "we won't jump that ditch until we come to it." And if his administration did inherit a war, "I must run the machine as I find it."[26] Piatt, however, did nothing to impress either Lincoln or his advisors on this trip, and was soon dropped from serious discussions regarding a cabinet position.

The train first stopped at Lincoln, Illinois, about 30 miles northeast of Springfield. Originally called Postville, the village was the county seat of Logan County and Lincoln had been a regular visitor here while riding the circuit. He often stayed at the Deskins Tavern, and spent many enjoyable hours at the nearby town square, playing townball (a predecessor of baseball) and pitching horseshoes. On August 27, 1857, Lincoln had drawn up city charter documents and, at the celebration that afternoon, officials named the new city in his honor. Lincoln then broke open a watermelon and christened his namesake with a stream of juice.[27] Now Lincoln and his party stepped off the train to stretch their legs, and as word spread that Lincoln was at the station a crowd quickly gathered and called for a speech. Lincoln obliged with a few words:

> Fellow citizens: I thank you for this mark of your kindness toward me. I have been shut up in Springfield for the last few months, and therefore have been unable to greet you, as I was formerly in the habit of doing. I am passing on my way to Chicago, and am happy in doing so to be able to meet so many of my friends in Logan County, and if to do no more, to exchange with you the compliments of the season, and to thank you for the many kindnesses you have manifested toward me. I am not in the habit of making speeches now, and I would therefore ask to be excused from entering upon any discussion of the political topics of the day. I am glad to see so many happy faces, and to listen to so many pleasant expressions. Again thanking you for this honor, I will pass on my journey.[28]

Later the train stopped at Bloomington, the home of Judge David Davis, and

Lincoln spoke again, this time peppering his remarks with a little politicking and a story:

> Fellow citizens of Bloomington and McLean County: I am glad to meet you after a longer separation than has been common between you and me. I thank you for the good report you made of the election in Old McLean. The people of the country have again fixed up their affairs for a constitutional period of time. By the way, I think very much of the people, as an old friend said he thought of woman. He said when he lost his first wife, who had been a great help to him in his business, he thought he was ruined — that he could never find another to fill her place. At length, however, he married another, who he found did quite as well as the first, and that his opinion now was that any woman would do well who was well done by. So I think of the whole people of this nation — they will ever do well if well done by. We will try to do well by them in all parts of the country, North and South, with entire confidence that all will be well with all of us.[29]

Lincoln and his party arrived in Chicago in the early evening and were immediately driven to the Tremont Hotel on Lake Street. After dinner Lincoln and Mary received Hannibal Hamlin, who had arrived that morning. Hamlin was born in Paris Hill, Maine, just six months after Lincoln, on August 27, 1809. After graduating from Hebron Academy he took over the family farm in Oxford County. But, like Lincoln, Hamlin quickly tired of manual labor, and found work as a surveyor, compositor in a printing office, and schoolteacher. He studied law and was admitted to the bar in 1833. A Jacksonian Democrat, Hamlin was elected to the Maine House of Representatives for the first time in 1836 and served as speaker for three terms.

Hamlin was elected to Congress in 1843 and reelected in 1847. He ran unsuccessfully for the Senate in 1846, but was elected in 1848 on an antislavery ticket. By 1856 Hamlin had become disillusioned with the Democratic Party and became a Republican, losing his chairmanship of the powerful commerce committee as a result. After a decade in the Senate, Hamlin resigned to become governor of Maine in January 1857. But the position did not suit him, and he resigned in March and returned to the Senate. He had not particularly wanted to be nominated for the vice presidency in 1860. It was, by tradition, a relatively powerless office; in fact, most presidents had at best a cool relationship with their vice presidents. But Hamlin had accepted the nomination for the good of the party, and hoped to foster a meaningful relationship with Lincoln in Washington. (He was to be disappointed in that regard. While he became relatively good friends with Lincoln, he played a secondary role in shaping policy. Hamlin became so frustrated with his inactivity that in the summer of 1864 he enlisted as a private in the Maine Coast Guard and took his place among the ranks during the summer encampment. He endured plenty of public criticism, and then the humiliation of being replaced on the Republican ticket that fall when Lincoln and his advisors, in an attempt to appeal to southern voters, named Tennessee governor Andrew Johnson as the vice-presidential candidate.)

But in the summer of 1860 Hamlin proved to be a loyal, dedicated Republican and an energetic campaigner. Maine's September general election was the first in the nation, and Republicans knew that an impressive victory there would provide the momentum toward a national victory in November. Hamlin tirelessly corresponded with prominent Republican leaders from all parts of the country, urging them to come to Maine and stump for the party. "We will do well in Maine," Hamlin wrote to Charles Sumner. "But the Slave Democracy are making super human exertions, and the moral effect of our election on N.Y. Con. & R.I. and elsewhere is important. We want to keep up our maj. to its present point and must work hard to do it. Do come and help us."[30] And unlike Lincoln, Hamlin was a visible figure during the campaign; donning a red cape and bearskin lumberjack's hat, Hamlin liked to march with the Bangor detachment of Wide Awakes at rallies throughout the Northeast.

But Lincoln was nervous about the outcome of the Maine election. In September he heard a disturbing rumor about his running mate and wrote to Hamlin: "I am annoyed some by a letter from a friend in Chicago, in which the following passage occurs: 'Hamlin has written Colfax that two members of Congress will, he fears, be lost in Maine — the first and sixth districts; and that Washburne's majority for governor will not exceed six thousand.' Such a result as you seem to have predicted in Maine ... would, I fear, put us on the down-hill track, lose us the State elections in Pennsylvania and Indiana, and probably ruin us on the main turn in November. You must not allow it."[31]

Hamlin immediately responded with a letter of his own, denying the rumor and predicting a Republican victory. "I regret that you or any of our friends should have been annoyed at any time which it is *supposed* I have written," he wrote to Lincoln. "I have neither said nor written any thing I should not, I am sure, nor any thing which could possibly annoy any one. I have not written to *Colfax at all*, nor to any one anything like the extract in your letter.... I have never been so busy thro' the Press and by personal effort endeavoring to strengthen the weak points all along the line — and I feel a confidence in the result of Monday which I will not express. New England will not disappoint our friends."[32]

Hamlin's confidence proved well-founded. The Republicans swept in Maine, and Hamlin immediately wrote to Lincoln. "We think Maine has come nobly up to the crisis and vindicated the right in a gallant manner," he wrote proudly. "It cannot fail to have a powerful moral effect every where.... I trust it is the pressage of our success, and the triumph of truth and justice."[33]

Hamlin had tried to keep his trip to Chicago a secret, as Lincoln had requested. When he boarded the train in Bangor on November 19, most assumed, and the Bangor *Jeffersonian* reported, that he was returning to Washington to resume his seat in the Senate until the inauguration.[34] But word leaked out, at least to Thurlow Weed, William Seward's political advisor, who met the train in New York. Weed told Hamlin that Seward would turn down the State Department post if offered it, and Hamlin should so instruct Lincoln. To avoid any misunderstanding, Weed was planning his own trip to Springfield in the near future and would speak with Lincoln about what role Seward might be willing to play in the new administration.

In Chicago Hamlin was warmly greeted by Lincoln, and the two men reminisced about their days in Congress. Lincoln recalled that he had heard Hamlin give a speech once, and had been impressed: "I was very much struck with that speech, senator — particularly struck with it — and for the reason that it was filled 'chock up' with the very best kind of anti-slavery doctrine." Hamlin also remembered hearing

Lincoln speak. "My one and first recollection of yourself," he said, "is of having heard you make a speech in the House, — a speech that was so full of good humor and sharp points that I, together with other of your auditors, was convulsed with laughter. And I see that you and I remain in accord in our anti-slavery principles."[35] The initial meeting between Lincoln and Hamlin, reported the newspapers, was "cordial in the highest degree."[36]

The next several days were busy ones for the two men. On the 22nd they visited several places of interest in Chicago, including the post office, custom house and the federal courthouse. They also insisted on viewing the Wigwam, where the two had been nominated at the raucous Republican convention six months earlier, and which was now in the process of being torn down. Lincoln, of course, had seen Chicago many times, but Hamlin had not been to the city in 25 years and was greatly impressed. "This place is a marvel indeed," he wrote to his wife Ellen. "It has a population of 110,000 and has all grown up…. The buildings are magnificent, some of them palaces." Mary Lincoln was apparently on her best behavior, for Hamlin was also impressed with her. "I think she is one of your kind of women exactly," he wrote.[37]

A massive reception at the Tremont House was scheduled for the next day. From early morning until noon Lincoln and Hamlin received a nonstop stream of callers in the parlor suites of the hotel; it was estimated that they shook 3,000 hands in the reception line. That evening the men dined with important political allies, including Lyman Trumbull, congressmen William Kellogg of Illinois and James Gurley of Ohio, and the ever-present Carl Schurz. The next day, Saturday, November 24, Lincoln, Hamlin and Trumbull traveled to suburban Lake View, where they were the guest of Lincoln's friend Judge Ebenezer Peck. Here, finally, serious discussions as regards the selection of the cabinet could take place.

Lincoln outlined his strategy to Hamlin, who agreed that all of the various factions of the Republican Party should be represented, if possible. Seward's role was particularly important. Lincoln was not shocked at the message Hamlin delivered from Thurlow Weed, but he was firm in his insistence that Seward must either accept a post in a show of party unity, or reject it only after publicly pledging support for Lincoln's administration and expressing a desire to continue the party's work in the Senate. Lincoln also sought Hamlin's advice for the Treasury Department position. Hamlin supported Chase, and like Lincoln was not swayed by Simon Cameron's claims that he had been promised the post by Lincoln's managers at the Chicago convention. Lincoln promised to consider Chase, although he remained curious about James Guthrie of Kentucky, who had served Franklin Pierce as secretary of the treasury and was a respected figure in an important border state. (Guthrie had been recommended to Lincoln by none other than Joshua Speed, who with his wife, Fanny, had come to Chicago to visit the Lincolns. Speed confidentially assured his old friend that he was in fine shape financially and neither needed nor sought a political appointment.)

Lincoln and Hamlin candidly discussed all the potential candidates under consideration, and others mentioned by Hamlin. Lincoln made no decisions, but appreciated Hamlin's counsel and told him so. Hamlin, in return, was gratified when

Lincoln promised that Hamlin could choose the New England member of the cabinet. Lincoln's preliminary list of potential nominees from that region had expanded to include Charles Francis Adams and Nathaniel P. Banks of Massachusetts, Amos Tuck of New Hampshire and Gideon Welles of Connecticut. Lincoln let it be known that he personally favored Banks, but that fact should not sway Hamlin's choice. "I shall always be willing to accept, in the very best spirit any advice that you, the Vice-President, may give me," he told Hamlin.[38]

The next morning Hamlin boarded a train for Washington, uncertain as to whether civil war was pending but assured that the new president was capable of handling any challenge he might face. Hamlin also felt confident, for the time being at least, that he would play a meaningful role in Lincoln's administration. Lincoln and Mary attended morning services at St. James Church in Chicago, and that afternoon Lincoln toured the Mission Sabbath School, where he enjoyed the company of the children. Later he sat for a photograph taken by Samuel Alschuler — requests for photographs were becoming more and more frequent — before dinner. Finally on the 26th Lincoln and his party boarded the nine o'clock train and traveled back to Springfield in a steady rain. This time Lincoln and Mary insisted on a private car and were accommodated. They arrived home at 6:30 that evening, and the newspapers reported that Lincoln's return "is the delight of the reporters and a number of office-seekers, who have been lying in wait for him since November 24th."[39]

Both Lincoln and his wife were glad to be home. Mary, in particular, looked forward to a final holiday season in Springfield and the entertaining that went with it. While her husband spent the next several days at his statehouse office, greeting an endless stream of visitors and answering an endless stream of mail, she planned and prepared a massive celebratory dinner. November 29 was Thanksgiving Day in Illinois (not yet a national holiday; Lincoln would proclaim it as such in 1863). "Mr. Lincoln, like the rest of Anglo-American mankind, feasted on roast turkey," reported the New York *Tribune,* "and having special cause to thank his Maker, attended Divine service."[40]

6

Standing Firm

James L. Buchanan — who preferred to be called "Old Buck" — could not wait to leave the White House, and could only hope that civil war, which he knew was inevitable, would wait at least until he finished his term. Born in 1791 in rural Pennsylvania, near Gettysburg, to an Irish immigrant who had prospered as a merchant, Buchanan had lived a life of privilege. He graduated from Dickinson College at the age of 18, where he excelled in debate, Greek and Latin, and then began to study law. After a brief service as a private in the War of 1812, Buchanan entered law practice in Lancaster, and his abilities, along with wise investing, quickly enabled him to build a fortune. He fell in love with a young lady named Ann Coleman, daughter of a wealthy coal manufacturer, and by 1819 they were engaged to be married. But an argument led to estrangement, and Ann died shortly thereafter, perhaps of suicide. Buchanan was heartbroken and never really recovered from his grief; he had no other meaningful relationships with women and never married, becoming the only bachelor to serve as president.

Buchanan turned his attentions to politics, embarking on a long and distinguished career in public service. A Democrat, he spent 10 years in Congress and then in 1831 was appointed by President Andrew Jackson as minister to Russia, where he negotiated a historic trade treaty with Czar Nicholas I. He returned to America in 1835 and was elected to the U.S. Senate, where he served until President James Polk appointed him secretary of state in 1845. A firm believer in manifest destiny — he once said that it would be easier to stop Niagara from flowing than to prevent Americans from crossing the Rocky Mountains — Buchanan's aggressive actions on behalf of statehood for Texas helped lead to the Mexican War.

In 1852, after an unsuccessful bid for the Democratic nomination for the presidency, President Franklin Pierce appointed Buchanan minister to Great Britain. He came home four years later to find his country embroiled over slavery and bloody unrest in the western territories. With John C. Breckinridge as his running mate, Buchanan was elected president, easily winning the electoral college 174-114 over John C. Fremont, candidate of the new Republican Party.

Buchanan hoped that his experience as a constitutional scholar, along with his considerable skills as a mediator, would help preserve the Union. He also was not above backroom politics. He lobbied southern members of the Supreme Court, encouraging them to decide that slaves were not to be considered citizens. Once the

Court definitively spoke on the slavery issue, he reasoned, the American people would accept the decision as binding law and the crisis would die down. Just days before his inauguration, Buchanan was secretly advised that the upcoming decision in *Dred Scott* would not only deny blacks the right to sue, but also strike down the Missouri Compromise as unconstitutional. In his inaugural address Buchanan confidently predicted that the Court was about to settle the territorial question "speedily and finally." All good citizens, cautioned Buchanan, ought to abide by the ruling that was imminent.

Buchanan also sought to appease the South by selecting slaveowners for his cabinet, naming Howell Cobb of Georgia as secretary of the treasury, John Floyd of Virginia as secretary of war and Jacob Thompson of Mississippi as secretary of the interior. But Buchanan's efforts to be seen as a voice of reason and architect of compromise were derided by nearly everyone. Northern moderates resented his shameless pandering to southern interests. Abolitionists were outraged at his endorsement of *Dred Scott*. And even members of his own Democratic Party were divided over Buchanan. When he endorsed the entry of Kansas as a slave state, he earned the wrath of Stephen Douglas, who insisted that Buchanan was not a true advocate of popular sovereignty as he routinely claimed. In 1858, amidst a nationwide economic recession, the Republicans took advantage of Buchanan's woes and gained control of Congress. Two years later Buchanan did not seek, and was not offered, the nomination of his own party for the presidency, and massive disruption within the Democratic Party enabled Lincoln to win the White House.

Now truly a lame duck in the months prior to a new administration, Buchanan would take no decisive action in the face of southern threats of secession. Congress reconvened, and on December 3 Buchanan delivered his State of the Union address, blaming the crisis on "the incessant and violent agitation of the slavery question" brought about by northern radicals. These muckrackers "inspired slaves with vague notions of freedom" and "had no more right to interfere (with slavery) than with similar institutions in Russia or in Brazil." In what some perceived as a reference to Lincoln, Buchanan stated that "it was beyond the power of any President ... to restore peace and harmony among the States."[1] No state had the right to secede from the Union, he maintained. But neither did the Constitution grant the federal government any power to prevent secession. He intended to collect revenues in slave states, he said, but practically speaking, since the federal judge, district attorney and marshal in South Carolina had already resigned their offices, there existed no machinery to execute and enforce federal laws. As president, said Buchanan, he was powerless to halt the crisis; remedies, if any existed, must come from Congress. He would continue his policy of cautious restraint and hope that the Constitution might be amended so as to appease southern slaveholders— perhaps by amendments guaranteeing the property rights of slave owners and assuring enforcement of fugitive slave laws.

Southerners gained no satisfaction from Buchanan's remarks. They disagreed with his assertion that unhappy states had no right to secede. The Union itself had been created by the various sovereign states, they believed, and any state could leave the Union if it so chose. Neither were southern states in a mood to wait months, or years, for a constitutional revision process to unfold. The Union would be broken, and soon, by force if necessary.

Northerners viewed Buchanan's address as weak and contradictory. Worse, his do-nothing policy—his insistence that he was in fact powerless to act—would only encourage an angry South to continue to mobilize in preparation for war. If southern states were allowed to establish their own government unencumbered by Washington's interference, that government would surely gain a measure of legitimacy in the eyes of foreign nations, further complicating the situation for the North.

In Springfield, Lincoln read a synopsis of Buchanan's remarks over the wire and was appalled. Buchanan's attempts to "straddle the fence" on secession were pathetic. Lincoln disagreed with the idea that southern unrest was merely the result of northern actions and attitudes toward slavery—this nonsense coming from a Pennsylvanian! Buchanan's conclusion that any state had the right to leave the Union was preposterous. The government had not been formed in anticipation of its eventual destruction and thus must have the inherent ability to preserve itself. Any attempt to dismember or destroy the Union could not be tolerated. Lincoln found guidance, or at least precedent, from the actions of President Andrew Jackson in the nullification crisis of 1832. Then, when South Carolina had threatened to leave the Union, Jackson sent federal troops to Charleston Harbor as a show of force, and the crisis was averted. (Lincoln ignored the fact that Jackson had asked for, and received, appropriations from Congress for his actions; Buchanan did not have that luxury.) Despite his anger over Buchanan's remarks, Lincoln maintained his silence.

If Buchanan would not act, at least some members of Congress felt compelled to find a solution as the session began. In an effort to reach a compromise, Senator Lazarus W. Powell of Kentucky introduced a resolution to create a Committee of Thirteen. The committee, appointed by Vice President Breckinridge, was composed of five southern Democrats (two of whom were from border states), three northern Democrats (including Stephen Douglas) and five Republicans (including William Seward). Kentuckian John J. Crittendon, the senior member of the Senate, led the efforts to come up with a workable solution to the crisis. At age 73, Crittendon, an old-time Henry Clay Whig, had served in the Senate for the better part of 40 years and had twice been a cabinet member. Lincoln had known Crittendon since his days in Congress, and even though Crittendon had supported Douglas for senator in 1858, Lincoln considered Crittendon a good friend. Crittendon saw disunion as the "greatest evil" that could befall the country, and worked hard to pull the divided factions together. The committee began its work on December 21 and continued throughout the winter. In its final form, Crittendon's plan called for reimplementing the Missouri Compromise and extending the line west through the territories all the way to the Pacific Ocean, prohibiting slavery above but permitting it below. The plan also called for a constitutional amendment protecting slavery where it existed. Even though it was endorsed by dozens of wealthy northern capitalists, including Jay Gould, Anthony Allen, John Brodhead and Charles Augustus Davis, the measure was defeated in committee; later, just two days before Lincoln's inauguration, another version of the plan was defeated by the entire Senate by a 20-19 vote.[2] Crittendon was disappointed in the failure to reach a compromise for personal, as well as patriotic reasons: his sons Thomas and George would serve as generals on opposite sides of the Civil War.

The House also made efforts to reach a compromise in the wake of Buchanan's address. A Committee of Thirty-three was established, its members coming from each state in the union. Thomas Corwin of Ohio chaired the committee, and while few saw any chance of real progress, Corwin took his job very seriously. "I have never, in my life, seen my country in such a dangerous position," he wrote Lincoln. "But I am resolved not to be paralyzed with dismay."[3] His efforts were not rewarded. The committee spent months crafting language in a series of proposals and resolutions, over 20 in the first week alone, none of which directly addressed the issues revolving around secession, slavery or even the extension of slavery. Finally it recommended similar actions as the Senate sommittee, but added that New Mexico could be admitted as a free state. The proposals went nowhere.

Lincoln kept a close eye on these committees and their activities. He communicated directly with selected loyal congressmen, including Elihu Washburne and Lyman Trumbull and, through Thurlow Weed, consulted with Seward. Initially Lincoln entertained offers of slight moderation of his positions. He agreed that, as a show of support to the slaveholder interests, he would urge that the fugitive slave law be more aggressively enforced. Further, he would endorse the repeal of any so-called "personal liberty" laws, enacted by northern states and meant to conflict with federal legislation (although he could scarcely see how a president might bring about that result himself). But he would not waiver on his opposition to the extension of slavery into the territories, and any such compromise was out of the question. How could he agree to reach such a middle ground, when do to so would be to admit that the principles upon which he had been elected were wrong? "Let there be no compromise on the issue of *extending slavery*," he wrote Trumbull. "If there be, all our labor is lost, and, ere long, must be done again. The dangerous ground — that into which some of our friends have a hankering to run — is Pop. Sov. Have none of it. Stand firm. The tug has to come, & better now, than any time hereafter."[4]

Buchanan could not even please members of his own cabinet. On December 8 his secretary of the treasury, Howell Cobb, resigned and went home to Georgia to advance the cause of secession. Two days later a contingent of South Carolina congressmen called on Buchanan and requested that he pledge not to reinforce federal forts in Charleston Harbor, pending further negotiations between the state and federal government. When Buchanan verbally agreed that he would not reinforce the forts, at least for the time being, Secretary of State Lewis Cass of Ohio resigned in protest. Buchanan continued to flounder. In a worried attempt to garner some support from those who ridiculed his inactivity, and to regain at least some credibility, he purported to adopt the Crittendon efforts. He sent Duff Green, a journalist and capitalist who had once served in President Jackson's "kitchen cabinet," to Springfield. Buchanan hoped that Green could convince Lincoln to endorse a compromise plan, thereby reassuring the public that both the president and president-elect were taking steps to halt disunion. Lincoln read the various Crittendon proposals that Green carried, and expressed his opinion that, if passed, they might temporarily quiet southern agitation. He did not believe, however, that unrest would disappear for long, but would surface again when and if Mexican territories were annexed by the United States, bringing the expansion of slavery question once again to the forefront. Lincoln promised Green that he would consider the matter further, and perhaps issue a letter stating his views.

Green returned to Washington and reported to Buchanan that his trip had been partially successful. Both men expected to hear from Lincoln shortly. Lincoln began, but did not finish, his letter. "I do not desire any amendment of the Constitution," he wrote, adding that the question ought to be settled by the "whole people" of the states, along with a declaration that the right of states to handle their own domestic affairs must not be taken away. He showed his draft letter to Trumbull and suggested that it should not be delivered, or published, unless six southern senators would call for a suspension of the secession movement. But Trumbull rightly pointed out that the letter broke no new ground. If delivered, it would likely only offend southerners; they would resent the implication that they would be gullible enough, and stupid enough, to suspend secession in exchange for a reiteration of the Republican Party's position.[5] Lincoln's letter was never sent, leaving Green feeling betrayed and Buchanan even more helpless.

Indeed, many in Congress felt that compromise was impossible, and their numbers were growing. On the 13th of December, a group met in the apartment of Congressman Reuben Davis of Mississippi and drafted a resolution entitled "To Our Constituents," which read: "The argument is exhausted. In our judgment, the Republicans are resolute in the purpose to grant nothing that will or ought to satisfy the South. We are satisfied that the honor, safety, and independence of the southern people require the organization of a southern confederacy — a result to be obtained only by separate state secession."[6] After some urging by his colleagues, Senator Jefferson Davis of Mississippi, previously a reluctant secessionist who was also a member of the Committee of Thirteen, signed the address, along with 29 others. Judah Benjamin of Louisiana could not see "how bloodshed is to be avoided." Robert Hatton of Kentucky agreed, stating that the country was "on the eve of a revolution." And Justin S. Morrill of Vermont invoked the infamous phrase that just a few years before had branded William Seward a radical and contributed to his failure to secure the Republican presidential nomination. "We must accept the truth," Morrill said, "that there is an 'irrepressible conflict' between our systems of civilizations."[7]

William Seward remained on Lincoln's mind. After losing the Republican nomination for the presidency — he blamed his defeat on Horace Greeley — Seward had gone into a brief exile, drinking heavily, preferring to face the "humiliation" of his defeat alone, even without his wife, Frances. He had written Thurlow Weed on June 26 that he was "content to quit with the political world, when it proposes to quit with me."[8] While Seward had pulled himself together enough to deliver a series of speeches advocating Republican causes during the fall campaign — including his own pet project, America's acquisition of Canada and Alaska — shortly after the election in November he declared, "I am without schemes, or plans, hopes, desires, or fears for the future that need trouble anybody, so far as I am concerned."[9]

Seward's moodiness cost him some support in the Senate, as Republicans looked to him for leadership and found none. Rumors had surfaced for several weeks that

Seward was in favor of compromise in the territories, and Lincoln and his supporters could not risk association with Seward if that were the case. When Weed published an editorial in the Albany *Evening Journal* supporting compromise, many, including Lincoln, assumed that Seward supported the idea. Seward traveled to New York City and met Weed at his residence at the Astor House, expressing his annoyance at the editorial and insisting that Weed publish another one, stating clearly that his views were not necessarily Seward's. Weed apologized and advised Seward that a cabinet position was still forthcoming—Lincoln could not govern without him. Weed then promised to clarify his editorial, but although this was done a few days later on November 30, some damage had already been done. James Watson Webb, editor of the New York *Courier and Enquirer*, endorsed Weed's position, sending a copy of his endorsement to every member of Congress.[10] Some Republican congressmen stated that they would now support territorial compromise if it would satisfy the South, and others called on Seward for clarification. Then the New York *Herald*, among other newspapers, published erroneously that Seward would soon "take the role of pacificator" on the compromise issue. And if that were true, it opined, Lincoln would not offer Seward a cabinet post, weakening the precarious political positions of both men. Finally Seward himself authorized that a denial of all such rumors be published, in the December 8 edition of the *Herald*: "Mr. Seward will make no speech immediately, and will submit no proposition. All rumors to the contrary are entirely unfounded. He is in no manner or form responsible for the various suggestions recently put forward in various newspapers, which have been supposed to reflect his views, and was not consulted concerning, or in any way privy to, their publication. His policy is to watch the development of events, and to direct them wisely at the proper time for peace and the preservation of the Union."[11]

The awkward political dance between Lincoln and Seward continued. Seward's written repudiation of the rumors satisfied Lincoln for the moment, and he acted in indirect fashion. Lincoln wrote to Hamlin and asked him to meet with Trumbull. Absent any objection from either men, he would offer Seward the post of secretary of state. Lincoln enclosed a letter to be delivered to Seward. Rumors had recently surfaced, wrote Lincoln, that he would tender the position only out of courtesy and that he expected Seward to decline. On the contrary, he had wanted Seward to lead the State Department since gaining the nomination in April, and now he showered him with praise. "Your position in the public eye," he wrote, "your integrity, ability, learning, and great experience, all combine to render it an appointment pre-eminently fit to be made."[12] Hamlin consulted with Trumbull as promised, and the two men agreed that, in view of the high stakes, the situation called for more delicate handling. They sent Senator Preston King to meet with Seward and learn how Seward might receive an offer. But Seward gave King no direct answers, and finally on December 13 Hamlin delivered to Seward both of Lincoln's letters.

Still embarrassed by his defeat at the hands of the lesser-known and unqualified politician from Illinois, Seward wanted time to consider the offer, along with his options. Despite his lingering depression he still wanted to control his political party. He was not sure that he wanted to associate himself with the upcoming administration, particularly when he had no idea how powerful a voice he would carry within it. If Lincoln proved to be a weak and ineffective leader, certainly Seward could assume *de facto* command at the White House and guide the country through whatever turbulence lay ahead. But if Lincoln surprised everyone and showed some strength, Seward would be left without his Senate leadership and his own political future in doubt.

Seward wrote to Lincoln and thanked him for the offer. He was concerned as to "the very anomalous condition of public affairs. I wish, indeed, that a conference with you upon them were possible. But I do not see how it could prudently be held under existing circumstances.... With your leave," he added, he would "reflect upon it a few days, and then give you my definite answer." He then wrote to Weed: "I have now the occasion for consulting you that you have expected."[13] Seward went to Albany to meet with his advisor, and was surprised to learn that, through David Davis and Leonard Swett, Lincoln had invited Weed to Springfield to discuss the entire matter. Despite the flap over Weed's recent editorials, Seward still trusted Weed enough to grant him permission to travel and confer with Lincoln on his behalf. Weed made plans to travel to Illinois within the week.

Lincoln's political problems continued. The *New York Times* suggested that Lincoln could reassure the South by finding a place for a southerner in his cabinet, an idea that was supported by a number of eastern Republicans, including Hannibal Hamlin.[14] Lincoln recognized that the South, as a significant region of the country, might deserve such representation in normal times, but he was skeptical of the proposition that such a move would mitigate the secession crisis. On December 12 he wrote a short editorial that appeared in the Illinois *Journal*, setting forth rhetorically a few of the questions that concerned him. "Is it known that any such (Southern) gentlemen would accept a place in the cabinet?... If yes, on what terms does he surrender to Mr. Lincoln, or Mr. Lincoln to him, on the political differences between them; or do they enter upon the administration in open opposition to each other?" Privately Lincoln was less polite. "Does any man think that I will take to my bosom an enemy?" he snapped in an unguarded moment.[15] Lincoln tried to take his mind off his troubles, at least for a while. On the evening of the 13th he escorted Mary to the wedding of his friend Ozias Hatch, but while the event was enjoyable, it provided only a temporary respite. The correspondent for the New York *Tribune* noted that Lincoln's appearance "has somewhat changed for the worse the last week." He now looks "pale and careworn."[16]

With the Seward matter still in the air, and pending Weed's arrival in Springfield, Lincoln was visited by Francis Preston Blair, long a powerful force in national politics. Born into wealth in Virginia, Blair was originally a journalist who edited the Washington *Globe* during the Jackson administration. As a Republican delegate in 1860 Blair had initially supported Edward Bates for President, but switched his allegiance to Lincoln and earned the candidate's ear. Lincoln relied upon Blair for advice, and Blair was not shy about offering it. He urged Lincoln to remain strong in his no-compromise stance. A realist, Blair told Lincoln that secession, and war, was coming soon. Winfield Scott's better days were behind him, he counseled, and it was not too soon for Lincoln to begin thinking about someone who might take command of Union forces. He knew of a fellow Virginian who showed great promise, named

Robert E. Lee (Lincoln later would in fact offer Lee the position, through Blair; Lee, of course, rejected the offer, believing his allegiance belonged to Virginia). Blair also had a person in mind for a cabinet post: his son, Montgomery.

The younger Blair was born in 1813. He graduated from West Point in 1835 and studied law at Transylvania University in Kentucky. Once a Democrat and briefly a Know-Nothing, Blair became a Republican solely because of the slavery issue. In 1857 he served as the attorney for Dred Scott, and helped secure counsel for John Brown in 1860. Like his father, Blair did not believe that blacks and whites could ever coexist in America, and like Lincoln, he favored colonization. Although many Republicans lobbied on behalf of former Whig Henry Winter Davis of Maryland, Lincoln selected Blair to be his postmaster general, and was a little relieved when Blair, through his father, accepted without hesitation. Lincoln finally had nailed down a member of his cabinet. Blair would serve honorably until 1864, when he resigned at Lincoln's request during the reelection campaign. His loyalty was not rewarded as he hoped, however. He expected to be nominated by Lincoln for the United States Supreme Court when Roger Taney died in 1864, but Salmon Chase was chosen instead.

The elder Blair also successfully lobbied Lincoln on behalf of another former Whig, Edward Bates of Missouri. Born in Virginia in 1793, Bates moved to St. Louis as a young man and became an attorney. He met Lincoln in 1847 when both men attended the Chicago River and Harbor Convention. Bates had Horace Greeley's support at the 1860 Republican convention, where his strategy was to trail Seward after the first ballot and then pick up defecting delegates as they sought a compromise candidate. But Bates did not count on Lincoln's managers doing the same thing to his own delegates, and more effectively. In June Bates endorsed Lincoln, calling him a "sound, safe, national man" who "could not be sectional if he tried," but did not campaign energetically for Lincoln. That was fine with Lincoln, who was wary of Bates' brief association with the Know-Nothing party and its anti-German stance. Now, however, the Blairs, Seward, Greeley and Schuyler Colfax of Indiana endorsed Bates for the cabinet. He met with Lincoln on December 15, and Lincoln offered him an unspecified position; in a few months Bates would officially become the attorney general. Like Lincoln, Bates did not believe that southern states would leave the Union. As the winter rolled along he wrote in his diary, "The news from the South, as to secession, does not improve. Still I think that ... it is all brag and bluster, hoping thus to make a better compromise with the timid patriotism of their opponents."[17]

Events quickly proved Bates wrong. On December 17 the 169 delegates to the South Carolina convention met at Columbia to consider an ordinance of secession. Gen. D.F. Jamison was elected president of the convention, and in his opening remarks to the assemblage he compared what was about to happen to the French Revolution, whose patriots' maxim was "dare, and again to dare, and without end to dare." When it was suggested that the roll be called, Jamison ruled that such formality was not necessary. "We came not to *make*, but to *unmake*, a government," he said.[18] The business had to wait a few days, however. A smallpox epidemic was raging in Columbia, and Jamison ordered the delegates to adjourn to Charleston immediately.

The next day the convention resumed at "Secession Hall," where the activities of the delegates were closely monitored by a large crowd. President Buchanan's address was read into the record, and it was suggested that a committee be established to determine the value of all federal property in South Carolina; when the state left the Union, it would then be entitled to an equal share of the property. The rest of the day, and the next, were devoted to speeches from delegates and visiting dignitaries. Robert Barnwell Rhett, the fire-eater who had so strongly called for this convention, spoke of the glorious nature of the slave system and his great fear that the new Republican administration would never endorse the fugitive slave law. Official representatives of Alabama and Mississippi assured the convention that their states would surely, and quickly, follow the lead of South Carolina. Everyone present believed that the matter at hand had been simmering for generations, and now was the time to act. Lawrence Keitt summed up the feelings of many. "I have been engaged in this movement ever since I entered political life," he said. "I am content with ... what will take place here. We have carried the body of this Union to its last resting-place, and now we will drop the flag over its grave."[19]

At quarter past one o'clock on the afternoon of December 20, the ordinance of secession was introduced and then passed by unanimous vote:

> We, the people of the State of South Carolina, in Convention assembled, do declare and ordain, and it is hereby declared and ordained, the Ordinance adopted by us in Convention, on the 23d day of May, in the year of our Lord 1788, whereby the Constitution of the United States of America was ratified, and also all Acts and parts of Acts of the General Assembly of this State ratifying the amendments of the said Constitution, are hereby repealed; and that the Union now subsisting between South Carolina and other States, under the name of the United States of America, is hereby dissolved.[20]

Through the delegates the people of South Carolina now "appealed to the Supreme Judge of the world for the rectitude of our intentions.... The State has resumed her position among the nations of the world, as a separate and independent State, with full power to levy war, conclude peace, contract alliances, establish commerce, and to do all other acts and things which independent States may of right do."[21]

Delegate W.F. De Saussure moved that "the passage of the Ordinance be proclaimed by the firing of artillery and the ringing of the bells of the city, and such other demonstrations as the people may deem appropriate on the passage of the great act of deliverance and liberty." The motion carried. Then each of the delegates proceeded to the front of the hall and signed the ordinance, in alphabetical order. Finally President Jamison affixed his signature to the document, and as he held it high above his head and waved it jubilantly he shouted, "The State of South Carolina is now and henceforth a free and independent commonwealth!"[22]

It was resolved that the secession ordinance be sent to each slave state via special messenger, to hasten cooperation and similar action. Three delegates were selected to travel to Washington and personally deliver a copy of the ordinance to President Buchanan. That night Charleston was alive in celebration as cannons roared, music played, and thousands of revelers danced in the streets of the city. Dr. Samuel

Crawford, a U.S. Army officer stationed at nearby Fort Sumter, wrote that "the whole city was wild with excitement as the news spread like wild-fire through the streets. Business was suspended everywhere; the peals of the church bells mingling with the salvos of artillery from the citadel. Bold men ran shouting down the street. Everyone entitled to it appeared at once in uniform. In less than fifteen minutes ... the principal newspaper of Charleston had placed in the hands of the eager multitude a copy of the Ordnance of Secession.... The heart of the city had spoken."[23]

"The Union is Dissolved!" shouted the Charleston *Mercury*. The following day, and for the next five years, the Charleston newspapers referred to any items of interest emanating from nonseceding states as "Foreign News."[24]

On the same day that South Carolina seceded, Thurlow Weed arrived in Springfield to discuss the appointment of William Seward to Lincoln's cabinet. Weed was hoping he could gain Lincoln's endorsement of territorial compromise; with it, he could convince Seward that the Union might thus be preserved peacefully. He also wanted to secure for Seward (and himself) some promise of control over the new administration, for he shared the view of many that Lincoln was wholly unprepared to handle the administrative duties the office required.

But Weed would be disappointed in that regard. While he was charmed by Lincoln's hospitality and humor, he found himself on the defensive. Lincoln chastised him for the *Evening Journal* editorial, calling it a "heavy broadside" that would do "some good or much mischief." Weed had "opened fire at a critical moment," Lincoln scolded, aiming at "friends and foes alike."[25] When pressed, Weed had to admit that his views were not endorsed by most Republicans, particularly in the East. Lincoln insisted that he would not compromise the territories. If that were the case, wondered Weed, perhaps a mere gesture toward compromise might soften southern attitudes. Would Lincoln name two southerners to his cabinet? Lincoln smiled and said that "he supposed that Weed had had some experience in cabinet-making." The process was "by no means easy," and was made even more difficult due to his "own want of acquaintance with the prominent men of the day." Also, Lincoln believed, "really great men are scarcer than they used to be." Though he wanted, and appreciated, Weed's advice, Lincoln voiced the same concerns he had written about just a week before in the *Journal* editorial. Besides, he asked, could such men be trusted to work in his administration if their home states had left the Union? Weed countered that he could personally vouch for certain southern men. "Well," said Lincoln. "Let us have the names of your white crows."[26]

Weed suggested two former congressmen from Virginia, William Cabell Rives and John Minor Botts, and five Tennesseans: Horace Maynard, Thomas Nelson, Emerson Etheridge, Meredith Gentry and Balie Peyton. Also mentioned were Randall Hunt of Louisiana (who happened to be Salmon Chase's brother-in-law), Mississippian William Sharkey, and Kenneth Rayner of North Carolina. Lincoln promised to consider the qualifications of each of these men, and appears to have thought seriously about them. Ultimately, however, he could not be sure that their allegiance would be to the government, and extended no offers.

Weed was not bashful about stating his concerns regarding other candidates. He was not impressed with Gideon Welles and thought that "several other gentlemen" would be "more acceptable to the people of New England," particularly Charles Francis Adams for Treasury. Weed also objected to Montgomery Blair, who "represents nobody" and "has no following." Weed was disappointed to learn, however, that Lincoln's mind was already made up about Blair. Lincoln asked Weed about Simon Cameron, the influential but controversial Pennsylvanian who was being considered for secretary of war. Weed liked Cameron personally but felt that he might be more of a hindrance than a help to Lincoln's administration. Lincoln gave no indication whether he would offer Cameron a position. By Weed's unofficial estimation Lincoln's cabinet might include former Democrats Seward, Chase, Bates and perhaps Welles. Cameron, Blair, and one other, perhaps Caleb Smith of Indiana, counted three former Whigs. Weed expressed his concern that former Democrats would outnumber former Whigs 4-3. "You seem to forget that *I* expect to be there," replied Lincoln. "And counting me as one, you see how nicely the cabinet would be balanced and ballasted."[27]

Word arrived the South Carolina had seceded. Lincoln, in his second day of meetings with Weed, took the news calmly. Henry Villard informed his New York readers that "the President elect did not did not experience any extraordinary shock.... It certainly does not make him any more willing to listen to compromises. Timidity is certainly no element in his composition."[28] Weed attempted to press the urgency of the matter upon Lincoln—this was no longer merely talk, but a real crisis—but Lincoln still saw no reason to change his views. While there were "loud threats" and "much muttering in the cotton states," he told Weed, "he hoped that by wisdom and forbearance the danger of serious trouble might be averted, as such dangers had been in former times."[29] He asked Weed to rally New York newspapers in support of the Union, particularly if war broke out, and Weed assured he would do all he could. Their meetings concluded, Lincoln reiterated his philosophy in a short statement that he wrote out and gave to Weed:

> Resolved: that the fugitive slave clause of the Constitution ought to be enforced by a law of Congress, with efficient provisions for that object, not obliging private persons to assist in its execution, but punishing all who resist it, and with the usual safeguards to liberty, securing freemen against being surrendered as slaves-
> That all state laws, if there be such, really or apparently, in conflict with such law of Congress, ought to be repealed; and no opposition to the execution of such law of Congress ought to be made-
> That the Federal Union must be preserved.[30]

Lincoln instructed Weed to carry the statement to Washington and discuss it with Trumbull and Hamlin. If all agreed, it was to be introduced as a Senate resolution by Seward, and Lincoln's name was not to be mentioned. Weed left Springfield late on the night of the 20th, traveling not directly to Washington but to Syracuse, where he was met by Seward, the two men then continuing on together to Albany. Seward was slightly surprised to hear that Lincoln fully and confidently intended to be president in fact as well as name, and at least a little disappointed to learn that Lincoln showed no predisposition to share control of the new administration. But Seward weighed his options and concluded that his love of Union must come before personal ambition. Within a week he accepted the position of secretary of state, telling his wife Frances, "I will try to save freedom and my country."[31] Then, as Lincoln insisted, he introduced the resolution (in slightly different form, yet true to the spirit of Lincoln's language), and voted against the Crittendon compromise plan, all but insuring that war would come.

And many felt that war might begin very soon, undoubtedly in South Carolina. Maj. Robert Anderson, an 1825 graduate of West Point who saw his first action in the Black Hawk War, was the new commander of three federal forts in Charleston Harbor: Moultrie, Sumter and Castle Pinckney (these forts, along with Pickens, Taylor and Jefferson in Florida constituted the only remaining garrisons that flew the Union flag in the South). Anderson had been specifically chosen in November to serve as commander in the Carolina region. He was born in Kentucky and was married to a Georgia woman,

Thurlow Weed, Republican activist and advisor to William Seward (the Lincoln Museum, Fort Wayne, Indiana, #2439).

and had for a time owned slaves. President Buchanan and his secretary of war, John Floyd of Virginia, hoped that Anderson's southern roots would forestall military action. Gen. Winfield Scott had confidence in Anderson for another reason: Anderson had been Scott's aide during the Mexican War and had survived bullet wounds on three separate occasions. Anderson knew that his position at Moultrie was precarious, for its location on Sullivan's Island was meant to protect Charleston from attack by sea; its guns were thus pointed westward, leaving it vulnerable to attack from the mainland. Anderson also recognized a painful irony. His father, Capt. Richard Anderson, had defended Fort Moultrie in Charleston Harbor during the American Revolution, and had surrendered to the British.

Since Lincoln's election Anderson had flooded Washington with urgent telegrams requesting instruction and assistance. Carolina authorities had stationed militiamen in Charleston in an effort to block the delivery of arms and munitions to the forts. Bands of armed secessionists patrolled the vicinity day and night, and rumors of attacks on federal positions increased. "The clouds are threatening," wrote Anderson, "and the storm may break at any moment."[32] After weeks of silence from Buchanan, finally in mid-December Floyd authorized Anderson to move his meager force of 82 federal troops—not quite two full companies—to the most defensible fort.

That fort was surely Sumter, an octagonal-shaped garrison of solid masonry, pierced on three sides with double rows of portholes for heavy guns and muskets and located on a small island just over three miles from Charleston. There were enough supplies at Sumter to last perhaps three months, and Sumter's guns could keep the harbor closed to southern shipping to and from the city while also answering the inevitable attack from southern forces. But as Anderson made plans to move his troops from Moultrie to Sumter, he received a confusing message from Floyd that seemed to suggest that he should surrender if attacked. Anderson decided, however, that Floyd's motives were suspect, and after South Carolina seceded on the 20th felt he had little time to waste. On Christmas Day he ordered his men and two dozen civilian workers to pack Moultrie's movable goods. One night of rain postponed the transfer, but on the night of the 27th the federal personnel left for Sumter under the light of a full moon. The lead boat was quickly intercepted by a secessionist patrol craft, but since the federal guns and muskets were concealed, the guard ship allowed it to pass. The last soldiers to leave Moultrie set fire to its wooden gun carriages, a strategy meant to eliminate the ability of secessionists to utilize the cannon. Once all his men were safely inside the walls of Sumter, Anderson knelt and offered a prayer of thanksgiving for their safe passage. The band played "Hail Columbia" and the troops presented arms. When the morning haze cleared, citizens of Charleston saw the smoke rising from Moultrie and the Stars and Stripes flying from the mast atop Sumter's ramparts. Secessionists took the action as a sure sign of northern aggression, and moved quickly. They seized the federal arsenal in Charleston, along with the post office and customs office, and then raised the palmetto flag over Fort Moultrie itself.

Despite increased pressure from Washington Anderson had no plans to surrender his position at Sumter. When news reached Springfield that Buchanan, through Floyd, had recommended that Anderson surrender if attacked, Lincoln reacted angrily. "If that is true they ought to hang him," he told Nicolay. But if any of the forts were taken, he believed, a plan should be immediately formulated to take them back. In the days before Christmas he wrote to General Scott and Elihu Washburne, among others, and stressed the point. On December 24 he wrote to Lyman Trumbull and expressed that, if the forts were attacked and seized, the result could actually steel the resolve of the North. "I will, if our friends at Washington concur, announce publicly at once that they are to be retaken after the inauguration. This will give the Union a rallying cry."[33]

The headaches surrounding Lincoln's cabinet selections continued. His managers at the Republican convention had apparently promised Simeron Cameron of Pennsylvania a position, and even if Lincoln ignored what had happened in Chicago, he still needed a representative of that important and populous state. With Cameron scheduled to visit Springfield on the 30th, Lincoln prepared as he might have for an important legal case: he drafted a memorandum to himself outlining Cameron's pros and cons.

On the plus side Cameron was bright, enthusiastic and experienced and, at age 60, still a relatively young and healthy man. His ancestors had been heroes in the American Revolution and Indian wars, and subsequently the Cameron name was well respected in Pennsylvania. He had followed successful careers in newspapers, construction, banking, iron production and insurance with election to the Senate in 1845, when he had filled the seat of the resigning James Buchanan. Outgoing and popular with the press, who appreciated his willingness to speak his mind on and off the record, Cameron proved to be an effective and influential Senator. He championed high tariffs and the development of internal improvements such as railroads and canals, positions that Lincoln could easily identify with. He also opposed the extension of slavery, and after his presidential hopes were dashed at the Chicago convention he had campaigned energetically for Lincoln. Cameron also had numerous friends, all wealthy and powerful, who lobbied Lincoln on his behalf.

But Cameron also carried some baggage. He had a history of switching party, including membership first in the Democratic Party, then the Whigs, then the Know-Nothings, before becoming a Republican in 1857. Rumors constantly swirled that he had profited by a settlement he negotiated as a state commissioner for Winnebago Indian claims; "the Great Winnebago Chief," he was sarcastically called. Many people wrote Lincoln in December criticizing him for dishonesty; even Hannibal Hamlin warned that the possibility of Cameron in the cabinet "had an odor about it that will damn us as a party."[34]

But on balance Lincoln decided that Cameron's positive attributes outweighed the negative. After a lengthy meeting at his home on the 30th, Lincoln decided to offer Cameron a post, although he was not sure which one. The next day, as Cameron boarded a train for home, Lincoln handed him a note. "I think fit to notify you now," it read, "that by your permission I shall at the proper time nominate you to the United States Senate for confirmation as Secretary of the Treasury, or as Secretary of War — which of the two I have not yet definitely decided."[35]

Cameron made no secret of Lincoln's tentative offer to politicos in Pennsylvania, which led to problems. Upon hearing the news a group of the state's most prominent men, including Governor Andrew Curtin, traveled to Springfield and protested vehemently against Cameron. Uncharacteristically, Lincoln changed his mind. On January 3 he wrote Cameron and withdrew the offer. "Since seeing you things have developed which make it impossible for me to take you into the cabinet," Lincoln wrote, and then gave Cameron a way out. "And now I suggest that you write to me declining the appointment, in which case I do not object to its being known that it was tendered you. Better do this at once, before things so change, that you can not honorably decline, and I be compelled to openly recall the tender. No person living knows, or has an intimation that I write this letter. Telegraph me instantly on receipt of this, saying 'All right.'"[36]

But Cameron refused to play that game, and did not respond to Lincoln. Instead, he had his supporters flood Lincoln with letters and telegrams, and dispatched several of his political friends to Springfield to personally lobby on his behalf. Cameron loyalists also gently reminded Lincoln of the promises made by David Davis and Leonard Swett at the Chicago convention, and Swett himself urged Lincoln to consider that "the Cameron influence, as much as anything, nominated you."[37] By mid-January Lincoln changed his mind yet again, and wrote to Cameron. "I wrote that letter (of January 3) under great anxiety," he explained. "And perhaps I was not so guarded in its terms as I should have been; but I beg you to be assured I intended no offense.... Destroy the offensive letter or return it to me. I say to you now I have not doubted that you would perform the duties of a Department ably and faithfully persisted."[38]

Lincoln now decided that he would not act officially in the Cameron matter until he reached Washington in March. Once there, he would quickly offer the secretary of war post to Cameron. With no military background to speak of, Cameron would prove to be ineffective, however, and lasted only until 1862, when he was replaced by Edwin Stanton. Lincoln appointed Cameron minister to Russia and he filled that position honorably for three years. He returned to America and to the Senate in 1864, where he remained a powerful legislator in the Republican Party. After Lincoln's assassination he served as an honorary pallbearer at Mary's request, and he was later able to secure for her a $3,000 pension. Cameron finally left public office in 1877, his political career having spanned some 40 colorful and controversial years. He died in 1889 at age 90, surrounded by his wife, five children and two dozen grandchildren.

Lincoln grew increasingly irritable in the waning days of December. To get away from the political headaches, the office seekers and the overwhelming mail he set aside some time to relax and think. Thomas D. Jones, a renowned sculptor from Cincinnati, arrived in Springfield and convinced Lincoln to sit for a bust, and Lincoln spent two or three hours each morning for two weeks in an improvised studio at the St. Nicholas Hotel. He bought handkerchiefs for Christmas presents for his friends, and spent Christmas Day at home with Mary and the children. On the 29th Lincoln and Nicolay moved out of the governor's office, Nicolay moving to a room in Johnson's building, across from the Chenery House, and Lincoln dividing his time between his home and the old law office. He watched anxiously for more signs from the South. It seemed certain that more states would follow South Carolina's lead and secede, but which ones? Probably the gulf states, he guessed, but what about the border states? If Virginia, Kentucky, Tennessee and Missouri remained loyal, perhaps the states of the Deep South would realize that secession was foolish, even suicidal, and return to the Union.

The precarious situation in the South and the struggles to formulate his cabinet left Lincoln feeling physically drained. He spent more and more time alone, quietly contemplating the calamity of war that most people believed was imminent. Friends remarked that he seemed to have aged 10 years in just a few months. He saw no reason to celebrate New Year's Eve and turned down several party invitations. The next day, the first day of 1861, when a visitor annoyed Lincoln he summarily threw him out of the house.[39]

7

"The Rubicon Is Now Crossed"

At six feet five inches and well over 300 pounds, Gen. Winfield Scott was so large he could no longer lift his leg to mount a horse. Now 74 years old and suffering from vertigo, fading eyesight, and speech that sometimes slurred, the best days of "Old Fuss and Feathers" were far behind him. He spent the better part of each day reclined on a couch, worrying about disunion while reviewing intelligence reports that described the mounting military buildup in the South. Despite his difficulty in getting around, Scott still commanded respect in governmental circles, and had many admirers who well remembered his exploits. He had fought heroically at the battles of Chippewa and Lundy's Lane in the War of 1812. Promoted to major general, he became an expert at military tactics. By 1841 Scott was commanding general of the entire U.S. Army, directing operations during the Mexican War and leading the invasion at Veracruz. He had briefly dabbled in politics, running unsuccessfully for president on the Whig ticket in 1852. Given to pomp and spectacle, Scott never appeared in public out of uniform, complete with shining gold braid and buttons, fancy epaulets and long plumed hat, so that he appeared to be "almost a parade by himself."[1]

But even as his health faded, the Virginia-born Scott's loyalty to the Union had never been stronger. As President Buchanan struggled to decide if and how to provision Fort Sumter without offending South Carolina, Scott took matters into his own hands. He considered sending four companies of troops from Fort Monroe to Sumter, along with three months' worth of provisions, and even ordered the USS *Brooklyn*—a deep-draft warship—to stand by. But Scott was concerned that the removal of troops from Monroe would weaken that garrison, making it easier for Virginia to secede, and so he decided on another, less conspicuous, plan. On January 5 he had his assistant adjutant general, Lorenzo Thomas, engage the merchant vessel *Star of the West* at cost of $1,250 per day, and then filled it with provisions and 200 New York troops. On January 5 the *Star*, commanded by Lt. Charles R. Woods and the troops hidden below deck, quietly left New York. Although Scott wanted secrecy, word of the ship's mission quickly leaked. On January 7, Senator Louis T. Wigfall of Texas telegraphed Governor Francis Pickens of South Carolina, warning him that the relief expedition's arrival at Charleston Harbor was imminent. When Jacob Thompson, Buchanan's secretary of the interior, heard the news he immediately resigned his cabinet post and went home to Louisiana to prepare for war.

Incredibly, at Fort Sumter Major Anderson first learned of the *Star's* mission by reading the January 8 edition of the Charleston *Mercury*. Unsure of the accuracy of the newspaper report, Anderson sent a dispatch to Joseph Holt, who had replaced John Floyd as secretary of war, advising that secessionists were building gun emplacements along the shore of the harbor. Holt believed the *Star* was in peril and tried to call her back, but it was too late. At 6 A.M. on January 9 the *Star* was spotted as it approached Morris Island, near the mouth of the harbor. Gunner George E. Haynsworth, a cadet at the Citadel, fired two cannon rounds, missing badly with what technically were the first shots of the Civil War. Seconds later a battery from Fort Moultrie, its guns now remounted, joined the shelling. Major Anderson watched the action from the parapet at Sumter but did not fire on the secessionists. Within minutes the *Star of the West* turned about and limped back to open sea, her mission ending in total failure.

The southern press hailed the encounter as a great victory. South Carolina, wrote Robert Barnwell Rhett, had the honor of firing "the opening ball of the Revolution.... She has not hesitated to strike the first blow, full in the face of her insulter. We would not exchange or recall that blow for millions! It has wiped out a half century of scorn and outrage."[2] Northerners were both incensed and humiliated. South Carolina's actions were "intolerable, dishonorable, vile," and must be met by "the whole power of the navy and army" if necessary.[3] But war was not to come yet. Major Anderson and Governor Pickens agreed to an uneasy truce until the issue of Sumter's possession was settled in Washington, and Pickens sent a negotiating team to meet with President Buchanan. In the meantime, Anderson was ordered only to fire defensively, and Pickens agreed not to fire unless further attempts were made to provision Sumter. In Springfield Lincoln watched pensively, and Henry Villard reported that Lincoln felt that "the Rubicon is now crossed."[4]

Secessionists in the South acted upon their momentum. On the same day that the *Star of the West* was repulsed in Charleston Harbor, a special state convention met in Jackson, Mississippi, and its delegates voted overwhelmingly, by a count of 84-15, to secede from the Union. The next day Florida also seceded, although the procedure there was more complicated. Voters had gone to the polls on December 22 and elected 69 delegates, most of whom favored immediate secession. But 27 delegates were "cooperationists" who were inclined to wait and see if any of the congressional compromise plans would be approved. Those efforts appeared doomed, however, and with the news of the action off the coast of Carolina most of the Florida cooperationists now went over to the secessionists. In Montgomery, Alabama, a preliminary vote of 100 delegates on January 7 had resulted in a narrow margin, only 54-46, of secessionists over cooperationists. Four days later, following news that Mississippi and Florida had left the Union and that the *Star of the West* had been repelled, the Alabama convention adopted an ordinance of succession by a wider vote of 61-39. On the 19th Georgia left the Union by vote of 208-89, and on the 28th Louisiana did the same by a vote of 113-17. Now the only state in the Deep South to not yet secede was Texas.

The secession story in Texas was a strange one, and it centered around one on the country's most colorful and amazing figures, Sam Houston. Houston was born in 1793 in Virginia. When he was 17 years old he ran away from home and lived for three years with the Cherokee Indians of Tennessee. He enlisted in the U.S. Army during the War of 1812, serving with distinction under Andrew Jackson. He practiced law in Nashville and served in the House of Representatives from 1823 to 1827, when he was elected governor. When Houston's wife left him, he resigned the governorship and went back to live with the Cherokee, who adopted him as a member of their nation. He put his experience to work, lobbying Congress on behalf of the Cherokee nation and exposing fraudulent governmental Indian agents.

In 1832 President Jackson appointed Houston to represent Indian tribes from Texas in their negotiations with the government. He became a leading figure in Texas' struggle for independence against Mexico, and in 1835 he led the Texan army into war. After the fall of the Alamo he captured San Jacinto and Mexican president Santa Anna. Now a hero, Houston was elected first president of the Republic of Texas, then U.S. senator when Texas was

Winfield Scott, a true American hero, whose best years were behind him at the time of Lincoln's election (the Lincoln Museum, Fort Wayne, Indiana, # 2131).

admitted into the Union in 1845. In 1859 his popularity enabled him to win the governorship of Texas even though he was opposed to secession. But Lincoln's election and recent news of the crisis in Carolina rallied Texas secessionists. Houston refused to call a convention to consider the idea, so the legislature called a special session to meet in Austin in late January. On February 1 the convention voted overwhelmingly to leave the Union, by a vote of 166-8. But because the convention had been irregularly called, the legislature submitted its decision to the people of Texas for ratification. On February 23 secession was ratified by a better than three to one margin. Governor Houston stubbornly refused to swear allegiance to the Confederacy, and on March 18, just 14 days after Lincoln was inaugurated, Houston was deposed as governor. He died unhappily two years later, his legacy overshadowed by the bitter events of disunion.

As the country broke apart, in Springfield Lincoln seemed to have decided upon another cabinet member. Widely respected Salmon Portland Chase was born in Cornish, New Hampshire, in 1808, the ninth of 11 children. By age 12 he was living with an uncle, Philander Chase, an Episcopal bishop in Ohio. After a year of seminary studies Chase entered Dartmouth College, where he graduated Phi Beta Kappa in 1826. He was admitted as an attorney three years later and began his legal career, soon becoming known as the "Attorney General of Fugitive Slaves" for his strong anti-slavery views. Like other abolitionists, Chase believed that slavery was a sin and that the Constitution afforded equal rights to both black and white Americans. A founding father of Ohio's Free-Soil Party, he served a single term in the Senate from 1848 to 1854, where he introduced the successful Pacific Railroad Act. Chase opposed the Kansas-Nebraska Act of 1854 and enthusiastically joined the Republican Party. He left the Senate and served two terms as Ohio's governor, advocating public education, prison reform, women's rights and, of course, the abolition of slavery, all the while keeping an eye on the White House. Chase was an unsuccessful candidate for the Republican presidential nomination in 1856 and 1860. It was said that he "never forgave Lincoln for the crime of having been preferred President over him," and from that moment on he was busy "laying pipe" to gain the nomination in 1864.[5]

Chase arrived in Springfield on January 4 for a personal interview with Lincoln, unsure, as many were, of the capabilities of the president-elect. Although he protested Lincoln's choice of William Seward as secretary of state, and had little respect for Simon Cameron, Chase was unexpectedly impressed with Lincoln's sincerity and conviction of purpose. Chase's rigid, upright style contrasted with Lincoln's affability and sense of humor. Lincoln looked beyond Chase's solemnity and saw a man who had overcome personal tragedies—he had been widowed three times—to excel in politics and the law. Lincoln later said that Chase "is about one hundred and fifty to any other man's hundred."[6] Lincoln was not yet ready, however, to directly offer Chase a cabinet appointment. He asked Chase to "accept the appointment of Secretary of the Treasury, without, however, my being exactly prepared to offer it to you." Chase was just as cagy in his reply. "I did not wish and was not prepared to say that I would accept the place if offered," he countered.[7] Lincoln knew he needed Chase to balance other, more controversial, choices. A few days later Lincoln settled on Chase as secretary of the treasury, although he would not make it official until March. Chase's political ambitions necessitated that the relationship between himself and Lincoln would always be an uneasy one. But Chase would prove to be an effective administrator, and he found ingenious methods of financing the most expensive war in U.S. history.

Although it had been a difficult and frustrating task thus far, Lincoln had made progress in the selection of his cabinet. He now had the makings of what he hoped would be a workable group: Seward at State, Bates at attorney general, Blair at postmaster general, possibly Cameron at War and Chase at Treasury. He still had to fill the positions of secretaries of the interior and the navy, and he wrestled with his thoughts. How should Indiana be rewarded for its support? Congressman Schuyler Colfax had campaigned energetically for Lincoln, was only 37 years old and dedicated to the Republican cause. But Lincoln's managers at the Chicago convention had apparently promised a position to Caleb B. Smith, a long-time Whig and dedicated Republican who had seconded Lincoln's nomination. Smith had served in the Indiana House of Representatives for 20 years and in Congress for six, and Lincoln approved of his track record of support for railroads and canals. But questions about Smith's health concerned Lincoln. And many people pushed Lincoln to reward his own state of Illinois with an appointment. Norman Judd had seemed a likely choice and had been on Lincoln's original list, but David Davis and Leonard Swett opposed him. And Mary Lincoln disliked Judd for purely personal reasons, even going so far as writing a confidential letter to Davis, condemning Judd and urging Davis to "speak to (Lincoln) on this subject and urge him not to give Judd so responsible a place."[8] Lincoln decided to let these unfinished matters settle for the time being. He would make no more cabinet choices until after he arrived in Washington.[9]

While Lincoln struggled with cabinet decisions, watched helplessly as southern states seceded and brooded over military actions in Carolina, Mary decided that she needed a shopping excursion. On January 11 she boarded a train for New York, accompanied by her brother-in-law C.W. Smith and former congressman Amos Tuck of New Hampshire. Tuck, who had given the Republican Party its name, had spent the last week in town lobbying Lincoln for cabinet appointments for his friends and a Boston collectorship for himself. Arriving in New York a few days later, Mary was met by her son Robert, over from Harvard, and the pair took a suite at the Astor House, the guests of Philip Dorsheimer, treasurer of the state of New York. Although she intended to stay for a week, Mary extended her stay for three more days, indulging herself in the city's finest stores, purchasing gowns and jewelry for herself and china and artwork for the White House, all on credit and most without the knowledge or approval of her husband. But she had convinced herself that no matter how grave the nation's problems might be, or how serious the criticisms of her husband might become, she would show the eastern intellectuals that a woman from Illinois could make a magnificent first lady. Mary also continued her attempts to manipulate her husband's political affairs. She accepted jewelry from one merchant, than later pressured Lincoln into awarding him with a customhouse position. The man was later indicted for fraud.[10]

After making arrangements for all her purchases to be shipped to Washington in March, Mary and Robert finally left for home on the 21st. There was a minor disturbance in Buffalo. Finding that no provision had been made for her trip, Mary complained loudly to everyone within earshot. Robert managed to locate R.N. Brown, superintendent of the State Line Railroad, and introduced himself. "My name is Bob Lincoln; I'm a son of Old Abe — the old woman is in the cars raising hell about her passes — I wish you would go and attend to her."[11] Brown acquiesced, and Mary and Robert completed their travels free of charge. Unaware that Mary had extended her trip, Lincoln drove his carriage to the Springfield train depot three straight nights and waited alone, in the snow and sleet, for his wife and son to arrive. Finally they appeared on the 25th, and Lincoln was too relieved to be angry.

Lincoln could feel that he was running out of time in Springfield, and he scrambled to attend to all his political commitments. On January 9 he was pleased to learn that the Illinois legislature reelected Lyman Trumbull as U.S. senator, and he attended an honoring ceremony at the statehouse, seated next to Governor Wood, members of the state supreme court, and other state officials. Five days later he attended the inauguration of new governor Richard Yates, although he found Yates' inaugural address so radical — Yates was also rumored to be slightly inebriated as he spoke — that Lincoln later declined to endorse it for the press.

On the 19th Lincoln was delighted to welcome Matias Romero, Mexican charge d'affaires in Washington, for a three-day visit to Springfield. Romero had been sent by President Benito P. Juarez to "proceed to the place of residence of President-elect Lincoln and in the name of this government ... to make clear ... the desire which animates President Juarez, of entering into the most cordial relations." Lincoln could not act officially, but was happy to express his "sincere wishes for the happiness, prosperity, and liberty of yourself, your government, and its people."[12] Next came George Fogg, secretary of the Republican National Executive Committee, who thoroughly briefed Lincoln on the status of compromise proposals in the Senate. And like visiting delegations from California, Pennsylvania, Indiana and many other places, Fogg attempted to convince Lincoln of the worthiness of his personal choice for any and all cabinet positions. Along with the personal visits came gifts in the mail: several suits of clothes, an overcoat, a bronze medallion of Henry Clay, and even a good-luck whistle made from a pig's tail.

Lincoln now began to work laboriously on a first draft of his inaugural address. He knew this speech would be of tremendous importance, for after months of silence since the election, and with the nation now divided, his remarks would be carefully scrutinized by northerners and southerners alike. He did not wish to offend secessionists, yet he had to reassure Unionists that he would not stray from the principles upon which he had been elected. He had also to convince the all-important border states that they must remain loyal to the government. The object was to sound fair and reasonable, yet firm and sure of purpose. There could be no room for misunderstanding; every word, every phrase, would be important. Along with the U.S. Constitution, Lincoln borrowed a copy of Herndon's *Statesmen's Journal* that contained the three documents he wished to review in order to prepare his address: Daniel Webster's celebrated second reply to Hayne of 1830, Andrew Jackson's proclamation against nullification, and Henry Clay's great compromise speech of 1850, all of which buttressed his position that secession was an impossibility.

In the late 1820s and early 1830s Congress enacted a series of high duties on imported goods, derided in the South as "Tariffs of Abominations." Stricken by a lack of manufacturing in the South, and encouraged by the U.S. vice president (and president of the Senate), John C. Calhoun, South Carolina's legislature published an exposition, or protest, claiming that the tariffs were unconstitutional. Senator Robert J. Hayne, who had previously been best known for his suppression of a slave revolt in Charleston in 1822, explained Calhoun's theory in a set of speeches delivered in the Senate in mid-January 1830. The Union was a contract between sovereign states, argued Haynes, and the central government was simply an agent of the states that had created it. Those states had acted to ratify the Constitution and could independently determine whether any act of Congress was unconstitutional, in effect nullifying improper congressional action. And ultimately, any nullifying state could exercise its right as a sovereign and secede from the Union.

Senator Daniel Webster rose to reply to Haynes. Born on a farm in Salisbury, New Hampshire, in 1782, Webster graduated from Dartmouth in 1801 and quickly became known as a skilled attorney and outspoken member of the Federalist Party. He was elected to the U.S. House of Representatives because of his opposition to the War of 1812, which had crippled the shipping trade in New England. While out of politics from 1816 to 1822, Webster —called "Black Dan" because of his dark eyes and "Godlike Daniel" because of his magisterial style — argued dozens of cases before the Supreme Court, including the landmark *McCulloch v. Maryland*, which recognized the authority of Congress to charter a national bank. Webster returned to Congress in 1822, and five years later he was elected U.S. senator from Massachusetts, where he championed nationalism and a strong centralized federal government.

Now in magnificent fashion Webster argued that Haynes' position was "founded in a total misapprehension of the origin of the government, and of the foundation on which it stands." The national government was created for one purpose, and state governments for another, each holding separate powers but without authority to arrest the operation of the others' laws. Only the national government, for example, could coin money, enter into treaties, or make war. The Constitution was authorized by the people, not just the several states, and was intended to be the supreme law of the land. The legality of any national law could be tested only through the judicial process, not by state proclamation, no matter how dissatisfied a state might be. Webster cautioned South Carolina, or any state, from trampling on that "gorgeous ensign of the republic," the American flag, for to do so would lead to civil war. He closed with the stirring sentence that would immortalize him: "Liberty and Union, now and forever, one and inseparable!"[13]

But the crisis over states' rights would not go away. In 1832 South Carolina passed an "ordinance of nullification" that declared federal tariffs null and void, and threatened that any congressional attempt to enforce such laws or close South Carolina's ports to commerce would be considered grounds for secession. On December 10, 1832, President Jackson issued a proclamation, warning the state that it was treading on dangerous grounds in attempting to usurp Congress, and would face severe consequences if it tried to enforce its ordinance. South Carolina had taken the "strange position," wrote Jackson, that it might choose which national laws it might observe and which it might ignore. If it disagreed with Congress the proper redress lay through other congressional action or the courts. The Constitution was adopted to form a more perfect union, and was expressly ratified by each state; no state, by such ratification, reserved the right to veto any law of the United States. The Constitution was the "object of our reverence, the bond of our Union, our defense in danger, the source of our prosperity in peace." Jackson forcefully stated that he considered any attempt to "annul a law of the United States, assumed by one State, incompatible with the existence of the Union, contradicted expressly by the letter of the Constitution, unauthorized by its spirit, inconsistent with every principle on which it was founded, and destructive of the great object for which it was formed."[14] Jackson's message carried great weight, and Congress, inspired by the tireless efforts of Kentuckian Henry Clay, was able to work out a compromise: the passage of a new taxation scheme that gradually lowered the objectionable duties. South Carolina was thus satisfied and repealed its ordinance.

It was to be just the first in a series of agreements engineered by Clay, who would become known as "The Great Compromiser" and "The Great Pacificator." Clay was born in 1777 in Hanover County, Virginia. As a young congressman he was one of the nation's most outspoken "war hawks" during the War of 1812, and then was part of the team that negotiated a treaty with Great Britain and ended the war. Clay became best known for the development of his American System, a government-sponsored economic development program that stressed internal improvements, particularly in the West, and the formation of a national bank. Clay was a slaveowner who favored gradual emancipation and ultimately colonization of freedmen, and condemned radical abolitionists. Above all else, Clay was a strong nationalist, and his love of the Union permeated his politics. A founding father of the Whig Party, Clay was an unsuccessful candidate for president in both 1832 and 1844.

The acquisition of California and the Southwest after the Mexican War brought the slavery question again to the forefront. With southern states threatening to secede if the regions were not opened to slavery, Clay engineered a sweeping compromise plan meant to settle the issue. Among other things, the compromise called for admitting California as a free state, organizing the territories of New Mexico and Utah without congressional conditions on slavery, abolishing the slave trade (but not slavery itself) in the District of Columbia, and strict enforcement of the fugitive slave law. In late February 1850, Clay delivered a speech in support of the plan on the floor of the Senate. "I wish to speak today, not as a Massachusetts man, nor as a Northern man, but as an American.... Peaceable secession? Peaceable secession? ...Heaven forbid! Where is the flag of the republic to remain? Where is the eagle still to tower?" Clay's plan called for the North to "make more liberal and extensive concession" than the South, but it could afford to because of sheer numerical superiority. The South, however, was at risk of losing "its social fabric, life, and all that makes life desirable and happy" if disunion occurred. At one point Clay held up a fragment of wood claimed to be taken from the coffin of George Washington. "The venerated father of the country is warning us from Mount Vernon," he said. "Do not destroy his handiwork!" In a dramatic conclusion Clay turned to Calhoun, sitting in his Senate presidential chair. "Sir, we may search the pages of history, and none so furious, so bloody, so implacable, so exterminating, from the wars of Greece down — none, none of them raged with such violence as will that war which shall follow that disastrous event — if that event ever happens—of dissolution."[15] Clay's proposals were not ratified en masse, but later that session each of his provisions were adopted, due in large part to the forceful work of Stephen Douglas, and secession was delayed for 10 years.

With this history of threatened secession, compromise and oratory, and guided by the distinguished remarks of Webster, Jackson and Clay, Lincoln went to work. For several hours of each day, beginning in mid-January, Lincoln took a small room in Johnson's building on the town square, above the drugstore of C.W. Smith, and drafted, and re-drafted, his inaugural address. When he completed a version that suited him, he asked William H. Bailhache, an owner of the *Illinois State Journal*, to print 20 copies, which were then secretly distributed to friends and associates for review.

The news from the South grew more ominous by the day. South Carolina, already in possession of Fort Moultrie, seized the U.S. Revenue Cutter *William Aiken*. Federal arsenals were seized by state authorities in Alabama, Mississippi and Florida. Forts Morgan, Gaines, Marion, Johnston, Caswell, Jackson and St. Philip, among others, surrendered. Louisiana soldiers seized the U.S. Marine Hospital below New Orleans. On January 21 five U.S. senators, David L. Yulee and Stephen R. Mallory of

Florida, Clement Clay and Benjamin Fitzpatrick of Alabama, and Jefferson Davis of Mississippi, resigned their seats.

Seward wanted Lincoln to come immediately to Washington. He believed that Lincoln could, merely by his presence there, assure a nervous public that he was in control of the volatile situation. But Lincoln put him off, believing that he should stay out of the Capitol until at least after February 13, the day when the electoral count was made official. He feared that southern Democratic senators, still in the majority despite several resignations, might fail to show up and legitimize his election. Still, Lincoln could not sit by much longer. Alarmed by reports that 10,000 malcontents in Maryland and Virginia were organizing with the aim to prevent his inauguration, Lincoln instructed John Nicolay to contact the governors of states surrounding Washington and request commitments of support "in the event of trouble or danger."[16] Within days Gen. Edwin Wilson of the Pennsylvania militia assured Lincoln that his forces would be on hand to meet any disturbance. More significantly, Winfield Scott positioned a garrison of regulars just outside the city limits at Fort Washington and ordered two more artillery units to stand by. He told a reporter that anyone who dared interfere with the electoral count "should be lashed to the muzzle of a twelve-pounder gun and fired out of a window of the Capitol" to "manure the hills of Arlington with his body." Further, Lincoln should feel free to "come to Washington when he is ready. Tell him I consider myself responsible for his safety. If necessary, I'll plant cannon at both ends of Pennsylvania Avenue, and if any should raise a finger I'll blow them to hell."[17] Scott was not intimidated when students at the University of Virginia in Charlottesville, just 200 miles from the capitol, hung him in effigy. "The old warrior is aroused," wrote Elihu Washburne to Lincoln, "and he will be equal to the occasion."[18]

Lincoln now felt better about the situation — at least now he believed he would actually be inaugurated — and so began to finalize plans for his journey to Washington. He determined that he would leave Springfield on February 11, one day before his 52nd birthday, and would travel to the capital in a roundabout way, proceeding through Indianapolis, Cincinnati, Columbus, Cleveland, Buffalo, Albany, New York, Harrisburg, Philadelphia and Baltimore and dozens of other, smaller towns (his original idea had been to take a more southerly route, through Cincinnati, Wheeling, and Baltimore, but the plan was rejected as too dangerous). Since he had not campaigned he felt the need to allow the people to see him. He asked Ward Lamon to coordinate security with railroad official William S. Wood. But there was one special person who must see him first, and whom he must see: his stepmother, Sally Bush Lincoln, widowed but still living near the old Goosenest Prairie homestead in Coles County.

Lincoln would make this journey alone. On January 30, faded carpetbag in hand and a shawl tossed over his shoulders, he quietly took a seat on a Great Western train, having received a free pass from Asa Bowen, the railroad supervisor. The train was late pulling into Mattoon and Lincoln missed his connection on a passenger train. Late in the afternoon a freight train pulled up, and Lincoln rode in the caboose to Charleston, arriving just after 6 P.M. A small crowd had received word of his trip and gathered at the station, most expressing surprise that the president-elect of the United

States would travel alone, with no security and no fanfare, and seem not to care in the least. An old friend, state senator Thomas A. Marshall, had happily agreed to allow Lincoln to spend the night at his home. The two men traveled in Marshall's buggy through sleet and snow, both men so glad to see each other that the weather wasn't noticed. That night, after supper, Lincoln received many old friends from his days on the circuit. One visitor was a man named A.P. Dunbar, an attorney who had gone up against Lincoln many times in court. Though they had been close friends, Dunbar was now nervous about how he should act in front of the man who would be president. "If he is dignified and formal," Dunbar thought to himself as he knocked on the door, "I must act accordingly." But he was pleasantly surprised when Lincoln answered and, recognizing him immediately, exclaimed, "Lord Amighty, Aleck, how glad I am to see you!"[19] Dunbar joined his friend as they sat by the fire late into the night, telling stories and laughing at Lincoln's jokes as in older days.

The next morning Lincoln borrowed Marshall's buggy and rode 12 miles south of town to the home of his stepsister Matilda, now Mrs. Ruben Moore. He spent the day there in an emotional visit with his stepmother, now 73 years old. Sally had known Thomas Lincoln, Abraham's father, as a young girl in Kentucky; some said that she had rejected Thomas for another. When Nancy Lincoln, Abraham's mother, died of milk sickness in Indiana in October 1818, leaving Thomas with 11-year-old Sarah and nine-year-old Abraham, he went back to Kentucky and found Sally, now a widow with three children of her own. He paid her debts and promised her happiness in Indiana. In December 1819 they married, and Thomas brought Sally back to his home on Little Pigeon Creek, where she found an 18-square-foot cabin with a dirt floor and stone fireplace. She also found Abraham and Sarah, dirty and unkempt and badly in need of a mother. Sally insisted that her husband put a floor in the cabin, and make real beds and furniture, and she saw that the family joined the Little Pigeon Baptist Church. Most important, Sally quickly grew to love her new stepchildren as her own.

Sally developed a special bond with Abraham, who she called "the best boy I ever saw" and who "never gave me a cross word or look."[20] She said that "his mind and mine — what little I had — seemed to run together (and) move in the same channel."[21] She recognized his potential, and she did what she could to nurture it. While his father was only interested in getting a good day's work in the fields out of his son, Sally encouraged Abraham to read and study and develop his intellect. Although formal schooling was seldom available in the wilderness— only if a teacher had moved into the area, and even then just between the fall harvest and spring planting seasons— Sally made certain that Abraham and the other children attended when possible. Abraham loved Sally and called her mother, always appreciating the kindness she showed him, and after he left home in 1831 he missed her greatly.

In 1840 Thomas moved his family to Coles County, Illinois, to the first of four farms, finally settling for good at Goosenest Prairie. There he built a double-room "saddlebag" log cabin, essentially two cabins joined together as one, with planks covering the space in between. Thomas raised corn, oats and wheat, and his livestock included horses, cattle, hogs and chickens. Abraham returned to visit only sporadically, although when he traveled the legal circuit he sometimes came through Charleston and then came out to the farm for short visits, perhaps out of courtesy only to his father, but out of deep affection for Sally.

Now Lincoln quietly reminisced with his stepmother, holding her hand as they talked of the years they had spent together. After his assassination five years later Sally would recall that she "did not want to see (him) run for Presd., not want him, elected—was afraid somehow or other ... that Something would happen (to) him. When he came down to see me after he was elected ... my heart told me ... that I should never see him again."[22] But Abraham reassured her. "No No Mama," he said. "Trust in the Lord and all will be well. We will see each other again."[23] He gave her a fur coat to keep her warm and remember him by.

At some point that day Lincoln drove out to Shiloh Cemetery, just a mile from the cabin, where his father was buried. Lincoln's relationship with his father had long been strained. Thomas could never understand his young son's eagerness to read and to study when there was so much farmwork to be done. Thomas was an honest, if not a restless man, and he knew no other way to success than through the sweat of his brow. As his son's intellect so quickly surpassed his own, and it became clear that Abraham wanted to leave his father's world behind him, Thomas no doubt became frustrated and a little intimidated. It is possible that Thomas was abusive toward young Abraham; Billy Herndon later interviewed people who commented that Thomas "slashed" or "whipped" his son when displeased.[24] Years later, after Lincoln had become a successful attorney, he loaned his father some money, but he seemed to be embarrassed that it was necessary and scolded his father for needing it. When Thomas was on his deathbed his stepbrother John Johnston had implored Lincoln to come and visit his father, but Lincoln had refused to make the trip. "I sincerely hope Father may yet recover his health," Lincoln wrote Johnston, "but at all events tell him to remember to call upon, our great, and good, and merciful Maker.... Say to him that if we could meet now, it is doubtful whether it would be more painful than pleasant."[25] Lincoln did not attend his father's funeral in 1851, claiming that his work schedule was too pressing. Thomas died without ever having met his daughter-in-law Mary or his grandsons. Now, 10 years later, Lincoln said a silent farewell to his father. He told friends that he intended to purchase a proper headstone for Thomas' grave, but he never did.

On his last night in Charleston, Lincoln attended a reception at a public hall. He received still more friends and supporters, including various members of the Hanks and Johnston families, and seemed in fine spirit. One guest vowed that he would shed the last drop of his blood to insure Lincoln's inauguration. That reminded Lincoln of a story. He'd heard of a young man, ready to go to war, whose sisters made him a belt embroidered with the motto "Victory or death." "No, no," the youth said, "don't put it quite that strong. Put it 'Victory or get hurt pretty bad.'"[26] Lincoln could not be persuaded to make a speech. The time for a public declaration of policy had still not come, he insisted. All he could do was express his gratitude to all the people who wished him well in Washington. The next day, alone again, Lincoln left for Springfield.

When he arrived he learned that Seward, along with Stephen Douglas, had convinced delegates from 20 Union states to gather in Washington, the objective being to debate still more compromise proposals while keeping border states occupied, forestalling their secession. But this "Peace Convention" was doomed to failure. None of the states of the Deep South agreed to send delegates; Lincoln himself refused to endorse the convention and urged Illinois representatives not to attend. The time for compromise had long passed, he believed. "I'm not going to buy my right to be peaceably inaugurated," he said. "I would rather die first."[27]

8

"The Power of the Lion, the Ravages of the Bear"

In the mid–19th century slaves outnumbered free white men in Montgomery County, Alabama, by better than two to one. Huge numbers of slaves were required to work the vast cotton fields that surrounded the capital city of Montgomery. More than 130,000 bales of cotton were harvested each year in the county, then transported via steamboat and railway to manufacturing plants and factories in the North. The cotton crop was the primary reason that county real estate was valued at more than $51 million, and with at least 30 plantation owners worth more than $100,000, Montgomery was per capita one of the wealthiest cities in the South.

Monday, February 4, 1861, brought unseasonably cool temperatures—barely above the freezing mark—to Montgomery. But the weather mattered little to 43 of the most distinguished and influential men of the South, who had gathered at the statehouse to form the provisional government of secessionist states. In age the group averaged 47 years, the youngest being 31-year-old "Jap" Campbell of Louisiana, the oldest 72-year-old Thomas Fearn of Alabama. Most of the men were college educated; included in the group were lawyers, judges, professors, politicians and one physician. Seventeen were farmers or plantation owners. At least half of the group were Democrats, and six were old-line Whigs. All but eight owned slaves; Duncan Kenner of South Carolina owned the most at 473.

At just past 12:30 P.M. The Reverend Basil Manly of the Montgomery Southern Baptist Church rose to deliver the invocation. Inwardly he worried that the God who had blessed America for nearly 100 years might not look with favor upon the convention. But he believed that the disunionists acted not as revolutionaries or rebels, but reformers, and his words pleased the delegates and the hundreds of spectators who had wedged their way into the seating gallery to watch history take place. So long as the sun and moon should last, Manly prayed, "allow the Union of these States to exist. Let truth, and justice, and equal rights be decreed to our government."[1]

Robert Barnwell Rhett moved that Howell Cobb of Georgia be elected president of the convention, and the motion passed by acclamation. In a brief acceptance speech Cobb, who had served as speaker of the house for the Thirty-first Congress and more recently as President Buchanan's secretary of the treasury, urged the delegates to make this most of this opportunity. The separation from the old Union would be "perfect, complete and perpetual," he said. Cobb appealed to the border states who had not yet committed to secession; those states "identified with us in interest, feeling and institutions," and must now be encouraged to join them. "Our responsibilities, gentlemen, are great," he concluded. "We will this day inaugurate for the South a new era of peace, security and prosperity."[2]

A secretary was quickly chosen, then a doorkeeper and messenger. A committee of five was selected to prepare the rules of the convention, Alexander Stephens to head the group. Finally, a name had to be chosen for the new nation. Many names were considered, including the Republic of Washington, Chicora, Atlanta, and the Georgia Confederacy. Even the "Southern United States of America" was suggested. The group reached a consensus on "the Confederate States of North America" and when Stephens proposed that the word "North" be dropped, the vote was unanimous. Then the gavel came down, ending the first day of the convention after only an hour. Most of the delegates retired to the Exchange Hotel, where they spent the rest of the day in the lobby and bar, congratulating themselves and accepting toasts from adoring crowds.

By the end of the week a great deal had been accomplished. Not satisfied with simply formulating the new government, the group also decided to assume legislative powers, although no one had bothered to ask the permission of any state. Most importantly, a committee of 12 delegates—two from each of the six participating states; the Texas delegates were not yet present—met in secret session and formulated a provisional constitution. This document, which was eventually adopted by the body as a whole, would be in place for 31 days, until a permanent constitution could be ratified by the states by vote. The U.S. Constitution, and to a lesser extent, the Articles of Confederation, were used as a model for the committee's deliberations. Because the delegates believed that they, and not their erring northern neighbors, were acting more in accordance with the revolutionary spirit of the founding fathers, only a few changes were necessary. Although the right to secession was not expressly set forth, the right was implied; each state was acting in "its sovereign and independent character" in adopting the document. The right to own slaves, however, was clearly expressed. The slave trade was abolished, for the importation of more slaves into the country, it was believed, would only decrease the value of the 4 million slaves already present. Slavery in the territories would be recognized, and the fugitive slave law was fortified.

Under the new constitution the president and vice president would serve six-year terms and would not be eligible for reelection. A supreme court would sit only when called upon by Congress to decide a case, and Congress would have the authority to remove a president by a two-thirds majority vote. Cabinet members would have seats on the floors of both houses, a concept loosely modeled on the British system of government. In recognition of the nullification struggles of several decades earlier the taxation on imports was prohibited.

With a framework in place the assemblage had to select a provisional president and vice president. For several days the delegates argued over the coveted post of chief executive. The most popular names under consideration included William Lowndes Yancey, Howell Cobb, Robert Toombs, Alexander Stephens, Robert Barnwell Rhett and Jefferson Davis, all men with particular strengths and weaknesses. The views of Yancey of Alabama, who dreamed of a slave empire that would encircle the Gulf of Mexico and the Caribbean, were seen as too extreme by many delegates. Cobb of Georgia, who had remained in Buchanan's cabinet until December 10, 1860, was distrusted by some because he had supported the Compromise of 1850. Toombs, the senior senator from Georgia but not even an official delegate to the convention, managed to offend almost everyone by drinking excessively all week long; he would serve for a brief time as Confederate secretary of war and later became a brigadier general in the Confederate army. Stephens had urged fellow Georgians not to secede only a few months ago, and his health was a concern. Rhett's passion for the new country was admirable — it was his idea to assemble in Montgomery — but the nation needed a statesman for its president, not a radical. Finally Davis of Mississippi was chosen. His military and political background would be essential if and when civil war came, and his unwavering support of states' rights would be an important inducement to those border states not yet committed to secession.

He was born Jefferson Finis Davis (the middle name given because he was the last of 10 children) in Christian County, Kentucky, on June 3, 1808, just eight months earlier and 100 miles away from Abraham Lincoln. His father Samuel, a Revolutionary War veteran, moved the family to Wilkinson County in the Mississippi Territory shortly thereafter, and Davis spent his childhood there on the farm. He attended Transylvania University in Kentucky for a time, but at his father's urging and upon the nomination of President James Monroe he entered the U.S. Military Academy at West Point in 1824. Davis was only moderately successful at West Point, not rising above the rank of private and graduating 23rd in a class of 34, behind other cadets such as Albert Sidney Johnston and Leonidas Polk. Two other cadets, one year younger, included Joseph E. Johnston and Robert E. Lee. All these men would later serve Davis well as Confederate officers.

After a stint at the Infantry School of Practice at Jefferson Barracks in Missouri, Davis's first assignments were to Forts Crawford and Winnebago on the Wisconsin frontier. He then moved on to Iowa and Illinois, where he established military posts, served as adjutant and quartermaster, and became a company commander. None of the work was glamorous, but he found that he enjoyed it. "I know of nothing else that I could do that I would like better," he wrote.[3] His burdens were eased by the presence of James Pemberton, a slave he acquired as a young man who accompanied him from post to post, and who on at least one occasion nursed him through a serious illness.[4] Davis fought in the Indian Wars and gradually matured into a respected leader of men. Along with a young lieutenant named Robert Anderson (the same man who now commanded Fort Sumter), Davis was given the honor by Col. Zachary Taylor of escorting the renegade Black Hawk to Jefferson Barracks after his capture in 1832. Davis treated Black Hawk with dignity and respect, a fact that the chief appreciated. Davis was "a good and brave young chief" Black Hawk later wrote in his autobiography, and he was "much pleased" with Davis's conduct.[5] Finally promoted to first lieutenant, Davis was placed in charge of a dragoons company and awaited his next assignment.

But then something unforeseen interrupted his now-promising military career:

he fell in love with the colonel's daughter, 16-year-old Sarah Knox Taylor, whom he called "Knoxie." While the elder Taylor respected Davis's abilities as a soldier, "Old Rough and Ready" did not view him as an appropriate suitor of his daughter. Offended, Davis challenged Taylor to a duel, then thought better of it and resigned his commission instead. He traveled immediately to Louisville and proposed to Knoxie, who accepted despite her father's disapproval. The wedding took place at the home of her aunt, and Davis took his new bride home to Mississippi.

Samuel Davis had died several years earlier, and now Jefferson looked to his older brother Joseph for guidance. Joseph had prospered as a cotton grower at his plantation he called The Hurricane. He gave his younger brother an adjoining 800-acre plantation called Brierfield, along with 14 slaves on credit. Davis put in a cotton crop and expected a bountiful harvest. But both he and Knoxie fell ill with malaria, and in September 1835 she died, having been a wife for just three months. Davis recovered, but never completely, it seemed; he would have the gaunt, pallid look of a convalescent the rest of his life.

For the next eight years Davis brooded, traveled, studied and built Brierfield into a thriving enterprise. In 1843 he met Varina Howell, the daughter of a Natchez lawyer and granddaughter of the governor of New Jersey. Despite their age difference — Davis was then 35, Varina just 17 — they were married in February 1845, and after a honeymoon in New Orleans returned to Brierfield. That same year Davis was elected to Congress as a Democrat, and served until the Mexican War began, when he resigned his seat and headed up a volunteer regiment called the Mississippi Rifles. Davis distinguished himself at Monterey and Buena Vista, guiding his troops to decisive victories despite being severely wounded in the foot. He returned home a hero, and was appointed U.S. senator by the governor of Mississippi.

His former father-in-law Zachary Taylor had been elected president in 1848, but this awkward circumstance did not seem to bother Davis, for he proved to be an effective politician, principled, disciplined and uncompromising. He chaired the committee on military affairs, supported construction of the Pacific railroad as a military necessity (but only if it was to be built through either Memphis or Vicksburg), advocated for the fugitive slave law and supported states' rights. Every position Davis took was dictated by his adherence to southern nationalism, and he prided himself as the political heir to John Calhoun.

His cold, aristocratic style impressed many colleagues and even some adversaries — he became close friends with William Seward, for example — but his intellectual arrogance and humorless nature also made him more than a few enemies. Senator James Hammond of South Carolina described him as "irascible ... vain as a peacock as ambitious as the Devil." Winfield Scott believed Davis to be "false by nature, habit, choice.... There is contamination in his touch." Sam Houston called him "as ambitious as Lucifer and as cold as a lizard."[6] Davis suffered from numerous physical ailments, including recurring infections in his foot and the loss of sight in his left eye. He was at times depressed over events both political and personal: his son Samuel, the first of five children, died unexpectedly, and Davis's grief never fully subsided.

After an unsuccessful run for governor of Mississippi in 1851, Davis was named secretary of war by President Franklin Pierce, where he worked tirelessly to improve the Army's infantry and made certain that supplies and fortifications were adequate. An innovator, it was Davis who proposed the use of camels in the desert regions of the Southwest. With the election of Buchanan as president in 1856 Davis returned to the Senate in 1857 and quickly reestablished himself as leader of that body. He loathed Stephen Douglas and his popular sovereignty concept and toured the country in 1858 and 1859, giving a series of speeches designed to unite the country while at the same time recognizing the autonomy of individual states. He tried to convince Bell, Breckenridge and Douglas that they must withdraw from the 1860 presidential race in the hope that an acceptable compromise candidate might be found. But the strategy that worked for the Republicans would not work for the Democrats, and Davis watched with disgust as Lincoln, a hated "Black Republican," was elected.

Davis held out hope for a compromise that might prevent disunion. He believed that secession would lead to civil war; his beloved Mississippi, among many southern states, was not prepared militarily to match a vengeful North and would surely be crushed. He offered advice to Buchanan regarding the ill-received State of the Union address in December, but was annoyed when the president declared that he would attempt to collect revenues from slave states, even those that might secede. When it became clear that the work of the Senate's Committee of Thirteen, of which he was a member, would end in failure, Davis knew that secession was inevitable. "The Union was dear to me when it was a Union of fraternal states," he said. "But that Union no longer exists. The abolitionists and Black Republicans have destroyed that Union."[7]

Davis was incensed when Buchanan refused to surrender Charleston Harbor in early January 1861, proof, he believed, of the North's intended aggression. On the 10th Davis took out his anger in a venomous speech on the Senate floor:

> Even after forty years of bitter debate, you still ask us what is the matter. I will tell you what is the matter.... Your platform on which you elected your presidential candidate denies us equality in the Union. It refuses us equal enjoyment of the territories, even though we've paid equally in their purchase and bled equally in their acquisition in war. Is this how you honor your compact with us? ... Whose fault is it if the Union be dissolved? Your votes refuse to recognize our domestic institutions ... our slave property which is guarded by the Constitution. You elect a candidate on the basis of sectional hostility, one who, in his speeches, now thrown broadcast over the country, made a distinct declaration of war upon our institutions. We care not whether that war be made by armies marching for invasion, or whether it be by proclamation, or whether it be by indirect and covert process. In all three modes, you declare your hostility.... And you dare to ask us, "What is the matter?" ... If we submit to you, we would surrender our birthright of freedom and become slaves ourselves. I don't care to quote your platform; I don't care to quote the speeches of your President-elect.... Our hands are stainless. It is *you* who are the aggressor.... If in the pride of power, if in contempt of reason and reliance upon force, you say we shall not go, but shall remain as subjects to you, then, gentlemen of the North, a war is to be inaugurated the likes of which men have not seen before.[8]

Davis developed a severe case of neuralgia and took to his bed for a week. Within days Mississippi seceded, and Governor John Pettus wired Davis, ordering him to return home and take command of the state militia and reorganize it into an army. Davis wrote a letter to his friend, former President Pierce: "I come to the hard task of announcing to you that the hour is at hand which closes my connection with the United States, for the independence and Union for which my father bled and in the service of which I have sought to emulate the example he set for my guidance. Mississippi not as a matter of choice but of necessity has resolved to enter on the trial of secession. When Lincoln comes in he will have but to continue in the path of his predecessor to inaugurate a civil war and leave a democratic administration responsible for the fact."[9]

On the 21st Davis ignored his doctor's advice and dragged himself from his bed, intent on addressing his colleagues in the Senate one final time. Four other senators, Clay and Fitzpatrick of Alabama, and Mallory and Yulee of Florida, had resigned their seats earlier in the day with little fanfare, but now the galleries were packed with people, including Varina, who had one of her slaves secure a place for her. The crowd hushed as Davis began to speak, his hands trembling and his face nervously twitching, his tone reflecting what he later called "the saddest day of my life":

> I rise, Mr. President, for the purpose of announcing to the Senate that I have satisfactory evidence the State of Mississippi, by a solemn ordinance of her people, in convention assembled, has declared her separation from the United States. Under these circumstances, of course, my functions are terminated here ... the occasion does not invite me to go into argument; and my physical condition would not permit me to do so, if it were otherwise; and yet it seems to become me to say something on the part of the State I here represent on an occasion as solemn as this.
>
> It has been a conviction of pressing necessity — it has been a belief that we are to be deprived in the Union of the rights which our fathers bequeathed to us — which has brought Mississippi to her present decision. She has heard proclaimed the theory that all men are created free and equal, and this made the basis of an attack upon her social institutions; and the Sacred Declaration of Independence has been invoked to maintain the position of the equality of the races. That declaration is to be construed by the circumstances and purposes for which it was made. The communities were declaring their independence; the people of those communities were asserting that no man was born — to use the language of Mr. Jefferson — booted and spurred, to ride over the rest of mankind; that men were created equal — meaning the men of the political community; that there was no divine right to rule; that no man inherited the right to govern; that there were no classes by which power and place descended to families; but that all stations were equally within the grasp of each member of the body politic.... When our Constitution was formed, the same idea was rendered more palpable; for there we find provision made for that very class of persons as property; they were not put upon the equality of footing with white men — not even upon that of paupers and convicts; but, so far as representation was concerned, were discriminated against as a lower caste, only to be represented in the numerical proportion of three-fifths. So stands the compact which binds us together.
>
> Then, Senators, we recur to the principles upon which our Government was founded; and when you deny them, and when you deny us the right to withdraw from a Government which, thus perverted, threatens to be destructive of our rights, we but tread in the path of our fathers when we proclaim our independence and take the hazard. This is done, not in hostility to others, not to injure any section of the country, not even for our own pecuniary benefit, but from the

high and solemn motive of defending and protecting the rights we inherited, and which it is our duty to transmit unshorn to our children.

I hope ... for peaceable relations with you, though we must part. They may be mutually beneficial to us in the future, as they have been in the past, if you so will it. The reverse may bring disaster on every portion of the country, and, if you will have it thus, we will invoke the God of our fathers, who delivered them from the power of the lion, to protect us from the ravages of the bear....

I carry with me no hostile remembrance. Whatever offense I have given which has not been redressed, or for which satisfaction has not been demanded, I have, Senators, in this hour of our parting, to offer you my apology for any pain which, in the heat of discussion, I have inflicted. I go hence unencumbered by the remembrance for any injury received, and having discharged the duty of making the only reparation in my power for any injury offered.

Mr. President and Senators, having made the announcement which the occasion seemed to me to require, it only remains for me to bid you a final adieu.[10]

There was a moment of silence; then the Davis supporters present in the gallery burst out in applause, joining the remaining southern senators. As he left the building Davis half-expected that he would be arrested for treason; in fact, he hoped he would be, for he wanted to test the constitutionality of secession in the courts. But he and Varina were allowed to travel unrestricted to Mississippi. At Jackson, Governor Pettus commissioned him a major general, and while he gladly assumed command of state forces he knew that not nearly enough arms had been procured to wage an effective war. "General," said Pettus, "you overrate the risk." "I only wish I did," Davis replied.[11]

Within days Davis received a telegram from the convention in Montgomery, asking if he would accept the position of provisional president of the new nation. He would much rather serve in a military capacity, he wired back; in fact, he could think of no greater honor than being named commander of the entire Confederate army. But he would serve in any capacity asked of him. On the afternoon of the 10th of February he was in the rose garden at Brierfield with Varina, trimming bushes, when a messenger on horseback galloped up. Davis read the message silently, such a pained expression on his face that Varina thought a loved one had died. Davis forlornly read the message aloud, as Varina later put it, "as a man might speak of a sentence of death":[12]

> Sir:
>   We are directed to inform you that you are this day unanimously elected President of the Provisional Government of the Confederate States of America, and to request you to come to Montgomery immediately. We send also a special messenger. Do not wait for him.
>   R. Toombs,
>   R. Barnwell Rhett....[13]

Davis left immediately for Montgomery, boarding the train at Vicksburg. Believing that war would come quickly, perhaps even before Lincoln's election, he decided to name his West Point friend Albert Sidney Johnston chief field commander of the Confederate army. He also decided upon his cabinet nominations, with each state of the Deep South represented: Toombs for secretary of state; Charles G. Memminger of South Carolina for Treasury; Leroy Pope Walker of Alabama for War; Stephen R. Mallory of Florida for Navy; Judah Benjamin of Louisiana for attorney general; and John H. Reagan of Texas for postmaster general. Davis made 25 stops en route to Montgomery, giving speeches to cheering crowds and before demonstrating militias; one reporter called the trip "one continuous ovation" for Davis.[14] The time for compromise had passed, Davis said, and the break from the Union was irreparable. He promised that England and France would grant diplomatic recognition to the new country. But, he cautioned, the struggle with the North promised to be long and bloody. All those opposed to the Confederate position would "smell Southern powder and feel Southern steel."[15]

At 10 P.M. on the 16th, Davis was met at the Montgomery train station by William Yancey, who escorted him to the Exchange Hotel. Yancey took him to a balcony and introduced him to a cheering crowd below. "We have the man we need now," Yancey exulted. "The man and the hour have met!" Although Davis was hoarse and exhausted, he spoke briefly: "Fellow citizens and brethren of the Confederate States of America — for now we are brethren, not in name merely, but in fact — men of one flesh, one bone, one interest, one purpose, and of identity of domestic institutions. We have henceforth, I trust, a prospect of living together in peace with our institutions the subject of protection and not of defamation.... If war should come, we shall show that Southern valor still shines as brightly as in the days of seventy-six. Rest assured, that as the sun disperses the crowds, the progress of the Southern Confederacy will carry us safely over the sea of troubles."[16]

Davis spent Sunday, February 17, alone in his room, composing his inaugural address. The next day dawned cold and cloudy as Davis was driven by carriage from the hotel to the capitol building, followed by governors of the seceding states, convention delegates, and city officials. Along the way a band played a new song called "I Wish I Was in Dixie Land," which although composed by a northern minstrel singer named Daniel Decatur Emmett, was fast becoming the unofficial theme song of the South. On the portico, Davis was introduced by Howell Cobb, and the crowd of over 5,000 people pushed forward to hear him.

Davis spoke of his hope for goodwill and kindness between the two American nations. "Our policy is peace, and the freest trade our necessities will permit," he said. But if the Confederacy was not allowed to pursue its separate course, if the North refused to see the "folly and wickedness" of aggression, and if "the integrity and jurisdiction of our territory be assailed, it will but remain for us with a firm resolve to appeal to arms and invoke the blessings of Providence upon a just cause.... You will not find in me wither a want of zeal or fidelity to a cause that has my highest hopes and most enduring affection.... Sanctified by justice and sustained by a virtuous people, let me reverently invoke the God of our fathers to guide and protect us in our efforts to perpetuate the principles which by His blessing they were able to vindicate, establish and transmit to their posterity, and with the continuance of His favor, ever to be gratefully acknowledged, let us look hopefully forward to success, to peace, and to prosperity."[17]

That night a reception was held at Estelle Hall, and Davis enjoyed himself as hundreds of well-wishers stood in line to shake his hand. The confidence he showed in public did not hint at the apprehension he felt inside. He wrote to Varina: "we are without machinery without means and threatened by powerful opposition but I do not despond and will not shrink from the task imposed upon me." In March Varina and the children joined Davis in Montgomery, and the family took up temporary residence at a two-story frame house across the street from the capitol. In May, after Virginia joined the Confederacy, the capitol was relocated to Richmond.

Although Davis had been careful to make no direct mention of slavery in his speech, his vice president saw no reason for restraint. Addressing a crowd at Savannah a few days later Alexander Stephens declared that the cornerstone of the Confederacy "rests upon the great truth, that the Negro is not equal to the white man; that slavery — subordination to the superior race — is his natural and normal condition. This, our new government, is the first in the history of the world based upon this great physical, philosophical, and moral truth."[18] Davis was mildly annoyed that Stephens would use such language, and it was not the first time Stephens would disappoint the president. Davis asked him to head a commission to persuade Arkansas to secede, and Stephens refused. He then suggested that Stephens travel to Washington and attempt to negotiate compensation for the seized federal forts and installations, and Stephens refused again. Relations between the two men thus were quickly strained; within weeks Stephens was privately complaining that Davis lacked the capacity to serve as president.

Davis did, however, write a letter to President-elect Lincoln on February 27, advising him that he was willing to negotiate the return of federal forts and other properties that had come under Confederate control, for appropriate compensation. He also sent a commission to Washington with instructions to meet personally with Lincoln. But while his envoys were able to communicate their positions to William Seward (through Supreme Court justice John A. Campbell, an Alabama native), Seward had no real authority to bind Lincoln, or the United States government, and only acted in hopes of forestalling military action. Lincoln did not respond to Davis's letter or his commission. Because secession was nothing but an act of rebellion against the Union, Lincoln did not recognize the Confederacy as a legitimate nation. And just as Lincoln never acknowledged the existence of the Confederate government, he never referred to Davis as its president.

There is no record of Lincoln's reaction to Davis's trip to Montgomery and his inauguration, although he surely followed the events through the newspapers and carefully analyzed Davis's speeches. But Lincoln had little time to ponder the political rise of his adversary; he had much to attend to in his last few days in Springfield. He cut back visiting hours to one and one-half hours each day, in the late afternoon. He met privately with Orville Browning, Carl Schurz, and Horace Greeley, who was on a nationwide lecture tour asserting his views on the state of the Union. Everyone asked Lincoln how the South could be satisfied. Only through the "surrender of everything worth preserving," he said.[19]

In preparation for the trip to Washington Mary spent many hours cleaning, sorting, and boxing personal and household items. She burned stacks of old letters and papers in the alley behind the house; a neighbor named Jared Irwin wandered by and asked for some of the letters to remember his friends by, and was accommodated. Lincoln took a valise filled with speeches and writings to Mrs. Elizabeth Todd Grimsley, a favorite cousin of Mary's, and asked her to care for it until he returned. If he did not return, Lincoln advised her, she was free to dispose of his "literary bureau" as she deemed appropriate. The Lincoln took out an advertisement in the *State Journal* announcing what was essentially a 19th century rummage sale:

> AT PRIVATE SALE — THE FURNITURE consisting of Parlor and Chamber Sets, Carpets, Sofas, Chairs, Wardrobes, Bureaus, Bedsteads, Stoves, China, Queensware, Glass, etc., etc., at the residence on the corner of Eighth and Jackson Streets.... For particulars apply on the premises at once.[20]

Druggist Samuel Melvin purchased most of the furniture, including a spring mattress for $26, a wardrobe for $20, six chairs for $2 each, a "whatnot" for $10, a stand for $1.50, four comforters for $2.00 each, and nine and one-half yards of stairway carpet for $4.75. Lincoln dutifully wrote out a receipt totaling $82.25. A neighbor from across the street, Allen Miller, purchased a marble-topped pier table, a mirror with gilded frame, and a set of six side chairs, and what was not sold was placed in storage.[21]

The house itself was leased to Lucian Tilton, the retired president of the Great Western Railroad, for $350 per year. The house was valued at $3,000, the carriage barn at $75, and the woodshed and privy at $175, and Lincoln insured the property with the Hartford Fire Insurance Company at a cost of $25 per year. He named Robert Irwin of the Springfield Marine and Fire Insurance Company his fiscal agent, authorizing him to collect payments and interest on various notes and mortgages that Lincoln owned, totaling just over $11,000.[22] He also instructed Irwin to pay any bills that might come in after he left for Washington. The family dog, a yellowish mongrel named Fido, was entrusted to the care of the John Roll family, who had young boys to take care of him. Lincoln sold his horse, Old Bob, to John Flynn, a Springfield drayman. In four years Old Bob would accompany Lincoln's funeral procession to Oak Ridge Cemetery.

On February 6 the Lincolns hosted a huge farewell reception at their home. The weather was mild, and the line of invited guests—700 of "the political elite of Illinois and the beauty and fashion of the area"—extended out to the street and down the block; it was estimated that it took 20 minutes to reach the front door. The guests were properly introduced and received by Lincoln as he stood at the parlor entrance. Mary stood at the center of the parlor, attended by her sisters and half sisters, Mrs. Charles Kellogg of Cincinnati, Mrs. Clark Smith and Mrs. William Wallace of Springfield, and Miss Elodie Todd of Kentucky. Mary looked radiant in a full trail gown of white moire antique silk and French lace collar. A single strand of pearls adorned her neck, and a delicate vine was arranged as a headdress. Mary's "splendid toilette," it was reported, "gave satisfactory evidence of extensive purchases during her late visit to New York."[23] The reception was a huge success and lasted well past the midnight hour. It was the last night the Lincoln family spent in the home at Eighth and Jackson. The next morning they checked into a second floor suite at the Chenery House, where they would spend their final weekend in Springfield.

There was still time to say goodbye to a few old friends, some of whom came in from New Salem. Lincoln was especially glad to see Hannah Armstrong, who had shown him so much kindness in the early days and whose son, Duff, had been acquitted of murder in the famous moonlight case. Hannah had heard rumors that Lincoln's life was in danger, and now she expressed her fear that she would never see her friend alive again. "Hannah," Lincoln joked with her, "if they do kill me I shall never die again." This was not to be the last communication between Lincoln and Hannah. After the war began Duff enlisted with the 85th Illinois Volunteers. Learning that her captured son was languishing in a Louisville hospital, Hannah appealed to Lincoln, who personally interceded and gained Duff's release. Another visitor was Isaac Cogsdale, one of New Salem's pioneers, and Lincoln enjoyed reminiscing about the community he loved. According to Billy Herndon, Lincoln confided to Cogsdale that he still cared for Ann Rutledge and had never really gotten over her death.[24] Many years later, when Mary read this account in Herndon's book, her dislike for him turned to hatred.

Despite his wife's feelings, Lincoln had to say a final farewell to his partner. On Sunday, February 10, Lincoln asked Herndon to meet him at the law office and have a talk. The two men went over various business matters, and Lincoln gave instructions on how certain cases ought to be handled. After a while Lincoln stretched out on the worn couch that rested against the wall. He looked up at the ceiling for some time and then spoke. "Billy, how long have we been together?" Over 16 years, Herndon told him. "We've never had a cross word during all that time, have we?" No, indeed we have not, was the reply. "Billy, there's one thing I have, for some time, wanted you to tell me, but I reckon I ought to apologize for my nerve and curiosity in asking it even now. I want you to tell me, how many times you have been drunk."

Herndon was more than a little surprised at the question and had no ready answer. Lincoln told Herndon that over the years other attorneys—"weak creatures"— had advised him to drop Herndon from the partnership. But Lincoln believed in him and would never consider it. Having made his point, Lincoln gathered up some books and papers and the two men prepared to leave. Nodding at the shingle of Lincoln & Herndon, he said, "Let it hang there undisturbed. Give our clients to understand that the election of a President makes no change in the firm of Lincoln and Herndon. If I live I'm coming back some time, and then we'll go right on practicing law as if nothing had ever happened."[25] Herndon watched as Lincoln walked away, not looking back, into the afternoon sun.

The next day, the day of departure, broke colder with low-hanging clouds and sleet and snow in the air. The Lincolns rose early for the breakfast that was brought up to their room. Mary's excitement over the long-awaited trip was dimmed when her husband told her they would not travel together on the same train, at least not right away. Repeated threats of violence against the president-elect had convinced his managers that Mary and the boys should meet Lincoln later, perhaps in New York. They argued, then finally settled on a compromise. Mary, Willie and Tad would take a separate train to St. Louis, ostensibly to do more shopping. They would meet Lincoln and Robert at Indianapolis, and the family would make the rest of the journey together. "The plucky wife of the President," reported one newspaper, "would see Mr. Lincoln on to Washington, danger or no danger."[26]

Lincoln walked downstairs to the hotel lobby and finished the task he had begun the night before. He tied ropes about several trunks of clothes, books and personal items. Taking some cards from the front desk he wrote: A. LINCOLN, WHITE HOUSE, WASHINGTON, D.C., then affixed the cards to the trunks. At half past seven a carriage arrived, and a drayman named Jameson Jenkins drove Lincoln to the Great Western Railroad depot, where he was surprised to find that a crowd of about 1,000 people had gathered. Lincoln nodded at familiar faces and walked into the depot's waiting room, where his closest friends and advisors were waiting, along with many prominent politicians of both parties. He stood quietly near the door of the overheated room as the people filed past him, some with tears in their eyes, saying their goodbyes. The mood, according to the Illinois *State Journal*, was "subdued and respectful," and Lincoln himself was pale and anxious.

President-elect Abraham Lincoln, February 9, 1861, Springfield, Illinois (the Lincoln Museum, Fort Wayne, Indiana, # 0-43).

Just before eight o'clock the boarding whistle sounded. Now the snow had turned to rain and Lincoln draped his gray shawl around his shoulders, then was led out the door by railway supervisor William Wood. His friends pressed close, some extending their hands, others quietly wishing him a safe journey. Lincoln climbed onto the rear platform and stood behind an iron grate, the protective Ward Hill Lamon standing alongside him, and looked out into the crowd. Mary's carriage arrived and she was assisted to the train by a friend, sculptor Thomas Jones, who opened an umbrella as she took his arm. Lincoln had not prepared a speech, but the moment seemed to require one. He paused for a few moments, and then, ignoring the rain, removed his hat and began to speak:

> Friends,
>   No one who has never been placed in a like position, can understand my feelings at this hour, nor the oppressive sadness I feel at this parting. For more than a quarter of a century I have lived among you, and during all that time I have received nothing but kindness at your hands. Here I have lived from my youth until now I am an old man. Here the most sacred ties of earth were assumed; here all my children were born; and here one of them lies buried. To you, dear friends, I owe all that I have, all that I am.
>   All the strange, chequered past seems to crowd now upon my mind. To-day I leave you; I go to assume a task more difficult than that which devolved upon General Washington. Unless the great God who assisted him, shall be with and aid me, I must fail. But if the same omniscient mind, and Almighty arm that directed and protected him, shall guide and support me, I shall not fail, I shall succeed.

The crowd applauded, but Lincoln was not quite finished. He held up his hand for silence and continued:

> Let us all pray that the God of our fathers may not forsake us now. To him I commend you all — permit me to ask that with equal security and faith, you all will invoke His wisdom and guidance for me. With these few words I must leave you — for how long I know not. Friends, one and all, I must now bid you an affectionate farewell.[27]

The train whistle sounded again and the steam from the *L.M. Wiley's* engine hissed loudly, muffling the hurrahs from the crowd. "We have known Mr. Lincoln for many years," reported the *State Journal*. "We have heard him speak upon a hundred different occasions; but we have never saw him so profoundly affected, nor did he ever utter an address, which seemed to us as full of simple and touching eloquence, so exactly adopted to the occasion, so worthy of the man and the hour. Although it was raining fast when he began to speak, every hat was lifted and every head bent forward to catch the last words of the departing chief."[28] Lincoln ducked into the railcar as the train slowly pulled away from the station. He would never see Springfield again.

9

"The Crisis Is All Artificial"

As soon as he entered the passenger car Lincoln was surrounded by newspapermen. Originally no representatives of the press were to make the trip, but Henry Villard had personally lobbied Lincoln to allow him and a few select others to come aboard. Now Villard, representing the New York *Herald*, joined Edward Baker of the Illinois *State Journal* and Henry M. Smith of the Chicago *Tribune* as press corps representatives. They had not expected Lincoln to make a farewell speech, much less one so emotional and moving, and were not prepared to write down what he said. They insisted that Lincoln repeat his speech so that they could wire it to their editors. Instead Lincoln took a pad and pencil and began to write. After four lines he decided that he would rather dictate; he handed the pad to Nicolay, who had trouble making the lines legible as the train picked up speed and bounced along the track. The newspapermen took Lincoln's speech and huddled with J.J.S. Wilson, superintendent of the Illinois-Mississippi telegraph lines, who carried a portable transmission instrument suitable for dispatches. In time Lincoln's impromptu farewell speech from Springfield would be considered one of his finest, the simple yet heartfelt words comparing even with his Gettysburg Address of 1863.

Lucian Tilton, president of the Great Western Railway and the man who had leased Lincoln's house, was on board, assisted by F.M. Bowen, road superintendent. The two men gave Lincoln a quick tour of the "Presidential Special." Ironically, the locomotive was named for L.M. Wiley, a slaveowner and secessionist who made a fortune growing cotton in South Carolina and for a time was a director of the railroad. Manufactured by the Hinkley Locomotive Works of Boston in 1855, the *Wiley* pulled a baggage car and a passenger car, both newly painted bright yellow, and could reach a speed of 30 miles per hour at full throttle. The coach was handsomely decorated with rich carpet, oaken furniture, comfortable chairs and couches. Red tassels adorned the window shades, and long strips of deep blue silk, studded with silver stars, hung from the walls.

Lincoln's advisors, acting on the recommendation of Thurlow Weed, had entrusted the administrative duties for the journey to William Wood, and had christened him "superintendent of arrangements." Wood had worked with the 18 railroads over whose tracks Lincoln would travel and prepared a timetable that had been distributed to newspapers, city officials and political organizations across the North. He had personally approved of all who rode with Lincoln, many of whom traveled for only

Lincoln's Inaugural Journey
February 11 - 23, 1861

Springfield · Cleveland · Buffalo · Albany · Indianapolis · Pittsburgh · New York · New York · Pennsylvania · Philadelphia · Ohio · Harrisburg · Indiana · New Jersey · Illinois · Cincinnati · Columbus · Delaware · Virginia · Maryland · Washington · Baltimore

Lincoln's inaugural journey, February 11–23, 1861 (map by Tim Mosbacher).

short distances. The passenger coach was jammed to capacity with at least 40 travelers besides Lincoln.

The Illinois delegation on board consisted of virtually all of Lincoln's closest advisors and associates, men who, more than any others, were responsible for his election: Norman Judd, David Davis, Ebenezer Peck, Orville Browning, O.M. Hatch, Jesse Dubois, John Moore, and Governor Richard Yates. Another group of 12 Illinois Democrats, including William Butler, also crowded into the car upon special invitation of Lincoln. The Illinois delegation would travel only as far as the Indiana border.

Because Lincoln was not yet a public official, the government did not pay for the trip or provide security. Lincoln's unofficial military escort on board consisted of volunteers Col. E.V. Sumner of the First United States Cavalry; Maj. David Hunter of Fort Leavenworth; Elmer Ellsworth; Col. James Burgess of Janesville, Wisconsin; and Ward Lamon. (Lamon, heavily armed with daggers and pistols, was the only member of the contingent who would travel the entire way to Washington.) Lincoln's physician and brother-in-law Dr. William Wallace also was on board, along with financial advisor Robert Irwin. Robert Lincoln and a young friend from Springfield, George Latham, were present, along with Nicolay and Hay. The conductor of the Presidential Special was Walter Whitney, who was assisted by engineer Edward H. Fralick, fireman Benjamin Gordon, brakeman Thomas Ross, and baggage master Platt Williamson.[1]

Heading east, the train puffed past the tiny Illinois towns of Jamestown, Dawson, Mechanicsburg, Lanesville, Illiopolis and Summit. All along the way crowds gathered, some on horseback or in wagons, others on foot, to cheer and wave as the train rumbled by, black smoke rising from the chimney stack, flags and streamers snapping in the wind. At Niantic a militia group stood smartly at attention, and at Harristown a brass band played. In about an hour and a half the train pulled into

Decatur, Macon County, its first stop. State law required that passenger trains stop at each county seat, and Lincoln was glad to step down from the train for a few minutes, shake hands and accept good wishes, before boarding again. Lincoln smiled as the train passed through Bement in Piatt County. Here, at the home of banker Frances Bryant, he had met with Stephen Douglas in 1858 and mapped out the schedule of their famous senatorial campaign debates. At Tolona the Great Western crossed the Illinois Central Railroad. As the Special took on firewood and water, Lincoln walked to a nearby grove of trees where a crowd had assembled. He climbed up on a bench and spoke:

> My friends, I am leaving you on an errand of national importance, attended, as you are aware, with considerable difficulties. Let us believe, as some poet has expressed it:
> Behind the cloud the sun is still shining.
> I bid you an affectionate farewell.[2]

The train passed through more prairie towns that Lincoln recognized from his traveling days on the old Eighth Circuit: Philo, Sydney, Homer, Salina, Catlin and Bryant. Crossing the Vermilion River the Special pulled into Danville, seat of Vermilion County and the home of Ward Lamon, who from 1852 to 1857 was Lincoln's associate in the law practice. Now Lamon appeared with Lincoln on the rear platform of the passenger car, and while he smiled and waved to many of his friends he did not speak, for the people only wanted to hear Lincoln. Lincoln told the crowd that "if he had any blessings to dispense, he would certainly dispense the largest and roundest to his good old friends of Vermilion County."[3]

At 12:38 P.M. the Special arrived at State Line, a town divided by the railroad roundhouse that served both the Great Western line, which ended here, and the Toledo and Wabash Railroad, which began. As a new locomotive was connected the entire entourage left the train and took lunch, "indifferent food at double the regular price," at the State Line Hotel.[4] After his meal Lincoln strolled back to the station by way of the public square. Many of the town's 600 residents had assembled there for a glimpse of him, and Lincoln spoke:

> Gentlemen of Indiana:
> I am happy to meet you on this occasion and enter again the state of my early life, and almost of maturity. I am under many obligations to you for your kind reception, and to Indiana for the aid she rendered our cause which is, I think, a just one. Gentlemen, I shall address you at greater length at Indianapolis, but not much greater. Again gentlemen, I thank you for your warm hearted reception.[5]

A delegation of important Indiana politicians had been given the honor of accompanying Lincoln from State Line to Indianapolis. Caleb Smith, Lincoln's nominee for secretary of the interior, and Schuyler Colfax, who had nearly been selected for a cabinet post, boarded the train. They were joined by Henry Lane, who had been elected U.S. senator in November; Thomas Nelson, who had been defeated in his bid for Congress but would be appointed minister to Chile by Lincoln; Gen. John Mansfield, who would become head of the state militia when the war came; and George

Steele, Indiana state senator and head of the legislative reception committee. For the next hour, as the train turned northeast toward the Wabash Valley, these men took their turns conversing with Lincoln. Meanwhile Lamon entertained the entire group by playing his banjo and singing songs, including his favorite "The Lament of the Irish Immigrant." At 2:30 P.M. the train pulled into the station at Lafayette and switched locomotives, and the politicians crowded behind Lincoln as he spoke to a large gathering from the rear platform of the passenger car:

> Fellow Citizens:
> We have seen great changes within the recollection of some of us who are the older. When I first came to the west, some 44 or 45 years ago, at sundown you had completed a journey of some 30 miles which you had commenced at sunrise, and thought you had done well. Now only six hours have elapsed since I left my home in Illinois where I was surrounded by a large concourse of my fellow citizens, almost all of whom I could recognize, and I find myself far from home surrounded by the thousands I now see before me, who are strangers to me. Still we are bound together, I trust by Christianity, civilization and patriotism, and are attached to our country and our whole country. While some of us may differ in political opinions, still we are all united in one feeling for the Union. We all believe in the maintenance of the Union, of every star and every stripe of the glorious flag, and permit me to express the sentiment that upon the Union of the States, there shall be between us no difference. My friends, I meet many friends at every place on my journey, and I should weary myself should I talk at length, therefore permit me to bid you an affectionate farewell.[6]

The train turned southeast through Indiana. Its next scheduled stop was at Thorntown, and Lincoln held up his hand for silence when the crowd shouted for a speech. He had no time for a speech, but would "tell you a story if you promise not to let it out." He had heard of a man, he said, who was a candidate for a county office. The man traveled the district on his horse, who was a steady mount but very slow. On the morning of the convention the man mounted his horse and started for the county seat, but his horse was slower than usual, lagging along despite the man's whip and spurs, biting at every bush. But at this point in the story the engine whistle sounded, and Lincoln had no time to finish. Within 20 minutes Lincoln's train arrived at Lebanon. Lincoln started his story over, but now had time to finish it before a new crowd. The candidate arrived late at the convention, he said, and was defeated. "If I stopped at every station and made a stump speech," said Lincoln, "I won't get to Washington until the inauguration is over." The crowd laughed and Lincoln ducked back inside as the train pulled away.[7]

At exactly 5:00 P.M. the Presidential Special arrived at Indianapolis, its approach harkened by the firing of a 34-gun salute, one for each state in the Union. Oliver P. Morton, Indiana's first native-born governor, was waiting along with a crowd estimated at 20,000 when the train arrived at the junction of West Washington and Missouri streets. As Lincoln appeared on the rear platform deck Morton stood up in an exquisitely styled barouche and delivered his welcome: "You are about to enter upon your official duties under circumstances at once novel and full of difficulty, and it will be the duty of all good citizens, without distinction of party, to yield a cordial and earnest support to every measure of your administration calculated to maintain the Union, promote the national prosperity and restore peace to our unhappy and distracted country."[8] Lincoln replied:

> Governor Morton and fellow citizens of the state of Indiana:
> Most heartily do I thank you for this magnificent reception, and while I cannot take to myself any share of the compliment thus paid, more than that which pertains to a mere instrument, an accidental instrument, perhaps I should say, of a great cause, I yet must look upon it as a most magnificent reception, and as such, most heartily do I thank you for it.
> You have been pleased to address yourselves to me chiefly, in behalf of this glorious Union in which we live, in all of which you have my hearty sympathy, and, as far as may be within my power, will have, one and inseparably, my hearty consideration. While I do not expect, upon this occasion, or on any occasion, till after I get to Washington, to attempt any lengthy speech, I will only say that to the salvation of this Union there needs but one single thing — the hearts of a people like yours. When the people rise in masses on behalf of the Union and the liberties of their country, truly may it be said, "The gates of hell shall not prevail against them."

These words of inspiration struck a chord with the large crowd and were met with cheers and vigorous applause. When the crowd quieted Lincoln continued:

> In all the trying positions in which I shall be placed, and doubtless I shall be placed in many trying ones, my reliance will be placed upon you and the people of the United States — and I wish you to remember now and forever, that it is your business, and not mine; that if the union of these States, and the liberties of this people, shall be lost, it is but little to any one man of fifty-two years of age, but a great deal to the thirty millions of people who inhabit these United States, and to their posterity in all coming time. It is your business to rise up and preserve the Union and liberty, for yourselves, and not for me. I desire they shall be constitutionally preserved.
> I, as already intimated, am but an accidental instrument, temporary, and to serve but for a limited time, but I appeal to you again to constantly bear in mind that with you, and not with politicians, not with Presidents, not with office-seekers, but with you, is the question, "Shall the Union and shall the liberties of this country be preserved to the latest generation?"[9]

As the crowd cheered and shouted in approval ("That's the talk" and "We've got a president now"), Lincoln climbed into the carriage and took a seat next to Morton. Accompanied by Indiana guardsmen, Zouaves, city fire and policemen and several brass bands, the carriage passed through the city's business district to the Bates House, where Lincoln and his guests would spend the night. The crowd of onlookers was so tightly packed near the entrance of the hotel that a human wedge had to form, with Lincoln in the middle, to get him inside. Within minutes Lincoln appeared on the balcony of the hotel, and the nearly overwhelming size of the crowd prompted him to deliver a speech now, instead of later in the evening to state legislators, as was planned. He took from his pocket an envelope labeled "For Indianapolis" and removed the speech he had prepared before he left Springfield:

> It is not possible, in my journey to the national capitol, to address assemblies like this which may do me the great honor to meet me as you have done, but very

briefly. I should be entirely worn out if I were to attempt it. I appear before you now to thank you for this very magnificent welcome which you have given me, and still more for the very generous support which your State recently gave to the political cause of the whole country, and the whole world. Solomon has said, that there is a time to keep silence. We know certain that they mean the same thing while using the same words now, and it perhaps would be as well if they would keep silence.

The words "coercion" and "invasion" are in great use about these days. Suppose we were simply to try if we can, and ascertain what, is the meaning of these words. Let us get, if we can, the exact definitions of these words—not from dictionaries, but from the men who constantly repeat them—what things they mean to express by the words. What, then, is "coercion"? What is "invasion"? Would the marching of an army into South Carolina, for instance, without the consent of her people, and in hostility against them, be coercion of invasion? I very frankly say, I think it would be invasion, and it would be coercion too, if the people of that country were forced to submit. But if the Government, for instance, but simply insists upon holding its own forts, or retaking those forts which belong to it, [*cheers*] or the enforcement of the laws of the United States in the collection of duties upon foreign importations, [*renewed cheers*] or even the withdrawal of the mails from those portions of the country where the mails themselves are habitually violated; would any or all of these things be coercion? Do the lovers of the Union contend that they will resist coercion or invasion of any State, understanding that any or all of these would be coercing or invading a State? If they do, then it occurs to me that the means for the preservation of the Union they so greatly love, in their own estimation, is of a very thin and airy character. (Applause.) If sick, they would consider the little pills of the homeopathist as already too large for them to swallow. In their view, the Union, as a family relation, would not be anything like a regular marriage at all, but only as a sort of free-love arrangement, [*laughter*] to be maintained on what that sect calls passionate attraction. [*Continued laughter.*] But, my friends, enough of this.

What is the particular sacredness of a State? I speak not of that position which is given to a State in and by the Constitution of the United States, for that all of us agree to—we abide by; but that position assumed, that a State can carry with it out of the Union that which it holds in sacredness by virtue of its connection with the Union. I am speaking of that assumed right of a State, as a primary principle, that the Constitution should rule all that is less than itself, and ruin all that is bigger than itself. [*Laughter.*] But, I ask, wherein does consist that right? If a State, in one instance, and a county in another, should be equal in extent of territory, and equal in the number of people, wherein is that State any better than the county? Can a change of name change the right? By what principle of original right is it that one-fiftieth or one-ninetieth of a great nation, by calling themselves a State, have the right to break up and ruin that nation as a matter of original principle? Now, I ask the question—I am not deciding anything [*laughter*] and with the request that you will think somewhat upon that subject and decide for yourselves, if you choose, when you get ready,—where is the mysterious, original right, from principle, for a certain district of country with inhabitants, by merely being called a State, to play tyrant over all its own citizens, and deny the authority of everything greater than itself? [*Laughter.*] I say I am deciding nothing, but simply giving something for you to reflect upon; and, with having said this much, and having declared, in the start, that I will make no long speeches, I thank you again for the magnificent welcome, and bid you an affectionate farewell. [*Cheers.*][10]

Eager newspaper reporters rushed to get Lincoln's speech out over the wires.

Finally he had hinted at the policy his administration might undertake. After months of maddening silence he had spoken, if only briefly, of his resolve to uphold federal authority by holding installations or retaking those seized by secessionists. Utilizing the logic of Webster, Jackson and Clay, and drawing on his skills and precision as a lawyer, Lincoln defined the problem, articulated the absurdity of the opposing position, and set forth the only acceptable solution. His speech was well received in the North. "This little speech has electrified the true Republicans," said the Chicago *Tribune*. The Philadelphia *Press* stated that "there can be no doubt of the general correctness of these opinions," and the New York *Times* opined that the Union must be, as Lincoln pointed out, unbreakable.[11] But many people, no matter their political persuasion, winced at Lincoln's reference to free love, which they perceived as vulgar and unseemly. The language reinforced the perception that Lincoln was an uncouth westerner, undoubtedly unfit to guide the country through its time of peril.

After his speech Lincoln was escorted through crowded hotel corridors to the dining room. He was besieged by well-wishers and autograph seekers even after he sat down; the room was so crowded with guests that Lincoln had to wait 30 minutes before his food arrived. After dinner he was supposed to meet the legislators at a private reception set up by local Republican officials. But security arrangements proved ineffective—"sadly deficient," according to Henry Villard—and the interior of the building was now jammed "like a beehive" with people.[12] Incredibly, 3,000 men and women jostled inside the hotel that evening and managed to meet Lincoln. "Outside my door," wrote John Nicolay to his fiancée, "I hear the crowd pushing and shouting in almost frantic endeavor to get to another parlor in the door of which Mr. Lincoln stands shaking hands with the multitude."[13] Lincoln wearily said that the task was "harder than mauling rails."[14]

Robert Lincoln was not annoyed with the crowd as his father was, but he was restless after a long day on the train. The "Prince of Rails," as he had been titled by Villard, looked for a chance to get away. He eagerly accepted an invitation from some young men his age and headed for a tour of local saloons.

Eventually Lincoln gained some privacy in his suite. He summoned Orville Browning to his parlor, intending to review with him his inaugural address before Browning turned home for Quincy the next day. But he had given the small black satchel containing the only copies of the address to Robert for safekeeping, and Robert was nowhere to be found. Lincoln panicked; he had visions of the press getting hold of his speech and printing it before it would be delivered, and now he paced impatiently for his son to return. At last Robert arrived from his gleeful carousing, and breezily informed his father that he had left the satchel downstairs with the hotel clerk, who had placed it behind the counter with other luggage. Lincoln fairly flew down the stairs to the lobby, and as an astonished clerk and an amused group of bystanders looked on, he began to rummage through the collection of bags and suitcases until he found the all-important satchel and its contents. Relieved, he returned to his room and thrust the empty bag to Robert. "Now, you keep it," he snapped. There was no time now to review anything with Browning, who had gone grumpily to bed. (The hotel was overcrowded and the entire presidential party had to squeeze into just a few rooms. "Had to sleep two in a bed, and accommodations were very poor," complained Browning in his diary. "It is just about as much of that sort of thing as I want."[15]) Lincoln finally retired himself; it had been a very long first day of the journey.

The next day was February 12th, Lincoln's 52nd birthday. He was awakened at dawn by the shouts of the crowd that had gathered outside his balcony. Lincoln appeared on the balcony, acknowledged the crowd, and went back inside. The crowd shouted for him again, and he repeated his appearance. Finally Lincoln appeared for the third time, this time with Robert, who waved to his father's admirers. A Wayne County legislator named Solomon T. Meredith appeared on the adjoining balcony with J.W.T. McMullen, a Methodist minister, who delivered a short speech. McMullen was tall and lanky, and some in the crowd mistook him for Lincoln, cheering his words. But Lincoln had managed to escape. He was driven to Governor Morton's mansion on Market Street for breakfast, and from there he went to the statehouse, where he met informally with politicians, both Democrat and Republican.

He was back at the hotel by midmorning. He met with Browning, who read the inaugural address draft and made a suggestion. He advised Lincoln to omit any mention of reclaiming federal property that had been seized by secessionists, for that would be taken for aggression. It would be enough, Browning felt, to simply express the government's intentions of holding what it already had. Lincoln agreed and made the change.

His old friends Jesse Dubois and Ebenezer Peck visited and offered words of encouragement, and snipped off a lock of Lincoln's hair as a keepsake. Before they said goodbye they cornered Ward Lamon and reminded him unnecessarily of the importance of protecting Lincoln on this trip. By 11:00 A.M. Lincoln and his party were back at the Union Depot. Former president Rutherford B. Hayes was in the audience, and noted with amusement Lincoln's habit of bowing uncomfortably to crowds: "His chin rises—his body breaks in two at the hips—there is bend of the knees at a queer angle." Like everyone else who had never seen Lincoln, Hayes commented on his appearance. "Homely as L. is," he wrote, "if you can get a good view of him by *day light* when he is talking he is by no means ill looking."[16] After some send-off speeches by local dignitaries, the train prepared to pull out.

Minutes before the whistle blew, Mary and the two younger boys arrived, having traveled all night from Springfield. She had been so afraid that they would miss the train at Indianapolis that she instructed the conductor to wire ahead, advising that they were on their way. Reunited with his family, Lincoln's mood brightened as the train pulled away. Now under the control of the Indianapolis and Cincinnati Railroad, the locomotive *Samuel Wiggins*, named for an Ohio banker, pulled four coaches, all festively decorated in red, white and blue bunting. A beautiful blue banner decorated with 34 stars encircled the smoke stack. Portraits of the previous 14 presidents and the newest president-elect, all surrounding a portrait of George Washington, covered the front of the locomotive, and a rosette, draped flags, and a gilded eagle adorned the rail of the rear. American flags flew from the sides of the entire train. The newly installed Loughbridge safety braking system was designed to eliminate rough, jarring stops, making travel much more comfortable than those systems still operating under the old link-and-pin coupling system.

Lincoln and his family now had their own private car, lavishly decorated with plush crimson walls draped with blue silk, and a hand-carved frescoed ceiling. Even Mary was impressed, reporters noting that she was "amiable and vivacious," and "kept up a spirited conversation during the entire journey, although much fatigued by night travel." The younger boys Willie and Tad amused themselves by asking people, "Do you want to see Old Abe?" and then pointing to anyone but their father. And Lincoln was "merriest among the merry"; his never-ending supply of jokes and stories "kept those around him in a continual roar of laughter."[17]

From Indianapolis the train rolled southeast, stopping briefly at Shelbyville and Greensburg. Lincoln showed himself from the rear car platform, waved to the crowds and listened appreciatively to glee clubs and brass bands. The last stop in Indiana was at Lawrenceburg, separated from Kentucky by the Ohio River. Encouraged by the crowd that had gathered at the station, Lincoln spoke:

> My fellow countrymen. You call upon me for a speech; I have none to give to you, and have not sufficient time to devote to it if I had. I suppose you are all Union men here [*cheers and cries of "Right"*], and I suppose that you are in favor of doing full justice to all, whether on that side of the river [*pointing to the Kentucky shore*], or on your own. [*Loud cheering and cries of "We are."*] If the politicians and leaders of parties were as true as the people, there would be little fear that the peace of the country would be disturbed. I have been selected to fill an important office for a brief period, and am now, in your eyes, invested with an influence which will soon pass away; but should my administration prove to be a very wicked one, or what is more probable, a very foolish one, if you, the people, are but true to yourselves and to the Constitution, there is but little harm I can do, thank God![18]

Lincoln had intended that the train pass through parts of his native Kentucky, but for unknown reasons that plan was altered, and the short speech he had prepared went undelivered.[19] Within minutes of leaving Lawrenceburg the Special crossed into Ohio, slowing down outside of the cemetery at North Bend so that Lincoln could pay his respects at the grave of former president William Henry Harrison. At just after 3:00 P.M. the train pulled into the Ohio and Mississippi Railroad depot in Cincinnati. A tremendous crowd cheered him, and Robert Hosea, acting as chairman of the welcoming committee, invited him to speak. Lincoln said:

> Mr. Chairman: I thank you, citizens of Cincinnati, Ohio, and Kentucky, for this reception. As I understand it is a part of the programme that I will address you a little more at length at the Burnet House, I will, for the present, postpone the making of any remarks. I will proceed at once from here. I remark here that it is not my purpose to make a lengthy speech.[20]

Lincoln stepped into a carriage with Mayor Richard Bishop as the crowd cheered. Drawn by six white horses and escorted by the Washington Dragoon Regiment and a police squadron, the carriage led a procession through downtown Cincinnati. Massive crowds lined the streets and looked on from windows and rooftops. Lincoln-Hamlin banners hung from flagpoles, and portraits of the pair adorned doorways and fenceposts. Bands played and ladies fluttered white handkerchiefs as Lincoln passed by, bowing and waving to his admirers. At the local orphanage a group of children sang "Hail, Columbia!" and waved miniature American flags, and as another group sang the "Star-Spangled Banner," Lincoln accepted a floral bouquet from their leader, then kissed her on both cheeks. Two hours later, after passing by an estimated 100,000 people, the procession finally arrived at the Burnet House.

Lincoln went immediately to a second-floor balcony, where he was introduced by Mayor Bishop, and read his prepared speech. He followed familiar themes: the importance of a perpetual national government, respect for political opposition, and reassurances to the people of the South (some of whom, Kentuckians, were in the crowd):

> Mr. Mayor, ladies and gentlemen: Twenty four hours ago, at the Capital of Indiana, I said to myself I have never seen so many people assembled together in winter weather. I am no longer able to say that. But it is what might reasonably have been expected–that this great city of Cincinnati would thus acquit herself on such an occasion. My friends, I am entirely overwhelmed by the magnificence of the reception which has been given, I will not say to me, but to the President-elect of the United States of America. [*Loud cheering.*] Most heartily do I thank you, one and all for it. [*Applause.*]
>
> I am reminded by the address of your worthy Mayor, that this reception is given not by any one political party, and even if I had not been so reminded by His Honor I could not have failed to know the fact by the extent of the multitude I see before me now. I could not look upon this vast assemblage without being made aware that all parties were united in this reception. [*Applause.*] This is as it should be. It is as it should have been if Senator Douglas had been elected. It is as it should have been if Mr. Bell had been elected–as it should have been if Mr. Breckinridge had been elected–as it should ever be when any citizen of the United States is constitutionally elected President of the Untied States. [*Great applause.*] Allow me to say that I think what has occurred here to-day could not have occurred in any other country on the face of the globe without the influence of the free institutions which we have unceasingly enjoyed for three-quarters of a century. [*Applause.*] There is no country where the people can turn out and enjoy this day precisely as they please, save under the benign influence of the free institutions of our land. [*Applause.*]
>
> I hope that, although we have some threatening National difficulties now–I hope that while these free institutions shall continue to be in the enjoyment of millions of free people of the United States, we will see repeated every four years what we now witness. [*Applause.*]
>
> In a few short years, I and every other individual man who is now living will pass away. I hope that our national difficulties will also pass away, and I hope we shall see in the streets of Cincinnati–good old Cincinnati–for centuries to come, once every four years her people give such a reception as this to the constitutionally elected President of the whole United States. [*Applause.*] I hope you shall all join in that reception, and that you shall also welcome your brethren far across the river to participate in it. We will welcome them in every State of the Union, no matter where they are from. From away South we shall extend them a cordial good will when our present differences shall have been forgotten and blown to the winds forever. [*Applause.*]
>
> I have spoken but once, before this, in Cincinnati. That was a year previous to the late Presidential election. On that occasion, in a playful manner, but with sincere words, I addressed much of what I said, to the Kentuckians. I gave my opinion that we, as Republicans, would ultimately beat them as Democrats; but that they could postpone that result longer by nominating Senator Douglas for the

Presidency than they could in any other way. They did not, in any true sense of the word, nominate Douglas, and the result has come certainly as soon as ever I expected. I also told them how I expected they would be treated, after they should have been beaten; and I now wish to re-call their attention to what I then said upon that subject. I then said: "When we do, as we say, beat you, you perhaps want to know what we will do with you. I will tell you, so far as I am authorized to speak for the opposition, what we mean to do with you. We mean to treat you, as near as we possibly can, as Washington, Jefferson, and Madison treated you. We mean to leave you alone, and in no way to interfere with your institution; to abide by all and every compromise of the constitution, and, in a work, coming back to the original proposition, to treat you, so far as degenerated men (if we have degenerated) may, according to the examples of those noble fathers–Washington, Jefferson and Madison. We mean to remember that you are as good as we; that there is no difference between us, other that the difference of circumstances. We mean to recognize, and bear in mind always, that you have as good hearts in your bosoms as other people, or as we claim to have, and treat you accordingly."

Fellow citizens of Kentucky–friends–brethren, may I call you–in my new position, I see no occasion, and feel no inclination, to retract a word of this. [*Applause.*] If it shall not be made good, be assured, the fault shall not be mine. [*Applause.*]

And now, fellow citizens of Ohio, have you, who agree with him who now addressed you, in political sentiment–have you ever entertained other sentiments towards our brethren of Kentucky than those I have expressed to you. [*Loud and continued cries of "No."*] If not, then why shall we not, as heretofore, be recognized and acknowledged as brethren again, living in peace and harmony one with another? [*Cries of "We will."*] I take your response as the most reliable evidence that it may be so, along with other evidence, trusting that the good sense of the American people, on all sides of all rivers in America, under the Providence of God, who has never deserted us, that we shall again be brethren, forgetting all parties–ignoring all parties. My friends I now bid you farewell. [*Long continued applause.*][21]

While Lincoln dined with his family that evening at the hotel, several thousand members representing 18 German industrial associations marched through the streets of Cincinnati to the music of brass bands, illuminated by torchlight, arriving at the Burnet at precisely 8:00 P.M. Shortly thereafter their leader, an iron molder named Frederick H. Oberkleine, appeared with Lincoln on the balcony, and introduced him to the group. "We, the Germans," said Oberkleine, "free workingmen of Cincinnati, avail ourselves of this opportunity to assure you, our chosen Chief Magistrate, of our sincere and heartfelt regard. You won our votes as the champion of free labor and free homesteads.... We trust you, the self-reliant, because self-made man will uphold the Constitution and the laws against secret treachery and avowed treason.... If to this end you should be in need of men, the German free workingmen, with others, will rise as one man and at your call, ready to risk their lives in the effect to maintain the victory already won by freedom over slavery."[22]

Lincoln did not wish to speak of war. Rather, he outlined his beliefs in equality for all men, including those born outside U.S. boundaries. He said:

> Mr. Chairman: I thank you and those whom you represent, for the compliment you have paid me, by tendering me this address. In so far as there is an allusion to our present national difficulties, which expresses, as you have said, the views of

the gentleman present, I shall have to beg pardon for not entering fully upon the questions, which the address you have now read, suggests.

I deem it my duty—a duty which I owe to my constituents—to you, gentlemen, that I should wait until the last moment, for a development of the present national difficulties, before I express myself decidedly what course I shall pursue. I hope, then, not to be false to anything that you have to expect of me.

I agree with you, Mr. Chairman, that the working men are the basis of all governments, for the plain reason that they are the most numerous, and as you added that those were the sentiments of the gentlemen present, representing not only the working class, but citizens of other callings than those of the mechanic, I am happy to concur with you in these sentiments, not only of the native born citizens, but also of the Germans and foreigners from other countries.

Mr. Chairman, I hold that while man exists, it is his duty to improve not only his own condition, but to assist in ameliorating mankind; and therefore, without entering upon the details of the question, I will simply say, that I am for those means which will give the greatest good to the greatest number.

In regard to the Homestead Law, I have to say that in so far as the Government lands can be disposed of, I am in favor of cutting up the wild lands into parcels, so that every poor man may have a home.

In regard to the Germans and foreigners, I esteem them no better than other people, nor any worse. [*Cries of "Good."*] It is not my nature, when I see a people borne down by the weight of their shackles—the oppression of tyranny—to make their life more bitter by heaping upon them greater burdens; but rather would I do all in my power to raise the yoke, than to add anything that would tend to crush them.

Inasmuch as our country is extensive and new, and the countries of Europe are densely populated, if there are any abroad who desire to make this the land of the adoption, it is not in my heart to throw aught in their way, to prevent them from coming to the United States.

Mr. Chairman, and Gentlemen, I will bid you an affectionate farewell.[23]

Lincoln returned to the dining hall. He refused to speak further but agreed to stand in a reception line and shook hands for an hour. Finally, exhausted, he was led upstairs to his suite where Mary and the boys were already asleep.

At 6:15 the next morning he was awakened for breakfast, then endured another long procession to the depot for the 9:00 sendoff. The Special now consisted of a locomotive, three coaches and one baggage car. The press and railroad personnel occupied the first coach, staff and political representatives the second, and Lincoln and his family the rear coach. A rumor circulated that threats had been made to blow up the train or at least throw it off its track. Thus a pilot engine preceded the Special as a precautionary measure. Traveling northeast en route to the Ohio state capitol at Columbus, where Lincoln would deliver a prepared speech to the legislature, the train stopped at Milford, Loveland, Miamiville, Morrow and Corwin, and although Lincoln showed himself to the assembled crowds he did not speak, for he had developed a cold and was growing increasingly hoarse. He seemed to grow increasingly uncomfortable the farther from home he went. While he "satisfied the public curiosity," wrote Henry Villard, "he disappointed, by his appearance, most of those who saw him for the first time. I could see that impression clearly written on the faces of his rustic audiences. Nor was this surprising, for they certainly saw the most unprepossessing features, the gawkiest figure, and the most awkward manners."[24] At Xenia a luncheon had been prepared for Lincoln and his party, but hungry people who had waited all morning for a glimpse of him had helped themselves to the food, and when the Special pulled into the depot at 1:00 P.M. there was nothing left to eat. Lincoln and the other travelers were forced to wait until dinner was served that evening.

At London, about 25 miles from Columbus, a uniformed brass band had assembled to serenade Lincoln, and he referred to it as he spoke:

> Fellow citizens: I do not appear before you to make a speech, and have not
> strength nor time to do so. If I were to undertake to make a speech at every sta-
> tion, I should be completely tuckered out before I reached the capital. I perceive a
> band of music present, and while the iron horse stops to water himself, I would
> prefer they should discourse in their more eloquent music than I am capable of.[25]

As the Special rolled northeast Lincoln had time to reflect on the connections he had with the state of Ohio, for although he had never resided there his legal and political connections with the state ran deep. An antislavery congressman from Jefferson, Ohio, named Joshua Giddings influenced the young Lincoln in the 1840s when both men roomed at Mrs. Spriggs' boarding house in Washington. Another Ohioan, Thomas Corwin of Lebanon, was the only senator to lobby on Lincoln's behalf in his unsuccessful bid to be named commissioner of the land office in 1848. That same year the head of the newly created Department of the Interior, Thomas Ewing of Cincinnati, offered Lincoln the governorship of Ohio, which he refused.

Lincoln occasionally practiced law in Ohio. In 1855, in a case involving the patent rights of the McCormick reaper, Lincoln was part of a team of attorneys hired by inventor John H. Manny. Lincoln prepared thoroughly for the case and traveled to Cincinnati for the trial, in which he fully expected to play an important role. But the other members of the team, which included Edwin Stanton, were unimpressed with the country lawyer's appearance and mannerisms, and shunned him. While Lincoln was ultimately impressed with how Stanton, in particular, handled the case (he would name Stanton, a Democrat, his secretary of war in 1862), he was so disillusioned by the entire experience that he vowed never again to return to Cincinnati.

Lincoln's embarrassment quickly faded. By 1859 many Ohio political leaders were touting him for the Republican presidential nomination, much to the chagrin of Governor Salmon Chase, who coveted the position for himself. At the convention in Chicago in May 1860, Lincoln's name was seconded into nomination by an Ohioan named Columbus Delano. After Lincoln's advisors made promises of cabinet posts for various candidates, Ohio delegation leader David Carrter announced the switch of four Ohio votes to Lincoln on the third ballot, and the nomination was his.

The Special neared Columbus. Just a week earlier, on February 7, Lincoln had written to Governor William G. Dennison, accepting his invitation to visit the State Capitol "with profound gratitude for the mark of respect and honor thus cordially tendered me by you." But, Lincoln had added in a postscript, "Please arrange no ceremonies which will waste time."[26] Dennison ignored the request, naming a joint legislative committee of House and Senate members to work cooperatively with the Columbus City Council and plan festivities. The committee worked feverishly to plan a suitable program, barely finishing in time for publication in the morning edition of the February 13 Ohio *State Journal*. Now at a few minutes after 2:00 P.M. the Special crossed the Scioto River bridge outside of town, and a lookout fired his weapon in welcome, the first in a 34-gun salute.

The Special pulled into Union Station, and when Lincoln, Mary and their three sons emerged from their car "the air was rent with a deafening shout."[27] Lincoln was taken directly to the state Capitol on High Street, and as his carriage slowly passed sidewalks filled with admirers he stood and bowed, acknowledging the cheers. Once inside, Lincoln walked unescorted to the front of the overflowing Assembly Chamber. "The impression which the appearance of the President-elect created was most agreeable," said the Ohio *State Journal*. "His great height was conspicuous even in the crowd of goodly men, and lifted him fully in view as he walked down the aisle. When he took the Speaker's stand, a better opportunity was afforded to look at the man upon whom more hopes hang than upon any other living. At first the kindness and amiability of his face strikes you; but as he speaks, the greatness and determination of his nature are apparent. Something in his manner, even more than his words, told how deeply he was affected by the enthusiasm of the people…. There was the simplicity of greatness in his unassuming and confiding manner that won its way to instant admiration. He looked somewhat worn with travel and the fatigues of popularity, but warmed to the cordiality of his reception."[28] Lincoln was introduced by Lieutenant Governor Robert C. Kirk:

> Sir: On this day, and probably this very hour, the Congress of the United States will declare the verdict of the people, making you their president. It is my pleasurable duty, in behalf of the people of Ohio, speaking through this General Assembly, to welcome you to their Capitol.
>
> Never in the history of this Government has such fearful responsibility rested upon the Chief Executive of the nation as will now devolve upon you. Never since the memorable time our patriotic fathers gave existence to the American Republic, have the people looked with such intensity of feeling to the inauguration and future policy of a President, as they do to yours.
>
> I need not assure you that the people of Ohio have full confidence in your ability and patriotism, and will respond to you in their loyalty to the Union and the Constitution. It would seem, sir, that the great problem of self-government is to be solved under your administration. All nations are deeply interested in its solution, and they wait with breathless anxiety to know whether this form of government which has been the admiration of the world is to be a failure or not.
>
> It is the earnest and united prayer of our people, that the same kind Providence which protected us in our colonial struggles and has attended us thus far in our prosperity and greatness, will so imbue your mind with wisdom, that you may dispel the dark clouds that hang over our political horizon, and thereby secure the return of harmony and fraternal feelings to our now distracted and unhappy country. God grant their prayer may be fully realized! Again I bid you a cordial welcome to our Capitol.[29]

Lincoln nodded in thanks, and then offered words of confidence and reassurance:

> Mr. President and Mr. Speaker and Gentlemen of the General Assembly:
> It is true, as has been said by the President of the Senate, that very great respon-

sibility rests upon me in the position to which the votes of the American people have called me. I am deeply sensible of that weighty responsibility. I cannot but know what you all know, that, without a name, perhaps without a reason why I should have a name, there has fallen upon me a task such as did not rest even upon the Father of his country, and so feeling I cannot but turn and look for the support without which it will be impossible for me to perform that great task. I turn, then, and look to the American people and to that God who has never forsaken them. Allusion has been made to the interest felt in relation to the policy of the new administration. In this I have received from some a degree of credit for having kept silence, and from others some deprecation. I still think that I was right. In the varying and repeatedly shifting scenes of the present, and without a precedent which could enable me to judge by the past, it has seemed fitting that before speaking upon the difficulties of the country, I should have gained a view of the whole field, to be sure, after all, being at liberty to modify and change the course of policy, as future events may make a change necessary. I have not maintained silence from any want of real anxiety. It is a good thing that there is no more than anxiety, for there is nothing going wrong. It is a consoling circumstance that when we look out there is nothing that really hurts anybody. We entertain different views upon political questions, but nobody is suffering anything. This is a most consoling circumstance, and from it we may conclude that all we want is time, patience and a reliance on that God who has never forsaken this people. Fellow citizens, what I have said, I have said altogether extemporaneously, and I will now come to a close.[30]

Lincoln's remarks were met with deafening applause. To his surprise, Governor Dennison stepped forward and announced that Lincoln would personally greet his supporters in the Capitol rotunda, and Lincoln was led wearily to the north stairs. The plan was for the people to proceed orderly past Lincoln and exit through the opposite door, but as soon as the doors were opened hundreds of people rushed in towards him. Lincoln did the best he could, shaking with both hands, nearly engulfed from the pressure, finally backing up the stairs. A fist fight broke out between two men, and then a woman fainted from the excitement. Lincoln retired to the safety of the governor's office.

Here Lincoln learned that in Washington the electoral vote had proceeded in an orderly fashion, and Congress had confirmed that he was now officially the president-elect of the United States. Lincoln had been concerned, with good reason, that the vote might not be tabulated. Rumors had flown, and intelligence reports had verified, that secessionist forces had half-heartedly conspired to prevent the vote. Armed seceders had planned to enter the House chamber just before the vote and stage a disturbance. In the meantime, the Capitol itself was to be seized just as Fort Moultrie and other federal installations had been taken. But a Peace Conference delegate had notified Winfield Scott, who posted armed guards at all Capitol entrances, checking visitors for any weapons and inspecting credentials. A regiment of army regulars roamed the floor, dressed in civilian clothes but armed with rifles, and an extra supply of arms and ammunition was locked in nearby conference rooms. There was no disturbance, and Vice President John Breckinridge calmly announced to a joint session of Congress that the electoral vote was now official.

That evening Lincoln and Mary were the guests of honor at a reception at the home of Governor Dennison, attended by local and state officials and members of the press. A lavish buffet table satisfied their hunger, and despite the day's ordeal Lincoln looked refreshed in dignified evening attire, while Mary struck one reporter as "a very pleasant lady, courteous, unassuming and with a smile for all, dressed in a very rich, dark-figured silk with headdress to match."[31] After dinner the Lincolns made brief appearances at the Capitol at a public reception, and then a military ball at Deshler Hall, where Lincoln twice led the grand promenade around the room.

After a short night's rest at the governor's residence, the next morning the Lincolns boarded the Special, now headed by the locomotive *Washington City*. Although it was raining steadily some 200 people showed up before the 8:00 A.M. departure, intent on riding along to the state line; they were quietly advised that this was not possible. The first stop was Newark, where local organizers anticipated erroneously that Lincoln would address the crowd. Lincoln gently corrected them:

> I understand that arrangements were made for something of a speech from me here, when the train moved down, but it has gone so far that it has deprived me of addressing the many fair ladies assembled, while it has deprived them of observing my very interesting countenance. It is impossible for me to make you a speech: there is not time, so I bid you farewell.[32]

At the tiny town of Cadiz Junction, Lincoln and his party were taken to a local hotel that featured a dining hall. Here a luncheon was prepared under the direction of Mrs. T.L. Jewett, wife of the president of the Steubenville and Indiana Railroad. After the meal Lincoln appeared at the rear platform and told the crowd that he could not speak because he was "too full for utterance" but that he hoped that they would "pass a vote of thanks to the lady of the house" for the wonderful dinner.[33]

The sun came out at Steubenville, where nearly 10,000 people, including a good number of Virginians from across the Ohio river, assembled around a carpeted stage built next to the train tracks. As cannon roared around him, Lincoln was led to the stage. He sat contentedly and listened to a ladies' choir sing "The Red, White and Blue." The Honorable W.R. Lloyd, circuit court judge, introduced Lincoln to the crowd, assuring him that "they were all attached to the Union…. To you, sir, we entrust our hopes with confidence." Lincoln replied:

> Mr. Chairman and Fellow-Citizens: The subject of the short address which has been made to me, though not an unfamiliar one, involves so many points, that in the short time allotted to me, I shall not be able to make a full and proper response. Though the people have made me, by electing me, the instrument to carry out the wishes expressed in the address, I greatly fear that I shall not be the repository of the ability to do so. Indeed I know I shall not, more than in purpose, unless sustained by the great body of the people, and by the Divine Power, without whose aid we can do nothing. We everywhere express devotion to the Constitution. I believe there is no difference in this respect, whether on this or on the other side of this majestic stream. I understand that on the other side, among our dissatisfied brethren, they are satisfied with the Constitution of the United States, if they can have their rights under the Constitution. The question is, as to what the Constitution means—"What are their rights under the Constitution?" That is all. To decide that, who shall be the judge? Can you think of any other, than the voice of the people? If the majority does not control, the minority must—would that be right? Would that be just or generous? Assuredly not! Though the majority

may be wrong, and I will not undertake to say that they were not wrong in elect-ing me, yet we must adhere to the principle that the majority shall rule. By your Constitution you have another chance in four years. No great harm can be done by us in that time — in that time there can be nobody hurt. If anything goes wrong, however, and you find you have made a mistake, elect a better man next time. There are plenty of them.

The whistle of the *Washington City* blew, and as smoke appeared from the stack. Lincoln concluded his remarks:

> These points involve the discussion of many questions which I have not time to consider. I merely give them to you for your reflection. I almost regret that I alluded to it at all.
>   Ladies, gentlemen and friends, I thank you for this kind and overwhelming reception, and bid you farewell.[34]

It was 2:30 in the afternoon. The next stop was Wellesville, about 20 miles straight north of Steubenville. Here Lincoln appeared on the rear platform and told the crowd he had no time for a speech. A drunken man pushed his way to the front of the crowd and caught Lincoln's attention, shouting loudly that he had voted for Douglas. Lincoln shook hands with the man and told him that "if he and the other friends of Mr. Douglas would assist in keeping the ship of state afloat, perhaps Mr. Douglas might be selected to pilot it sometime in the future. But if it were allowed to go to pieces now, Mr. Douglas would, of course, stand no chance hereafter." As the crowd laughed and cheered, Lincoln promised that he "would do what he could to preserve the Union, and if the people would do the same, the thing would be accomplished."[35] The Special turned east and crossed over into Pennsylvania. It stopped at Rochester, just outside of Pittsburgh, and Lincoln made his usual brief remarks. As he turned to go back into the car a voice shouted out "What will you do with the secessionists then?" Lincoln turned toward the voice and replied, "My friend, that is a matter which I have under very grave consideration."[36]

Just outside of Freedom, Pennsylvania, a freight train had broken down, block-ing the track. The Special sat for several hours while the track was cleared, and it became obvious that Lincoln and his party would not make the scheduled 5:00 P.M. arrival time in Pittsburgh. As the party waited it began to rain, adding to the frus-tration of everyone. Finally, after a three-hour wait, the Special began to move again. It pulled into Pittsburgh at 8:00 P.M., and because of the late arrival the crowd had thinned, and the welcoming parade was cancelled. Instead Lincoln was taken directly to the Monongahela House, where he would spend the night. Despite the hour many supporters had gathered inside the hotel lobby, and when someone found Lincoln a chair he stood on it and addressed the boisterous crowd:

> Fellow citizens: We had an accident upon the road to-day, and were delayed till this late hour. I am sorry for this, inasmuch as it was my desire and intention to address the citizens of Pennsylvania, briefly, this evening, on what is properly styled their peculiar interest. And I still hope that some arrangement may be made to-morrow morning which will afford me the pleasure of talking to a larger num-ber of my friends than can assemble in this hall. [*"Go on now; there's enough*

here."] I have a great regard for Allegheny County. It is "the banner county of the Union" [*cheers*], and rolled up an immense majority for what I, at least, consider a good cause. By a mere accident, and not through any merit of mine, it happened that I was the representative of that cause, and I acknowledge with all sincerity the high honor you have conferred on me. [*"Three cheers for Honest Abe," and a voice saying "It was no accident that elected you, but your own merits, and the worth of the cause."*] I thank you, my fellow citizen, for your kind remark, and trust that I feel a becoming sense of the responsibility resting upon me. [*"We know you do."*]

I could not help thinking, my friends, as I traveled in the rain through your crowded streets, on my way here, that if all that people were in favor of the Union, it can certainly be in no great danger — it will be preserved. [*A voice — "We are all Union men." Another voice — "That's so." A third voice — "No compromise." A fourth — "Three cheers for the Union."*] But I am talking too long, longer than I ought. [*"Oh, no! Go on; split another rail." Laughter.*] You know that it has not been my custom, since I started on the route to Washington, to make long speeches; I am rather inclined to silence, [*"That's right"*] and whether that be wise or not, it is at least more unusual now-a-days to find a man who can hold his tongue than to find one who cannot. [*Laughter, and a voice — " no railery Abe."*] I thank you, sincerely, for the warm reception I have received, and in the morning, if an arrangement can be made, of which I am not yet certain, I may have something to say to you of that "peculiar interest of Pennsylvania" before mentioned. [*"Say it now, we are all attention."*] Well, my friends, as it is not much I have to say, and as there may be some uncertainty of another opportunity, I will utter it now, if you will permit me to procure a few notes that are in my overcoat pocket. [*"Certainly we will," and cheers.*][37]

Lincoln was taken upstairs to his room, but hunger and fatigue overcame him. He stepped out onto the balcony and announced that his speech must wait until morning:

> Fellow citizens, I have been prevailed upon by your committee to postpone my intended remarks to you until to-morrow, when we hope for more favorable weather, and I have made my appearance now only to afford you an opportunity of seeing, as clearly as may be, my beautiful countenance! [*Loud laughter, and cheers.*] In the morning at half-past eight o'clock I propose speaking to you from this place. Until then, I bid you all good night.[38]

Tired and hungry, Lincoln had a quiet supper with Mary and went to bed. As he promised, the next morning, Friday the 15th, he appeared on the same balcony with Pittsburgh mayor George Wilson. Although it was still raining steadily, an enormous crowd had gathered below, some with umbrellas and some without, and Lincoln delivered the speech he had prepared in Springfield, at 30 minutes the longest speech of the trip:

> Mayor Wilson and Citizens of Pennsylvania: I most cordially thank his Honor Mayor Wilson, and the citizens of Pittsburgh generally for this flattering reception. It is the more grateful, because I know that, while it is not given to me alone, but to the cause which I represent, yet it is given under circumstances which clearly prove to me that there is good will and sincere feeling at the bottom of it.
> And here, fellow citizens, I may remark that in every short address I have made to the people, and in every crowd through which I have passed of late, some allusion has been made to the present distracted condition of the country. It is natu-

rally expected that I should say something upon this subject, but to touch upon it at all would involve an elaborate discussion of a great many questions and circumstances, would require more time than I can at present command, and would not yet be fully developed themselves. [*Immense cheering, and cries of "good!" "That's right!"*]

The condition of the country, fellow-citizens, is an extraordinary one, and fills the mind of every patriot with anxiety and solicitude. My intention is to give this subject all the consideration which I possibly can before I speak fully and definitely in regard to it — so that, when I do speak, I may be as nearly right as possible. And when I do speak, fellow-citizens, I hope to say nothing in opposition to the spirit of the Constitution, contrary to the integrity of the Union, or which will in any way prove inimical to the liberties of the people or the peace of the whole country. And, furthermore, when the time arrives for me to speak on this great subject, I hope to say nothing which will disappoint the reasonable expectations of any man, or disappoint the people generally throughout the country, especially if their expectations have been based upon anything which I may have heretofore said.

Lincoln pointed south towards Virginia and continued, his voice rising:

Notwithstanding the troubles across the river, there is really no crisis, springing from anything in the government itself. In plain words, there is really no crisis except an artificial one! What is there now to warrant the condition of affairs presented by our friends "over the river?" Take even their own view of the questions involved, and there is nothing to justify the course which they are pursuing. I repeat it, then — there is no crisis, excepting such a one as may be gotten up at any time by designing politicians. My advice, then, under such circumstances, is to keep cool. If the great American people will only keep their temper, on both sides of the line, the troubles will come to an end, and the question which now distracts the country will be settled just as surely as all other difficulties of like character which have originated in this government have been adjusted. Let the people on both sides keep their self-possession, and just as other clouds have cleared away in due time, so will this, and this great nation shall continue to prosper as heretofore. But, fellow citizens, I have spoken longer on this subject than I had intended in the outset — and I shall say no more at present.

Lincoln now moved to another area of interest — taxation. Playing to his audience of Pennsylvanians, and with full understanding of the importance of a tariff policy to the mining industry, he continued:

Fellow citizens, as this is the first opportunity which I have had to address a Pennsylvania assemblage, it seems a fitting time to indulge in a few remarks upon the important question of a tariff — a subject of great magnitude, and one which is attended with many difficulties, owing to the great variety of interests which it involves. So long as direct taxation for the support of government is not resorted to, a tariff is necessary. The tariff is to the government what a meal is to the family; but, while this is admitted, it still becomes necessary to modify and change its operations according to new interests and new circumstances. So far there is little difference of opinion among politicians, but the question as to how far imposts may be adjusted for the protection of home industry, gives rise to various views and objections. I must confess that I do not understand this subject in all its multiform bearings, but I promise you that I will give it my closest attention, and endeavor to comprehend it more fully. And here I may remark that the Chicago platform contains a plank upon this subject, which I think should be regarded as law for the incoming administration. In fact, this question, as well as all other subjects embodied in that platform, should not be varied from what we gave the people to understand would be our policy when we obtained their votes. Permit me, fellow citizens, to read the tariff plank of the Chicago platform, or rather, to have it read in your hearing by one who has younger eyes than I have.

John Hay then stepped forward and read the 12th section of the Republican platform adopted at the convention in Chicago:

"That, while providing revenue for the support of the General Government by duties upon imposts, sound policy requires such an adjustment of the imposts as to encourage the development of the industrial interest of the whole country, and we commend that policy of national exchanges which secures to the working men liberal wages, to agriculture remunerating prices, to mechanics and manufacturers an adequate reward for their skill, labor and enterprise, and to the nation commercial prosperity and independence."

Lincoln continued:

Now, fellow citizens, I must confess that there are shades of difference in construing even this plank of the platform. But I am not now intending to discuss these differences, but merely to give you some general ideas upon this subject. I have long thought that if there be any article of necessity which can be produced at home with as little or nearly the same labor as abroad, it would be better to protect that article. Labor is the true standard of value. If a bar of iron, got out of the mines of England, and a bar of iron taken from the mines of Pennsylvania, be produced at the same cost, it follows that if the English bar be shipped from Manchester to Pittsburgh, and the American bar from Pittsburgh to Manchester, the cost of carriage is appreciably lost. [Laughter.] If we had no iron here, then we should encourage its shipment from foreign countries; but not when we can make it as cheaply in our own country. This brings us back to our first proposition, that if any article can be produced at home with nearly the same cost as abroad, the carriage is lost labor.

The treasury of the nation is in such a low condition at present that this subject now demands the attention of Congress, and will demand the immediate attention of the new Administration. The tariff bill now before Congress may or may not pass at the present session. I confess I do not understand the precise provisions of this bill, and I do not know whether it can be passed by the present Congress or not. It may or may not become the law of the land—but if it does, that will be an end of the matter until a modification can be effected, should it be deemed necessary. If it does not pass [and the latest advices I have are to the effect that it is still pending] the next Congress will have to give it their earliest attention.

According to my political education, I am inclined to believe that the people in the various sections of the country should have their own views carried out through their representatives in Congress, and if the consideration of the Tariff bill should be postponed until the next session of the National Legislature, no subject should engage your representatives more closely than that of a tariff. And if I have any recommendation to make, it will be that every man who is called upon to serve the people in a representative capacity, should study this whole subject thoroughly, as I intend to do myself, looking to all the varied interest of our common country, so that when the time for action arrives adequate protection can be extended to the coal and iron of Pennsylvania, the corn of Illinois, and the "reapers of Chicago." Permit me to express the hope that this important subject may receive such consideration at the hands of your representatives, that the interests of no part of the country may be overlooked, but that all sections may share in common the benefits of a just and equitable tariff. {Applause.}

But I am trespassing upon your patience — [*cries of "no! "no!" "Go on — we'll listen!"*] and must bring my remarks to a close. Thanking you most cordially for the kind reception which you have extended me, I bid you all adieu. [*Enthusiastic applause.*][39]

His speech played well to the Pittsburgh audience, and Republican newspapers throughout the North also reacted favorably to his comments. But Democratic papers ridiculed him for vagueness, and as proof of his lack of political sophistication pointed out that he admitted he "did not understand the precise provisions" of the tariff bill in question. Henry Villard was also critical. Lincoln's remarks about tariffs were "really nothing but crude, ignorant twaddle, without point or meaning. It proved him to be the veriest novice in economic matters...."[40] Edward Everett, the former governor of Massachusetts (and the man who would be the featured speaker in 1863 at the dedication of the Gettysburg cemetery) was blunt in his criticism of all of Lincoln's remarks on the trip. "His speeches thus far have been of the most ordinary kind, destitute of everything, not merely of felicity and grace, but of common pertinence. He is evidently a person of very inferior cast of character," wrote Everett.[41]

Lincoln immediately left for the train depot and his 10:00 A.M. departure. The station was crowded with admirers, and despite the gloomy weather spirits were high. One man managed to pass his tiny baby son over people's heads so that Lincoln might kiss him, and Lincoln did so. Three pretty young ladies also received a kiss from their hero, and the crowd laughed when Robert and his young male friends were denied the same opportunity.

Now pulled by the locomotive *Meteor*, which was adorned by an immense jib-boom rigged to the engine and shaped like an American flag, the Special roared back through Ohio, stopping briefly at Canton and Salem. At Alliance Lincoln appeared, repeating what had become familiar comments:

Ladies and Gentlemen: I appear before you merely to greet you and say farewell. I have no time for long speeches, and could not make them at every stopping place without wearing myself out. If I should make a speech at every town, I would not get to Washington until some time after the inauguration. [*Laughter.*] But as I am somewhat interested in the inauguration, I would like to get there a few days before the 4th of March.[42]

From Alliance the Special headed north, past Berlin Lake and into Ravenna, seat of Portage County and about 15 miles east of Akron. Lincoln thanked the crowd that had gathered to see him, and acknowledged the voters of Ohio who had supported the Republican cause. He also referred to the incident of the day before, which apparently he found amusing:

But let me tell to those who did not vote for me, an anecdote of a certain Irish friend that I met yesterday. He said he did not vote for me, but went for Douglas. "Now," said I to him, "I will tell you what you ought to do in that case. If we all turn in and keep the ship from sinking this voyage, there may be a chance for Douglas on the next; but if we let it go down now, neither he nor anybody else will have an opportunity of sailing in it again." Now, was not that good advice? ["*Yes, yes,*" "*that's the talk.*"] Once more, let me say good-bye.[43]

At Hudson Lincoln appeared only to tell the crowd that his voice was hoarse, and he could not make a speech.[44] At Painesville Lincoln noted that while "so many good-looking ladies" had turned out to see him, he had "the best of the bargain."[45] Lincoln's cold was no better, and his long speech in Pittsburgh had made his throat raw. He rode now in silence, reading newspapers, intending to save his voice for major audiences the rest of the way. Lamon kept the entourage entertained with his banjo, and everyone marveled at the large crowds that continued to turn out at Wellsville, Salineville and Bayard. At Alliance a fine meal was served at Sourbeck's Hotel, courtesy of John N. McCullough, president of the Cleveland, Zanesville and Cincinnati Railroad, and members of the press decided that the food was the best they had sampled on the entire trip. The food was so good, in fact, that some members of Lincoln's party ignored Wood's call to board, and had to run after the moving train as it pulled away. After Lincoln left the dining hall his table was quickly cleared, not by waiters, but by admirers who wanted Lincoln's plates and silverware as souvenirs.

At Canton a company of Zouaves fired a cannon salute as the Special pulled into the depot, and the intensity of the blast shattered a car window, spraying broken glass on Mary, who happened to be sitting close by. She was shaken but not injured, and after a repair was quickly made to the window the Special continued on through small towns choked with cheering crowds.

But no crowd compared with the immense throng that had begun to gather in Cleveland early that morning, at first centered around the Euclid Street station and then extending outward along the streets toward downtown's public square. At 4:30 P.M. news spread that the Special was finally arriving, and excitement mounted. To loud cheers Lincoln emerged from his car and stepped into a waiting carriage, part of an enormous parade that would take him to the Weddell House, where he would spend the night. Leading the procession were wagons of the American and United States Express Companies, filled with employees; a fully rigged miniature schooner carrying a cannon and crew; buses of the Forest City Tool Company workers; buses carrying 75 Cuyahoga Steam Furnace workers who held a banner that read: "We forge bonds to bind the Union"; a volunteer fire brigade; 40 young men on horseback who escorted Robert Lincoln; Cleveland's famed Light Dragoons, a Light Artillery brigade, and the Cleveland Grays on horseback; and finally Lincoln's spacious carriage that also held his advisors, city councilmen, and party officials.

The procession made its way more than two miles through city streets clogged with mud and rain. Thirty thousand people crammed every inch of sidewalk and window space, and most buildings were adorned with flags and banners. Leland's Brass Band, a Cleveland favorite, played festively, and young boys threw firecrackers. Although a drizzling rain fell Lincoln rested his stovepipe hat on his lap as he smiled and waved to the crowd. At 5:00 Lincoln arrived at the Weddell House and immediately made his way to a balcony, where he was welcomed by acting Mayor J.N. Masters:

> Honored Sir — The pleasant duty devolves upon me to extend to you on behalf of the citizens of the city of Cleveland through their municipal representatives, a cordial welcome to this city and community.
>
> In extending this welcome I am but speaking the voice of our men of business, our merchants— whose numerous representatives are around me — of farmers who have largely gathered here, of men of all trades, avocations, professions and parties, who merge all distinctions. In that name common to them all — American citizen, they bid me welcome you as the official representative of their country, chosen in accordance with the Constitution which they venerate and love. They bid me express to you their unconditional loyalty to the Constitution and country which their fathers transmitted to them and which they fervently hope may, by the blessings of God, be transmitted, unimpaired, to their children and children's children.
>
> Again, I bid you a hearty welcome.[46]

Judge Sherlock J. Andrews then formally introduced the guest of honor:

> Mr. Lincoln — Sir — I have the honor, on behalf of the citizens of Cleveland, to repeat the welcome you have already received through their official organs of the city, and to express the great satisfaction that we all derive from this personal interview.
>
> We come to-day, sir, forgetful of party distinctions, and as citizens of a common country, to tender to you, the homage of our sincere respect, both for your personal character and for the high station to which you have been called by the popular will; and through unexampled difficulties and embarrassments stand upon the threshold of your administration, we still cherish the hope that by the blessing of Divine Providence you may be enabled so to execute the great trust confided in you as to allay excitement, correct misapprehension, restore harmony, and reinstate this glorious Union of ours in the affections and confidence of the whole people. It is true, indeed, that in the late peaceful contest for the Chief Magistracy, we have acted under various political organizations and have differed as to men and measures. Yet, sir, in every enlightened effort to support the prerogatives and honor of the General Government, in every determination to uphold the supremacy of law, in every measure wisely designed to maintain unimpaired the constitutional rights of all the States or of any of the States, and in every concession, consistent with truth and justice, that looks to the promotion of peace and concord, there is not a man in the vast multitude here assembled to do you honor who will not give you his cordial and earnest support.
>
> Such, I am persuaded sir, are the views of those I represent, and to whom, for any further expression of their sentiments, I shall now refer you.
>
> Fellow citizens, I have the honor on introducing to you the Honorable Abraham Lincoln, the President-elect of the United States.[47]

Lincoln bowed in appreciation and spoke in a raspy voice:

> Mr. Chairman and fellow citizens of Cleveland: We have been marching about two miles through snow, rain, and deep mud. The large numbers that have turned out under these circumstances testify that you are in earnest about something or other. But do I think so meanly of you as to suppose that the earnestness is about me personally? I would be doing you injustice to suppose you did. You have

assembled to testify your respect to the Union, the constitution and the laws, and here let me say that it is with you, the people, to advance the great cause of the Union and the Constitution, and not with any one man. It rests with you alone. This fact is strongly impressed on my mind at present. In a community like this, whose appearance testifies to their intelligence, I am convinced that the cause of liberty and the Union can never be in danger. Frequent allusion is made to the excitement at present existing in our national politics, and it is as well that I should also allude to it here. I think that there is no occasion for any excitement. The crisis, as it is called, is altogether an artificial crisis. In all parts of the nation there are differences of opinion and politics. There are differences of opinion even here. You did not all vote for the person who now addresses you. What is happening now will not hurt those who are farther away from here. Have they not all their rights now as they ever have had? Do they not have their fugitive slaves returned now as ever? Have they not the same constitution that they have lived under for seventy odd years? Have they not a position as citizens of this common country, and have we any power to change that position? [*Cries of "No."*] What then is the matter with them? Why all this excitement? Why all these complaints? As I said before, this crisis is all artificial. It has no foundation in fact. It was not argued up, as the saying is, and cannot, therefore, be argued down. Let it alone and it will go down of itself [*Laughter*].

I have not strength, fellow citizens, to address you at great length, and I pray that you will excuse me; but rest assured that my thanks are as cordial and sincere for the efficient aid which you gave to the good cause, is working for the good of the nation, as for the votes which you gave me last fall.

There is one feature that causes me great pleasure; and that is to learn that this reception is given, not alone by those with whom I chance to agree, politically, but by all parties. I think that I am not selfish when I say this is as it should be. If Judge Douglas had been chosen President of the United States, and had this evening been passing through your city, the Republicans ought, in the same manner, to have come out to receive him. If we don't make common cause and save the good old ship, nobody will. And this should be so. It is a matter of interest to you all that it be so.

To all of you then, who have done me the honor to participate in this cordial welcome, I return most sincerely my thanks, not for myself, but for Liberty, the Constitution, and the Union.

I bid you all an affectionate farewell.[48]

Lincoln's remarks were met with tremendous applause. His words, said the Cleveland *Leader*, were "fitly spoken, like apples of gold in pictures of silver."[49] Lincoln accepted several bouquets of flowers and was led into a large banquet room inside the hotel that was decorated with flags, bunting, and beautifully colored lamps suspended from the ceiling. For the next three hours Lincoln shook hands with hundreds of Cleveland's civic and political elite. One man named Abner McIllrath stood out from the rest. He was the tallest man Lincoln had ever seen; when the two men stood back to back McIllrath towered four inches above Lincoln. "A man of my high stature in the community might also look forward to the Presidential chair," McIllrath said, and Lincoln laughingly agreed.[50] Meanwhile, a separate levee was held next door in Mary's honor.

Twenty suites at the Weddell House, newly and ornately furnished, had been reserved for Lincoln's party, and many happily and gratefully retired. Lincoln and Mary, however, agreed to sit for a private interview with J. W. Gray, the editor of the

Cleveland *Plain Dealer*. The details of the conversation were not revealed, but Gray wrote in his newspaper the next day that he was "most favorably impressed with both. If mistakes do occur in the Executive Government of the country, we are satisfied they will not be chargeable to design."[51]

The next morning, February 16, was a bright and sunny one. After a bountiful breakfast Lincoln was escorted to the depot by the Cleveland Greys, again to the unrestrained cheers of thousands, for his 9:00 departure. All felt that the stop in Cleveland had been the highlight of the trip thus far. "There is but one sentiment among the recipients of the hospitality of the Forest City," wrote Henry Villard. "They all agree that as to splendor of pageantry, kindliness and heartiness of welcome her inhabitants eclipsed anything witnessed since the departure from Springfield."[52]

Its occupants rested and happy, the Special headed east, stopping at Willoughby, Mentor and Geneva. At Ashtabula members of the crowd called for Mary Lincoln to appear at the back of the train, but she declined. "I have never succeeded very well in getting her to do anything she didn't want to," said Lincoln, and the crowd laughed. Here Lincoln also met briefly with Joshua Giddings, a strong antislavery congressman who had been forced to resign because of poor health. Lincoln later appointed Giddings consul-general to the British North American Colonies, as Canada was then called. At Conneaut, the last stop in Ohio, an elderly man called out, "Don't give up the ship!" as the train pulled away from the station. "With your aid I never will as long as life lasts," said Lincoln.[53]

10

"I Bring a Heart True to the Work"

Just a few miles inside the New York state line, the Presidential Special stopped at the small town of Westfield. Lincoln stepped onto the rear platform and noticed several thousand ladies among the large crowd that greeted him. "I am glad to see you," he said, repeating a joke he used frequently. "I suppose you are to see me; but I certainly think I have the best of the bargain." When the laughter and applause faded Lincoln told the crowd that he had a special appreciation for one of Westfield's female residents. "Some three months ago," he said, "I received a letter from a young lady here; it was a very pretty letter, and she advised me to let my whiskers grow, as it would improve my personal appearance; acting partly upon her suggestion, I have done so; and now, if she is here, I would like to see her; I think her name was Miss Barlly." A small boy, sitting on a post near the railroad car, excitedly cried out, "There she is, Mr. Lincoln." He pointed to a blushing little girl with black eyes standing by her father. Lincoln left the car and made his way through the people so that he could personally meet the little girl.[1] The letter Lincoln had received read:

Hon A Lincoln …
 Dear Sir
 My father has just come from the fair and brought home your picture and Mr. Hamlin's I am a little girl only 11 years old, but want you should be President of the United States very much so I hope you wont think me very bold to write to such a great man as you are. Have you any little girls about as large as I am if so give them my love and tell her to write to me if you cannot answer this letter. I have got 4 brother's and part of them will vote for you any way and if you let your whiskers grow I will try and get the rest of them to vote for you you would look a great deal better for your face is so thin. All the ladies like whiskers and they would tease their husband's to vote for you and then you would be President. My father is going to vote for you and if I was a man I would vote for you to but I will try to get every one to vote for you that I can I think that rail fence around your picture makes it look very pretty I have got a baby sister she is nine weeks old and is just as cunning as can be. When you direct your letter direct to Grace Bedell Westfield Chatauqua County New York
 I must not write any more answer this letter right off. Good bye
 Grace Bedell[2]

Lincoln was very much amused by Grace's letter, and just four days later, on the 19th, he wrote to her:

> Miss Grace Bedell
>   My dear little Miss
>   Your very agreeable letter of the 15th is received — I regret the necessity of saying I have no daughters — I have three sons — one seventeen, one nine, and one seven years of age — They, with their mother, constitute my whole family — As to the whiskers, having never worn any, do you not think people would call it a piece of silly affection if I were to begin it now?
> > Your very sincere well wisher
> > A. Lincoln[3]

Now in Grace's hometown Lincoln lifted her up and kissed her as the crowd shouted in delight. The next day newspaper headlines across the country announced Lincoln's actions: "Old Abe Kisses Pretty Girl," and "Whiskers Win Winsome Miss." The story of Grace Bedell and Lincoln's beard has charmed many generations and become a part of his legend. While the story is true, in actuality Lincoln was urged to grow his beard by other admirers at almost exactly the same time. On October 12 a group calling themselves the "True Republicans" of New York wrote to him:

> To the
>   Hon. Abm. Lincoln
>   Dear Sir
>   Allow a number of very earnest Republicans to intimate to you, that after oft-repeated views of the daguerreotypes; which we wear as tokens of our devotedness to you; we have come to the candid determination that these medals would be much improved in appearance, provided you would cultivate whiskers and wear standing collars.
>   Believe us nothing but an earnest desire that "our candidate" should be the best looking as well as the best of the rival candidates, would induce us to trespass upon your valued time.
> > Your most
> > Sincere & earnest
> > Well wishers
> > True Republicans[4]

The Special rolled on across New York. At Dunkirk 15,000 people turned out to see the president-elect. A triumphal arch had been erected over the tracks, and beside it flew an American flag. Lincoln stood next to the flagpole and said, "Standing as I do with my hand upon this staff, and under the folds of the American flag, I ask you to stand by me so long as I stand by it!" "We will! We will!" shouted the crowd in return as Lincoln reboarded the Special and waved goodbye. At Silver Creek, when the Special passed by the station an artillery salute was fired, and a young man named William Hazen lost his arm in the explosion.[5]

Within the hour the Special reached Buffalo, the final stop of the day. Among the large crowd gathered at the Exchange Street station was the city's most celebrated resident, former president Millard Fillmore. Like Lincoln, Fillmore had been born in a log cabin, in Cayuga County, New York, on January 7, 1800. To escape his family's poverty Fillmore had apprenticed out to a firm of cloth-dressers and managed to enroll in an academy at New Hope. He quickly began a clerkship in the office of a local judge, and by 1823 gained admission to the bar. Always interested in politics, Fillmore aligned himself with the anti-Masonic movement, and through those circles formed a friendship with Thurlow Weed and William Seward. He was first elected to Congress in 1832 on the anti-Masonic ticket, and shortly thereafter became a Whig.

In the 1840s Fillmore led the antislavery wing of the Whig Party while also developing strong antiforeignist views. He eyed the vice presidential spot on the 1844 ticket with Henry Clay, but was instead persuaded to run for governor of New York, which he lost. His chance came four years later, when he was elected vice president as the running mate of Zachary Taylor. But in the summer of 1850 Taylor died, and Fillmore became President. He supported the 1850 Compromise while also affirming states' rights, walking a political tightrope of appeasement. His administration's most impressive victory was the authorization of Commodore Matthew Perry's unprecedented expedition to Japan. But a divided Whig Party in 1852 cast Fillmore aside in favor of Winfield Scott and the antislavery position, and Fillmore left the party in disgust. In 1856 his hatred of Catholics earned him the Know-Nothing party's nomination for president, but he ran a distant third to Democrat James Buchanan and Republican John Fremont, and his political career was over.

Like Lincoln, Fillmore cast an imposing figure. He was tall and powerfully built, and carried himself with an impressive authoritarian air. As Lincoln emerged from his car he shook hands with Fillmore and other members of the welcoming committee. Although the party was protected by Company D of the Seventy-fourth Infantry Regiment, as well as a few local policemen, the crowd of people surged forward, hoping to get a better look at Lincoln, and the guard was overpowered. Villard noted with disgust that "a scene of the wildest confusion ensued. To and fro the ruffians swayed and cries of distress were heard on all sides. The pressure was so great that it is really a wonder that many were not crushed and trampled to death."[6] Fortunately only one member of Lincoln's party was injured: Maj. David Hunter's arm was dislocated.

At last Lincoln was led to a waiting carriage and the processional parade began. Riding with him to the American House hotel were Lamon, Buffalo Mayor A.S. Bemis, and A.M. Clapp, chairman of the welcoming committee. It was a beautiful winter day, and the previous night's snowfall glistened in the sun. At the hotel all was in order, and to Lincoln's appreciation a protective squadron of police formed a barrier from carriage to entrance. As he had on other occasions he went directly to a second-floor balcony and appeared before thousands of cheering people:

> Mr. Mayor, and Fellow Citizens of Buffalo and the State of New York: — I am here to thank you briefly for this grand reception given to me, not personally, but as the representative of our great and beloved country. [*Cheers.*] Your worthy Mayor has been pleased to mention in his address to me, the fortunate and agreeable journey which I have had from home, on my rather circuitous route to the Federal Capitol. I am very happy that he was enabled in truth to congratulate myself and companions on that fact. It is true we have had nothing, thus far, to mar the plea-

sure of the trip. We have not been met alone by those who assisted in giving the election to me — I say not alone — but by the whole population of the country through which we have passed. This is as it should be.

Had the election fallen to any other of the distinguished candidates instead of myself, under the peculiar circumstances, to say the least, it would have been proper for all citizens to have greeted him as you now greet me. It is evidence of the devotion of the whole people to the Constitution, the Union, and the perpetuity of the liberties of this country. [*Cheers.*] I am unwilling, on any occasion, that I should be so meanly thought of, as to have it supposed for a moment that I regard these demonstrations as tendered to me personally. They should be tendered to no individual man. They are tendered to the country, to the institutions of the country, and to the perpetuity of the country for which these institutions were made and created.

Your worthy Mayor has thought fit to express the hope that I may be able to relieve the country from its present — or I should say, its threatened difficulties. I am sure I bring a heart true to the work. [*Tremendous applause.*] For the ability to perform it, I must trust in that Supreme Being who has never forsaken this favored land, through the instrumentality of this great and intelligent people. Without that assistance I shall surely fail. With it I cannot fail.

When we speak of threatened difficulties to the country, it is natural that there should be expected from me something with regard to particular measures. Upon more mature reflections, however, others will agree with me that when it is considered that these difficulties are without precedent, and have never been acted upon by any individual situated as I am, it is most proper I should wait, see the developments, and get all the light I can, so that when I do speak authoritatively I may be as near right as possible. [*Cheers.*] When I shall speak authoritatively, I hope to say nothing inconsistent with the Constitution, the Union, the rights of all the States, of each State, and of each section of the country, and not to disappoint the reasonable expectations of those who have confided to me their votes.

In this connection allow me to say that you, as a portion of the great American people, need only to maintain your composure. Stand up to your sober convictions of right, to your obligations to the Constitution, act in accordance with those sober convictions, and the clouds which now arise in the horizon will be dispelled, and we shall have a bright and glorious future; and when this generation has passed away, tens of thousand will inhabit this country where only thousands inhabit it now.

I do not propose to address you at length — I have no voice for it. Allow me again to thank you for this magnificent reception, and bid you farewell.[7]

Back in the hotel Lincoln was introduced to other members of Buffalo's welcoming committee, and learned that five members of Governor Edwin Morgan's staff would accompany him to the state capital at Albany, his next destination. That evening Lincoln was guest of honor at a reception, and he stood for two hours as people filed past him, while Mary received her guests in another parlor nearby. Again security was lax, as hundreds of uninvited people entered through the kitchen door and managed to meet the president-elect and his wife. When the levees concluded, Lincoln was introduced to Jacob Beyer, head of the city's German Republican delegation, who welcomed him to Buffalo and wished him a safe passage to Washington. "I am gratified with this evidence of the feelings of the German citizens of Buffalo," replied Lincoln. "My own idea about our foreign citizens has always been that they were no better than anyone else, and no worse. And it is best that they should forget they are foreigners as soon as possible."[8] Lincoln and Mary were then serenaded with German ballads by the *Saengerbund* (choral society) and *Liedertafel* (glee club) before they retired to their room.

Sunday, February 17, was the most relaxing day of the trip. Lincoln slept in, and at 10:00 A.M. Fillmore arrived and took him by carriage to the Unitarian Church, of which Fillmore was a member, for morning services conducted by The Reverend George Hosmer. They returned to the American House and picked up Mary, and then went to the Fillmore residence for lunch. Mary was a great admirer of Fillmore and enjoyed the time she spent with him and his wife, Abigail. Lincoln and Fillmore also got along well on a personal level. (Politically, however, Fillmore had no confidence in Lincoln's abilities and was critical of his administration and policies throughout the war. In 1864 Fillmore supported Democrat George McClellan for president.) The Lincolns spent the afternoon at the hotel, then enjoyed a quiet supper together. In the evening Lincoln attended another service, this one conducted by Father John Beason, who spoke of his experiences with Indian tribes of various western reservations and territories.

The next day brought a 5:45 A.M. departure, the earliest of the journey. The locomotive *Dean Richmond*, named for the vice president of the New York Central Railroad (and who also happened to be the chairman of the state Democratic Party), now pulled two coach cars, as well as dining and baggage cars. The car occupied by Lincoln and his family included a modern ventilation system that had specially designed and constructed, not for Lincoln, but for the Prince of Wales, who had traveled in the car few months ago on his American tour.

The Special made many stops at small towns along the way, including Batavia, Clyde, and Fonda, and larger ones like Little Falls, Syracuse and Utica. At each of these Lincoln appeared, made a few brief remarks, and the train pulled out again.[9] At Schenectady Lincoln was introduced by state Supreme Court justice Platt Potter, who expected that Lincoln would make a speech from a large platform erected for that purpose. Lincoln declined. He had no prepared speech to make, he said, and no time to make one. He did not wish to disappoint the crowd, but he must.[10] The scene was repeated at Fonda when Lincoln again refused to mount a platform. He wanted it distinctly understood, he joked, that he would never shrink from a platform on which he properly belonged.[11] At almost exactly the same time that Lincoln made these remarks, Jefferson Davis, newly selected president of the Confederate States of America, was delivering his inaugural address in Montgomery, Alabama.

The Special arrived in Albany right on time at 2:20 P.M., a unit of artillerymen keeping watch from the heights outside of town and announcing Lincoln's arrival with cannon fire. But the Special, now pulled by the locomotive *Erastus Corning, Jr.*, came only as far as the Broadway crossing and stopped. As an enormous crowd surrounded the car and jostled with policemen, Mayor George Thatcher came on board and tried to coax Lincoln to appear, but William Wood would not allow it, insisting that a military escort take Lincoln to the Capitol Building. After a 30-minute wait Company B of the Twenty-fifth Infantry Regiment marched up, accompanied by a military band. Lincoln then joined Thatcher in a carriage that took the men along Broadway to State Street and up the hill to the Capitol. Here Lincoln made two

speeches, the first a reply to Governor Edwin D. Morgan's welcome,[12] and then an
address to the state legislature:

> Mr. President and Gentlemen of the Legislature of the State of New York: It is
> with feelings of great diffidence, and I may say with feelings of awe, perhaps
> greater than I have recently experienced, that I meet you here in this place. The
> history of the great State, the renown of those great men who have stood here,
> and spoke here, and been heard here, all crowd around my fancy, and incline me
> to shrink from any attempt to address you. Yet I have some confidence given me
> by the generous manner in which you have invited me, and by the still more gen-
> erous manner in which you have received me to speak further. You have invited
> and received me without distinction of party. I cannot for a moment suppose that
> this has been done in any considerable degree with reference to my personal ser-
> vices, but that it is done in so far as I am regarded at this time as the representa-
> tive of the majority of this great nation. I doubt not this is the truth and the
> whole truth of the case, and this is as it should be. It is much more gratifying to
> me that this reception has been given to me as the representative of a free people
> than it could possibly be if tendered me [merely] as an evidence of devotion to
> me, or to any one man personally, and now I think it were more fitting that I
> should close these hasty remarks. It is true that while I hold myself without mock
> modesty, the humblest of all individuals that have ever been elevated to the Presi-
> dency, I have a more difficult task to perform than any one of them. You have gen-
> erously tendered me the united support of the great Empire State. For this, in
> behalf on the nation, in behalf of the present and future of the nation, in behalf on
> the civil and religious liberty for all time to come, most gratefully do I thank you.
> I do not propose to enter into an explanation of any particular line of policy as to
> our present difficulties to be adopted by the incoming administration. I deem it
> just to you, to myself and to all that I should see everything, that I should hear
> everything, that I should have every light that can be brought within my reach, in
> order that when I do so speak, I shall have enjoyed every opportunity to take cor-
> rect and true ground; and for this reason I don't propose to speak at this time of
> the policy of the Government; but when the time comes I shall speak as well as I
> am able for the good of the present and future of this country — for the good of
> both the North and the South of this country — for the good of the one and the
> other, and of all sections of the country. [Rounds of applause.] In the mean time, if
> we have patience; if we restrain ourselves; if we allow ourselves not to run off in a
> passion, I still have confidence that the Almighty, the Maker of the Universe will,
> through the instrumentality of this great and intelligent people, bring us through
> this as He has through all the other difficulties of our country. Relying on this, I
> again thank you for this generous reception. [Applause and cheers.][13]

That evening Lincoln was once again guest at a reception at his hotel, the Del-
evan House. Originally a separate reception for women had been planned for the following morning. But an unexpected late winter thaw had released ice floes from the
Hudson River, demolishing bridges and sending water overflowing into the streets,
and the festivities were cancelled. So on Tuesday Lincoln's party left Albany at 7:45
A.M., pulled by the wood-burning locomotive *Union* and then the *Constitution,* and
behind the pilot engine *Young America*, heading south toward New York City.[14]

Lincoln had time to reflect on the strange role the state, and the city, had played
in his election. Upstate New York was considered a solid Republican region, but even
after his triumph at Cooper Union the party had no expectation of doing well in the

city. Many of Manhattan's wealthy bankers, merchants and other businessmen backed a Democratic fusion ticket that was calculated to defeat Lincoln, reasoning that southern unrest over a Lincoln victory would trigger market chaos and a massive panic on Wall Street. On election day, Democratic merchants closed their places of business so that their workers could go to the polls, warning them that if Lincoln was elected "the South will withdraw its custom from us and you will get little work and bad prices."[15] Democratic newspapers also used financial concerns to justify their antiabolitionist views. James Gordon Bennett's *Tribune* predicted that "if Lincoln is elected you will have to compete with the labor of four million emancipated negroes." The New York *Daily News* agreed, writing that if Lincoln was elected "we shall find negroes among us thicker than blackberries swarming everywhere." Horace Greeley's editorials fanned the flames. "The moneybags of Wall Street," he wrote in his *Tribune*, "the rich Jews and other money lenders" and the "great dry goods and other commercial houses" feared Lincoln just as much as the slaveholders.[16]

Statewide the New York vote was split between city and country. The Union ticket won a 30,000 majority of New York City's votes; put another way, 62 percent of the city's voters voted for candidates other than Lincoln.[17] But the Republicans' strength in rural areas was too much for urban Democrats to overcome, and Lincoln carried the state on the whole by a relatively healthy margin.

Six weeks after the election over 2,000 New York City merchants drafted a resolution reassuring southern leaders that, on matters of race (and therefore business), their views were the same: "If ever a conflict arises between races, the people of the city of New York will stand by their brethren, the white race."[18] Further, if secession was the chosen course, the businessmen of the city would support a peaceful departure.

But southern merchants had no interest in cooperating even with sympathetic northerners. After the new year, most southerners repudiated debts owed the North, began to bypass northern ports and ignored northern merchandise flowing south. The *Herald* estimated northern losses to be $478 million in a matter of weeks.[19] In panicked response the city sent two delegations, representing each of the two major political parties, to Washington to lobby for a compromise. President Buchanan responded only by appointing a New Yorker, John A. Dix, as secretary of the treasury, a move that proved to be merely symbolic. Social commentators predicted that bread lines would soon form on the streets of New York.

With this background Lincoln was thus unsure of the reception he would receive in New York City. At 3:00 P.M. on the 19th the Special arrived at New York's Hudson River Railroad Station on 10th Street. Perhaps sensing her husband's apprehension, Mary smoothed his coarse hair and kissed him.[20] Lincoln stepped out of his car and was met by city Alderman Charles G. Cornell. He took his place in an open carriage next to Judge David Davis and military aide Col. Edwin Sumner, and the procession of 11 carriages began its trip toward the Astor House on Broadway's west side. Although some 250,000 New Yorkers had turned out to catch a glimpse of the president-elect (a large crowd, but not as massive as the one that greeted the Prince of Wales months earlier), the mood was subdued, almost gloomy, in great contrast to the excitement that had surrounded much of the trip thus far. No bands played, no military companies marched, and only one small police unit had been organized to accompany the procession. Occasionally cheers were heard, and Lincoln smiled and waved, but everyone in his party noticed the lack of enthusiasm that was displayed.

Within the hour Lincoln's carriage pulled up to the front of the magnificent Astor House, a six-story, 300-room hotel built in 1836 by John Jacob Astor, the city's first millionaire, a butcher's son from Germany who got his start selling musical instruments and made his fortune in fur trading. The hotel, which received the country's and the world's most distinguished guests, stood across the street from City Hall Park and close to another New York landmark, P.T. Barnum's American Museum. Flags, banners and murals adorned that structure, but not in honor of Lincoln's arrival; rather, they served as advertising for the great showman's collection of oddities. Broadway itself was choked with the traffic of carriages, stages and pedestrians, all fighting for room to maneuver their way across town. Now some 30,000 other New Yorkers gathered near the Astor House, hoping to catch a glimpse of Lincoln.

One of these spectators was perched atop an omnibus stalled in the traffic. Walt Whitman was a 41-year-old poet from Brooklyn who had astonished the country six years earlier with his *Leaves of Grass*, but had since fallen into a pathetic near-oblivion. Whitman spent his days with teamsters and cabdrivers, negotiating the city's bustling streets while observing the sometimes wonderful, sometimes wretched human condition of the city he called *Mannahatta*. He spent his nights in Pfaff's beer cellar, drinking and consorting with other earthy, raunchy "bohemians," male and female. He had recently been fired from his job as editor of the Brooklyn *Daily Times*, and had ended a love affair with a young man many years his junior; both experiences, along with the resignation that the country he had celebrated in *Leaves of Grass* was self-destructing, left him feeling more despondent than ever before. But now he gazed for the first time at a man whose actions would transform his life and give it real meaning. Whitman noted the "sulky, unbroken silence" of the crowd as Lincoln stepped from the coach onto the pavement, later noting in his diary that "I had, I say, a capital view of it all, and especially of Mr. Lincoln, his look and gait — his perfect composure and coolness — his unusual and uncouth height, his dress of complete black, stovepipe hat push'd back on the head, dark-brown complexion, seam'd and wrinkled yet canny-looking face, black, bushy head of hair disproportionately long neck, and his hands held behind him as he stood observing the people. He look'd with curiosity upon that immense sea of faces and the sea of faces return'd the look with similar curiosity." Whitman was aware that rumors were circulating that Lincoln's life was in danger, and he worried that Lincoln might not live to see the White House. As Lincoln made his way to the entrance of the Astor House Whitman noted that "many an assassin's knife and pistol lurk'd in hip or breast-pocket there, ready, as soon as break and riot came."[21]

Whitman would gaze at Lincoln many more times over the next four years. When war broke out his brother George Washington Whitman enlisted. After the bloody encounter at Fredericksburg in December 1862, the Whitman family feared that George had been killed or wounded, and Walt went to search him out among the dozens of Washington's army hospitals. Happily, he found his brother; perhaps more significantly, Whitman's period of "personal stagnation" was over. He found his calling as a sort of male Florence Nightingale, tirelessly visiting hospitals and surgical sites, comforting the thousands of wounded and near-dying soldiers. His spirit rekindled, Whitman began to write again. And he developed the habit of waiting and watching, on the streets near the White House, for Lincoln to emerge. Although the men never spoke, Whitman became one of Lincoln's greatest admirers, memorializing him after his death in poems such as "When Lilacs Last in the Dooryard Bloom'd" and "Oh Captain, My Captain." Now Whitman watched as Lincoln climbed a few steps to the hotel entrance and entered, pausing again to silently gaze back at the crowd before he went inside.

Lincoln was taken to room number 43 on the second floor, above the main entrance facing Broadway. Mary and the boys, who had been driven directly to the hotel, occupied a room down the hall, separated from Lincoln by a private dining room. Lincoln stood with his back to a roaring fire and gratefully accepted some lozenges that had been procured to ease his sore throat. He greeted members of the city council and other officials, complimenting Police Commissioner John Kennedy on the security arrangements. "A man ought to be thanked when he does his duty right well," he said.[22] He was informed that while most of the crowd outside had dispersed, several hundred of his supporters remained on the street. He stepped onto the balcony and addressed the people below:

> Fellow Citizens—I have stepped before you merely in compliance with what appeared to be your wish, and with no purpose of making a speech. In fact, I do not propose making a speech this afternoon. I could not be heard by any but a very small fraction of you at best; but what is still worse than that is, that I have nothing just now to say worth your hearing. I beg you to believe that I do not now refuse to address you through any disposition to disoblige you, but the contrary. But at the same time I beg of you to excuse me for the present.[23]

At six P.M. dinner was served in the dining room, the table beautifully decorated with camellias, roses and violets, an enormous cut-glass chandelier hanging above. A painting of Washington crossing the Delaware adorned the mantelpiece. Lincoln and his family enjoyed their meal, sampling from generous portions of boiled salmon, turkey, duck and quail, potatoes and vegetables, cream cakes and ice cream. A sterling silver buffet held fruits and chilled wine coolers. The dinner was so elegant that the entire menu was reprinted in the New York *Herald*.[24]

After dinner there were more introductions, now in a large reception room on the first floor. The state's electoral college representatives and Republican committee members, Wide-Awake members, campaign workers and state and local bureaucrats, numbering some 400 people, crowded into the room to meet Lincoln while Mary hosted a smaller reception for the wives in a private parlor. E. Delafield Smith, chairman of New York's Republican central committee, climbed up on a table and asked for quiet. "It is a remarkable incident," he said, "that there should have been but two receptions in this room. One was to Daniel Webster, the other to Henry Clay, and third now to Abraham Lincoln. But, Mr. President, we meet you tonight, not as partisans, but as Americans and as citizens of the greatest and most glorious Republic...."[25] Lincoln appreciated the reference to his political heroes, and spoke extemporaneously:

Mr. Chairman and Gentlemen: — I am rather an old man to avail myself of such an excuse as I am now about to do, yet the truth is so distinct and presses itself so distinctly upon me that I cannot well avoid it, and that is that I did not understand when I was brought into this room that I was brought here to make a speech. It was not intimated to me that I was brought into the room where Daniel Webster and Henry Clay had made speeches, and where one in my position might be expected to do something like those men, or do something unworthy of myself or my audience. I therefore will beg you to make very great allowance for the circumstances under which I have been by surprise brought before you. Now, I have been in the habit of thinking and speaking for some time upon political questions that have for some years past agitated the country, and if I were disposed to do so, and we could take up some one of the issues as the lawyers call them, and I were called upon to make an argument about it to the best of my ability, I could do that without much preparation. But that is not what you desire to be done here to-night. I have been occupying a position, since the Presidential election, of silence, of avoiding public speaking, of avoiding public writing. I have been doing so because I thought, upon full consideration, that was the proper course for me to take. [*Great applause.*] I am brought before you now and required to make a speech, when you all approve, more than anything else, of the fact that I have been silent — [*loud laughter, cries of "Good — good," applause*] — and now it seems to me from the response you give to that remark it ought to justify me in closing just here. [*Great laughter.*] I have not kept silent since the Presidential election from any party wantonness, or from any indifference to the anxiety that pervades the minds of men about the aspect of the political affairs of this country. I have kept silence for the reason that I supposed it was peculiarly proper that I should do so until the time came when, according the customs of the country, I should speak officially. [*Voice, partially interrogative, partially sarcastic, "Custom of the country?"*] I heard some gentleman say, "According to the custom of the country;" I alluded to the custom of the President elect at the time of taking his oath of office. That is what I meant by the custom of the country. I do suppose that while the political drama being enacted in this country at this time is rapidly shifting in its scenes, forbidding an anticipation with any degree of certainty to-day what we shall see to-morrow, that it was peculiarly fitting that I should see it all up to the last minute before I should take ground, that I might be disposed by the shifting of the scenes afterwards again to shift. [*Applause.*] I said several times upon this journey, and I now repeat it to you, that when the time does come I shall then take the ground that I think is right — [*interruption by cries of "Good," "good," and applause*] — the ground I think is right for the North, for the South, for the East, for the West, for the whole country — [*cries of "Good," "Hurrah for Lincoln", and great applause*]. And in doing so I hope to feel no necessity pressing upon me to say anything in conflict with the Constitution, in conflict with the continued union of these States— [*applause*] — in conflict with the perpetuation of the liberties of these people — [*cheers*] — or anything in conflict with anything whatever that I have ever given you reason to expect from me. [*Loud cheers.*] And now, my friends, have I said enough? [*Cries of "No, no," "Go on", &c.*] Now, my friends, there appears to be a difference of opinion between you and me, and I feel called upon to insist upon deciding the question myself. [*Enthusiastic cheers.*][26]

The next day was Wednesday, February 20. At just past eight o'clock in the morning Lincoln climbed into a carriage beside Thurlow Weed, Rhode Island governor William Sprague and James Watson Webb, editor of the New York *Courier*, and rode to the Moses Grinnell mansion on Fifth Avenue. The Grinnell family had amassed a fortune in mercantiles, whaling and railroads, among other enterprises, and Lincoln was given a tour of the ornate residence. Lincoln enjoyed a breakfast with a hundred of New York's most wealthy and influential merchants, including National Bank owner James Gallatin, City Bank magnate Moses Taylor, former governor and senator Hamilton Fish, attorney William Evarts, trader and philanthropist Robert Minturn, railroad financier William Aspinwall and John Jacob Astor Jr., himself. Lincoln was impressed with the influence these men held, but not necessarily by their wealth. When someone remarked on the staggering number of millionaires present, Lincoln said, "Well, that's quite right. I'm a millionaire myself. I got a minority of a million in the votes last November."[27]

Despite his reply Lincoln would certainly come to appreciate New York money in the near future. By July 1861 Secretary of the Treasury Salmon Chase would report that the Union had just $2 million available for the war effort; the estimated need was $320 million. Chase's pleas to East Coast bankers were successful. Their offers of conciliation rebuffed by southern plantation owners, a consortium of New York bankers led by Gallatin and Taylor, along with several Philadelphia and Boston financiers, loaned the government $150 million at 7.3 percent interest (two or three points higher than the normal rate). Nearly one-fifth of this amount came from New York's 39 participating banks, and came in gold. By the end of the year the government was ready to default on its payments, and in response Congress authorized the issuance of legal tender, or "greenbacks," a figure that grew to $450 million in just two years. A new, national banking system, complete with Federal regulatory rules, was then established, and not coincidentally the system's center found its permanent home in New York City — yet another reason why the city came to so strongly support the federal government in the war.[28]

After the two-hour breakfast meeting Lincoln returned to the Astor House, where he met still more of the city's personalities. Among the most notable figures was 94-year-old Joshua Dewey of Brooklyn. Dewey had been a drummer boy in the Revolutionary War and had voted in every presidential election since George Washington's. Later he graduated from Yale University and served in the New York legislature. Lincoln was so impressed that he called Mary in to meet Dewey, as well, and Dewey gave the couple a photograph of himself.

At 11:00 A.M. Lincoln was off again, this time to the City Hall where he was presented to controversial Mayor Fernando Wood and the rest of the council. Lincoln was familiar with Wood's political adventures. He began his career in the 1830s as a saloon keeper on the waterfront, catering to immigrants and working classes. After an unremarkable stint in Congress he returned to his element in the city, eventually leasing merchant ships and trading with southern markets. His second wife was wealthy, and Wood built upon his fortune by supplying 49ers with supplies during the California gold rush. He speculated in city land and built stores and homes in every ward, then invested his profits in banks, railroads and insurance companies. His motives and ethics were questioned at every turn, but official investigations yielded no indictments, to the dismay of his critics. A millionaire, he was elected mayor in 1854, and re-elected in 1856, running as a Democrat and friend of the working class. (The Irish, it seemed, were particularly strong supporters. In the Irish sixth ward Wood tallied 4,000 more votes than there were registered voters.)

Trying to shake off his scandalous reputation, Wood became a reform mayor. He overhauled and centralized the police department (approving the hiring of hundreds of Irish; by 1857 they comprised 27 percent of the force). He crusaded against prostitution and Sunday closing laws, cleaned city streets, strengthened building codes, and improved sanitary conditions. He championed the call for a great Central Park and a new City Hall, and supported city colleges and universities, even for women. "No good government can exist in a city like this," he proclaimed, "containing so many thousands of the turbulent, the vicious, and the indolent, without a Chief Officer with necessary power to see the faithful execution of the laws."[29]

But the financial panic of 1857, massive unemployment and widespread dissatisfaction over Woods' catering to the working class brought trouble to his administration. He was voted out of office in 1858 as the upper class unified against him. But two years later he was returned to office as Tammany Hall splintered, riding the support of James Gordon Bennett's *Herald* and arguing against the "kid-glove, scented, silk-stalking, poodle-headed, degenerate aristocracy."[30] Wood quickly found a new cause. In the wake of southern secession, in January 1860 Wood proposed to the Common Council that New York City itself declare its independence. Adopting southern fears and reactions to Lincoln's election, Wood believed that a northern assault on the southern institution of slavery was imminent; not only was the assault unconstitutional, but the damage done to the city's traders and merchants would be catastrophic. His new city-state, to be called Tri-Insula, would be free of oppressive federal tariffs, continue unbridled trade with the "aggrieved brethren of southern slave states," and sever pesky ties with meddling Puritans from upstate. But Wood generated little support from merchants, who feared that the move might only trigger new rounds of economic recession. From Springfield Lincoln scoffed at the plan, joking that it would be "some time before the front door sets up house-keeping on its own account."[31]

But there would be no partisan bickering on this day. Wood now stood in the governor's room at City Hall, behind a lectern that had been used by George Washington and under portraits of Presidents Washington, Monroe, Taylor and Fillmore, and William Seward. Addressing the council, city officials and members of the press, Wood graciously introduced the president-elect, referring to the split in the Union and expressing hope that the crisis might be averted. Lincoln replied:

> Mr. Mayor: It is with feelings of deep gratitude that I make my acknowledgment for this reception which has been given me in the great commercial city of New York. I cannot but remember that this is done by a people who do not by a majority agree with me in political sentiments. It is all the more grateful to me because in this reception I see that, in regard to the great principles of our government, the people are very nearly or quite unanimous.
> In reference to the difficulties that confront us at this time, and of which your Honor thought fit to speak so becomingly, and so justly as I suppose, I can only say that I fully concur in the sentiments expressed by the Mayor. In my devotion to the Union I hope I am behind no man in the Union; but as to the wisdom with which to conduct affairs tending to the preservation of the Union, I fear that even too great confidence may have been reposed in me. I am sure I bring a heart devoted to the work.

> There is nothing that can ever bring me willingly to consent to the destruction
> of this Union, under which not only the commercial city of New York, but the
> whole country has acquired its greatness, unless it were to be that thing for which
> the Union itself was made. I understand a ship to be made for the carrying and
> preservation of the cargo, and so long as the ship can be saved, with the cargo, it
> should never be abandoned. This Union should likewise never be abandoned
> unless it fails and the probability of its preservation shall cease to exist without
> throwing the passengers and cargo overboard. So long, then, as it is possible that
> the prosperity and the liberties of the people can be preserved in the Union, it
> shall be my purpose at all times to preserve it. Thanking you for the reception
> given me, allow me to come to a close. [32]

Lincoln returned to the Astor House where hundreds more people awaited him.
He was particularly glad to meet 30 veterans of the War of 1812, and greeted them
enthusiastically. Two city hatters presented him with new silk stovepipe hats. When
asked which hat was worth more, Lincoln said that "they mutually surpassed each
other" in value, and the New York press took careful note of Lincoln's famous wit.
Seeing that the line of people was long, Lincoln encouraged Mary to take the boys
go across the street and visit P.T. Barnum's American Theater.

Barnum had been expecting Lincoln himself. He had been something of a pest
at the previous evening's reception, trying to hold Lincoln's attention while many
other people waited for their chance, and would not leave until he had elicited a half-
promise that Lincoln might visit his museum the next day. "Don't forget you're Honest Old Abe; I shall rely upon you, and I'll advertise you," Barnum said. He then left
the Astor House and placed announcements for Lincoln's visit in several newspapers.
"Those who would see him should come early," the advertisement read. Barnum
knew that Lincoln would be a curious attraction for ticket buyers, but he was also
keenly interested in politics. He had been a Jackson Democrat most of his adult life,
but a tour of the South with singing sensation Jenny Lind in the 1850s gave him a
glimpse of the horrors of slavery — he "abhorred the curse from witnessing its fruits,"
he said — and he became an abolitionist. In 1860 he supported Lincoln for president,
participating in rallies and marching with Wide-Awake groups.[33]

Mary and the boys spent the afternoon wandering through the museum's five
floors and seven showrooms, gazing at stuffed elephants, leopards, giraffes, and exotic
birds. Behind glass cases were tropical plants and reptiles, sharks' teeth, butterflies
and rhinoceros horns. They watched "Ned the Learned Seal" play musical instruments, and gawked at dozens of "living curiosities" including giants, dwarfs, albinos,
skeleton men, bearded ladies, missing links, and Aztec children of lost civilizations.
They viewed wax figures of Chang and Eng, Barnum's famous Siamese Twins (who
had recently retired from touring and settled on a North Carolina plantation, where
they married, fathered 22 children between them and owned 33 slaves), and marveled at the uniform of 25-inch-tall General Tom Thumb, who would meet Lincoln
at a White House reception in 1863. They topped off the afternoon by attending the
children's play *Woman in White*, sitting with Barnum in his private box.[34]

That evening the Lincolns dined with Hannibal Hamlin and his wife, who had
just arrived from Maine. Joining them were Mary's sister from Springfield, Mrs. Ninian Edwards, and her daughter Elizabeth, who would travel on to Washington to

assist Mary in inaugural social events and ceremonies. After dinner Mary, her sister, and Mrs. Hamlin hosted a reception in the parlor of the Astor House, attended by 500 guests.

Tired of receptions, Lincoln joined Judge Davis and Alderman Cornell at the Academy of Music for a performance of Verdi's new opera *Un Ballo in Maschera (A Masked Ball)*. They arrived late and took their seats in the proscenium box on the second tier. After the first act the crowd of 3,000 noticed Lincoln and applauded; embarrassed, Lincoln took two bows. After the second act the audience joined the cast in "The Star-Spangled Banner" and then "Hail, Columbia" as Lincoln left the theater. He returned to the hotel and listened to serenades from a Hoboken, New Jersey, German quartet who had positioned themselves outside his door. Just as he was about to fall asleep, the 54-piece Seventh Regiment band began to play on the street below, accompanied by 150 Wide-Awake club members. Between numbers they shouted loudly for Lincoln to appear. He did not, but Hannibal Hamlin came to his window instead, thanking the revelers and telling them that "with your heads, your hearts, and your hands, you will rally to [the Government's] support in sunshine and in storm."[35]

Lincoln and his party were scheduled to leave New York the next day, the 21st. Henry Villard wrote that he was sick of the "traveling show" Lincoln's trip had become, and stayed in New York; he would come to Washington for the inauguration in two weeks.[36] Lincoln was so anxious to leave the city that he had his departure time pushed ahead one hour, to 8:00 A.M. He had felt uncomfortable from the moment he arrived in the city. People made fun of his language and mannerisms. He was vulgar and uncouth, they said, and lacked the polish of a statesman. The newspapers did not provide detailed analysis of his speeches or discuss his prospects of healing a divided country without war; rather, they noted, Lincoln had the audacity to wear black kid gloves to the opera.[37]

11

Plums and Nuts

Thursday, February 21, was the busiest day of the journey. Precisely at 8:00 A.M. Lincoln and his entourage departed from the Cortlandt Street Ferry near Manhattan's lower tip amidst artillery salvos and a respectful crowd. The brand new ferry boat *John P. Jackson*, piloted by Commodore Charles F. Woolsey, made its way across the Hudson River to Jersey City, where Lincoln was to address the legislature. Part of New Jersey was below the Mason-Dixon line, and its sympathies were with the southern people. New Jersey had traditionally been a Democratic state, and in the 1860 election Stephen Douglas, making effective use of the proslavery Jersey City *Courier and Advertiser* and the *American Standard* newspapers, had carried it by some 4,500 votes. (New Jersey was, the New York *Times* scornfully proclaimed, the "only free state to be untrue to freedom.")[1] Public opinion was to remain anti-Union throughout the war; McClellan carried the state in the 1864 election by 7,600 votes, and in 1877 it elected him governor.

Despite their state's political leanings, the Jersey City dignitaries that comprised the welcoming committee were determined to give the president-elect a proper greeting. The entire committee of 10 city politicians, led by Mayor Cornelius Van Vorst, had crossed the river and boarded the ferry with Lincoln in New York. En route back to Jersey City, Mayor Van Vorst addressed Lincoln:

> We are commissioned by the municipal authorities of Jersey City to receive and escort you to the soil of New Jersey. With that high respect so eminently due to a chosen chief of a mighty nation, her people await to welcome you in your progress through their state to assume the chair of Washington. It is a pleasure thus to greet the future President of the republic. Devoted in their attachment to the union of these states, they ever cling to it with fidelity as the ark of their political safety. It is their prayer that the republic may be immortal; and that he who holds in His hands the destinies alike of individuals and of nations may guide and sustain you in all your acts for the conservation of the public weal.[2]

Lincoln nodded in appreciation but made no speech. Instead he approached the one member of the welcoming committee he recognized, Dudley S. Gregory Sr. Gregory was an industrialist who had served with Lincoln in Congress, then returned home to become Jersey City's first mayor, then president of the Provident Savings Bank. The two old friends shook hands warmly and chatted for the rest of the short ride.

Lincoln was surprised to see a large crowd awaiting his arrival at the Exchange Place landing. To the delight of many he picked up a little girl and kissed her cheek. "We cheerfully welcome the little lambs," he said as the crowd applauded and made room for him to enter the train depot of the New Jersey Railroad and Transportation Company. It was an imposing two-story building, 500 by 100 feet long, built on 10 acres of land reclaimed from the river four years earlier. Now it was decorated with red, white and blue bunting and filled with a throng of 25,000 people, many of whom waved American flags. Lincoln climbed to the top of a passenger car that had been converted to a stage, where he was greeted by state Attorney General William L. Dayton (who had been, in 1856, the vice-presidential running mate of John Fremont on the first Republican ticket, and who would later be appointed by Lincoln as ambassador to France). Dayton spoke:

> In the absence of the governor, and by his authority, I give you a cordial welcome to the soil of New Jersey. We may not hope to equal in the demonstrations of our attention those magnificent ovations which have accompanied your journey elsewhere, but in cordiality of greeting, we are second to none. We desire to testify our sincere respect and high appreciation of your character and public position, and to assure you of the loyalty and unwavering fidelity of this people to the laws and constitution. I am sure, sir, I do not tread on forbidden or doubtful ground when I say that our people prefer one union, one flag and one destiny. But, they look to you as possessing the great requirements of integrity and public virtue, and with their sympathy and support will uphold you in all rightful measures you may undertake to perpetuate the union and the cordial feeling which should exist in all parts of our common country. We desire to live in harmony with our brothers as of old, asking from them only what is fair, and giving them the same in return; this, I am sure sir, is the unanimous sentiment of the people of New Jersey. Upon you, sir, rests a great responsibility, but this united people will follow you to the capital, with their best wishes, their brightest hopes and most fervent prayers.[3]

Lincoln waited for the applause to cease, then replied, being careful to make reference to his friend Dayton:

> Ladies and gentlemen of the State of New-Jersey, I shall only thank you briefly for this very kind and cordial reception — not as given to me individually, but as to the representative of the chief magistracy of this great nation. I cannot make any speech now to you, as I shall be met frequently to-day in the same manner as you have received me here, and, therefore, have not the strength to address you at length. I am here before you care-worn, for little else than to greet you, and to say farewell. You have done me to very high honor to present your reception of me through your own great man — a man with whom it is an honor to be associated anywhere — a man with whom no State could be poor. [*Applause, long continued.*] His remarks of welcome, though brief, deserve an hour's well-considered reply; but time, and the obligations before me, render it necessary for me to close my remarks — allow me to bid you a kind and grateful farewell.

The crowd cheered and waved their handkerchiefs and flags. Some called out for Hannibal Hamlin, who was not present. Many then rushed the stage in attempts to get closer to Lincoln, but policemen held them back. Cries of "Lincoln, Lincoln" began and picked up momentum, and in response Lincoln held up his hand and spoke again:

> There appears to be a desire to see more of me, and I can only say that from my position, especially when I look around the gallery [*bowing to the ladies*], I feel that I have decidedly the best of the bargain, and in this matter I am for no compromises here. [*Applause and much laughter.*][4]

Two Cunard liners sounded their whistles, Lincoln's cue to go. Upon the order of Col. Dudley S. Gregory Jr., the Hudson Guard fired a salute, and as factory whistles sounded, Dodsworth's Band played "The Star-Spangled Banner." Waving a final goodbye, Lincoln and his party boarded the New Jersey edition of the Presidential Special, pulled by the brand-new locomotive *Governor Pennington*. The smokestack was decorated in red, white and blue; a banner read "The Union" on one side and "1776" on the other.

Lincoln settled into one of two luxurious private train cars that had been made available for him and his companions. Seven more cars followed, filled with politicians and an ever-increasing number of journalists. Each of the two lead cars featured a hot-air furnace, gas fixtures, four sofas, rich carpeting, marble-top tables, and numerous plush easy chairs. Bouquets of flowers adorned every corner of the cars, all courtesy of the railroad company. As Dodsworth's Band played "Hail, Columbia!" and a cannon sounded a 34-round salute, the Special pulled away from the Jersey City station, heading straight west toward Newark Bay.

A half-hour later the Special arrived in Newark, and in response to the welcome of Mayor Moses Bigelow Lincoln repeated familiar themes:

> Mr. Mayor: I thank you for the reception to your city, and would say in response, that I bring a heart sincerely devoted to the work you desire I should do. With my own ability I cannot succeed, without the sustenance of Divine Providence, and of this great, free, happy, and intelligent people. Without these I cannot hope to succeed; with them I cannot fail. Again I return you my thanks. [*Cheers.*][5]

Snow began to fall as Lincoln climbed into a barouche and was driven up Broad Street to Newark's upper depot, where he repeated his remarks before a crowd estimated at 30,000. Quickly aboard again, the Special turned south, rolling through the quiet towns of Elizabeth, Rahway and New Brunswick, where Lincoln appeared and acknowledged cannon salutes, brass bands, fireworks and cheering crowds. At Princeton the college men's chorus serenaded Lincoln, much to his delight. Snow drifted onto the tracks at a few places, slowing the train's progress, and it was nearly noon when the Special pulled into Trenton, the state capital, where Lincoln was scheduled to address both houses of the legislature. The sun came out as he was paraded through town, where an estimated 20,000 people lined the streets from the station to the statehouse. Order was maintained by a number of mounted policemen, adorned with special white satin badges on their hats. Lincoln was taken first to the Senate Chamber, and after a short introduction he spoke, his words taking on a far more personal tone than usual. John Hay noticed the difference in his speech and delivery, as well; Lincoln's voice was "as soft and sympathetic as a girl's," and although "not lifted above the tone of average conversation, it was distinctly audible through-out the entire hall"[6]:

> Mr. President and Gentlemen of the Senate of the State of New-Jersey: I am very grateful to you for the honorable reception of which I have been the object. I cannot but remember the place that New-Jersey holds in our early history. In the early Revolutionary struggle, few of the States among the old Thirteen had more of the battle-fields of the country within their limits than old New-Jersey. May I be pardoned if, upon this occasion, I mention that away back in my childhood, the earliest days of my being able to read, I got hold of a small book, such a one as few of the younger members have ever seen, "Weem's Life of Washington." I remember all the accounts there given of the battle fields and struggles for the liberties of the country, and none fixed themselves upon my imagination so deeply as the struggle here at Trenton, New-Jersey. The crossing of the river; the contest with the Hessians; the great hardships endured at that time, all fixed themselves on my memory more than any single revolutionary event; and you all know, for you have all been boys, how these early impressions last longer than any others. I recollect thinking then, boy even though I was, that there must have been something more than common that those men struggled for. I am exceedingly anxious that that thing which they struggled for; that something even more than National Independence; that something that held out a great promise to all the people of the world to all time to come; I am exceedingly anxious that this Union, the Constitution, and the liberties of the people shall be perpetuated in accordance with the original idea for which that struggle was made, and I shall be most happy indeed if I shall be a humble instrument in the hands of the Almighty, and of this, his almost chosen people, for perpetuating the object of that great struggle. You give me this reception, as I understand, without distinction of party. I learn that this body is composed of a majority of gentlemen who, in the exercise of their best judgment in the choice of a Chief Magistrate, did not think I was the man. I understand, nevertheless, that they came forward here to greet me as the constitutional President of the United States — as citizens of the United States, to meet the man who, for the time being, is the representative man of the nation, united by a purpose to perpetuate the Union and liberties of the people. As such, I accept this reception more gratefully than I could do did I believe it was tendered to me as an individual.[7]

The gallery erupted in applause as Lincoln finished. He shook hands with each member of the Senate and then was led across the hall to the assembly chamber, where he addressed the House. Here he spoke extemporaneously:

> Mr. Speaker and Gentlemen: I have just enjoyed the honor of a reception by the other branch of this Legislature, and I return to you and them my thanks for the reception which the people of New-Jersey have given, through their chosen representatives, to me, as the representative, for the time being, of the majesty of the people of the United States. I appropriate to myself very little of the demonstrations of respect with which I have been greeted. I think little should be given to any man, but that it should be a manifestation of adherence to the Union and the Constitution. I understand myself to be received here by the representatives of the people of New-Jersey, a majority of whom differ in opinion from those with whom I have acted. This manifestation is therefore to be regarded by me as expressing their devotion to the Union, the Constitution and the liberties of the people. You, Mr. Speaker, have well said that this is a time when the bravest and wisest look with doubt and awe upon the aspect presented by our national affairs.

> Under these circumstances, you will readily see why I should not speak in detail of the course I shall deem it best to pursue. It is proper that I should avail myself of all the information and all the time at my command, in order that when the time arrives in which I must speak officially, I shall be able to take the ground which I deem the best and safest, and from which I may have no occasion to swerve. I shall endeavor to take the ground I deem most just to the North, the East, the West, the South, and the whole country. I take it, I hope, in good temper—certainly no malice toward any section. I shall do all that may be in my power to promote a peaceful settlement of all our difficulties. The man does not live who is more devoted to peace than I am. [*Cheers.*] None who would do more to preserve it. But it may be necessary to put the foot down firmly.

Lincoln spoke these words, according to Hay, "with great deliberation and with a subdued intensity of tone," and to emphasize their meaning he "lifted his foot lightly, and pressed it with a quick, but not violent, gesture upon the floor. He evidently meant it."[8] This remark—that he may have to "put the foot down firmly"—was Lincoln's clearest statement yet that military action might be necessary to hold the Union together, and newspapers across the country quoted him in the next day's editions. Those assembled broke out into thunderous cheers which lasted several minutes. Finally he was able to continue:

> And if I do my duty, and do right, you will sustain me, will you not? [*Loud cheers, and cries of "Yes," "Yes", "We will."*] Received, as I am, by the members of a Legislature the majority of whom do not agree with me in political sentiments, I trust that I may have their assistance in piloting the ship of State through this voyage, surrounded by perils as it is; for, if it should suffer attack now, there will be no pilot ever needed for another voyage.
>
> Gentlemen, I have already spoken longer than I intended, and must beg leave to stop here.[9]

Hay had never seen "an assemblage more thoroughly captivated and entranced by a speaker than were listeners ... by the grim and stalwart Illinoisan."[10] As the crowd applauded Lincoln was whisked away to the Trenton House, where he had lunch with Mary and Mr. and Mrs. Dayton, who had traveled from Jersey City. Lincoln was apparently impressed with the food, and he asked to be taken to the kitchen, where he chatted with the chefs and their staff. Hay, however, did not care for the service. The lunch was "imperfectly arranged; those who had forks could find but little to put those utensils into; those surrounded by all the luxurious varieties of cold cuts had no forks."[11] Lincoln declined an offer to make a formal speech, and by 2:30 P.M. was back on the train, bound for Philadelphia.

The Special pulled into the Kensington depot at Philadelphia at precisely 4:00 P.M., Lincoln's arrival announced by a 34-gun salute fired by a militia group called the Minute Men of '76. One hundred thousand people lined the streets leading from the depot to the Continental Hotel, viewing a carriage procession that numbered over 200 politicians and dignitaries, all honoring Lincoln. The crowd around the entrance to the hotel was pushed back, and Lincoln was immediately escorted to a balcony on the second floor, where he responded to an introduction by Mayor Alexander Henry:

Mr. Mayor and Fellow Citizens of Philadelphia — I appear before you to make no lengthy speech. I appear before you to thank you for the reception. The reception you have given me to-night is not to me, the man, the individual, but the man who temporarily represents, or should represent, the majesty of the nation. [*Applause.*] It is true, as your worthy Mayor has said, that there is great anxiety amongst the citizens of the United states at this time. I say I deem it a happy circumstance that the dissatisfied portion of our fellow citizens do not point us to anything in which they are being injured, or about to be injured, from which I have felt all the while justified in concluding that the crisis, the panic, the anxiety of the country at this time is artificial. If there be those who differ with me upon this subject, they have not pointed out the substantial difficulty that exists. [*Tremendous cheering.*]

I do not mean to say that this artificial panic has not done harm. That it has done much harm I do not deny. The hope that has been expressed by your worthy Mayor, that I may be able to restore peace and harmony and prosperity to the country, is most worthy in him; and most happy indeed shall I be if I shall be able to fulfill and verify that hope. [*Cheers.*]

I promise you in all sincerity, that I bring to the work a sincere heart. Whether I will bring a head equal to that heart, will be for future time to determine. It were useless for me to speak of the details of the plans now. I shall speak officially on next Monday week, if ever. If I should not speak, then it were useless for me to do so now. When I do speak, as your worthy Mayor has expressed the hope, I will take such grounds as I shall deem best calculated to restore peace, harmony and prosperity to the country, and tend to the perpetuity of the nation, and the liberty of these States and all these people. [*Applause.*]

Your worthy Mayor has expressed the wish, in which I join with him, that if it were convenient for me to remain with you in your city long enough to consult your merchants and manufacturers or, as it were, to listen to those breathings rising withing the consecrated walls where the Constitution of the Unites States, and, I will add, the Declaration of American Independence was originally framed, I would do so.

I assure you and your Mayor that I had hoped on this occasion, and upon all occasions during my life, that I shall do nothing inconsistent with the teachings of those holy and most sacred walls.

I have never asked anything that does not breathe from those walls. All my political warfare has been in favor of the teachings coming forth from that sacred hall. May my right hand forget its cunning and my tongue cleave to the roof of my mouth, if ever I prove false to those teachings.

Fellow citizens, I have addressed you longer than I expected to do, and allow me now to bid you good night.

The cheering was so loud throughout the speech, observed the Baltimore *Sun*, that "we are confident not one person in the crowd below heard one word from Lincoln's speech."[12] Lincoln enjoyed a quiet dinner with Mary, who had learned that they were to stay in private accommodations in Washington — Trumbull and Washburne had rented a house for the family — before they would move into the White House. That would not do, she advised her husband, and so plans were changed; they would stay at Willard's Hotel, the finest in the city. Lincoln had been looking forward to the temporary respite from the crowds that private lodging might offer, but did not put up a fuss. He supposed that he was "public property" now, and "a public place is where people can have access to me."[13]

After dinner Lincoln endured a three-hour reception in the main floor parlor.

Hundreds of Philadelphia's finest moved past him, shaking his hand, offering congratulations, wishing him well. William S. McCaulley, chairman of a delegation from Wilmington, Delaware, was not satisfied with just a handshake. He somehow quieted the room, then formally invited Lincoln to visit his city the following day. Lincoln graciously declined.[14] At about 11:00 P.M. he retired to his room, but not to sleep. As a brass band played boisterously, and a fireworks show exploded to the delight of the 20,000 people who still lingered about, Lincoln's mood was anything but festive. He learned that a serious plot to assassinate him in Baltimore had been uncovered, and he was being advised to drastically alter his travel plans.

Lincoln's advisors had long believed that southern sympathizers wanted to do him harm before he could be sworn in as president. The danger seemed particularly high in Maryland, which John Breckenridge had carried in the 1860 election, and where some 90,000 blacks were held in bondage. Governor Thomas Hicks had gone to Washington in mid-February, testifying before a House committee that secret organizations, formed to wreak havoc against the government and do harm to Lincoln, existed in his state. He was powerless to stop them, he told the committee, and requested that Winfield Scott provide him 2,000 rifles to "meet an emergency if it shall arise."[15] Specifically, Baltimore was described as a "nest of conspirators" teeming with secessionist fever, and the severe recession that wracked the city since the election added to the sentiment.[16] The request was denied. While Lincoln's trip thus far had been free

Allan Pinkerton (in front), who may have saved Lincoln from an assassination attempt in Baltimore (the Lincoln Museum, Fort Wayne, Indiana, # 2193).

from danger, anti-Lincoln sentiment seemed to be everywhere in Baltimore, and now it seemed that the worst fears of Davis, Judd, Lamon and the others might be coming true.

Plans to deal with the Baltimore problem first surfaced in January, only weeks before Lincoln departed from Springfield. Samuel Morse Felton, the president of the Philadelphia, Wilmington and Washington Railroad, had heard rumors that secessionist groups in and around Baltimore—Blood Tubs, they called themselves, and Plug Uglies—were planning to blow up his railroad line and destroy locomotives, cutting off supply lines between northern factories and Washington, D.C. Felton could expect little help from the Maryland legislature, which was planning to meet and discuss secession; neither could he depend upon Baltimore law enforcement, headed by secessionist Marshal George P. Kane, who would later become a Confederate officer. Instead, Felton wrote a letter to Allan Pinkerton, head of the Chicago detective agency that bore his name, asking him to come to New York City to discuss these matters.

Pinkerton was a man who took threats and rumors seriously. Born in Glasgow, Scotland, in 1807, the son of a Calvinist police sergeant, he apprenticed as a barrelmaker. He came to America as a young man and settled in Cook County, Illinois. But cutting wood bored him, and in 1846 he took a job with the police department, where he quickly discovered that his interest lay in detective work. By 1850 he founded America's first private detective agency, Pinkerton & Company (its motto, "We Never Sleep" was almost literally true; Pinkerton got by on two or three hours of sleep per night for most of his life). Specializing in security and undercover work, the agency grew quickly, and within a few years counted many major railroads, insurance companies, and the U.S. Post Office among its clients. Pinkerton developed a close friendship with George McClellan, vice president of the Illinois Central and later president of the Ohio and Mississippi railways, and also came to know the corporate lawyer for the Illinois Central, Abraham Lincoln of Springfield. Politically, Pinkerton became a strong antislavery and Union man.

Now Pinkerton instructed Felton to order 200 of his most trusted employees to guard the line connecting Susquehanna and Baltimore. By day the group whitewashed the line bridges with salt and alum, rendering them fireproof. By night they conducted armed drills and maneuvers, preparing for expected trouble. Pinkerton also had Felton find men who could infiltrate Maryland militia groups and determine who might be disloyal to the Union. Meanwhile, Pinkerton embarked on his own plan. It was essential, he felt, to monitor the plans of secessionist groups closely, and "gain a controlling power over the mind of the suspected parties."[17] He chose some of his most trusted detectives, Timothy Webster, Hattie Lawton, Kate Warne, and Harry Davies, and headed to Maryland.

Just 39 years old, Timothy Webster was born in New Haven, Sussex County, England. He came to New Jersey with his parents in 1833 and learned to be a machinist. By 1853, however, he had begun a career in law enforcement, serving as a policeman at the World's Crystal Palace Exposition (the World's Fair) in New York City, where his able work came to the attention of Pinkerton. Webster accepted a detective's position with the Agency in Chicago. Eager to accept any new assignment,

Webster gladly followed Pinkerton's orders and traveled to Perryville, north of Baltimore, with a female detective named Hattie Lawton. Webster enlisted in a Confederate militia cavalry and easily infiltrated a group called the Knights of the Golden Circle, and learned that they hoped to assassinate Lincoln as he passed through Baltimore. Lawton kept Pinkerton advised of Webster's activities. (Both Webster and Lawton went on to serve as spies for the federal government during the war. Webster successfully infiltrated the Confederacy, gaining employment as an agent with the War Department, where he intercepted numerous rebel military communications and relayed them to Washington. He was exposed and hanged as a spy in Richmond, Virginia in April 1862. Lawton also was captured, sentenced to one year in prison, and then exchanged for a captured Confederate agent.)

Pinkerton traveled to Baltimore with Harry Davies and checked into a hotel as J.H. Hutcheson of Charleston, South Carolina. He rented a small office and posed as a businessman, but spent most of his time in rough saloons and hotels of the city, meeting and mingling with secessionists, and taking on the role of a Blood Tub. He became acquainted with a militant named Luckett, discovering that Luckett enjoyed frequenting taverns and was prone to loose talk after a few drams of beers. Through Luckett, Pinkerton learned, as Webster had, that certain railroads were targeted for attack, and that President-elect Lincoln was to be killed.

Luckett introduced Pinkerton to a bizarre man named Cypriano Ferrandini, a barber at Barnum's Hotel who spoke loudly of the right of the southern people to revolt. Ferrandini was a recent immigrant from Italy, where he had been implicated in a plot to kill Napoleon III. He had escaped law enforcement there and brought his violent nature with him to America. He was a captain in a Maryland militia company that had organized to assist the Confederacy, and he also joined the militant groups Constitutional Guards and National Volunteers, armed irregulars who would commit acts of rioting and murder across the state in the coming months. Ferrandini told Pinkerton that "murder of any kind is justifiable and right to save the rights of the Southern people." Ferrandini was "a man well calculated for controlling and directing the ardent-minded," Pinkerton later wrote. "Even I, myself, felt the influence of this man's strange power, and wrong though I knew him to be, I felt strangely unable to keep my mind balanced against him."[18]

While Pinkerton was getting close to Ferrandini, Davies was working another angle. Operating under the name Joe Howard, he befriended an associate of Ferrandini's named Hillard, and after several nights of revelry at Baltimore taverns and brothels, Hillard advised Davies that the plan was to assassinate Lincoln "as he walked through a narrow tunnel to the waiting Washington express," later determined to be the Calvert Street Station in Baltimore, where Lincoln would change trains en route to Washington.[19] Hillard was, he told Davies, "ready and willing to die to rid his country" of the tyrant Lincoln.[20] So convincing was Davies' portrayal as a Blood Tub that he was invited to a meeting of 30 potential assassins, headed by Ferrandini, where secret ballots were drawn: the plotter who drew the red ballot would have the honor of killing Lincoln. The conspirators did not know that Ferrandini had rigged the outcome, marking eight ballots, not just one, thereby increasing the likelihood that Lincoln would die.

By February 11, the very day of Lincoln's departure from Springfield, Pinkerton had learned enough. He telegraphed Norman Judd, informing him that trouble was brewing, and promised to keep him updated in coming days. He telegraphed Judd again when Lincoln's entourage reached Columbus, and sent Kate Warne, the head of Pinkerton's Female Detective Force, to New York City a few days later to confer personally with Judd. Warne convinced Judd that the threat of assassination was real, and Judd promised to make Lincoln available for a meeting with Pinkerton in Philadelphia, on February 21.

But now, in his suite at the Continental Hotel in Philadelphia, Lincoln could not be convinced that the plot was legitimate. It was difficult for the pragmatic Lincoln to take seriously the idea that a fanatical barber from Italy was the mastermind of an assassination attempt. Besides, Lincoln had engagements at Independence Hall the next morning, where he would raise the American flag (the first with 34 stars, including one for newly admitted Kansas), and later at Harrisburg where he was to address the legislature. Although Pinkerton insisted that Lincoln secretly travel through Baltimore, unannounced and at night, Lincoln would not agree.

But then, suddenly, corroboration of the Ferrandini plot came from another, unexpected source. Frederick Seward, the son of William Seward, arrived in Philadelphia on the 10:00 P.M. train and hastened to the Continental Hotel to meet Lincoln and the others. He had been sent by his father, who had consulted with Col. Charles P. Stone, inspector general of the District of Columbia Militia. Stone, in turn, had been advised by John Kennedy, New York City's police superintendent, that Lincoln's life would indeed be in danger in Baltimore; the information had been channeled from the House investigating committee (the very committee that had taken the testimony of Governor Hicks). Scott, Stone, Kennedy and Seward were all men Lincoln trusted. Too tired to argue, he reluctantly agreed to take Pinkerton's advice. He would alter his travel plans through Baltimore and sneak into Washington. He was weary and went to bed, letting Pinkerton arrange the details for the final leg of his journey.

Lincoln slept only a few hours that night. At sunrise on the 22nd cannon boomed across Philadelphia in celebration of George Washington's birthday. Lincoln rose, dressed and went to the lobby of the Continental, where his advisors were waiting. There was no time for breakfast. Lincoln stepped out into the cold, crisp morning air and climbed into a carriage that took him down Chestnut Street to Independence Hall, accompanied by the Scott Legion, heroes of the Mexican War. A large crowd was waiting for Lincoln, and a brass band played patriotic music. When the carriage arrived the ladies in the audience waved their kerchiefs and the men shouted, and Lincoln smiled and waved in return, then quickly stepped inside. He could not help but feel awed to be standing in the very room where America's founders had signed the Declaration of Independence, and walking to the center of the room began to speak to the group of politicians and dignitaries assembled there:

> Mr. Cuyler:—I am filled with deep emotion at finding myself standing here in the place where were collected together the wisdom, the patriotism, the devotion to principle, from which sprang the institutions under which we live. You have kindly suggested to me that in my hands is the task of restoring peace to our dis-

tracted country. I can say in return, sir, that all the political sentiments I entertain have been drawn, so far as I have been able to draw them, from the sentiments which originated, and were given to the world from this hall in which we stand. I have never had a feeling politically that did not spring from the sentiments embodied in the Declaration of Independence. [*Great cheering.*] I have often pondered over the dangers which were incurred by the men who assembled here and adopted that Declaration of Independence — I have pondered over the toils that were endured by the officers and soldiers of the army, who achieved that Independence. [*Applause.*] I have often inquired of myself, what great principle or idea it was that kept this Confederacy so long together. It was not the mere matter of the separation of the colonies from the mother land; but something in that Declaration giving liberty, not alone to the people of this country, but hope to the world for all future time. [*Great applause.*] It was that which gave promise that in due time the weights should be lifted from the shoulders of all men, and that all should have an equal chance. [*Cheers.*] This is the sentiment embodied in that Declaration of Independence.

The disturbing news of the night before, that his life was in danger, was clearly on Lincoln's mind. He continued:

Now, my friends, can this country be saved upon that basis? If it can, I will consider myself one of the happiest men in the world if I can help to save it. If it can't be saved upon that principle, it will be truly awful. But, if this country cannot be saved without giving up that principle — I was about to say I would rather be assassinated on this spot than to surrender it. [*Applause.*]

Now, in my view of the present aspect of affairs, there is no need of bloodshed and war. There is no necessity for it. I am not in favor of such a course, and I may say in advance, there will be no bloodshed unless it be forced upon the Government. The Government will not use force unless force is used against it. [*Prolonged applause and cries of "That's the proper sentiment."*]

My friends, this is a wholly unprepared speech. I did not expect to be called upon to say a word when I came here — I supposed I was merely to do something towards raising a flag. I may, therefore, have said something indiscreet, [*cries of "no, no"*], but I have said nothing but what I am willing to live by, and, in the pleasure of Almighty God, die by.[21]

The politicians crowded around Lincoln, anxious to shake his hand and offer words of congratulations and encouragement, but he all but dismissed them. He strolled around the Hall, gazing at the portraits of American heroes and patriots, the men he had idolized his entire life. His brief tour complete, Lincoln was led outside where, just a few feet from the entrance to the Hall, a platform six feet high had been erected. A large crowd gathered around, and at least one small boy had climbed up a tree for a better view of the festivities. A huge American flag, adorned with 34 stars and folded neatly, rested on the rail. Lincoln nodded at Tad, who had managed to secure a spot on the platform just to the left of his father, and spoke:

Fellow Citizens: — I am invited and called before you to participate in raising above Independence Hall the flag of our country, with an additional star upon it. [*Cheers.*] I propose now, in advance of performing this very pleasant and complimentary duty, to say a few words. I propose to say that when that flag was originally raised here it had but thirteen stars. I wish to call your attention to the fact, that, under the blessing of God, each additional star added to that flag has given additional prosperity and happiness to this country until it has advanced to its present condition; and its welfare in the future, as well as in the past, is in your hands. [*Cheers.*] Cultivating the spirit that animated our fathers, who gave renown and celebrity to this Hall, cherishing that fraternal feeling which has so long characterized us as a nation, excluding passion, ill-temper and precipitate action on all occasions, I think we may promise ourselves that not only the new star placed upon the flag shall be permitted to remain there to our permanent prosperity for years to come, but additional ones shall from time to time be placed there, until we shall number as was anticipated by the great historian, five hundred millions of happy and prosperous people. [*Great applause.*] With these few remarks, I proceed to the very agreeable duty assigned to me.

The Reverend Henry S. Clarke offered a short prayer, and Lincoln took off his overcoat, took hold of the halyard, and pulled it hand-over-hand style until the flag reached the top of the flagpole. A photographer recorded the scene, and the band played "The Stars and Stripes Are Still Unfurled," a brand new anthem composed in honor of Maj. Robert Anderson, commander at Fort Sumter. The Scott Legion presented arms, and an artillery detachment fired a salute. The crowd cheered wildly as Lincoln stepped back into his carriage and returned to the Continental Hotel. It was just past 7:00 A.M., and in two hours he was back at the West Philadelphia Station, ready to board the train again.

It was 115 miles due west from Philadelphia to Harrisburg, the state capital, a four and one-half hour trip. The excitement of the flag-raising ceremony quickly passed, and Lincoln sat quietly, alone with his thoughts. At Leaman Place, the Special's first stop, he declined to make a speech. There were repeated calls for Mary, and Lincoln coaxed her out onto the train's rear platform. "Now you have the long and short of it," Lincoln said, and the crowd laughed. At Lancaster, a pleasant town just north of the mighty Susquehanna River, the crowd shouted so loudly and persistently for Lincoln that he appeared and offered a few words:

> Ladies and Gentlemen of Old Lancaster: I appear not to make a speech. I have not time to make them at length, and not strength to make them on every occasion, and, worse than all, I have none to make. I come before you to see and be seen and, as regards the ladies, I have the best of the bargain; but, as to the gentlemen, I cannot say as much. There is plenty of matter to speak about in these times, but it is well known that the more a man speaks the less he is understood — the more he says one thing, his adversaries contend he meant something else. I shall soon have occasion to speak officially, and then I will endeavor to put my thoughts just as plain as I can express myself, true to the Constitution and Union of all the States, and to the perpetual liberty of all the people. Until I so speak, there is no need to enter upon details. In conclusion, I greet you most heartily, and bid you an affectionate farewell.[22]

The Special pulled into Harrisburg at 2:00 P.M., and Lincoln was met be a delegation headed by Pennsylvania governor Andrew Gregg Curtin, a man who would play an essential role in the Union's war effort. Curtin's father was a Scottish immigrant iron worker, his mother the daughter of U.S. senator Andrew Gregg. Curtin received an excellent education in private schools in Pennsylvania, completing his studies at the Dickinson School of Law in Carlisle. He practiced criminal law, was appointed the state's superintendent of public instruction, and joined the Whig Party. In 1860 he became a Republican (known as the People's Party in Pennsylvania), and in January 1861, at the age of 43, was elected governor, defeating his Democratic opponent by a landslide 30,000 votes.

Governor Curtin never wavered in his support for Lincoln's policies. Pennsylvania's railroads, iron and steel industry, and shipbuilding and agricultural resources played vital parts in the Federal cause. Immediately after the Confederates fired on Fort Sumter, Lincoln called for 16 volunteer regiments from Pennsylvania; it sent 25. Five militia companies were sent directly to Washington, and they became known as "The First Defenders." Over the course of the war nearly 350,000 Pennsylvanians, including 8,600 African-Americans, served in the Union army. In Harrisburg, more military units were organized than in any other northern recruiting point, at an 80-acre outpost that came to be called "Camp Curtin." In 1862 Curtin called northern governors to a conference in Altoona, where he encouraged them to support the president and successfully lobbied that the timid General McClellan be replaced as commander of the Union forces.

Despite suffering a mild nervous breakdown in early 1863, in November of that year Curtin authorized the purchase of 17 acres on Gettysburg's Cemetery Hill, and arranged for Lincoln to "make a few remarks" at the dedication for the burial grounds. (Lincoln's Gettysburg Address, just two minutes in length, was to become perhaps the greatest speech in American history.) After the war Curtin was named minister to Russia by President Ulysses S. Grant, but his disgust over the widespread corruption of the Grant administration led him to leave the Republican Party, and he served as a Democratic congressman from 1881 to 1887.

Now Governor Curtin escorted Lincoln to the Jones House, Harrisburg's finest hotel, and enjoyed a private luncheon with Lincoln and his family. In the afternoon Lincoln was told that a tremendous crowd still lingered outside the hotel, and at Curtin's request he appeared on the second-floor balcony where, after Curtin's rousing introduction, he addressed his admirers:

> Gov. Curtin and citizens of the State of Pennsylvania: Perhaps the best thing that I could do would be simply to endorse the patriotic and eloquent speech which your Governor has just made in your hearing. [*Applause.*] I am quite sure that I am unable to address to you anything so appropriate as that which he has uttered.
>
> Reference has been made by him to the distraction of the public mind at this time and to the great task that lies before me in entering upon the administration of the general Government. With all the eloquence and ability that your Governor brings to this theme, I am quite sure he does not — in his situation he cannot — appreciate as I do the weight of that great responsibility. I feel that, under God, in the strength of the arms and wisdom of the heads of these masses, after all, must be my support. [*Immense cheering.*] As I have often had occasion to say, I repeat to you — I am quite sure I do not deceive myself when I tell you I bring to the work an honest heart; I dare not tell you that I bring a head sufficient for it. [*A voice — "we are sure of that."*] If my own strength should fail, I shall at least fall back upon these masses, who, I think, under any circumstances will not fail.
>
> Allusion has been made to the peaceful principles upon which this great Commonwealth was originally settled. Allow me to add my meed of praise to those

peaceful principles. I hope no one of the Friends who originally settled here, or who lived here since that time, or who live here now, has been or is a more devoted lover of peace, harmony and concord than my humble self.

While I have been proud to see to-day the finest military array, I think, that I have ever seen, allow me to say in regard to those men that they give hope of what may be done when war is inevitable. But, at the same time, allow me to express the hope that in the shedding of blood their services may never be needed, especially in the shedding of fraternal blood. It shall be my endeavor to preserve the peace of this country so far as it can possibly be done, consistently with the maintenance of the institutions of the country. With my consent, or without my great displeasure, this county shall never witness the shedding of one drop of blood in fraternal strife.

And now, my fellow-citizens, as I have made many speeches, will you allow me to bid you farewell?[23]

It was just after 2:00 P.M. Lincoln was taken via military escort to the statehouse, where he addressed the entire General Assembly:

Mr. Speaker of the Senate and also Mr. Speaker of the House Of Representatives, and Gentlemen of the General Assembly of the State of Pennsylvania, I appear before you only for a very few brief remarks in response to what has been said to me. I thank you most sincerely for this reception, and the generous words in which support has been promised me upon this occasion. I thank your great Commonwealth for the overwhelming support it recently gave — not me personally — but the cause which I think a just one, in the late election. [*Loud applause.*]

Allusion has been made to the fact — the interesting fact perhaps we should say — that I for the first time appear at the Capitol of the great Commonwealth of Pennsylvania, upon the birthday of the Father of his Country. In connection with that beloved anniversary connected with the history of this country, I have already gone through one exceedingly interesting scene this morning in the ceremonies at Philadelphia, in old Independence Hall, [*enthusiastic cheering*], to have a few words addressed to me there and opening up to me an opportunity of expressing with much regret that I had not more time to express something of my own feelings excited by the occasion — somewhat to harmonize and give shape to the feelings that had been really the feelings of my whole life.

Besides this, our friends there had provided a magnificent flag of the country. They had arranged it so that I was given the honor of raising it to the head of its staff [*applause*]; and when it went up, I was pleased that it went to its place by the strength of my own feeble arm. When, according to the arrangement, the cord was pulled and it flaunted gloriously to the wind without an accident, in the bright glowing sun-shine of the morning, I could not help hoping that there was in the entire success of that beautiful ceremony, at least something of an omen of what is to come. [*Loud applause.*] Nor could I help, feeling then as I often have felt, that in the whole of that proceeding I was a very humble instrument. I had not provided the flag; I had not made the arrangement for elevating it to its place; I had applied but a very small portion of even my feeble strength in raising it. In the whole transaction, I was in the hands of the people who had arranged it, and if I can have the same generous co-operation of the people of this nation, I think the flag of our country may yet be kept flaunting gloriously. [*Enthusiastic, long continued cheering*].

I recur for a moment but to repeat some words uttered at the hotel in regard to what has been said about the military support which the general government may expect from the Commonwealth of Pennsylvania, in a proper emergency. To guard against any possible mistake do I recur to this. It is not with any pleasure that I contemplate the possibility that a necessity may arise in the country for the use of the military arm. [*Applause.*] While I am exceedingly gratified to see the manifestation upon your streets of your military force here, and exceedingly gratified at your promise here to use that force upon a proper emergency, while I make these acknowledgments, I desire to repeat, in order to preclude any possible misconstruction, that I do most sincerely hope that we shall have no use for them [*loud applause*] — that it will never become their duty to shed blood, and most especially never to shed fraternal blood. I promise that, in so far as I may have wisdom to direct, if so painful a result shall in any wise be brought about, it shall be through no fault of mine. [*Cheers.*]

　　Allusion has also been made, by one of your honored Speakers, to some remarks recently made by myself at Pittsburgh, in regard to what is supposed to be the especial interest of this great Commonwealth of Pennsylvania. I now wish only to say, in regard to that matter, that the few remarks which I uttered on that occasion were rather carefully worded. I took pains that they should be so. I have seen no occasion since to add to them or subtract from them. I leave them precisely as they stand; [*applause*] adding only now that I am pleased to have an expression from you, gentlemen of Pennsylvania, significant that they are satisfactory to you.

　　And now, gentlemen of the General Assembly of the Commonwealth of Pennsylvania, allow me again to return to you my most sincere thanks. [*Prolonged cheering.*][24]

　　Lincoln was relieved to learn that no reception was planned, and within the hour he was back at the Jones House, where he hoped to rest until dinner was served. But there was no time to relax. Pinkerton had assembled Lincoln's advisors and security personnel for a meeting to discuss travel plans to Washington. Present in Lincoln's room were Judd, Judge Davis, Colonel Sumner, Major Hunter, Captain Pope and Lamon. Pinkerton set forth the plan that he had developed with Judd in detail. That evening after dinner, rather than spending the night as a guest of Governor Curtin, Lincoln was to slip out of the hotel and take the 10:50 P.M. train from Harrisburg to Washington. He would pass through Baltimore, but in the middle of the night when no one expected him. He would pose as the invalid brother of Kate Warne, Pinkerton's agent, and would enter the capital in secrecy. Arrangements had been made with D.L. Franciscus, general manager of the Pennsylvania Railroad, who would see to it that no other trains would be on the tracks that night, and Edward S. Sanford of the American Telegraph Company, who gave his assurance that wires would be cut, negating communications between any conspirators.

　　Lamon later recalled that the plan "was a great surprise to all of us." Colonel Sumner was adamantly opposed to any change in the schedule. "That proceeding," he said, "will be a damned piece of cowardice." If lack of security was the problem, he told Pinkerton, "I'll get a squad of cavalry, sir, and *cut* our way to Washington, sir!" Judd tried to calm Sumner down. "Probably before that day comes the Inauguration day will have passed. It is important that Mr. Lincoln should be in Washington on that day." Judge Davis knew that the final decision rested with Lincoln. "What is your judgment on the matter?" he asked. Lincoln now agreed to play it safe. "Unless there are some other reasons besides fear of ridicule," he said. "I am disposed to carry out Judd's plan."[25]

Mary Lincoln did not take the news easily, and "fear threw her into an unreasoning panic." How could her husband leave her now, when danger was all around them? Her place, and the children's, was by his side. But Lincoln would "run no risk where no risk was required." The plans could not be changed now. He assured Mary that she and the boys would be safe, and that Lamon would see him safely to Washington.[26]

Dinner was served at five o'clock in the dining room at the Jones House. Shortly before six Judd came to Lincoln's table and ushered him out of the room. Lincoln quietly pulled on an overcoat and donned a brown soft wool hat called a "Tam o' Shanter." Holding a shawl over his arm, and flanked by Lamon and Sumner, he followed Judd out a side door of the hotel where a carriage waited. In the darkness Lincoln climbed inside, as did Lamon. Sumner tried to follow but Judd intervened, and as Sumner protested the carriage quickly pulled away. Judd hurried to send a telegraph to Philadelphia before the wires were cut: he let "Plums" (Pinkerton) know that "Nuts" (Lincoln) was on his way.

Lincoln and his bodyguard traveled alone on a special train to West Philadelphia, where they were met at the Pennsylvania Station by Pinkerton. The three men rode to the Philadelphia, Wilmington & Baltimore depot, and boarded the last sleeping car, Lincoln stooping to disguise his height, the collar of his overcoat turned up. Lincoln climbed into a berth reserved for Kate Warne's "invalid brother" and pulled the shabby curtain closed; the berth was so small that he had to nearly double up his legs. The car was full, warmed by two wood stoves and dimly lit by small candle lamps. The train pulled out and Lincoln lay in silence, unable to sleep, as Lamon stood guard outside. Pinkerton stood on the rear platform, and as the train passed each town he raised his lantern to signal his operatives that all was well. At 3:15 A.M. the morning the train arrived in Baltimore, the angry city now quiet and asleep. Lincoln's car was left at Camden Station, where it would be picked up by another night train. Lincoln and his companions waited uneasily for that train to arrive; the only noise came from a drunken man on the platform, just a few feet from Lincoln's berth, who sang "Dixie" over and over again in his stupor. "No doubt there will be a great time in Dixie by and by," Lincoln murmured. Finally the train arrived, and Lincoln was again on his way, now bound for Washington.[27]

As dawn broke the train pulled into the capital city. Lincoln, Lamon and Pinkerton walked briskly through Union Station, Lincoln still dressed in his hat and overcoat, the shawl now pulled over his shoulders. A broad-shouldered figure stepped out from behind a pillar and startled the group. "Lincoln, you can't play that on me!" said the man, and Pinkerton raised his fist before Lincoln stopped him.[28] It was Elihu Washburne, the congressman from Illinois. The men took a hack down Pennsylvania Avenue to Willard's Hotel. Pinkerton immediately telegraphed Judd back in Harrisburg: "Plums arrived with Nuts this morning."[29]

Lincoln was shown to Suite 6 on the corner of the second floor, where he would stay until the inauguration one week away. Relieved that he had made it safely to Washington but worried about Mary and the boys, Lincoln glanced wearily around the room and noticed a letter waiting for him on the desk. Lincoln sighed as he read line after line of profane abuse directed at him, the letter ending with the words: "You are nothing but a Goddam Black Nigger."[30]

12

The First Trick

Although rumors were spreading in Baltimore that Lincoln had already passed through the city, a crowd of nearly 15,000 people gathered to meet his scheduled train at the Calvert Street station on the morning of February 23. A good many of those assembled were anti-Union and wanted to tell Lincoln how they felt, although Mayor George Brown, who was also on hand, nervously hoped that there would be no trouble. Just before noon the train carrying Mary and the boys arrived, and many rushed to meet it even before it came to a stop. Angry men ran alongside and tried to cling to the sides of the cars, peering through windows, cursing and shouting. A few managed to climb aboard and tried to enter Mary's suite, but Robert and John Hay barricaded the door as Mary trembled in fear. After an anxious few minutes and when the crowd became satisfied that Lincoln was not present, order was restored, and Mary was taken by carriage to the home of John S. Gittings, the president of the B & O railroad. Back at the station after lunch Mary was greeted by more jeering, — "oaths, obscenity, disgusting epithets and unpleasant gesticulations, were the order of the day," reported the New York *Times*— and her train proceeded toward Washington. The next day's newspapers expressed indignation that the president-elect had snubbed their city, leaving his wife and family to face detractors without him. He had entered Washington "like a thief in the night," sneered the Baltimore *Sun*. "Had we any respect for Lincoln (this) would have utterly destroyed it."[1]

Baltimore would be the scene of another incident in coming weeks, this one far uglier. On April 19, after President Lincoln issued a call for 75,000 men to enlist in the Union army, one of the first regiments to respond, the Sixth Massachusetts, arrived in Baltimore en route to Washington. As the soldiers attempted to pass through the city a wild mob of secessionists carrying Confederate flags blocked Pratt Street, then began throwing bricks and stones. The horses pulling the soldiers' cars panicked, and the men got out and started to march toward Camden Yard. As the melee escalated some young soldiers fired into the crowd, and shots were returned. City police tried to calm the scene and ultimately the regiment reached the station, but not before four soldiers and 12 civilians were killed and dozens more wounded. The Baltimore Riot, as it came to be known, produced the first casualties of the Civil War. The northern press was outraged over the incident, and Horace Greeley wrote that the entire city should be burned to the ground. Three weeks later federal troops entered the city and declared martial law. The police chief and city commissioners were arrested for their alleged participation in the riot. Many other suspected secession-ists, including several state legislators, were arrested and held without charges. Fed-eral forces occupied Baltimore for the remainder of the war.[2]

William Seward was, with Washburne, supposed to meet Lincoln at Union Sta-tion in Washington, but overslept. Annoyed with himself, he invited Pinkerton and Lamon to his home and heard their accounts of the strange trip through Baltimore, and then took the men to Willard's, where Lamon began drinking and bragging about his role in the excursion. Soon the story of Lincoln's entrance into Washington was revealed, and he became the object of much ridicule. Was this an example of the lead-ership Lincoln would provide, wondered newspapers from both North and South? He was a coward, a charlatan, a disgrace. The facts of Lincoln's "disguise" became garbled; Joseph Howard Jr. of the New York *Times* wrote that Lincoln wore a Scot-tish plaid cap and matching military cloak, and this story came to be accepted as true. *Harper's Weekly* ran a panel of cartoons, depicting a terrified, scarecrowish Lin-coln dancing in his outlandish costume. The Louisville *Courier* told its readers that Lincoln traded clothing with his wife and rode through Baltimore in a skirt instead of a kilt. The Charleston *Mercury* wrote that "Everybody here is disgusted at this cow-ardly and undignified entry." Other Democratic newspapers ran a poem that played on "Yankee Doodle Dandy":

> Uncle Abe had gone to bed,
> The night was dark and rainy
> A laurelled night-cap on his head,
> "Way down in Pennsylvany.
>
> They went and got a special train
> At midnight's solemn hour,
> And in a cloak and Scottish plaid shawl,
> He dodged from the Slave-Power.
>
> Lanky Lincoln came to town
> In night and wind, and rain, sir
> Wrapped in a military cloak,
> Upon a special train, sir.[3]

Pinkerton never forgave Lamon for his indiscretion in leaking the story of the "Great Lincoln Escapade," and for the ridicule that followed. In his memoirs Pinker-ton called Lamon a "brainless egotistical fool."[4]

In light of Lincoln's awkward and embarrassing entrance into Washington, Seward saw more clearly than ever that he must take control. Convinced that he should spend as much time with Lincoln as possible, for his sake and the sake of the country, Seward rarely left Lincoln's side for the next week (all of which irritated Han-nibal Hamlin, who wondered whether the country would have a "Seward adminis-tration for the benefit of Mr. Seward or a Lincoln administration").[5] On Lincoln's first morning in Washington Seward accompanied him to breakfast, and boasted of how he had almost single-handedly held the government together from the election in November through the recent tally of electoral votes. He took Lincoln to the White House where they met briefly with President Buchanan and several members of the outgoing cabinet. Next they called on Winfield Scott, who was not home, and then Seward returned Lincoln to Willard's Hotel where he rested before the onslaught of visitors began to arrive. Seward promised Lincoln that he would greet Mary and the boys at Union Station that afternoon, and was true to his word.

Nathaniel Hawthorne observed that "the Willard Hotel more justly could be called the center of Washington than either the Capitol or the White House or the State Department." Built on property that had once been farmland, in 1816 an entrepreneur named John Tayloe built a row of two-story houses on the site. Thirty years later three Willard brothers of Vermont, Henry, Edwin and Joseph, bought the property from the Tayloe estate and united the houses architecturally, then gradually expanded the structure into a five-story hotel. Ornately decorated, Willard's was the hub of Washington's social and political scene, counting dozens of influential and famous people among its guests. This week before the inauguration was no exception. Many influential businessmen were registered, as were dozens of newspaper reporters. Most of the Peace Conference delegates, including former president John Tyler, were also there, still scrambling to come up with a compromise that might prove acceptable. Lincoln had first visited Willard's in 1849, when he attended a meeting of subscribers to President Zachary Taylor's inaugural ball and was elected to the board of managers. The prices had gone up since then. Suites now cost almost $100 per night, and were well worth it; Willard's was the first hotel in the country to feature running water in every room.[6]

While Willard's regularly received rave reviews, the city of Washington was something of a mess. It was, according to Congressman Albert Riddle of Ohio, "as unattractive, straggling, sodden a town, wandering up and down the left bank of the yellow Potomac, as the fancy can stretch." Pennsylvania Avenue was the only paved street in the city; all others were made of dirt or sand that turned to mud when it rained. None of the streets had gutters, and the city had no sewage system. Instead, each home, business or shack had open drains extending directly from their back doors into canals, which emptied untreated into the Potomac River. Malaria was commonplace, particularly in the hot summer months when mosquitoes and tadpoles abounded. Garbage was strewn everywhere, and pigs rooted about in the filth. The stench of dead and dying animals was almost overpowering. Only a few public buildings existed: the White House, a smallish State Department building, the War and Navy Department buildings, the Post Office and the Department of the Interior. The Washington Monument, begun in 1855, was only half completed. The Capitol itself was unfinished; huge cranes stood motionless against the outline of the rotunda, lumber and slabs of stone lay scattered around the grounds, and within the fenced area to the east stood a sickly grove of maple trees. Washington was home to about 61,000 people; one-quarter of those were African-Americans, and one-fifth of those were slaves.[7]

As Mary and the boys settled into the suite, Lincoln received the first wave of guests. Francis Blair and his son Montgomery, who sought reassurance that Montgomery would be appointed postmaster general, and Stephen Douglas, who headed an Illinois delegation of politicians, were among Lincoln's first callers. Then General Scott arrived, in such sad physical shape that he could barely climb one flight of stairs. The number of federal troops in Washington, Scott advised, was now 653, including infantry, cavalry and artillerymen. More were arriving nearly every day to fortify the city and protect the president-elect at all costs (nationwide, only 15 of the Army's 198 companies were located east of the Mississippi).[8] The Corps of Engineers, as well as the regular garrison, had been summoned from West Point, and joined regular troops in constant drill and maneuver exercises around the city. Washington "looked more like a Camp Ground than a City," grumbled one resident. "Was there ever such Tom foolery."[9] But rumors of a slave uprising heightened the anxiety of many, including General Scott, who was determined to assure a safe inaugural, now just days away. Lincoln would meet with Scott regularly in the coming months, discussing the state of the military and security measures needed in anticipation of a possible Confederate invasion of the city (on some of these visits Lincoln would meet with Scott outside, on the White House driveway, to save him the embarrassment of being unable to walk upstairs to Lincoln's office).

In the midafternoon, upon the request of *Harper's Weekly*, Lincoln went to Matthew Brady's studio at 352 Pennsylvania Avenue and had his portrait taken. He wearily climbed three flights of stairs, passing the reception room with its stereoscopic viewing box on the second floor, and the finishing and mounting rooms on the third. The portrait gallery at the top of the building was filled with cameras, chairs, mirrors, curtains and other props and accessories. Lincoln sat on a black chair, his stovepipe hat resting upside down on the table beside him, as the window curtains overhead were adjusted with a long pole to allow the proper amount of light illumination. He was plainly exhausted. During the five different poses that Brady took Lincoln sat quietly, closing his eyes for long periods of time, scarcely moving. His hair had grown long, his beard now fully developed. His right hand was swollen from shaking thousands of hands over the past two weeks, and he tried to hide it behind an armrest. Brady's young assistant, an artist named George H. Story, was present in the studio, and later recalled that Lincoln "seemed absolutely indifferent to all that was going on about him, and he gave the impression that he was a man who was overwhelmed with anxiety and fatigue and care."[10]

That evening Lincoln and Mary dined at the Seward residence, along with the increasingly wary Hamlin. Long lines of visitors crowded every free space at Willard's waiting for Lincoln to return. Lincoln was "overwhelmed with callers," said James Harlan. "The room in which he stood, the corridors and halls and stairs leading to it, were crowded full of people, each one, apparently, intent on obtaining an opportunity to say a few words to him *privately*."[11] He greeted as many people as he could, shaking with both of his hands, getting so caught up in the rush that he forgot to take off his hat. After two hours of this he was led into a private room by Salmon Chase, soon to be secretary of the treasury, and Lucius Chittendon of Vermont, who introduced him to each member of the Peace Conference. Lincoln was polite and listened attentively to summaries of the pending compromise proposals, but offered no assurances that he would support any of them. Almost all of the southern delegates were unimpressed with Lincoln's coarse style, but at least one, the elderly William C. Rives of Virginia, saw him in a different light. Lincoln "had been both misjudged and misunderstood by the Southern people. They have looked upon him as an ignorant, self-willed man, incapable of independent judgment, full of prejudices, willing to be used as a tool by more able. This is all wrong. He will be the head of his administration, and he will do his own thinking."[12] A group of New York businessmen got Lincoln's attention as they presented a plan to restore commerce with secessionist states. One businessman and delegate named William C. Dodge (who had himself given up Suite 6 to Lincoln) worried that, if war came, the country would go bankrupt and "grass shall grow in the streets of our cities." Lincoln replied, "If it depends upon me, the grass shall not grow anywhere except in the fields and the meadows." He added that "the Constitution shall not be preserved and defended unless it is enforced and obeyed in every part of every one of the United States. It *must* be so enforced, obeyed, enforced and defended, let the grass grow where it may."[13] At 10:00 P.M. members of Buchanan's cabinet, whom Lincoln had met that morning, returned the visit, after which he insisted that he must retire for the evening.

The next morning was Sunday, February 24. Lincoln and his family attended services at St. John's Episcopal Church, where they would sporadically worship throughout the next four years, and then relaxed the rest of the morning at Seward's home. Lincoln gave Seward a copy of his draft inaugural address and asked for his comments. The men read newspapers that detailed the speeches Lincoln had given during his week-long journey from Springfield. They also discussed recent events in the South: U.S. arsenals had been seized in Georgia, Florida, Louisiana and Arkansas; federal troops in Texas, under the command of Brevet Maj. Gen. David Emmanuel Twiggs—one of the four highest officers in the U.S. Army—surrendered to state authorities. (For this "treachery to the flag of his country" Twiggs was dismissed from the army. He was later commissioned a major general in the Confederate army.) The Provisional Congress of the Confederacy authorized Jefferson Davis to contract for the purchase and manufacture of army materiel; U.S. revenue cutters *Robert McClelland*, *Lewis Cass* and *Henry Dodge* were surrendered to southern authorities, their commanders ignoring specific orders from the War Department "defend the vessel and flag"; U.S. Army and Navy officers were resigning their commissions and returning to their home states in the South to prepare for war; the Choctaw Indian Nation declared its allegiance to the Confederacy.[14] Back at the hotel that afternoon, another steady stream of visitors, including vice president and failed presidential candidate John Breckenridge, filed past Lincoln. That evening before bed Lincoln and Mary enjoyed a serenade from the Marine Band.

On Monday Seward took Lincoln to the Capitol. Republican members greeted Lincoln warmly, but except for Douglas and William Bigler of Pennsylvania, the Democrats were cool toward him. Andrew Johnson of Tennessee (who would become Lincoln's vice president in 1865) was the only southerner who seemed anxious to meet him. Still unsure of a number of his cabinet selections, Lincoln took an informal poll of Republicans: did they prefer Chase or Cameron for secretary of the treasury? Of the 19 senators polled, 11 favored Chase, only three favored Cameron, while others suggested either William Dayton or James Simmons of Rhode Island.[15] Lincoln said nothing but now had made up his mind: he would offer Treasury to Chase and either War or Interior to Cameron. Seward then escorted Lincoln to the building's old Senate chambers where the Supreme Court was housed, and where the justices, headed by Chief Roger Taney, author of the *Dred Scott* decision, waited for him.

Roger Brooke Taney was born in Maryland in 1777, the second son of a tobacco-growing aristocrat who happened to be Roman Catholic. His older brother inherited the family plantation, and Roger was educated at Dickinson College and groomed for a career in law. In 1806 he married Anne Key, and together they raised six children, all girls. (Anne's brother Francis Scott wrote "The Star-Spangled Banner" after Britain's bombing of Fort McHenry in the War of 1812.) Taney's successful practice in Annapolis and Frederick precluded his election, as a member of the Federalist Party, to the House of Delegates and then the state Senate. His early political career was dominated by interests in banking, finance and agriculture, and by his support of federal authority over financial institutions. A slaveowner by inheritance, he was also a strong supporter of states' rights, believing that only individual states, and not the federal government, had the power to regulate slavery.

By 1826 Taney had become a Democrat and was elected Maryland's attorney general. Five years later President Jackson appointed him U.S. attorney general and then, in 1833, to the Supreme Court, where he replaced the legendary John Marshall. In just three years he was named chief justice, a position he held for nearly 30 years. He presided over a Court that drew careful lines between state and federal powers; generally, his opinions reflected the belief that states could regulate their own affairs provided they did not interfere with federal legislation. By the late 1850s the Court was dominated by southerners, slaveholders and southern sympathizers, and saw its chance to settle the slavery question in 1857s *Dred Scott* case. Taney authored the opinion that declared that blacks were not citizens, but property, protected by the Constitution, and that the Missouri Compromise was illegal. It was this inflammatory opinion that brought about Lincoln's return to the political arena. When Lincoln suspended the writ of habeas corpus in 1861 Taney issued an ex parte opinion that declared the action unconstitutional; the Lincoln administration ignored the ruling.

Three southerners joined Taney on the Court. John Archibald Campbell of Georgia was an intellectual giant who enrolled at the University of Georgia at the age of 11 and graduated with honors three years later. In 1853 Franklin Pierce nominated him to the Supreme Court, and the Senate confirmed the appointment unanimously. When the war began in April 1861 Campbell resigned and served the Confederacy as assistant secretary of war. He was imprisoned at Fort Pulaski for four months after the southern surrender at Appomattox. Upon his release he established a prosperous law practice, taking cases to the Supreme Court on many occasions. Another southern justice, James Moore Wayne of Georgia, was a slaveholder who regularly voted in the interests of slaveholders. But unlike Campbell, Wayne did not leave the Court for the war. Viewed as a traitor by his home state, Wayne saw his property confiscated by Confederate authorities. The last southern justice, John Catron of Tennessee, also remained on the bench after the war began. When the

Court completed its term in the spring of 1861, however, Catron returned home and unsuccessfully tried to prevent his state from seceding.

The North was also represented on the Supreme Court. John McLean of Ohio, Lincoln's personal choice for the Republican nomination for president in 1860, had been named to the Supreme Court by Andrew Jackson in 1828. A federalist, he authored the dissent in *Dred Scott*. In ill health, McLean would pass away on April 4, 1861, and his seat would remain unfilled until January 1862, when Lincoln nominated Noah Swayne of Ohio to replace him. Justice Samuel Nelson of New York, whose specialty was in admiralty and patent law, was nominated to the Court by President John Tyler in 1845 and had concurred in *Dred Scott*. Nathan Clifford of Maine was appointed U.S. attorney general by President James Polk in 1846, and a few years later was named ambassador to Mexico. A Buchanan appointee to the Supreme Court in 1857, his nomination was opposed by northern members of the Senate because of his southern sympathies and barely confirmed by a vote of 26 to 23.[16] Finally, Robert Cooper Grier was a Pennsylvania doughface who identified with the southern wing of the Court. It was Grier who allowed himself to be lobbied by President Buchanan and disclosed, prior to Buchanan's inaugural address of 1857, the direction the Court would take in *Dred Scott*.

The rest of Lincoln's week was filled with meetings with politicians, merchants and lobbyists (Willard's quickly became known as the "little White House" since matters of importance were discussed more frequently there than at the real Executive Mansion). "It was bad enough in Springfield," Lincoln complained, "but it was child's play compared to this tussle here. I hardly have a chance to eat or sleep. I am fair game for everybody of that hungry lot."[17] Lincoln's only private time came in the early morning hours before breakfast, and he took long walks around Washington, sometimes with Robert and Nicolay, enjoying the solitude before the daily crush of visitors. Former Massachusetts governor Nathaniel Banks, Senator-elect Ira Harris of New York (who was to replace Seward), and Frank Blair came by to endorse themselves, or others, for cabinet posts. Senator John Crittendon of Kentucky, desperately striving to reach a compromise through the efforts of the Peace Convention, was a frequent visitor. Although he had supported Douglas in the election of 1858 — Lincoln believed that it cost him the victory — Lincoln had a high regard for Crittendon and admired his attempts to assume the mantle of another Kentuckian, the great compromiser Henry Clay. But Lincoln could not support any compromise plan that permitted the extension of slavery into new territories, and Crittendon's plans were doomed to failure. Although the convention disbanded on the 27th, Lincoln appreciated and remembered Crittendon's efforts to keep Kentucky in the Union, and nearly nominated him to the Supreme Court a year later.

Representatives of the all-important border states came to see Lincoln. Virginian George W. Summers joined William Rives, along with Alexander W. Doniphan of Missouri, and James Guthrie and Charles S. Morehead of Kentucky. These men, too, supported compromise. Morehead took the lead, arguing that Lincoln must immediately withdraw federal troops from Fort Sumter; once done, Morehead believed, the border states might convince the secessionists to rejoin the Union. Lincoln responded with an attempt at humor. The situation reminded him an Aesop fable, he said. A lion wanted to enter society so badly that he had his claws cut off and his teeth pulled in hopes of soothing the fears of the other animals. Still distrustful, however, those animals beat the lion to death with a club. Morehead could not understand how Lincoln could joke in the face of crisis. "I appeal to you, apart from these jests, to lend us your aid and countenance," he said. When Lincoln offered no meaningful response Rives stood up in an excited state. If Lincoln resorted to the use of force at Fort Sumter, he said, his voice shaking, Virginia had no choice but to secede and he would join in the fight. Finally aware that his mannerisms had offended Rives, who he impressed just days before, Lincoln rushed over to him and tried to soothe him. "Mr. Rives, Mr. Rives," he said, "if Virginia will stay in, I will withdraw the troops from Fort Sumter."[18] But the party went away disappointed and frustrated at Lincoln's demeanor. A few days later Lincoln was asked about the encounter with Rives. "A fort for a state is no bad business," Lincoln said.[19]

Visitors reacted to Lincoln in different ways. Many were impressed, often unexpectedly so, at his charm, his pleasant nature, and his ability to put people at ease. Congressman-elect Albert Gallatin Riddle of Ohio, who had ridden part of the way to Washington on the Presidential Special, found Lincoln to often be in "wonderful spirits ... his face fairly radiant, his wit and humor at flood-tide. His marvelous faculty of improvising illustrated stories was at its best. They followed each other with great rapidity."[20] Others perceived genuine intellect and unwavering dedication underneath his coarse exterior. Charles Francis Adams described Lincoln as a "tall, ill-favored man, with little grace of manner or polish of appearance," and a "plain, good-natured, frank expression which rather attracts one to him." But some criticized everything about him. He was "a cross between a sandhill crane and an Andalusian jackass ... vain, weak, puerile, hypocritical, without manners, without moral grace," said a Virginia politician.[21] Sumner took note of Lincoln's remarkable "flashes of thought and bursts of illuminating expression," but was exasperated by Lincoln's insistence on turning every conversation into a joke or a story. It particularly galled Sumner that Lincoln enjoyed measuring anyone who came close to his six-feet four-inch height, insisting that the men stand back to back for the measurement. In view of the crisis, said Sumner, this was "the time for uniting our fronts against the enemy and not our backs."[22]

On the 27th Lincoln received Washington mayor James G. Berret and the city's Common Council, who welcomed him and also expressed their concerns that he might tamper with slavery in the District. Lincoln knew that the group had opposed his election and now assured them that he had no intention of interfering with their customs:

> Mr. Mayor—I thank you, and through you the municipal authorities of this city by whom you are accompanied for this welcome; and as it is the first time in my life, since the present phase of politics has presented itself in this country, that I have said any thing publicly within a region of country where the institution of slavery exists, I will take this occasion to say, that I think very much of the ill feeling that has existed and still exists between the people of the section from whence I came and the people here, is owning to a misunderstanding between each other which unhappily prevails, I therefore avail myself of this opportunity to assure you, Mr. Mayor, and all the gentle men present, that I have not now, and never

have had, any other that as kindly feelings towards you as to the people of my own section. I have not now, and never have had, any disposition to treat you in any respect otherwise than as my own neighbors. I have not now any purpose to withhold from you any of the benefits of the constitution, under any circumstances, that I would not feel myself constrained to withhold from my own neighbors, and I hope, in a word, when we shall become better acquainted — and I say it with great confidence — we shall like each other the more. Again I thank you for the kindness of this reception.[23]

The next day Lincoln was visited by his old friend and adversary Stephen Douglas, who had been part of the Illinois delegation two days before but now wanted to speak privately. Douglas looked and sounded even worse than he did at the end of last fall's presidential campaign. Overweight and fatigued, his eyes puffy and bloodshot, Douglas pleaded in a hoarse voice for Lincoln to approve a compromise plan and avert bloodshed. He urged Lincoln "in God's name, to act the patriot, and to save our children a country to live in."[24] But Lincoln had long felt that the time for compromise had passed and could give no such assurance. Douglas would not give up. He understood that Seward was floating a proposal for a national convention to address the issues that divided the country. Again, Lincoln had no confidence that such a plan was workable.

Still, Douglas pledged his support for Lincoln and the new administration. This was no time for partisan bickering, he told Lincoln, and he would do all in his power to assure that the Democrats did not gain political advantage because of the pending crisis. "Our Union must be preserved," he said in parting. "Partisan feeling must yield to patriotism. I am with you, Mr. President, and God bless you."[25] Lincoln was moved by Douglas's statements. "With all my heart I thank you," he said. "The people with us and God helping us all will yet be well." Lincoln thought about his friend for a long while. "What a noble man Douglas is!" he said later that evening.[26] While he could not agree with Douglas's pleas for compromise, Lincoln was worried that his health was in rapid decline. He knew that Douglas was drinking more heavily than usual, a reaction to the stress he felt over disunion. In fact, Douglas had but a few months to live; he would pass away on June 3, 1861, at the age of 48.

On Thursday evening Lincoln and Hamlin were guests of honor at a dinner at the National Hotel, hosted by Elbridge G. Spaulding, a New York congressman. At one point someone brought to Lincoln's attention the remarks of a Georgia secessionist, who had been quoted in the papers as saying he would never wear clothes produced under a Republican administration. Lincoln joked that he would like to see a Georgian clad only in clothes made in that state — a shirt collar and a pair of spurs. When the laughter died down Lincoln was serenaded by a men's chorus known as the Republican Association. When the group was finished Lincoln said:

> My Friends— I suppose that I may take this as a compliment paid to me, and as such please accept my thanks for it. I have reached this city of Washington under circumstances considerably differing from those under which any other man has ever reached it. I have reached it for the purpose of taking an official position amongst the people. almost all of whom were opposed to me, and are yet opposed to me, as I suppose. [*Several voices, "No, no." Other voices, "Go on, sir; you are*

mistaken in that, indeed you are."] I propose no lengthy address to you now. I only propose to say, as I did say on yesterday, I believe, when your worthy Mayor and Board of Aldermen called upon me, that I thought much of the ill feeling that has existed between you and the people of your surroundings and that people from amongst whom I come, has depended, and now depends, upon a misunderstanding. [*Several voices — "That's so;" and applause.*] I hope that if things shall go along as prosperously as I believe we all desire they may, I may have it in my power to remove something of this misunderstanding—[*Cries of "Good," and loud applause*]—that I may be enabled to convince you, and the people of your section of the country, that we regard you as in all things being our equals—in all things entitled to the same respect and to the same treatment that we claim for ourselves—[*cries of "Good," and applause*]—that we are in no wise disposed, if it were in our power, to oppress you or deprive you of any of your rights under the constitution of the United States or even narrowly to split hairs with you in regard to these rights. [*Loud and prolonged cheering.*] But are determined to give you, so far as lies in our hands, all your rights under the constitution, not grudgingly, but fully and fairly. [*Cries of "Good," and applause.*] I hope that by thus dealing with you we will become better acquainted and be better friends with these very few remarks, I again return my thanks for this compliment, and expressing my desire to hear a little more of your good music, I bid you good night.[27]

On the first day of March Lincoln met with Simon Cameron and offered him the War Department post. It was not Cameron's first choice — he had hoped for Interior — but he accepted anyway. At the same time, word of Lincoln's straw vote in the Senate had gotten out, and it became known that he was prepared to offer Salmon Chase the position of secretary of the treasury. The selections angered Seward; for all the personal attention he had lavished on Lincoln this week, he still had not been able to convince him that Cameron and Chase were not fit for the positions. Seward had his advisors set up a meeting with Lincoln to try to change his mind.

That evening Lincoln was the dinner guest of Rudolph Schleiden, the minister from Bremen. At least one of the other guests, J.W. Schulte, minister from Holland, was unimpressed. "His conversation consists of vulgar anecdotes at which he himself laughs uproariously," complained Schulte. But others, including Lord Richard Lyon, minister from Britain, enjoyed Lincoln's company. Mary did not join her husband for dinner; she accompanied Justice McLean's wife, Sarah, to the White House, where they visited with Harriet Lane, the president's niece and hostess. Harriet was unimpressed; she found Mary to be "awfully *Western*, loud & unrefined."[28]

The next morning Lincoln was presented with a new carriage, a gift from New York businessmen. He happily took the carriage for a drive, but when he returned he was met by Simeon Draper and other friends of Seward. Chase in particular must not be offered a cabinet post, they argued. He lacked a conciliatory approach to seceding states, and his advocacy for free trade would further jeopardize the business interests of the North. It seemed that Lincoln was preparing a "compound cabinet" of old Whigs and Democrats, and Seward did not believe the formula would be viable. The differences between Chase and Seward were so significant that Seward could not serve in the same cabinet with him. Lincoln remarked somewhat caustically that he might consider a slate of candidates that omitted Seward's name, rather than Chase's. Would

Seward consider the post of minister to England? There was no reasoning with this man, Draper felt, and he and his friends left in a foul mood.

Later that day Seward sent a note to Lincoln. "Circumstances which have occurred since I expressed ... my willingness to accept the office of Secretary of State seem to me to render it my duty to ask leave to withdraw that consent," he wrote. Lincoln knew that the letter, written just two days before the inauguration, was meant by Seward as a direct challenge to his leadership as well as an attempt to control policy. While he had to have the New Yorker in his cabinet, Lincoln told Nicolay, "I can't afford to let Seward take the first trick."[29]

Lincoln did not attend church services on Sunday, March 3, disappointing a crowd that waited by Willard's side door in hopes of seeing him. Instead, he spent the bulk of the day alone in his parlor, still polishing his inaugural address. He received only two visitors. The first, Gideon Welles, Hamlin's friend from Connecticut, was offered the post of secretary of navy and accepted. The other was Seward, who reminded Lincoln that it was he who had kept the party, and the country, together since the election. He had assumed "the responsibility of averting disasters ... a sort of dictatorship for defense." He alone recognized the dangers the secession crisis brought about, and while seven states had left the Union, he believed that they would come back under appropriate circumstances. Further, the border states remained in the Union and it seemed to him unlikely that they would secede; in recent weeks Virginia's voters had voted down secession, as had those in Tennessee, Arkansas, Missouri and North Carolina. In Maryland, Governor Hicks stubbornly resisted a movement to call the legislature into convention. And, Seward reminded Lincoln, he had worked intimately with Edwin Stanton, who kept him secretly appraised of Buchanan's efforts in the White House, and he had won over the confidence of Winfield Scott. In the words of Henry Adams, Seward had, "during these months of chaos, fought a fight which might go down to history as one of the wonders of statesmanship."[30]

Seward's advisor Thurlow Weed later claimed that Lincoln begged Seward to stay on as his secretary of state, and promised him that no matter what other cabinet members might do or say, he would never disagree with Seward on important policy questions. This seems unlikely, but certainly Lincoln forcefully urged Seward to accept the position and serve in the cabinet alongside of Chase. But Seward would not give Lincoln a final answer.

Later that afternoon Lincoln and Mary received Horatio Taft, chief examiner for the U.S. Patent Office, and his wife. Mrs. Taft could not help but notice that Mrs. Lincoln's social calendar seemed rather sparse, noting later that the Lincolns were "not welcome" in Washington.[31] Others noted the same thing. "The cold shoulder is given to Mr. Lincoln," wrote William Howard Russell, Washington correspondent for the London *Times*. His embarrassing entry into town was still the subject of ridicule. "People take particular pleasure in telling how he come towards the seat of his Government disguised."[32]

That evening Lincoln hosted a dinner for his would-be cabinet members, now all together for the first time: Chase, Welles, Blair, Cameron, Smith, Bates, and finally Seward, who was cordial but still gave no indication whether he would serve. These

A portrait of Lincoln and his cabinet in 1864: Edwin M. Stanton, who had replaced Simon Cameron; Salmon P. Chase; Lincoln; Gideon Welles; Caleb B. Smith; William A. Seward (seated); Montgomery Blair; Edward Bates (the Lincoln Museum, Fort Wayne, Indiana, # 2825d).

men (who had all been on Lincoln's original list compiled back in Springfield) were Lincoln's final selections, he told them, and the next day their names would be forwarded to the Senate for confirmation. The cabinet contained all who had been his chief rivals for the Republican nomination for president. The ill-assorted group would never work together well, and was called " a violent mixing ... of inimical and repulsive forces" and nothing but "a bunch of poor sticks."[33] After the meal was finished Lincoln went to the Capitol, alone, and sat quietly in the Senate gallery. He listened as John Crittendon, who had struggled so desperately to forge a compromise that would keep the country from breaking apart, gave his farewell speech.

13

Inauguration

After his efforts with Peace Conference ended in failure, former president John Tyler returned home to Virginia, where he became active in the state's secession movement. The only former president to embrace the Confederacy, Tyler was quickly elected to the Confederate Congress, serving until his death one year later. At sunrise on Monday, March 4, 1861, Tyler's granddaughter Letitia Christian Tyler climbed to the top of the Capitol Building in Montgomery and unfurled the Confederate flag, the first time that the Stars and Bars were displayed for public view.[1]

That very day was inauguration day in Washington. Lincoln and his wife were awakened by the sound of artillery wagons, cavalry horses and soldiers tramping down the streets below their suite at Willard's Hotel. In the distance cannon fire could be heard; Winfield Scott was making sure that any potential troublemakers were aware of the army's presence. Storm clouds threatened overhead and the wind blew steadily from the northwest, and many of the thousands of people milling about expected rain at any moment.

After breakfast Lincoln gathered his family and read aloud his address, then asked to be left alone. He wrote a note to William Seward, purposely mislabeling it the "Executive Mansion, March 4, 1861." Acknowledging Seward's letter of two days earlier, Lincoln wrote, "It is the subject of the most painful solicitude with me; and I feel constrained to beg that you will countermand the withdrawal. The public interest, I think, demands that you should; and my personal feelings are deeply enlisted in the same direction." He asked for a final answer from Seward by nine o'clock the next morning.[2] As usual, dozens of people wished to see him, but he admitted only David Davis, Gideon Welles and Edward Bates. Later that morning Lincoln dressed in a new black suit. For once his black boots had been shined and matched his suit and silken stovepipe hat. He grabbed his gold-headed cane — it had been a gift that he felt obligated to use on this important day — and went to the lobby to wait for President Buchanan, who would escort him to the Capitol for the ceremony.

Buchanan spent the morning attending to last-minute matters of his presidency. Congress had worked until five o'clock in the morning and managed to pass a flurry of bills; the most important created the territories of Nevada and Dakota, and duties on wool and iron were increased from 5 percent to 10 percent. Buchanan signed them into law. His cabinet was with him, except for Secretary of War Joseph Holt, and Buchanan's mood seemed fairly bright.[3] But then Holt burst in and handed Buchanan

United States of America
March 4, 1861

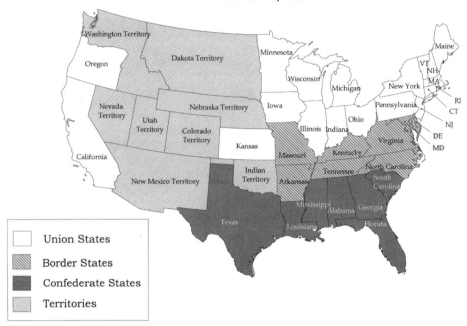

- ☐ Union States
- ▨ Border States
- ■ Confederate States
- ▨ Territories

The United States of America on March 4, 1961 (map by Tim Mosbacher).

a note, who glanced at it and frowned. It was another urgent message from Major Anderson at Fort Sumter. Buchanan put the note in his pocket, deciding that neither he, nor Lincoln, should be troubled with such matters on inauguration day. He called for his carriage and started for Willard's.

At just past 12 o'clock the carriage arrived at the hotel. The President's Mounted Guard, along with the Georgetown Mounted Guard, presented arms as Lincoln emerged from the building at the Fourteenth Street entrance. A nearby band, not part of the procession, was playing "Dixie" but an army band struck up "Hail to the Chief," drowning out the smaller group. Lincoln was led to the magnificent open barouche and climbed inside, next to Buchanan and across from his old friend Senator Edward Baker of Oregon and Senator James Pearce of Maryland, members of the Committee on Arrangements for the ceremony.[4] Flanked by double-files of cavalry the carriage took its place in a formal procession. The men rode in silence along the cobblestoned Pennsylvania Avenue toward Capitol Hill.

Infantry soldiers from West Point marched immediately in front of and behind the carriage, commanded by marshals smartly outfitted in blue scarves and white rosettes. After Lincoln's carriage came a succession of congressmen, diplomats, governors, department heads and clergymen, horse-drawn floats and military bands, all interspersed with detachments of army and naval forces. Members of the Peace Conference walked alongside carriages carrying veterans of the Revolutionary War and the War of 1812. Four white horses pulled a float constructed for the Republican Association, which was loaded with 34 young ladies in white frocks, one for each state in the Union. Mary and the boys boarded a carriage in the middle of the procession, and they noticed that despite the efforts of the parade's organizers the mood was anything but festive. Hundreds of soldiers had deployed throughout the area on the orders of General Scott, who stubbornly described the procession as little more than a military movement. Dozens of sharpshooters stood on the roofs of buildings, and mounted cavalrymen closed off intersections. At Scott's order all saloons had been closed for the day, as were schools, businesses and public buildings. Crowds of onlookers stood six or seven deep on the sidewalks, soldiers scattered throughout. The crowd was strangely silent, and Lincoln only occasionally looked out and nodded at expressionless people. Once or twice he took off his hat and waved it half-heartedly at the crowd. Faces peered out of some of the windows from above; other windows were closed in defiance. Gusts of wind kicked up yellow dust from the dry street, adding to the surreal atmosphere.

As the procession marched toward the Capitol, General Scott rode in his coupe on E Street, roughly parallel to Lincoln. He stopped briefly at Seward's house — perhaps delivered Lincoln's note — and advised him that all seemed satisfactory so far. Scott then was quickly taken to the east portico of the Capitol, where an artillery battery was stationed; he would direct operations from there. His military secretary, Erasmus Keyes, skulked about in civilian clothes, eavesdropping on conversations that might hint at trouble. By a quarter of one Lincoln's carriage arrived, and he was hurried by private entrance into the Senate chamber. Attendants beat the street dust from his suit as he nodded appreciatively. Most of the senators were present, as were all the members of the Supreme Court, to observe as Hannibal Hamlin was administered the vice-presidential oath by John Breckenridge. Lincoln sat with Buchanan at the secretary's desk, saying nothing. He looked "grave and impassive as an Indian martyr."[5]

At exactly one o'clock a procession was formed with the marshal of the District of Columbia at the head, followed by the members of the Supreme Court, the Senate sergeant-at-arms and Baker's committee. Next came Buchanan and Lincoln, who walked arm in arm down a corridor and out to a massive platform, decorated with red, white and blue bunting, that rested on the east portico. Underneath stood squads of infantrymen who had spent the night there, Scott's response to the rumor that militants might try to blow up the platform as Lincoln spoke. A second battery, commanded by John E. Wool, positioned itself strategically around the plaza. At each window of the Capitol sharpshooters peered out at the crowd of 30,000, who stood passively about the grounds.

Lincoln took his place at the center of the platform, next to Buchanan. They were flanked by Hamlin, Chief Justice Taney and the Supreme Court clerk, William Thomas Carroll, and surrounded by 300 congressmen, military personnel, judges, diplomats and their guests. Mary sat proudly nearby, her sons next to her, Stephen Douglas and his wife, Adele, next to them. The sun was shining now, but the wind was still brisk, kicking up small whirlwinds of dust and debris around the plaza. The temperature neared 50 degrees.

Inauguration Day, March 4, 1861 (the Lincoln Museum, Fort Wayne, Indiana, # 0-54).

Baker moved forward to the podium and quickly introduced the guest of honor. "Fellow citizens," he said, "I introduce to you Abraham Lincoln, the President-elect of the United States."[6] There was a smattering of polite applause as Lincoln stepped awkwardly to the front of the platform and rested his cane against a corner of the stand. He removed his hat and looked around for a place to set it. Finding none, Douglas rose and offered to hold it for him on his lap, and Lincoln nodded as Mary smiled. Lincoln removed the galleys of his address from his vest pocket, laid it on the speaker's table, and adjusted his reading glasses. He then began to speak in his high-pitched twang, a voice that always surprised those who were hearing it for the first time. Journalist Henry Watterson of the Louisville *Journal*, who was sitting within a few yards of Lincoln, marveled at how calm he seemed as he spoke words that were as eagerly awaited as any speech an incoming president had ever given. "He delivered that inaugural," wrote Watterson, "as if he had been delivering inaugural addresses all his life."[7]

> Fellow citizens of the United States:
>   In compliance with a custom as old as the government itself, I appear before you to address you briefly, and to take, in your presence, the oath prescribed by the Constitution of the United States, to be taken by the President before he enters on the execution of his office.
>   I do not consider it necessary, at present, for me to discuss those matters of administration about which there is no special anxiety, or excitement.

Apprehension seems to exist among the people of the Southern States, that by the accession of a Republican Administration, their property, and their peace, and personal security, are to be endangered. There has never been any reasonable cause for such apprehension. Indeed, the most ample evidence to the contrary has all the while existed, and been open to their inspection. It is found in nearly all the published speeches of him who now addresses you. I do but quote from one of these speeches when I declare that "I have no purpose, directly or indirectly, to interfere with the institution of slavery in the States where it exists. I believe I have no lawful right to do so, and I have no inclination to do so." Those who nominated and elected me did so with full knowledge that I had made this, and many similar declarations, and had never recanted them. And more than this, they placed in the platform, for my acceptance, and as a law to themselves, and to me, the clear and emphatic resolution which I now read:

"Resolved, That the maintenance inviolate of the rights of the States, and especially the right of each State to order and control its own domestic institutions according to its own judgment exclusively, is essential to that balance of power on which the perfection and endurance of our political fabric depend; and we denounce the lawless invasion by armed force of the soil of any State or Territory, no matter under what pretext, as among the gravest of crimes."

"Good, good," muttered Stephen Douglas to himself. Lincoln was reminding his listeners that he would not abandon the platform upon which he had been elected. There would be no surprises, no radical departures in policy from those which had appealed to the people — at least to the majority that had elected him — only four months ago.

I now reiterate these sentiments: and in doing so, I only press upon the public attention the most conclusive evidence of which the case is susceptible, that the property, peace and security of no section are to be in anywise endangered by the now incoming Administration. I add too, that all the protection which, consistently with the Constitution and the laws, can be given, will be cheerfully given to all the States when lawfully demanded, for whatever cause — as cheerfully to one section, as to another.

There is much controversy about the delivering up of fugitives from service or labor. The clause I now read is as plainly written in the Constitution as any other of its provisions:

"No person held to service or labor in one State, under the laws thereof, escaping into another, shall, in consequence of any law or regulation therein, be discharged from such service or labor, but shall be delivered up on claim of the party to whom such service or labor may be due."

It is scarcely questioned that this provision was intended by those who made it, for the reclaiming of what we call fugitive slaves; and the intention of the lawgiver is the law. All members of Congress swear their support to the whole Constitution — to this provision as much as to any other. To the proposition, then, that slaves whose cases come within the terms of this clause, "shall be delivered up," their oaths are unanimous. Now, if they would make the effort in good temper, could they not, with nearly equal unanimity, frame and pass a law, by means of which to keep good that unanimous oath?

There is some difference of opinion whether this clause should be enforced by national or by state authority; but surely that difference is not a very material one. If the slave is to be surrendered, it can be of but little consequence to him, or to others, by which authority it is done. And should anyone, in any case, be content that his oath shall go unkept, on a merely unsubstantial controversy as to how it shall be kept?

Again, in any law upon this subject, ought not all the safeguards of liberty known in civilized and humane jurisprudence to be introduced, so that a free man be not, in any case, surrendered as a slave? And might it not be well, at the same time, to provide by law for the enforcement of that clause in the Constitution which guarantees that "The citizens of each State shall be entitled to all privileges and immunities of citizens in the several States?"

I take the official oath to-day, with no mental reservations, and with no purpose to construe the Constitution or laws, by any hypercritical rules. And while I do not choose now to specify particular acts of Congress as proper to be enforced, I do suggest, that it will be much safer for all, both in official and private stations, to conform to, and abide by, all those acts which stand unrepealed, than to violate any of them, trusting to find impunity in having them held to be unconstitutional.

Douglas again nodded his head in approval. The Senate had just voted to endorse the fugitive slave act, and Lincoln was reaffirming his support of this all-important law. This news could only reassure, and not panic, the South. It mattered little that Lincoln hoped and expected that slavery would eventually fade away on its own. What did matter was that Lincoln would not use the instruments of his administration to bring about the end of slavery now. If the secessionists could only be made to see the truth of this principle the crisis could be averted.

Now Lincoln got the very heart of his position, that the Union could not lawfully be broken:

It is seventy-two years since the first inauguration of a President under our national Constitution. During that period fifteen different and greatly distinguished citizens, have, in succession, administered the executive branch of the government. They have conducted it through many perils; and, generally, with great success. Yet, with all this scope for precedent, I now enter upon the same task for the brief constitutional term of four years, under great and peculiar difficulty. A disruption of the Federal Union heretofore only menaced, is now formidably attempted.

I hold, that in contemplation of universal law, and of the Constitution, the Union of these States is perpetual. Perpetuity is implied, if not expressed, in the fundamental law of all national governments. It is safe to assert that no government proper, ever had a provision in its organic law for its own termination. Continue to execute all the express provisions of our national Constitution, and the Union will endure forever — it being impossible to destroy it, except by some action not provided for in the instrument itself.

"That's right," thought Douglas. Give them the logic, just as you would if explaining your position to a jury back in Illinois. This was the pragmatic Lincoln, the "most worthy adversary" that Douglas respected above all other politicians. Douglas was listening so intently to Lincoln that he failed to notice how badly he was shivering in the cold wind. Lieutenant Governor Gustave Koerner of Illinois noticed Douglas's discomfort and draped a heavy shawl over his shoulders.

Again, if the United States be not a government proper, but an association of States in the nature of contract merely, can it, as a contract, be peaceable unmade, by less that all the parties who made it? One party to a contract may violate it — break it, so to speak; but does it not require all to lawfully rescind it?

Descending from these general principles, we find the proposition that, in legal contemplation, the Union is perpetual, confirmed by the history of the Union itself. The Union is much older than the Constitution. It was formed in fact, by the Articles of Association in 1774. It was matured and continued by the Declaration of Independence in 1776. It was further matured and the faith of the then thirteen States expressly plighted and engaged that it should be perpetual, by the Articles of Confederation in 1778. And finally, in 1787, one of the declared objects for ordaining and establishing the Constitution, was "To form a more perfect union."

But if destruction of the Union, by one, or by a part only, of the States, be lawfully possible, the Union is less perfect than before the Constitution, having lost the vital element of perpetuity.

It follows from these views that no State, upon its own mere motion, can lawfully get out of the Union, that resolves and ordinances to that effect are legally void; and that acts of violence, within any State or States, against the authority of the United States, are insurrectionary or revolutionary, according to circumstances.

I therefore consider that, in view of the Constitution and the laws, the Union is unbroken, and, to the extent of my ability, I shall take care, as the Constitution itself expressly enjoins upon me, that the laws of the Union be faithful executed in all the States. Doing this I deem to be only a simple duty on my part; and I shall perform it, so far as practicable, unless my rightful masters, the American people, shall withhold the requisite means, or, in some authoritative manner, direct the contrary, I trust this will not be regarded as a menace, but only as the declared purpose of the Union that it will constitutionally defend, and maintain itself.

This was Seward's idea. Lincoln must not appear to be the aggressor. Rather, his language must send a clear message that he would run the federal government without in any way usurping the rights of the southern people.

In doing this there needs to be no bloodshed or violence; and there shall be none, unless it be forced upon the national authority. The power confided to me, will be used to hold, occupy, and possess the property, and places belonging to the government, and to collect the duties and imposts; but beyond what may be necessary for these objects, there will be no invasion — no using of force against, or among the people anywhere. Where hostility to the United States, in any interior locality, shall be so great and so universal, as to prevent competent resident citizens from holding the Federal offices, there will be no attempt to force obnoxious strangers among the people for that object. While the strict legal right may exist in the government to do so would be so irritating, and so nearly impracticable with all, that I deem it better to forego, for the time, the uses of such offices.

The mails, unless repelled, will continue to be furnished in all parts of the Union. So far as possible, the people everywhere shall have that sense of perfect security which is most favorable to calm thought and reflection. The course here indicated will be followed, unless current events, and experience, shall show a modification, or change, to be proper; and in every case and exigency, my best discretion will be exercised, according to circumstances actually existing, and with a view and a hope of a peaceful solution of the national troubles, and the restoration of fraternal sympathies and affections.

Lincoln now spoke directly to the secessionists. Even the most enthusiastic fireeaters, he believed, might reconsider if they would only take the time to reflect on the reckless nature of what they were advocating, and the consequences that would surely follow.

> That there are persons in one section, or another who seek to destroy the Union at all events, and are glad of any pretext to do it, I will neither affirm or deny; but if there be such, I need address no word to them. To those, however, who really love the Union, may I not speak?
>
> Before entering upon so grave a matter as the destruction of our national fabric, with all its benefits, its memories, and its hopes, would it not be wise to ascertain precisely why we do it? Will you hazard so desperate a step, while there is any possibility that any portion of the ills you fly from, have no real existence? Will you, while the certain ills you fly to, are greater than all the real ones you fly from? Will you risk the commission of so fearful a mistake?
>
> All profess to be content in the Union, if all constitutional rights can be maintained. Is it true, then, that any right, plainly written in the Constitution, has been denied? I think not. Happily the human mind is so constituted, that no party can reach to the audacity of doing this. Think, if you can, of a single instance in which a plainly written provision of the Constitution has even been denied. If, by the mere force of numbers, a majority should deprive a minority of any clearly written constitutional right, it might, in a moral point of view, justify revolution — certainly would, if such right were a vital one. But such is not our case. All the vital rights of minorities, and of individuals, are so plainly assured to them, by affirmations and negations, guarantees and prohibitions, in the Constitution, that controversies never arise concerning them. But no organic law can ever be framed with a provision specifically applicable to every question which may occur in practical administration. No foresight can anticipate, nor any document of reasonable length contain express provisions for all possible questions. Shall fugitives from labor be surrendered by national or by State authority? The Constitution does not expressly say. May Congress prohibit slavery in the territories? The Constitution does not expressly say. Must Congress protect slavery in the territories? The Constitution does not expressly say.
>
> From questions of this class spring all our constitutional controversies, and we divide upon them into majorities and minorities. If the minority will not acquiesce, the majority must, or the government must cease. There is no other alternative; for continuing the government, is acquiescence on one side or the other. If a minority, in such case, will secede rather than acquiesce, they make a precedent which, in turn, will divide and ruin them, for a minority of their own will secede from them, whenever a majority refuses to be controlled by such minority. For instance, why may not any portion of a new confederacy, a year or two hence, arbitrarily secede again, precisely as portions of the present Union now claim to secede from it. All who cherish disunion sentiments, are now being educated to the exact temper of doing this. Is there such perfect identity of interests among the States to compose a new Union, as to produce harmony only, and prevent renewed secession?

Horace Greeley, who had managed to secure for himself a seat at the rear of the platform, later wrote that Lincoln was the "victim of a grave delusion," if he believed that his words could dissuade the angry South. "His faith in Reason as a moral force was so implicit that he did not cherish a doubt that his Inaugural Address, whereon he had bestowed much thought and labor, would, when read throughout the South, dissolve the Confederacy as frost is dissipated by a vernal sun."[8]

Plainly, the central idea of secession, is the essence of anarchy. A majority, held in restraint by constitutional checks, and limitations, and always changing easily, with deliberate changes of popular opinions and sentiments, is the only true sovereign of a free people. Whoever rejects it, does, of necessity, fly to anarchy or to despotism. Unanimity is impossible; the rule of a minority, as a permanent arrangement, is wholly inadmissible, so that, rejecting the majority principle, anarchy, or despotism in some form is all that is left.

I do not forget the position assumed by some, that constitutional questions are to be decided by the Supreme Court; nor do I deny that such decisions must be binding in any case, upon the parties to a suit, as to the object of that suit, while they are also entitled to very high respect and consideration, in all parallel cases, by all other departments of the government. And while it is obviously possible that such decision may be erroneous in any given case, still the evil effect following it, being limited to that particular case, with the chance that it be over-ruled, and never become a precedent for other cases, can better be borne than could the evils of a different practice. At the same time the candid citizen must confess that if the policy of the government, upon vital questions, affecting the whole people, is to be irrevocably fixed by decisions of the Supreme Court, the instant they are made, in ordinary litigation between parties, in personal actions, the people will have ceased, to be their own rulers, having, to that extent, practically resigned their government, into the hands of that eminent tribunal. Nor is there, in this view, any assault upon the court, of the judges. It is a duty, from which they may not shrink, to decide cases properly brought before them; and it is not fault of theirs, if others seek to turn their decisions to political purposes.

Now Lincoln repeated the arguments he had been making for many months, but which, inexplicably, the secessionists had chosen to ignore. Maybe they would listen now.

One section of our country believes slavery is right, and ought to be extended, while the other believes it is wrong, and ought not to be extended. This is the only substantial dispute. The fugitive slave clause of the Constitution, and the law for the suppression of the foreign slave trade, are each as well enforced, perhaps, as any law can ever be in a community where the moral sense of the people imperfectly supports the law itself. The great body of the people abide by the dry legal obligation in both cases, and a few break over in each. This, I think, cannot be perfectly cured; and it would be worse in both cases after the separation of the sections, than before. The foreign slave trade, now imperfectly suppressed, would be ultimately revived without restriction, in one section; while fugitive slaves, now only partially surrendered, would not be surrendered at all, by the other.

Physically speaking, we cannot separate. We cannot remove our respective sections from each other, nor build an impassable wall between them. A husband and wife may be divorced, and go out of the presence, and beyond the reach of each other; but the different parts of our country cannot do this. They cannot but remain face to face; and intercourse, either amicable or hostile, must continue between them. Is it possible then to make that intercourse more advantageous, or more satisfactory, after separation than before? Can aliens make treaties easier than friends can make laws? Can treaties be more faithfully enforced between aliens, than laws can among friends? Suppose you go to war, you cannot fight always; and then, after much loss on both sides, and no gain on either, you cease fighting, the identical old questions, as to terms of intercourse, are again upon you.

This country, with its institutions, belongs to the people who inhabit it. Whenever they shall grow weary of the existing government, they can exercise their constitutional right of amending it, or their revolutionary right to dismember , or overthrow it. I can not be ignorant of the fact that many worthy, and patriotic citizens are desirous of having the national constitution amended. While I make no recommendation of amendments, I fully recognize the rightful authority of the people over the whole subject, to be exercised in either of the modes prescribed in the instrument itself; and I should, under existing circumstances, favor, rather than oppose, a fair opportunity being afforded the people to act upon it.

I will venture to add that, to me, the convention mode seems preferable, in that it allows amendments to originate with the people themselves, instead on only permitting them to take, or reject, propositions, originated by others, not especially chosen for the purpose, and which might not be precisely such, as they would wish to either accept or refuse. I understand a proposed amendment to the Constitution — which amendment, however, I have not seen, has passed Congress, to the effect that the federal government, shall never interfere with the domestic institutions of the States, including that of persons held to service. To avoid misconstruction of what I have said, I depart from my purpose not to speak of particular amendments, so far as to say that, holding such a provision to now be implied constitutional law, I have no objection to its being made express, and irrevocable.

The Chief Magistrate derives all his authority from the people, and they have conferred none upon him to fix terms for the separation of the States. The people themselves can do this also if they choose; but the executive, as such, has nothing to do with it. His duty is to administer the present government, as it came to his hands, and to transmit it, unimpaired by him, to his successor.

Why should there not be a patient confidence in the ultimate justice of the people? Is there any better, or equal hope, in the world? In our present differences, is either party without faith of being in the right? If the Almighty Ruler of nations, with his eternal truth and justice, be on your side of the North, or on yours of the South, that truth, and that justice, will surely prevail, by the judgment of this great tribunal, the American people.

By the frame of the government under which we live, this same people have wisely given their public servants but little power for mischief, and have, with equal wisdom, provided for the return of that little to their own hands at very short intervals.

While the people retain their virtue, and vigilance, no administration, by any extreme of wickedness or folly, can very seriously injure the government, in the short space of four years.

My countrymen, one and all, think calmly and well, upon this whole subject. Nothing valuable can be lost by taking time. If there be an object to hurry any of you, in hot haste, to a step which you would never take deliberately, that object will be frustrated by taking time; but no good object can be frustrated by it. Such of you as are now dissatisfied, still have the old Constitution unimpaired, and, on the sensitive point, the laws of your own framing, under it; while the new administration will have no immediate power, if it would, to change either. If it were admitted that you who are dissatisfied, hold the right side in the dispute, there still is no single good reason for precipitate action. Intelligence, patriotism, Christianity, and a firm reliance on Him, who has never yet forsaken this favored land, are still competent to adjust, in the best way, all our present difficulty.

Lincoln had stated his position, and his policy, as plainly and as firmly as he could. He continued to believe held that the differences between the two regions of the country could be resolved without bloodshed. There was no need, and certainly no justification, for war. He had avoided any reference to the so-called Confederate States of America, for that nation did not exist. Those states that comprised the folly could still come to their senses and again acknowledge the perpetuity of the Union. The next move, if there was to be one, was up to the secessionist states. Seward had suggested that Lincoln offer "some words of affection, some of calm and cheerful confidence."[9] He concluded poetically, the idea Seward's, the language his own:

> In your hands, my dissatisfied fellow countrymen, and not in mine, is the momentous issue of civil war. The government will not assail you. You can have no conflict, without being yourselves the aggressors. You have no oath registered in Heaven to destroy the government, while I shall have the most solemn one to "preserve, protect and defend" it.
>   I am loath to close. We are not enemies, but friends. We must not be enemies. Though passion may have strained, it must not break our bonds of affection. The mystic chords of memory, stretching from every battle field, and patriot grave, to every living heart and hearthstone, all over this broad land, will yet swell the chorus of the Union, when again touched, as surely they will be, by the better angels of our nature.[10]

Lincoln had spoken for 30 minutes. As the audience applauded, Justice Taney feebly stood and held out a Bible, gilt-clasped and bound in cinnamon velvet. The men on the platform removed their hats as Lincoln placed his left hand on the Bible and raised his right; then Taney administered the oath of office as he had to seven previous presidents since 1836. "*I do solemnly swear,*" said Lincoln, "*that I will faithfully execute the office of President of the United States, and will, to the best of my ability, preserve, protect, and defend the Constitution of the United States.*" Artillery boomed from the hilltop and militia rifles fired an answering volley, announcing that Lincoln was now officially the 16th president of the Republic.

As the Marine Band played "God Save Our President" the crowd shuffled off, and the plaza was empty in a matter of minutes. Newspaper reporters from around the country rushed to transmit copies of Lincoln's address to their editors. The speech would be considered rational and cooperative in the North, and aggressive and combative in the South. But the inauguration had come off without incident, a fact that surprised many. Horace Greeley wrote that he had fully expected to hear "the crack of a rifle aimed at (Lincoln's) heart; but it pleased God to postpone the deed, thought there was forty times the reason for shooting him in 1860 than there was in '65, and at least forty times as many intent on killing or having him killed. No shot was then fired, however; for his time had not yet come."[11] "Thank God," said General Scott as he watched the crowd disperse. "We now have a government."[12]

Lincoln and Mary were driven to the White House with Buchanan, who was anxious to leave the fate of the country in the hands of someone else. Turning down the Lincolns' offer to spend a final night in the Executive Mansion, Buchanan would depart that afternoon for his estate in Pennsylvania. "My dear sir," Buchanan said to Lincoln at the front door, "if you are as happy in entering the White House as I shall feel on returning to Wheatland, you are a happy man indeed."[13]

Lincoln, Mary and the boys were given a tour of their new home, closely watched by a guard of United States marshals. Later, while Mary supervised the unpacking of the luggage, Lincoln issued his first presidential directive: he signed John Nico-lay's appointment as private secretary (Nicolay would earn $2,500 per year — one-tenth the amount of Lincoln's salary, and $900 more than John Hay would eventually make).[14] That evening Lincoln and Mary hosted their first formal dinner in the White House for 17 guests, all prominent Republicans. Lincoln's meal was interrupted once when nearly a thousand visitors from New York demanded an audience with him before they returned home. Lincoln stepped into the entryway and spoke to them:

> Fellow citizens: I thank you for this visit. I thank you that you call upon me, not in any sectional spirit, but that you come, without distinction of party, to party, to pay your respects to the President of the United States. I am informed that you are mostly citizens of New York. [*Cries of "All, all."*] You all appear to be very happy. May I hope that the public expression which I have this day given to my senti-ments, may have contributed in some degree to your happiness. [*Emphatic excla-mations of assent.*] As far as I am concerned, the loyal citizens of every State, and of every section, shall have no cause to feel any other sentiment. [*Cries of "good, good."*] As towards the disaffected portion of our fellow-citizens, I will say, as every good man throughout the country must feel, that there will be more rejoic-ing over one sheep that is lost, and is found, than over the ninety-and-nine which have gone not astray. [*Great cheering.*] And now, my friends, as I have risen from the dinner-table to see you, you will excuse me for the brevity of my remarks, and permit me again to thank you heartily, and cordially, for this pleasant visit, as I rejoin those who await my return.[15]

That evening Lincoln and Mary attended the inaugural ball. Mary was attended by her sisters, and Lincoln was assisted by Hamlin and Senator Henry B. Anthony of Rhode Island. The ball was held in a temporary structure located behind City Hall. The plain wooden building, dubbed "Union Hall" for the event, was lavishly deco-rated with flowers and evergreens. American flags hung from the ceiling, spaced between five gas chandeliers, and some of the guests laughingly said that the hall looked like the Palace of Aladdin. Lincoln and Mary made their entrance at nine o'clock and then dutifully stood in place in the reception line, Lincoln absent-mind-edly tugging at his white kid gloves.[16] He did not seem to be enjoying himself. Still, he was proud of Mary, who looked radiant in a blue gown, gold necklace and bracelets, blue feather in her hair, and who did not seem to mind that "most of the distinguished ladies of Washington society" had declined to attend the ball.[17] Precisely at 11 the band struck up "Hail to the Chief," and Lincoln led the Grand March around the hall, his arm linked with Washington Mayor Berret. Stephen Douglas followed, escorting Mary, and while Lincoln watched approvingly Douglas and Mary danced the quadrille, as they often had in Springfield many years ago.

By one o'clock Lincoln was too fatigued to carry on, and leaving Mary with her sisters he had a carriage drive him to the White House. Almost as soon as he walked in the door he was handed the telegraph that Major Anderson had sent earlier to Joseph Holt. Things were urgent at Fort Sumter, Anderson had written. Supplies were running low and the Confederates had strengthened their positions. Anderson needed at least 20,000 troops to continue to hold the fort. An accompanying note from Winfield Scott recommended that Sumter be surrendered. Lincoln would con-vene his would-be cabinet the next morning to discuss the pending crisis. He went to sleep, his first night as president, with the growing realization that no matter what he did, or what he said, the country would soon be at war. His burden, John Hay later wrote, had become "heavier than that which Atlas bears." Hay wondered if Lincoln, in his heart, "does not wish himself back in the quiet village of Springfield once again."[18]

Notes

Prologue

1. Daily Illinois *State Journal*, August 4, 1860.
2. *Ibid.*, August 4, 1860. The storm was so severe that Lincoln mentioned it in a letter to his friend Simeon Francis: "We had a storm here last night which did considerable damage, the largest single instance of which, was to the Withies. A wall of their brick shop building was thrown in and, it is said destroyed ten thousand dollars worth of carriages. I have heard of no personal injury done." *Abraham Lincoln: Speeches and Writings, 1859–1865*, (New York: The Library of America, 1989), pp. 174, 175.
3. Daily Illinois *State Journal*, August 5,1860.
4. *Ibid.*
5. *Ibid.*
6. *Honest Old Abe: Song and Chorus*, words by D. Wentworth, Esq., music by a Wide-Awake, Buffalo, N.Y., Blodgett & Bradford, 1860, from *We'll Sing to Abe Our Song!* Sheet Music about Lincoln, Emancipation, and the Civil War from the Alfred Whital Stern Collection of Lincolniana.
7. Illinois *State Journal*, August 9, 1860. Trumbull spoke at the Wigwam on both August 4 and August 8, 1860.
8. *Ibid.*
9. David Herbert Donald, *Lincoln's Herndon* (New York: Alfred A. Knopf, 1948), pp. 139–140.
10. *Ibid.*
11. Illinois *State Journal*, August 4, 1860.
12. *Ibid.*
13. Chicago *Journal*, quoted in the Daily Illinois *State Journal*, July 16, 1860.
14. Illinois *State Journal*, August 9, 1860.
15. *Ibid.*
16. *Ibid.*
17. *Ibid.*
18. *Forward! Forward! Is the Word!* Words and music composed for the "N.Y. Rail-Splitters' Glee Club," by J.J. Clarke, The Wide-Awake Vocalist; or, *Rail-Splitters' Song Book* (New York: E.A. Daggett, 1860), original owned by the Chicago Historical Society.
19. Illinois *State Journal*, August 9, 1860.
20. Allan Nevins, *The Emergence of Lincoln* (New York: Scribner's, 1950), p. 305.
21. Don E. Fehrenbacher, editor, *Abraham Lincoln: Speeches and Writings, 1859–1865* (New York: Library of America, 1989), pp. 175–176.
22. David Herbert Donald, *Lincoln* (London: Jonathan Cape, 1995), p. 254
23. Michael Burlingame, editor, *Lincoln's Journalist: John Hay's Anonymous Writings for the Press, 1860–1864* (Carbondale: Southern Illinois University Press, 1997), p. 6.
24. *The Wide Awakes Lyrics* by O.P.Q. (New York: H. De Marsan), original owned by the University of Chicago, 1860.
25. Burlingame, p. 6.
26. Illinois *State Journal, August 9, 1860.*
27. *Ibid.*
28. Burlingame, p. 3.
29. Illinois *State Journal*, August 9, 1860.

Chapter 1

1. William Henry Herndon, *Herndon's Life of Lincoln* (Cleveland: World, 1942; New York: Da Capo, 1983), p. 377.
2. *Ibid.*, p. 69.
3. *Ibid.*, p. 61.
4. Kenneth J. Winkle, *The Young Eagle: The Rise of Abraham Lincoln* (Dallas: Taylor, 2001), p. 77.
5. Don Davenport, *In Lincoln's Footsteps: A Historical Guide to the Lincoln Sites in Illinois, Indiana, and Kentucky* (Madison, Wisconsin: Prairie Oak Press, 1991), p. 57.
6. Douglas L. Wilson, *Honor's Voice: The Transformation of Abraham Lincoln* (New York: Alfred A. Knopf, 1998), p. 70.
7. David Herbert Donald, *Lincoln* (London: Jonathan Cape, 1995), p. 40.
8. Winkle, p. 67.
9. *Ibid.*, p. 41
10. Albert A. Woldman, *Lawyer Lincoln* (New York: Carroll & Graf, 1994), p. 22.
11. *Ibid.*, p. 12.
12. Donald, p. 43.
13. Herndon, p. 85.
14. Donald, p. 43.
15. Benjamin P. Thomas, *Abraham Lincoln: A Biography* (New York: Alfred A. Knopf, Inc., 1952), p. 31.
16. Donald, p. 45.
17. Eventually Black Hawk was captured by General James Henry and his militia, and the war ended.
18. Herndon, p. 86.

19. Donald, p. 46.

20. *Ibid.*, p. 54.

21. Carl Sandburg, *Abraham Lincoln: The Prairie Years and the War Years 1809–1865* (New York: Dell, 1954), p. 85.

22. Herndon, p. 93.

23. Philip B. Kunhardt, Jr., Philip B. Kunhardt III, Peter Kunhardt, *Lincoln: An Illustrated Biography* (New York: Alfred A. Knopf, 1992), p. 48.

24. Donald, *Lincoln*, p. 64.

25. Ida M. Tarbell, *The Life of Abraham Lincoln,* Volume One (New York: S.S. McClure Company, 1895), p. 153.

26. Paul M. Angle, *"Here I Have Lived": A History of Lincoln's Springfield, 1821–1865* (Springfield, Illinois: The Abraham Lincoln Association, 1935), p. 14.

27. Sandburg, p. 104.

28. Woldman, p. 87.

29. Kunhardt, et al., p. 52.

30. *Ibid.*

31. Donald, p. 68.

32. Douglas L. Wilson, *Honor's Voice: The Transformation of Abraham Lincoln* (New York: Alfred A. Knopf, Inc., 1998), p. 135.

33. Donald, p. 68.

34. *Ibid.*, p. 69.

35. *Ibid.*, p. 84.

36. Winkle, p. 169.

37. Tarbell, p. 170.

38. Some sources place the first meeting at a party celebrating the completion of the new state capitol building in Springfield.

39. Jean Baker, *Mary Todd Lincoln: A Biography* (New York: W.W. Norton, 1987), pp. 82, 83, 85.

40. *Ibid.*, p. 79.

41. Stephen B. Oates, *With Malice Toward None: A Life of Abraham Lincoln* (New York: HarperPerennial, 1994), p. 55.

42. Donald, p. 85.

43. Baker, p. 84.

44. Oates, p. 53.

45. *Ibid.*, p. 56.

46. *Ibid.*, p. 69

47. Letter from James C. Conkling to Mercy Levering, quoted in Earl Schenck Miers and C. Percy Powell, editors, *Lincoln Day by Day: A Chronology, 1809–1865* (Dayton, Ohio: Morningside, 1991), p. 156.

48. Letters to Mary Speed, September 27, 1841, and Joshua Speed, c. January, 1842, quoted in Don E. Fehrenbacher, editor, *Abraham Lincoln: Speeches and Writings, 1859–1865* (New York: Library of America, 1984), pp.75, 77.

49. *Ibid.*

50. Justin G. Turner and Linda Levitt Turner, *Mary Todd Lincoln: Her Life and Letters* (New York: Alfred A. Knopf, 1972), pp. 25–28.

51. Oates, p. 60.

52. Kunhardt et al., p. 64.

53. *Ibid.*, p.62.

54. Oates, p. 63.

55. Baker, p. 99.

56. *Ibid.*, p. 102.

57. *Ibid.*, p. 103

58. Angle, p. 108.

59. Baker, 120.

60. *Ibid.*, p. 122

61. Kunhardt et al., p. 91.

62. Woldman, p. 50.

63. Kunhardts et al., p. 70.

64. *Ibid.*

65. Oates, p. 80.

66. *Ibid.*, p. 89.

Chapter 2

1. Douglas L. Wilson and Rodney O. Davis, editors, *Herndon's Informants: Letters, Interviews, and Statements about Abraham Lincoln* (Urbana and Chicago: University of Illinois Press, 1998), p. 771.

2. Jean Baker, *Mary Todd Lincoln: A Biography* (New York: W.W. Norton, 1987), p. 128.

3. David Herbert Donald, *Lincoln* (London: Jonathan Cape, 1995), p. 142.

4. Stephen B. Oates, *With Malice Toward None: A Life of Abraham Lincoln* (New York: HarperPerennial, 1994), p. 102.

5. Philip B. Kunhardt, Jr., Philip B. Kunhardt III and Peter W. Kunhardt, *Lincoln: An Illustrated Biography* (New York: Alfred A. Knopf, 1992), p. 107.

6. Stephen E. Ambrose, *Nothing Like It in the World: The Man Who Built the Transcontinental Railroad, 1863–1869* (New York: Simon and Schuster, 2000), p. 29.

7. Albert A. Woldman, *Lawyer Lincoln* (New York: Carroll & Graf, 1994), p. 179.

8. Kenneth J. Winkle, *The Young Eagle: The Rise of Abraham Lincoln* (Dallas: Taylor, 2001), p. 251.

9. Oates, p. 39.

10. *Ibid.*, p. 38.

11. Donald, p. 168.

12. *Ibid.*

13. Mark E. Neely, Jr., *The Abraham Lincoln Encyclopedia* (New York: McGraw-Hill, 1982), p. 86.

14. Oates, p. 108.

15. Winkle, p. 294.

16. Donald, p. 192.

17. William Henry Herndon, *Herndon's Life of Lincoln* (New York: Da Capo, 1983), pp. 312, 313.

18. Neely, p. 171

19. Don E. and Virginia Fehrenbacher, editors, *Recollected Words of Abraham Lincoln* (Stanford: Stanford University Press, 1996), p. 44.

20. Benjamin P. Thomas, *Abraham Lincoln: A Biography* (New York: Alfred A. Knopf, 1952), p. 172.

21. Oates, p. 133.

22. Philip Van Doren Stern, editor, *The Life and Writings of Abraham Lincoln* (New York: Random House, 1940), p. 438.

23. Kunhardts et al., p. 108.

24. Donald, p. 209; Oates, p. 145.

25. Oates, p. 153.

26. Kunhardts et al., p. 110.

27. *Ibid.*

28. *Ibid.*

29. Neely, p. 129

30. Thomas, p. 204–205.

31. Stern, pp. 590, 591.

32. Kunhardts et al., p. 114.

33. Thomas, p. 209, 210; Kunhardts et al., p. 120.

34. Oates, p. 178.

35. Stern, p. 594.

36. Oates, p. 178.

37. Thomas, p. 210.

38. Oates, p. 179
39. *Ibid.*

Chapter 3

1. Eighth United States Census, Springfield, Illinois, 1860. The census incorrectly lists Mary Lincoln's age as 35; in fact she was 42 in July 1860. Robert turned 17 on August 1st, 1860. William turned 10 on December 21, 1860, and Thomas turned 7 on April 4, 1860. The servant is listed as "M. Johnson." In their book *Seventeen Years at Eighth and Jackson*, Thomas J. Dyba and George L. Painter refer to her as "Emma," the name used here.
2. Ward Hill Lamon, *Recollections of Abraham Lincoln: 1847–1865* (A.C. McClurg, 1895; reprint, Lincoln, Nebraska: University of Nebraska Press, 1994), p. 21.
3. Thomas J. Dyba and George L. Painter, *Seventeen Years at Eighth and Jackson: The Lincoln Family in Their Springfield Home* (Lisle, Illinois: Illinois Benedictine College Publications, 1985), p. 57.
4. Michael Burlingame, editor, *Lincoln's Journalist: John Hay's Anonymous Writings for the Press, 1860–1864* (Carbondale: Southern Illinois University Press, p.13.
5. Letter to Simeon Francis, August 4, 1860, in Don E. Fehrenbacher, editor, *Abraham Lincoln: Speeches and Writings, 1859–1865* (New York: Library of America, 1989), p.175.
6. Philip Shaw Paludan, *The Presidency of Abraham Lincoln* (Lawrence: University Press of Kansas, 1994), p. 35.
7. These letters and many more appear in David Mearns, *The Lincoln Papers* (Garden City, New York: Doubleday, 1948).
8. *Ibid.*, pp. 295–299.
9. *Ibid.*, p. 293
10. Letter to Daniel Gardner, September 28, 1860, *Abraham Lincoln: Speeches and Writings, 1859–1865*, p. 180.
11. Herbert Mitgang, editor, *Lincoln as They Saw Him* (New York: Rinehart, 1956), p. 201.
12. Maury Klein, *Days of Defiance: Sumter, Secession, and the Coming of the Civil War* (New York: Vintage, 1999), p. 34.
13. Springfield *Daily Illinois State Journal*, November 6, 1860.
14. Illinois *State Register*, August 11, 1860.
15. *Ibid*, November 7, 1860.
16. Mitgang, p. 216.
17. William Henry Herndon, *Herndon's Life of Lincoln* (New York: Da Capo, 1983), p. 257.
18. Luther E. Robinson, *Ephraim Elmer Ellsworth: First Martyr of the Civil War* (Springfield, Illinois: Illinois State Historical Society, 1924), p. 9.
19. Mark E. Neely, Jr., *The Abraham Lincoln Encyclopedia* (New York: McGraw-Hill, 1982), pp. 102, 103.
20. Neely, p. 87.
21. Mitgang, p. 204.
22. *Ibid.*
23. *Ibid.*, p. 301
24. Stephen B. Oates, *With Malice Toward None: A Life of Abraham Lincoln*, (New York: Harper-Perennial, 1994), p. 190.

25. Mitgang, pp. 214–215.
26. Mearns, p. 303.
27. Letter of Mercy Levering Conkling, quoted in Ruth Painter Randall, *Mary Lincoln: Biography of a Marriage* (Boston: Little, Brown, 1953), p.187.
28. *Ibid.*, p. 186.
29. Carl Sandburg, *Abraham Lincoln: The Prairie Years and the War Years, 1809–1865* (New York: Dell, 1954), p. 161.
30. David Herbert Donald, *Lincoln* (London: Jonathan Cape, 1995), p. 256

Chapter 4

1. Electors from South Carolina were not elected in a popular vote in 1860, but appointed by the state legislature.
2. Phillip Shaw Paludan, *The Presidency of Abraham Lincoln* (Lawrence: University Press of Kansas, 1994), pp. 1–9.
3. *Ibid.*, p. 10.
4. James M. McPherson, *Battle Cry of Freedom: The Civil War Era* (New York: Oxford University Press, 1988), pp. 225, 226.
5. Quoted in William Barringer, *A House Dividing* (Springfield, Illinois: The Abraham Lincoln Association, 1945), p. 60.
6. Harrisburg *Telegraph*, November 7–8, 1860.
7. St. Louis *Democrat*, November 7, 1860, and reprinted in the Illinois *Journal*, November 8, 1860.
8. New York *Weekly Tribune*, November 17, 1860.
9. New York *Tribune*, November 9, 1860.
10. Ida M. Tarbell, *The Life of Abraham Lincoln*, Volume One (New York: Doubleday, 1900), p. 365.
11. David C. Mearns, *The Lincoln Papers* (Garden City, New York: Doubleday & Company, 1948), p. 261.
12. New York *Herald*, November 8, 1860.
13. Tarbell, p. 369.
14. Joseph Schafer, editor, *Intimate Letters of Carl Schurz, 1841–1869* (Madison, Wisconsin: 1928), pp. 230–32, and quoted in Maury Klein, *Days of Defiance: Sumter, Secession, and the Coming of the Civil War* (New York: Vintage, 1999), p. 21; Mark E. Neely, Jr., *The Abraham Lincoln Encyclopedia* (New York: McGraw-Hill, 1982), p. 268.
15. Klein, p. 23.
16. Mearns, p. 302.
17. Klein, p. 21.
18. *Ibid.*
19. Roy Morris, Jr., *The Better Angel: Walt Whitman in the Civil War* (New York: Oxford University Press, 2000), pp.11–12.
20. Lee Soltow, *Men and Wealth in the United States 1850–1870* (1975), p. 65, cited in McPherson, p. 97.
21. McPherson, p. 99.
22. Paludan, pp. 18, 19.
23. McPherson, p. 228.
24. Charles Eugene Hamlin, *The Life and Times of Hannibal Hamlin* (Cambridge: Riverside), pp. 354, 355.
25. William C. Davis, *"A Government of Our Own": The Making of the Confederacy* (Baton Rouge: Louisiana State University Press, 1994), p. 6.
26. John McCardell, *The Idea of a Southern Nation* (1979), pp. 323–24, quoted in Klein, p. 24.

27. Davis, p. 6.

28. Harold Holzer, *Witness to War: The Civil War: 1861–1865* (New York: Perigee, 1996), pp. 12–13.

29. Robert S. Harper, *Lincoln and the Press* (New York: McGraw-Hill, 1951), pp. 67–70.

30. See Holzer, p. 12.

31. *Ibid.*

32. *Ibid.*

33. Klein, p. 25.

34. Harper, pp. 67–70.

35. *Ibid.*, pp. 8–10

36. David Potter, *Lincoln and His Party in the Secession Crisis* (New Haven: Yale University Press, 1942), p. 57.

37. *Ibid.*, p. 11

38. *Ibid.*

39. *Ibid.*, p. 10.

40. *Ibid.*, p. 14.

41. Albert Shaw, *Abraham Lincoln: The Year of His Election* (New York: Review of Reviews, 1929), p. 37.

42. Quoted in Horace Greeley, *The American Conflict: A History of the Great Rebellion of the United States of America* (Hartford: O.D. Case, 1864), p. 335.

43. *Ibid.*, pp. 330–331.

44. Shaw, p. 136.

45. *Ibid.*, p. 336.

46. *Ibid.*

47. Davis, p. 7.

48. Philip B. Kunhardt, Jr., Philip B. Kunhardt III, Peter W. Kunhardt, *Lincoln: An Illustrated Biography* (New York: Alfred A. Knopf, Inc.,1992), p. 130.

Chapter 5

1. Paul M. Angle, editor, *The Lincoln Reader* (New Brunswick, New Jersey: Rutgers University Press, 1947), p. 297.

2. Technically Lincoln was not yet president-elect, and would not be until the electors of the various states voted so in mid-February.

3. Ida M. Tarbell, *The Life of Abraham Lincoln,* Volume One (New York: Lincoln Memorial Association), p. 390.

4. Don E. Fehrenbacher, editor, *Abraham Lincoln: Speeches and Writings, 1859–1865* (New York: Library of America, 1984), p. 183.

5. Roy P. Basler, editor, *The Collected Works of Abraham Lincoln* (New Brunswick, New Jersey: The Abraham Lincoln Association, 1953), pp. 138, 139.

6. *Ibid.*

7. David M. Potter, *Lincoln and his Party in the Secession Crisis* (New Haven: Yale University Press, 1942), p. 118.

8. Basler, p. 138.

9. *Ibid.*, p. 140

10. *Ibid.*, p.137

11. Fehrenbacher, pp. 186, 187.

12. Basler, p. 142.

13. *Ibid.*, pp. 142, 143.

14. *Ibid.*, pp.145, 146

15. *Ibid.*

16. Fehrenbacher, p. 194.

17. Basler

18. *Ibid.*

19. *Ibid.*, p. 136.

20. Henry Villard, *Lincoln on the Eve of '61: A Jour-*

nalist's Story, edited by Harold G. and Oswald Garrison Villard (New York: Alfred A. Knopf, 1941), p. 10.

21. *Ibid.*, pp. 6, 7.

22. *Ibid.*, pp. 13–14.

23. *Ibid.*, p. 11.

24. *Ibid.*, p. 21.

25. *Echoes* magazine article, undated, "Buckeyes Look at Lincoln," courtesy Fred Schuld, Cleveland, Ohio.

26. Stephen B. Oates, *With Malice Toward None: A Life of Abraham Lincoln* (New York: HarperPerennial, 1994), pp. 197–198.

27. Don Davenport, *Lincoln's Footsteps: A Historical Guide to the Lincoln Sites in Illinois, Indiana, and Kentucky* (Madison, Wisconsin: Prairie Oak, 1991), pp. 125–129.

28. *Ibid.*, p. 143.

29. *Ibid.*, pp. 143, 144

30. H. Draper Hunt, *Hannibal Hamlin of Maine: Lincoln's First Vice-President* (Syracuse, New York: Syracuse University Press, 1969), p. 124.

31. *Ibid.*, p. 125.

32. *Ibid.*, pp. 124, 125.

33. *Ibid.*, p. 125.

34. *Ibid.*, p. 126.

35. Charles Eugene Hamlin, *The Life and Times of Hannibal Hamlin* (Cambridge, Massachusetts: Riverside), p. 367.

36. Earl Schenck Miers and C. Percy Powell, editors, *Lincoln Day by Day: A Chronology, 1809–1865* (Dayton, Ohio: Morningside, 1991), p. 298.

37. Hunt, p. 127.

38. *Ibid.*, p. 129.

39. Miers and Powell, quoting the Chicago *Journal* of November 26 and the New York *Tribune* of November 27, 1860, p. 299.

40. *Ibid.*, p. 299.

Chapter 6

1. The State of the Union address was hand-delivered to members of Congress and major newspapers. Not until 1913 did President Woodrow Wilson personally appear and deliver the address in the House Chamber, beginning a tradition that is still in use today.

2. For a full discussion of northern capitalist pressures on the efforts of compromise see David M. Potter, *Lincoln and His Party in the Secession Crisis* (New Haven: Yale University Press, 1942), pp. 119–123.

3. Maury Klein, *Days of Defiance: Sumter, Secession, and the Coming of the Civil War* (New York: Vintage, 1999).

4. Philip Van Doren Stern, editor, *The Life and Writings of Abraham Lincoln* (New York: Random House, 1940), p. 190.

5. Potter, pp. 145, 146.

6. Stephen B. Oates, *The Approaching Fury: Voices of the Storm, 1820–1861* (New York: HarperPerennial, 1996), p. 351.

7. Klein, p. 130.

8. Potter, p. 83.

9. *Ibid.*, p. 83.

10. *Ibid.*, p. 128.

11. *Ibid.*, pp. 85, 86.

12. Stern, pp. 188–189.

13. Glyndon G. Van Deusen, *William Henry Seward* (New York: Oxford University Press, 1967), pp. 240–241.

14. Potter, pp. 146, 147.

15. *Ibid.*

16. Earl Schenck Miers and C. Percy Powell, editors, *Lincoln Day by Day: A Chronology, 1809–1865* (Dayton, Ohio: Morningside, 1991), p. 301.

17. Potter, p. 79.

18. Horace Greeley, *The American Conflict: A History of the Great Rebellion of the United States of America, 1860–1864* (Hartford: O.D. Case, 1864), p. 345.

19. *Ibid.* pp. 345–347.

20. *Ibid.*

21. *Ibid.*

22. *Ibid.*

23. Harold Holzer, *Witness to War: The Civil War, 1861–1865* (New York: Perigee, 1996), pp. 16–17.

24. *Ibid.*

25. Thurlow Weed, *The Autobiography of Thurlow Weed*, edited by Harriet A. Weed (Boston: Houghton Mifflin, 1883), p. 604.

26. Potter, p. 148, and Weed, pp. 606–614.

27. Weed, p. 610.

28. William Lee Miller, *Lincoln's Virtues: An Ethical Biography* (New York: Alfred A. Knopf, 2002), p. 441.

29. Weed, p. 605.

30. Potter, pp. 167, 168.

31. Van Deusen, p. 241.

32. William C. Davis, editor, *The Civil War: Brother Against Brother* (Alexandria, Virginia: Time-Life Books, 1983), pp. 120, 121.

33. Miller, p. 441.

34. David Herbert Donald, *Lincoln* (London: Jonathan Cape, 1995), p. 266.

35. Albert Shaw, *Abraham Lincoln: The Year of His Election* (New York: Review of Reviews, 1929), p. 216.

36. Stern, p. 195.

37. Donald, p. 266.

38. Shaw, p. 217.

39. Miers and Schenck, 1861 section, p. 3.

Chapter 7

1. Carl Sandburg, *Abraham Lincoln: The War Years* (New York: Dell, 1954), p. 167.

2. William C. Davis, editor, *The Civil War: Brother Against Brother* (Alexandria, Virginia: Time-Life, 1983), p. 127.

3. *Ibid.*, pp. 127–128.

4. Earl Schenck Miers and C. Percy Powell, editors, *Lincoln Day by Day: A Chronology 1809–1865* (Dayton, Ohio: Morningside, 1991), 1861 section, p. 4.

5. John C. Waugh, *Reelecting Lincoln: The Battle for the 1864 Presidency* (New York: Da Capo, 1997), p. 37.

6. David Herbert Donald, *Lincoln* (London: Jonathan Cape, 1995), p. 264.

7. *Ibid.*

8. Justin G. Turner and Linda Levitt Turner, *Mary Todd Lincoln: Her Life and Letters* (New York: Alfred A. Knopf, 1972), p. 162.

9. Lincoln eventually decided that Illinois had received enough credit for his election, eliminating Judd, and then chose Smith for secretary of the interior.

10. Maury Klein, *Days of Defiance: Sumter, Secession, and the Coming of the Civil War* (New York: Vintage, 1999), pp. 183, 184.

11. Jean Baker, *Mary Todd Lincoln: A Biography* (New York: W.W. Norton, 1987), p. 166; Miers and Powell, 1861 section, p. 5, quoting the Baltimore *Sun*, February 22, 1861.

12. Roy P. Basler, editor, *The Collected Works of Abraham Lincoln* (New Brunswick, New Jersey: Rutgers University Press, 1953), pp. 177, 178.

13. See Michael F. Holt, *the Rise and Fall of the American Whig Party: Jacksonian Politics and the Onset of the Civil War* (New York: Oxford University Press, 1999), pp. 21–22.

14. *Ibid.*, and see Donald, p. 270.

15. See generally Holt, pp. 476–482, and note that Clay addressed the Senate twice, first on January 29, 1850, then again a few days later.

16. Miers and Powell, pp. 6, 7.

17. Klein, p. 193.

18. *Ibid.*

19. Sandburg, *Abraham Lincoln: The Prairie Years*, p. 416

20. Don Davenport, *In Lincoln's Footsteps: A Historical Guide to the Lincoln Sites in Illinois, Indiana, and Kentucky* (Madison, Wisconsin: Prairie Oak, 1991), p. 35.

21. William Lee Miller, *Lincoln's Virtues: An Ethical Biography* (New York: Alfred A. Knopf, 2002), p. 59.

22. Davenport, p. 171.

23. Donald, p. 271.

24. Douglas L. Wilson and Rodney O. Davis, editors, *Herndon's Informants: Letters, Interviews, and Statements about Abraham Lincoln* (Urbana: University of Illinois Press, 1998), pp. 39, 41.

25. Philip Van Doren Stern, editor, *The Life and Writings of Abraham Lincoln* (New York: Random House, 1940), p. 256.

26. Donald, p. 271.

27. Stephen B. Oates, *With Malice Toward None: A Life of Abraham Lincoln* (New York: HarperPerennial, 1994), p. 205.

Chapter 8

1. William C. Davis, *"A Government of Our Own": The Making of the Confederacy* (Baton Rouge: Louisiana State University Press, 1994), p. 73.

2. *Ibid.*, p. 76.

3. William J. Cooper, Jr., *Jefferson Davis, American* (New York: Vintage, 2001), p. 51.

4. *Ibid.*, p. 54.

5. *Ibid.*, p. 60.

6. Maury Klein, *Days of Defiance: Sumter, Secession, and the Coming of the Civil War* (New York: Vintage, 1999), p. 249.

7. Oates, *The Approaching Fury: Voices of the Storm, 1820–1861* (New York: HarperPerennial, 1996), p. 351.

8. *Ibid.*, pp. 368–369.

9. *Ibid.*, p. 370.

10. Jefferson Davis' Farewell Speech to the U.S. Senate, January 21, 1861.

11. Shelby Foote, *The Civil War: A Narrative* (New York: Vintage, 1958), p. 16.

12. Cooper, p. 352.

13. *Ibid.*, p. 17.

14. *Ibid.*, p. 353.

15. Albert Shaw, *Abraham Lincoln: The Year of His Election* (New York: Review of Reviews, 1929), p. 179.

16. *Ibid.*, and Oates, p. 380.

17. Inaugural Address of Jefferson Davis, Southern Historical Society Papers, vol. 1, Richmond, Virginia.

18. Shaw, p. 178.

19. Oates, p. 207

20. Illinois *State Journal*, January 30, 1861, and quoted in Thomas J. Dyba and George L. Painter, *Seventeen Years at Eighth and Jackson: The Lincoln Family in Their Springfield Home* (Lisle, Illinois: Illinois Benedictine College Publications, 1985), p. 65.

21. *Ibid.*, p. 65, and David Herbert Donald, *Lincoln* (London: Jonathan Cape, 1995), p. 272.

22. Lincoln owned notes representing loans to a number of Springfield residents, including Norman Judd, all at 10 percent interest. He also owned one certificate of six shares of the Alton & Sangamon Railroad and one "certificate of scholarship" in Illinois State University. Roy P. Basler, editor, *The Collected Works of Abraham Lincoln* (New Brunswick, New Jersey: Rutgers University Press, 1953), pp. 188–189.

23. Donald, *Lincoln*, p. 272.

24. William Henry Herndon, *Herndon's Life of Lincoln* (New York: Da Capo, 1983), p. 389.

25. *Ibid.*, pp. 392–393, and Donald, p. 272.

26. Oates, p. 207.

27. At least two versions of Lincoln's farewell speech exist. The version printed here was reported in the February 12, 1861, Illinois *State Journal*. The second was written by Lincoln and John Hay as the train departed the station, and is most often quoted in books about Lincoln: "My friends— No one, not in my situation, can appreciate my feeling of sadness at this parting. To this place, and the kindness of these people, I owe every thing. Here I have lived a quarter of a century, and have passed from a young to an old man. Here my children have been born, and one is buried. I now leave, not knowing when, or whether ever, I may return, with a task before me greater than that which rested upon Washington. Without the assistance of the Divine Being, who ever attended him, I cannot succeed. With that assistance I cannot fail. Trusting in Him, who can go with me, and remain with you and be every where for good, let us confidently hope that all will yet be well. To His care commending you, as I hope in your prayers you will commend me, I bid you an affectionate farewell."

28. *Ibid.*

Chapter 9

1. Victor Searcher, *Lincoln's Journey to Greatness: A Factual Account of the Twelve-Day Inaugural Trip* (Philadelphia: John C. Winston, 1960), pp. 7–9.

2. 2. Roy P. Basler, editor, *The Collected Works of Abraham Lincoln* (New Brunswick, New Jersey: Rutgers University Press, 1953), p. 191.

3. *Ibid.*, pp. 191, 192.

4. Searcher, p. 13.

5. Basler, quoting the Lafayette *Courier*, February 12, 1861, p. 192.

6. *Ibid.*

7. *Ibid.*, p. 192, and Searcher, p. 23.

8. Searcher, p. 24.

9. Basler, pp. 193, 194, citing the Indianapolis *Journal* and the Cincinnati *Daily Gazette* of February 12, 1861, and the Cincinnati *Daily Commercial*, February 13, 1861.

10. Basler, citing the Indianapolis *Daily Sentinel* of February 12, 1861.

11. Searcher, pp. 33–35.

12. Henry Villard, *Lincoln on the Eve of '61: A Journalist's Story*, edited by Harold G. Villard and Oswald Garrison Villard (New York: Alfred A. Knopf, 1961), p. 77.

13. Searcher, p. 29.

14. *Ibid.*

15. Searcher, p. 37.

16. David Herbert Donald, *Lincoln* (London: Jonathan Cape, 1995), p. 274.

17. *Ibid.*, p. 43.

18. Basler, p. 197, quoting the Cincinnati *Daily Commercial*, February 13, 1861.

19. This fragment of Lincoln's speech intended for Kentuckians was later found with a copy of his first Inaugural Address:

I am grateful, for the opportunity your invitation affords me to appear before an audience of my native state. During the present winter it has been greatly pressed upon me by many patriotic citizens, Kentuckians among others, that I could in my position, by a word, restore peace to the country. But what word? I have many words already before the public; and my position was given me on the faith of those words. Is the desired word to be confirmatory of these; or must it be contradictory to them? If the former, it is useless repetition; if the latter, it is dishonorable and treacherous.

Again, it is urged as if the word must be spoken before the fourth of March. Why: Is the speaking the word a "sine quo non" to the inauguration? Is there a Bell-man, a Breckinridge-man, or a Douglas man who would tolerate his own candidate to make such terms, had he been elected? Who amongst you would not die by the proposition, that your candidate, being elected, should be inaugurated, solely on the conditions of the constitution, and laws, or not at all. What Kentuckian, worthy of his birth place, would not do this? Gentlemen, I too, am a Kentuckian.

Nor is this a matter of mere personal honor. No man can be elected President without some opponents, as well as supporters; and if when elected, he can not be installed, till he first appeases his enemies, by breaking his pledges, and betraying his friends, this government, and all popular government, is already at an end. Demands for such surrender, once recognized, and yielded to, are without limit, as to nature, extent, or repetition. They break the only bond of faith between public, and public servant; and they distinctly set the minority over the majority. Such demands acquiesced in , would not merely be the ruin of a man, or a party; but as a precedent they would ruin the government itself.

I do not deny that the people may err in an election; but if they do, the true [*remedy*] is in the next election, and not in the treachery of the person elected.

Basler, pp. 200–201.
20. Basler, p. 197.
21. *Ibid.*, pp. 197–199, quoting the Cincinnati *Daily Gazette*, February 13, 1861.
22. Searcher, p. 54.
23. Basler, pp. 201, 202, quoting the Cincinnati *Daily Commercial*, February 13, 1861.
24. Henry Villard, *Memoirs of Henry Villard, Journalist and Financier 1835–1900* (Boston: Houghton, Mifflin, 1904), p. 153.
25. Basler, pp. 203, 204, quoting the London *National Democrat*, February 14, 1861.
26. *Ibid.*
27. Robert S. Harper, *"During Two Journeys"* (Columbus: Ohio Lincoln Sesquicentennial Committee, Ohio State Museum, 1959), p. 3.
28. *Ibid.*, p. 4.
29. *Ibid.*, pp. 5, 6.
30. Basler, pp. 204, 205, quoting the New York *Herald*, February 14, 1861.
31. Searcher, p.
32. Basler, p.
33. *Ibid.*
34. *Ibid.*
35. From the steps of the capitol Lincoln said:

Ladies and Gentlemen: I appear before you only to address you briefly. I shall do little else than to thank you for this very kind reception, to greet you and bid you farewell. I should not find strength, if I were otherwise inclined, to repeat speeches of very great length, upon every occasion similar to this—although few so large—which will occur on my way to the Federal Capitol. The General Assembly of the great State of Ohio has just done me the honor to receive me, and to hear a few broken remarks from myself. Judging from what I see, I infer that that reception was one without party distinction, and one of entire kindness—one that had nothing in it beyond a feeling of the citizenship of the United States of America. Knowing, as I do, that any crowd, drawn together as this has been, is made up of the citizens near about, and that in this county of Franklin there is great difference of political sentiment, and those agreeing with me having a little the shortest row [*laughter,*] from this, and the circumstances I have mentioned, I infer that you do me the honor to meet me here without distinction of party. I think this is as it should be. Many of you who were not favorable to the election of the distinguished Senator from the State in which I reside. If Senator Douglas had been elected to the Presidency in the late contest, I think my friends would have joined heartily in meeting and greeting him on his passage through your Capital, as you have me to-day. If any of the other candidates had been elected, I think it would have been altogether becoming and proper for all to have joined in showing honor, quite as well to the office, and to the country, as to the man. The people are themselves honored by

such a concentration. I am doubly thankful that you have appeared here to give me this greeting. It is not much to me, for I shall very soon pass away from you; but we have a large country and a large future before us, and the manifestations of good-will towards the government, and affection for the Union which you may exhibit are of immense value to you and your posterity forever. [*Applause.*] In this point of view it is that I thank you most heartily for the exhibition you have given me, and with this allow me to bid you an affectionate farewell.

Basler, quoting the New Lisbon, Ohio, *Buckeye State*, February 21, 1861.
36. *Ibid.*, quoting the Beaver, Pennsylvania, *Argus*, February 20, 1861.
37. *Ibid.*, quoting the Pittsburgh *Dispatch*, February 15, 1861.
38. *Ibid.*
39. *Ibid.*
40. Villard, *Memoirs of Henry Villard*, p. 152.
41. John C. Waugh, *Reelecting Lincoln: The Battle for the 1864 Presidency* (New York: Da Capo, 1997), p. 49.
42. Basler, quoting the Portage, Ohio, *Republican*, February 21, 1861.
43. *Ibid.*, quoting the Portage, Ohio, *Sentinel*, February 20, 1860.
44. Lincoln said:
"Ladies and Gentlemen:—I stepped upon this platform to see you, and to give you an opportunity of seeing me, which I suppose you desire to do. You see by my voice that I am quite hoarse. You will not, therefore, expect a speech from me.—Basler, quoting the Akron, Ohio, *Summit County Beacon*, February 21, 1861.
45. Lincoln said:

Ladies and Gentlemen:—I have stepped out upon this platform that I may see you and that you may see me, and in the arrangement I have the best of the bargain. The train only stops for a few minutes, so that I have time to make but few remarks, and the condition of my voice is such that I could not do more if there were time. We are met by large crowds of people at almost every ten miles, but in few instances where there are so many as here, or where there are so many [*turning towards them and bowing*] good-looking ladies. I can only say now that I bid you good morning and farewell.

Then, turning towards it, he said, "Let us have the better music from the Band."
Basler, quoting the Painesville *Telegraph*, February 21, 1861.
46. Basler, quoting the Cleveland *Leader*, February 16, 1861.
47. *Ibid.*
48. *Ibid.*, quoting the Cleveland *Morning Leader*, February 16, 1861.
49. *Ibid.*
50. *Ibid.*
51. *Ibid.*, quoting the Cleveland *Plain Dealer*, February 16, 1861.
52. Villard, *Lincoln on the Eve of '61*, pp. 86–87.
53. Basler, quoting the Cleveland *Plain Dealer*, February 16, 1861.

Chapter 10

1. The incident with Grace Bedell was reported in several newspapers, including the Philadelphia *Inquirer*, February 20, 1861.

2. David C. Mearns, *The Lincoln Papers* (Garden City, New York: Doubleday, 1948), p.

3. *Ibid.*, p.

4. *Ibid.*, p.

5. Earl Schenck Miers and C. Percy Powell, editors, *Lincoln Day by Day: A Chronology 1809–1865* (Dayton, Ohio: Morningside, 1991), 1861 section, p. 16.

6. Henry Villard, *Lincoln on the Eve of '61: A Journalist's Story*, edited by Harold G. Villard and Oswald Garrison Villard (New York: Alfred A. Knopf, 1952), p. 89.

7. Roy P. Basler, editor, *The Collected Works of Abraham Lincoln* (New Brunswick, New Jersey: Rutgers University Press, 1953), quoting the Buffalo *Morning Express*, February 18, 1861.

8. Victor Searcher, *Lincoln's Journey to Greatness: A Factual Account of the Twelve-Day Trip* (Philadelphia: John C. Winston, 1963), p. 126.

9. At Rochester Lincoln said:

I confess myself, after having seen large audiences since leaving home, overwhelmed with this vast number of faces at this hour of the morning. I am not vain enough to believe that you are here from any wish to see me as an individual, but because I am, for the time being, the representative on the American people. I could not, if I would, address you at any length. I have not the strength, even if I had the time, for a speech at these many interviews that are afforded me on my way to Washington. I appear merely to see you, and to let you see me, and to bid you farewell. I hope it will be understood that it is from no disposition to disoblige anybody, that I do not address you at greater length.

At Syracuse Lincoln said:

Ladies and Gentlemen: I see you have erected a very fine and handsome platform here for me, and I presume you expected me to speak from it. If I should go upon it you would imagine that I was about to deliver you a much longer speech than I am. I wish you to understand that I mean no discourtesy to you by thus declining. I intend discourtesy to no one. But I wish you to understand that though I am unwilling to go upon this platform, you are not at liberty to draw any inferences concerning any other platform with which my name has been or is connected. [*Laughter and applause.*] I wish you a long life and prosperity individually, and pray that with the perpetuity of those institutions under which we have all so long lived and prospered, our happiness may be secured, our future made brilliant, and the glorious destiny of our country established forever. I bid you a kind farewell.

Ibid., quoting the New York *Times, Tribune*, and *Herald*, February 19, 1861.

At Utica Lincoln said:

Ladies and Gentlemen: — I have but a short speech to make you. I have no time to make remarks of any length. I appear before you to bid you farewell — to see you, and to allow you all to see me. At the same time I acknowledge, ladies, that I think I have the best of the bargain in the sight. I only appear to greet you, and to say farewell. I will come out again on the platform before the train leaves, so that you may see me.

[*Mr. Lincoln was then introduced to a number of gentlemen on the car, passing around at the same time, until he reached the north side, when he made the following remarks*]:

Gentlemen — I come around to say to you what I did to those on the other side, which was but a few words, and little more than good morning, as it were, and farewell. I can't however say here, exactly what I did on the other side, as there are no ladies on this side. I said that there were so many ladies present that I had the best part of the sight, but bear in mind I don't make any such admission now. Farewell!

Ibid., quoting the Utica *Evening Telegraph*, February 18, 1861.

At Little Falls, New York, Lincoln said:

Ladies and Gentlemen: I appear before you merely for the purpose of greeting you, saying a few words and bidding you farewell. I have no speech to make, and no sufficient time to make one if I had; nor have I the strength to repeat a speech, at all the places at which I stop, even if all the other circumstances were favorable. I have come to see you and allow you to see me [*applause*] and in this so far [as] regards the Ladies, I have the best of the bargain on my side. I don't make that acknowledgment to the gentlemen, [*Increased laughter*] and now I believe I have really make my speech and am ready to bid you farewell when the cars move on.

Ibid., quoting the Herkimer, New York, *Democrat*, February 20, 1861.

10. *Ibid.*, quoting the Schenectady *Daily Evening Star*, February 18, 1861.

11. New York *Times*, February 19, 1861.

12. Lincoln said:

Mr. Governor — I was pleased to receive an invitation to visit the capital of the great Empire State of this nation on my way to the federal capita, and I now thank you, Mr. Governor, and the people of this capital and the people of the State of New York, for this most hearty and magnificent welcome. If I am not at fault, the great Empire State at this time contains a greater population than did the United States of America at the time she achieved her national independence. I am proud to be invited to pass through your capital and meet them, as I now have the honor to do. I am notified by your Governor that this reception is given without distinction of party. I accept it more gladly because it is so. Almost all men in this country, and in any country where freedom of thought is tolerated, attach themselves to political parties. It is but ordinary charity to attribute this to the fact that in so attaching himself to the party which his judgment prefers, the citizen believes he thereby promotes the best interests of the whole country; and when an election is passed, it is altogether befitting a free people, that until the next election, they should be as one people. The reception you have extended to me to-day is not given to me personally. It should not be so, but as the representative for the time being of the majority of the nation. If the election had resulted in the selection of either of the other candidates, the same cordiality should have been extended him, as is extended to me this day, in their testimony of the devotion of the whole people to the Constitution and to the whole Union, and of their desire to perpetuate our institutions, and to hand them down in their perfection to succeeding generations. I have neither the voice nor the strength to address you at any greater length. I beg you will accept my most grateful thanks for ths devotion, not to me, but to this great and glorious free country.

Ibid., pp. 224–225.

13. *Ibid.*, quoting the New York *Times, Herald* and *Tribune,* February 19, 1861.

14. At Troy Lincoln said:

Mr. Mayor and Fellow Citizens of Troy, New York: — I am here to thank you for this noble demonstration of the citizens of Troy, and I accept this flattering reception with feelings of profound gratefulness. Since having left home, I confess, sir, having seen large assemblages of the people, but this immense gathering more than exceeds anything I have ever seen before. Still, fellow citizens, I am not so vain as to suppose that you have gathered to do me honor as an individual, but rather as the representative for the fleeting time of the American people. I have appeared only that you might see me and I you, and I am not sure but that I have the best of the sight.

Again thanking you, fellow citizens, I bid you an affectionate farewell.

At Hudson Lincoln said:

Fellow Citizens: I see that you have provided a platform, but I shall have to decline standing on it. [*Laughter and applause.*] The Superintendent tells me I have not time during our brief stay here to leave the train. I had to decline standing on some very handsome platforms prepared for me yesterday. But I say to you, as I said to them, you must not on this account draw the inference that I have any intention to desert any platform I have a legitimate right to stand on. I do not appear before you for the purpose of making a speech. I come only to see you and to give you the opportunity to see me; and I say to you, as I have before said to crowds where there sere so many handsome ladies as there are here, I have decidedly the best of the bargain. I have only, therefore, to thank you most cordially for this kind reception, and bid you all farewell.

At Poughkeepsie Lincoln said:

I cannot expect to make myself heard by any considerable number of you, my friends, but I appear here rather for the purpose of seeing you and being seen by you. [*Laughter.*] I do not believe that you extend this welcome — one of the finest I have ever received — to the individual man who now addresses you but rather to the person who represents for the time being the majesty of the constitution and the government. [*Cheers.*] I suppose

that here, as everywhere, you meet me without distinction of party, but as the people. [*Cries of "yes," "yes".*] It is with your aid, as the people, that I think we shall be able to preserve — not the country, for the country will preserve itself, [*cheers*], but the institutions of the country — [*great cheering*]; those institutions which have made us free, intelligent and happy — the most free, the most intelligent and the happiest people on the globe. [*Tremendous applause.*] I see that some, at least, of you are of those who believe that an election being decided against them is no reason why they should sink the ship. ["*Hurrah."*] I believe with you, I believe in sticking to it, and carrying it through; and, if defeated at one election, I believe in taking the chances next time. [*Great laughter and applause.*] I do not think that they have chosen the best man to conduct our affairs, now — I am sure they did not — [*here the speaker was interrupted by noise and confusion in another part of the crowd*] — but acting honestly and sincerely, and with your aid, I think we shall be able to get through the storm. [*Here Mr. Sloan caught hold of Mr. Lincoln's arm and pulled him around to see the locomotives — the Union and Constitution — which passed gaily dressed with flags. Turning hastily, Mr. Lincoln continued*] — In addition to what I have said, I have only to bid you farewell. [*Cheers and a salute, amid which the train moved on.*]

At Fishkill Lincoln said:

Ladies and Gentlemen: I appear before you not to make a speech. I have no sufficient time, if I had the strength, to repeat speeches at every station where the people kindly gather to welcome me as we go along. If I had the strength, and should take the time, I should not get to Washington until after inauguration, which you must be aware would not fit exactly. [*Laughter.*] That such an untoward event might not transpire, I know you will readily forego any further remarks; and I close by bidding you farewell. [*Loud cheers.*]

At Peekskill Lincoln said:

Ladies and Gentlemen: I have but a moment to stand before you to listen to and return your kind greeting. I thank you for this reception and for the pleasant manner in which it is tendered to me by our mutual friends. I will say in a single sentence, in regard to the difficulties that lie before me and our beloved country, that if I can only be as generously and unanimously sustained as the demonstrations I have witnessed indicate I shall be, I shall not fail; but without your sustaining hands I am sure that neither I nor any other man can hope to surmount those difficulties. I trust that in the course I shall pursue I shall be sustained, not only by the party that elected me, but by the patriotic people of the whole country.

Ibid., The Collected Works of Abraham Lincoln, quoting the Troy *Daily Budget,* February 19, 1861; New York *Herald,* February 20, 1861; New York *Herald,* February 20, 1861 New York *Tribune,* February 20, 1861; New York *Herald,* February 20, 1861.

15. Edwin G. Burrows and Mike Wallace, *Gotham: A History of New York City to 1898* (New York: Oxford University Press, 1999), p.

16. *Ibid.*, p. 865.
17. *Ibid.*, p. 864.
18. *Ibid.*
19. *Ibid.*, p. 866.
20. *Ibid.*; Miers and Powell, 1861 section, p. 18.
21. Roy Morris, Jr., *The Better Angel: Walt Whitman in the Civil War* (New York: Oxford University Press, 2000), p. 15.
22. Searcher, p. 187.
23. Basler, quoting the New York *Herald*, February 20, 1861.
24. Searcher, pp. 188, 189.
25. *Ibid.*, p. 193.
26. Basler, quoting the New York *Herald*, February 20, 1861.
27. Burrows and Wallace, p. 867.
28. *Ibid.*, p. 876.
29. *Ibid.*, p. 832.
30. *Ibid.*, p. 862.
31. *Ibid.*, p. 868.
32. Basler, *The Collected Works of Abraham Lincoln*, quoting the New York *Herald*, February 21, 1861.
33. Philip B. Kunhardt, Jr., Philip B. Kunhardt III, and Peter W. Kunhardt, *P.T. Barnum: America's Greatest Showman* (New York: Alfred A. Knopf, 1995), pp. 140, 141, 153.
34. *Ibid.*
35. Searcher, p. 212.
36. Henry Villard, *Memoirs of Henry Villard: Journalist and Financier, 1835–1900* (Boston: Houghton Mifflin, 1904), p. 152.
37. Miers and Powell, p. 19.

Chapter 11

1. The quote is from the New York *Times* headline of November 8, 1860. The source of much of the information in this chapter regarding Lincoln's visit to New Jersey is a 2002 article by Anthony Olszewski entitled "Abraham Lincoln Spoke in Jersey City," as well as other sources cited below.
2. Olszewski.
3. *Ibid.*
4. *Ibid.*; and Roy P. Basler, editor, *The Collected Works of Abraham Lincoln* (New Brunswick, New Jersey: Rutgers University Press, 1953), p. 234.
5. Basler, p. 234.
6. Michael Burlingame, editor, *Lincoln's Journalist: John Hay's Anonymous Writings for the Press, 1860–1864* (Carbondale: Southern Illinois University Press), p. 40.
7. Basler,
8. *Ibid.*, p. 40.
9. *Ibid.*
10. Burlingame, p. 40.
11. *Ibid.*, p. 41.
12. Baltimore *Sun*, February 22, 1861.
13. Ward Hill Lamon, *Recollections of Abraham Lincoln: 1847–1865* (A.C. McClurg, 1895; reprint, Lincoln: University of Nebraska Press, 1994), p. 35.
14. Lincoln said: Mr. Chairman — I feel highly flattered by the encomiums you have seen fit to bestow upon me. Soon after the nomination of Gen. Taylor I attended a political meeting in the city of Wilmington, and have since carried with me a fond remembrance of the hospitalities of the city on that

occasion. The programme established provides for my presence in Harrisburg in twenty-four hours from this time. I expect to be in Washington on Saturday. It is, therefore, an impossibility that I should accept your kind invitation. There are no people whom I would more gladly accommodate than those of Delaware; but circumstances forbid, gentlemen. With many regrets for the character of the reply, I am compelled to give you, I bid you adieu.
Basler, quoting the Philadelphia *Inquirer*, February 22, 1861.
15. *Ibid.*
16. *Ibid.*
17. James Mackay, *Allan Pinkerton: The Eye Who Never Slept* (Edinburgh: Mainstream Publishing, 1996), p. 98.
18. *Ibid.*, pp. 98–99.
19. *Ibid.*, p. 99.
20. *Ibid.*
21. Basler, quoting the Philadelphia *Inquirer*, February 23, 1861.
22. *Ibid.*, quoting the Lancaster *Evening Express*, New York *Tribune* and New York *Times*, February 23, 1861.
23. *Ibid.*, quoting the Harrisburg, Pennsylvania, *Daily Telegraph*, February 23, 1861.
24. *Ibid.*
25. This version of the meeting in Lincoln's room at the Jones House is taken from Lamon, pp. 41–43. Some sources place the meeting on the train between Harrisburg and Philadelphia.
26. Stephen B. Oates, *With Malice Toward None: A Life of Abraham Lincoln* (New York: HarperPerennial, 1994), p. 211.
27. *Ibid.*
28. *Ibid.*
29. *Ibid.*
30. *Ibid.*

Chapter 12

1. Maury Klein, *Days of Defiance: Sumter, Secession, and the Coming of the Civil War* (New York: Vintage, 1999), p. 273.
2. E.B. Long and Barbara Long, *The Civil War Day by Day: An Almanac 1861–1865* (New York: Doubleday, 1971), p. 62.
3. Robert S. Harper, *Lincoln and the Press* (New York: McGraw-Hill, 1951), p. 91.
4. Klein, p. 274.
5. *Ibid.*, p. 275.
6. The actual bill, which included private dinners, entertaining, liquor and cigars for numerous guests, came to $773. 75. Lincoln paid the bill on April 19 with his first Presidential paycheck. See Earl Schenck Miers and C. Percy Powell, editors. *Lincoln Day by Day: A Chronology, 1808–1865*, (Dayton, Ohio: Morningside, 1991), 1861 section, pp. 22, 36.
7. Paul M. Angle, editor, *The Lincoln Reader* (New Brunswickk, New Jersey: Rutgers University Press, 1947), pp. 318–319.
8. Albert A. Nofi, *The Civil War Notebook* (Conshohocken, Pennsylvania: Combined, 1993), p. 14.
9. Klein, p. 282.
10. Philip B. Kunhardt, Jr., Philip B. Kunhardt III and Peter W. Kunhardt, *Lincoln: An Illustrated Biog-*

raphy (New York: Alfred A. Knopf, 1995), pp. 14, 15.

11. Ida M. Tarbell, *The Life of Abraham Lincoln* (New York: Lincoln Memorial Association), p. 423.

12. *Ibid.*, p. 276.

13. *Ibid.*

14. See E.B. Long and Barbara Long.

15. David Herbert Donald apparently places the meeting with Republican Senators and the straw poll at Willard's Hotel. See David Herbert Donald, *Lincoln* (London: Jonathan Cape, 1995), at page 281. In *Days of Defiance* at page 278 Maury Klein places the meeting at the Capitol.

16. The source for the information on the members of the Supreme Court is Kermit L. Hall, *The Oxford Companion to the Supreme Court of the United States* (New York: Oxford University Press, 1992).

17. Stephen B. Oates, *With Malice Toward None: A Life of Abraham Lincoln* (New York: HarperPerennial, 1994), pp. 213–214.

18. David Detzer, *Allegiance: Fort Sumter, Charleston, and the Beginning of the Civil War* (San Diego: Harvest, 2001), p. 212.

19. *Ibid.*

20. Albert Shaw, *Abraham Lincoln: The Year of His Election* (New York: Review of Reviews, 1929), p. 263.

21. Donald, p. 280.

22. Klein, p. 277.

23. Roy P. Basler, editor, *The Collected Works of Abraham Lincoln,* (New Brunswick, New Jersey: Rutgers University Press, 1953), quoting the New York *Herald*, February 28, 1861.

24. Oates, p. 214.

25. Donald, p. 280.

26. *Ibid.*

27. Basler, p. 247, quoting the New York *Herald* of March 1, 1861.

28. Klein, p. 275.

29. *Ibid.*, p. 282.

30. David M. Potter, *Lincoln and His Party in the Secession Crisis* (New Haven: Yale University Press, 1942), pp. 310–312.

31. Miers and Powell, 1861 section, p. 24.

32. Ward, Geoffrey C., Ric Burns and Ken Burns, *The Civil War* (New York: Alfred A. Knopf, 1990), p. 33.

33. John C. Waugh, *Reelecting Lincoln: The Battle for the 1864 Presidency* (New York: Da Capo, 1997), p. 33.

2. Albert Shaw, *Abraham Lincoln: The Year of His Election* (New York: Review of Reviews, 1929), p. 265.

3. Holt was originally Buchanan's postmaster general and became secretary of war in 1858. A Kentuckian, he remained loyal to the Union after the war started, and Lincoln rewarded him by appointing his as the country's first judge advocate general of the Army in 1862. He successfully prosecuted the Lincoln assassins in June 1865.

4. Baker and Pearce, along with Senator Solomon Foot, comprised the Senate Committee of Arrangements for the Inauguration ceremony.

5. Information regarding the ceremony from Joseph Bucklin Bishop, *Our Political Drama* (New York: Scott-Thaw Co., 1904) and *An American Time Capsule: Three Centuries of Broadsides and Other Printed Ephemera.*

6. Paul M. Angle, editor, *The Lincoln Reader* (New Brunswick, New Jersey: Rutgers University Press, 1947), p. 334.

7. *Ibid.*, p. 336.

8. Harold Holzer, editor, *Abraham Lincoln As I Knew Him: Gossip, Tributes and Revelations from His Best Friends and Worst Enemies* (Chapel Hill, North Carolina: Algonquin, 1999), p. 110.

9. Carl Sandburg, *Abraham Lincoln: The War Years* (New York: Dell, 1954), p. 186.

10. Roy P. Basler, editor, *The Collected Works of Abraham Lincoln* (New Brunswick, New Jersey: Rutgers University Press, 1953), pp. 262–271

11. Holzer, p. 110.

12. Stephen B. Oates, *With Malice Toward None: A Life of Abraham Lincoln* (New York: HarperPerennial, 1994), p. 219.

13. Buchanan first went to the home of a friend, Senator Robert Ould of Virginia. William K. Klingaman, *Abraham Lincoln and the Road to Emancipation* (New York: Viking, 2001), p. 34.

14. Harold Holzer, *Dear Mr. Lincoln: Letters to the President* (Reading, Massachusetts: Addison-Wesley, 1994), pp. 8, 9.

15. Basler, p. 272.

16. Sandburg, p. 188.

17. Michael Burlingame, editor, *Lincoln's Journalist: John Hay's Anonymous Writings for the Press, 1860–1864* (Carbondale: Southern Illinois University Press), p. 47.

18. *Ibid.*, p. 50.

Chapter 13

1. Russell F. Weigley, *A Great Civil War: A Military and Political History, 1861–1865* (Bloomington: University of Indiana Press, 2000), p. 10.

Bibliography

Ambrose, Stephen E. *Nothing Like It in the World: The Men Who Built the Transcontinental Railroad, 1863–1869*. New York: Simon & Schuster, 2000.

Anderson, David D. *Abraham Lincoln*. Boston: Twayne, 1970.

Angle, Paul M. *Abraham Lincoln: An Authentic Story of His Life*. Springfield, Illinois: Springfield Life Insurance Company, 1926.

_____. *"Here I Have Lived": A History of Lincoln's Springfield, 1821–1865*. Springfield, Illinois: Abraham Lincoln Association, 1935.

_____, editor. *The Lincoln Reader*. New Brunswick, New Jersey: Rutgers University Press, 1947.

Baker, Jean. *Mary Todd Lincoln: A Biography*. New York: W.W. Norton, 1987.

Barringer, William. *A House Dividing*. Springfield, Illinois: Abraham Lincoln Association, 1945.

Burrows, Edwin G., and Mike Wallace. *Gotham: A History of New York City to 1898*. New York: Oxford University Press, 1999.

Catton, Bruce. *The American Heritage New History of the Civil War*. New York: Metrobooks, 2001.

Charnwood, Lord. *Abraham Lincoln*. Garden City, New York: Doubleday, 1938.

Coolidge, Olivia. *The Apprenticeship of Abraham Lincoln*. New York: Scribner's, 1974.

Cooper, Jr., William J. *Jefferson Davis, American*. New York: Vintage, 2001.

Cuomo, Mario M., and Harold Holzer, editors. *Lincoln on Democracy: His Own Words, with Essays by America's Foremost Historians*. New York: HarperPerennial, 1991.

Current, Richard N. *Lincoln and the First Shot*. Philadelphia: J.P. Lippincott, 1963.

_____. *The Lincoln Nobody Knows*. New York: McGraw-Hill, 1958.

Davenport, Don. *In Lincoln's Footsteps: A Historical Guide to the Lincoln Sites in Illinois, Indiana, and Kentucky*. Madison, Wisconsin: Prairie Oak, 1991.

Davis, William C. *"A Government of Our Own": The Making of the Confederacy*. Baton Rouge: Louisiana State University Press, 1994.

_____, editor. *The Civil War: Brother Against Brother*. Alexandria, Virginia: Time-Life Books, 1983.

de Borchgrave, Alexandra Villard, and John Cullen. *Villard: The Life and Times of an American Titan*. New York: Doubleday, 2001.

Detzer, David. *Allegiance: Fort Sumter, Charleston, and the Beginning of the Civil War*. San Diego: Harvest, 2001.

Donald, David Herbert. *Lincoln*. London: Jonathan Cape, 1995.

_____. *Lincoln at Home: Two Glimpses of Abraham Lincoln's Family Life*. New York: Simon & Schuster, 1999.

_____. *Lincoln's Herndon*. New York: Alfred A. Knopf, 1948.

_____. *"We Are Lincoln Men": Abraham Lincoln and His Friends*. New York: Simon & Schuster, 2003.

Dyba, Thomas J., and George L. Painter. *Seventeen Years at Eighth and Jackson: The Lincoln Family in Their Springfield Home*. Lisle, Illinois: Illinois Benedictine College Publications, 1985.

Fehrenbacher, Don E., and Fehrenbacher, Virginia, editors. *Recollected Words of Abraham Lincoln*. Stanford: Stanford University Press, 1996.

Foner, Eric. *Free Soil, Free Labor, Free Men: The Ideology of the Republican Party Before the Civil War*. New York: Oxford University Press, 1995.

Foote, Shelby. *The Civil War: A Narrative*. New York: Vintage, 1958.

Garrison, Webb. *Lincoln's Little War*. Nashville: Rutledge Hill, 1997.

Greeley, Horace. *The American Conflict: A History of the Great Rebellion of the United States of America, 1860–1864.* Hartford: O.D. Case, 1864.

Hall, Kermit L., editor. *The Oxford Companion to the Supreme Court of the United States.* New York: Oxford University Press, 1992

Hamlin, Charles Eugene. *The Life and Times of Hannibal Hamlin.* Cambridge, Massachusetts: Riverside Press.

Harper, Robert S. *"During Two Journeys."* Columbus: Ohio Lincoln Sesquicentennial Committee, Ohio State Museum, 1959.

_____. *Lincoln and the Press.* New York: McGraw-Hill, 1951.

Hay, John. *Lincoln's Journalist: John Hay's Anonymous Writings for the Press, 1860–1864.* Ed. Michael Burlingame. Carbondale: Southern Illinois University Press, 1997.

_____, and John R. Turner Ettlinger, editors. *Inside Lincoln's White House: The Complete Civil War Diary of John Hay.* Carbondale: Southern Illinois University Press, 1997.

Herndon, William Henry. *Herndon's Life of Lincoln.* New York: Da Capo, 1983.

Hertz, Emanuel, editor. *Lincoln Talks: An Oral Biography.* New York: Viking, 1939.

Holt, Michael F. *The Rise and Fall of the American Whig Party: Jacksonian Politics and the Onset of the Civil War.* New York: Oxford University Press, 1999.

Holzer, Harold. *Witness to War: The Civil War, 1861–1865.* New York: Perigee, 1996.

_____, editor. *Dear Mr. Lincoln: Letters to the President.* Reading, Massachusetts: Addison-Wesley, 2003.

_____, editor. *Lincoln as I Knew Him: Gossip, Tributes, and Revelations from His Best Friends and Worst Enemies.* Chapel Hill, North Carolina: Algonquin,1999.

Hunt, H. Draper. *Hannibal Hamlin of Maine: Lincoln's First Vice-President.* Syracuse, New York: Syracuse University Press, 1969.

Jaffa, Harry V. *A New Birth of Freedom: Abraham Lincoln and the Coming of the Civil War.* Lanham, Maryland: Rowman & Littlefield, 2000.

Johnson, William J. *Abraham Lincoln the Christian.* New York: Eaton & Mains, 1913.

Klein, Maury. *Days of Defiance: Sumter, Secession, and the Coming of the Civil War.* New York: Vintage, 1999.

Klingaman, William K. *Abraham Lincoln and the Road to Emancipation, 1861–1865.* New York: Viking, 2001.

Kunhardt, Dorothy Meserve, and Philip B.

Kunhardt, Jr. *Twenty Days.* New York: Castle, 1993.

Kunhardt, Philip B., Jr., Philip B. Kunhardt III and Peter W. Kunhardt. *Lincoln: An Illustrated Biography.* New York: Alfred A. Knopf, 1991.

_____, _____ and _____. *P.T. Barnum: America's Greatest Showman.* New York: Alfred A. Knopf, 1995.

Lamon, Ward Hill. *Recollections of Abraham Lincoln, 1847–1865.* A.C. McClury, 1895; reprint, Lincoln: University of Nebraska Press, 1994.

Lincoln, Abraham. *Abraham Lincoln: Speeches and Writings, 1859–1865.* Eds. Don E. Fehrenbacher and Virginia Fehrenbacher. New York: Library of America, 1984.

_____. *The Collected Works of Abraham Lincoln.* Ed. Roy P. Basler. New Brunswick, New Jersey: Rutgers University Press, 1953.

_____. *The Life and Writings of Abraham Lincoln.* Ed. Philip Van Doren Stern. New York: Random House, 1940.

Long, E.B., and Barbara Long. *The Civil War Day by Day: An Almanac 1861–1865.* Garden City, New York: Doubleday, 1971.

Loving, Jerome. *Walt Whitman: The Song of Himself.* Berkeley: University of California Press, 1999.

Mackay, James. *Allan Pinkerton: The Eye Who Never Slept.* Edinburgh: Mainstream, 1996.

McPherson, James M. *Battle Cry of Freedom: The Civil War Era.* New York: Oxford University Press, 1988.

Mearns, David C. *The Lincoln Papers.* Garden City, New York: Doubleday, 1948.

Miers, Earl Schenck, and C. Percy Powell, editors. *Lincoln Day by Day: A Chronology: 1809–1865.* Dayton, Ohio: Morningside, 1991.

Miller, William Lee. *Lincoln's Virtues: An Ethical Biography.* New York: Alfred A. Knopf, 2002.

Mitgang, Herbert. *Abraham Lincoln: A Press Portrait.* New York: Fordham University Press, 2000.

_____, editor. *Lincoln As They Saw Him.* Toronto: Clarke, Irwin, 1956.

Morris, Jr., Roy. *The Better Angel: Walt Whitman in the Civil War.* New York: Oxford University Press, 2000.

Morrow, Honore. *Great Captain.* New York: William Morrow, 1927.

Neely, Mark E., Jr. *The Abraham Lincoln Encyclopedia.* New York: McGraw-Hill, 1982.

_____. *The Last Best Hope of Earth: Abraham Lincoln and the Promise of America.* Cambridge, Massachusetts: Harvard University Press, 1993.

_____, and R. Gerald McMurtry. *The Insanity File: The Case of Mary Todd Lincoln.* Carbondale: Southern Illinois University Press, 1986.

Nevins, Allan. *The Emergence of Lincoln.* New York: Scribner's, 1950.

Newman, Ralph G., editor. *Lincoln for the Ages.* Garden City, New York: Doubleday, 1960.

Nicolay, John G. *The Outbreak of Rebellion.* New York: Da Capo, 1995.

Nofi, Albert A. *The Civil War Notebook.* Conshohocken, Pennsylvania: Combined Books, 1993.

Oates, Stephen B. *The Approaching Fury: Voices of the Storm, 1820–1861.* New York: Harper-Perennial, 1996.

_____. *With Malice Toward None: A Life of Abraham Lincoln.* New York: HarperPerennial, 1994.

Paludan, Phillip Shaw. *The Presidency of Abraham Lincoln.* Lawrence: University Press of Kansas, 1994.

Potter, David M. *Lincoln and His Party in the Secession Crisis.* New Haven: Yale University Press, 1942.

Randall, J.G. *Lincoln the President.* New York: Dodd, Mead, 1945.

Randall, Ruth Painter. *Mary Lincoln: Biography of a Marriage.* Boston: Little, Brown, 1953.

Robinson, Luther E. *Ephraim Elmer Ellsworth: First Martyr of the Civil War.* Springfield: Illinois State Historical Society, 1923.

Sandburg, Carl. *Abraham Lincoln: The Prairie Years and the War Years, 1809–1865.* New York: Dell, 1954.

_____. *Mary Lincoln: Wife and Widow.* New York: Harcourt, Brace, 1932.

Schurz, Carl. *Intimate Letters of Carl Schurz, 1841–1869.* Ed. Joseph Schafer. Madison, Wisconsin: 1928).

Searcher, Victor. *Lincoln's Journey to Greatness: A Factual Account of the Twelve-Day Inaugural Trip.* Philadelphia: John C. Winston, 1963.

Shaw, Albert. *Abraham Lincoln: The Year of His Election.* New York: Review of Reviews, 1929.

Stevens, Walter B. *A Reporter's Lincoln.* Lincoln: University of Nebraska Press, 1998.

Strozier, Charles B. *Lincoln's Quest for Union: Public and Private Meanings.* Urbana: University of Illinois Press, 1987.

Tarbell, Ida M. *The Life of Abraham Lincoln.* New York: Lincoln Memorial Association.

Thomas, Benjamin P. *Abraham Lincoln: A Biography.* New York: Alfred A. Knopf, 1952.

Turner, Justin G., and Linda Levitt Turner. *Mary Todd Lincoln: Her Life and Letters.* New York: Alfred A. Knopf, 1972.

Van Deusen, Glyndon G. *William Henry Seward.* New York: Oxford University Press, 1967.

Villard, Henry. *Lincoln on the Eve of '61: A Journalist's Story,* edited by Harold G. Villard and Oswald Garrison Villard. New York: Alfred A. Knopf, 1941.

_____. *Memoirs of Henry Villard: Journalist and Financier, 1835–1900.* Boston: Houghton Mifflin, 1904.

Walsh, John Evangelist. *The Shadows Rise: Abraham Lincoln and the Ann Rutledge Legend.* Urbana: University of Illinois Press, 1993.

Ward, Geoffrey C., Ric Burns and Ken Burns. *The Civil War.* New York: Alfred A. Knopf, 1990.

Waugh, John C. *Reelecting Lincoln: The Battle for the 1864 Presidency.* New York: Da Capo Press, 1997.

Weed, Thurlow. *The Autobiography of Thurlow Weed.* Edited by Harriet A. Weed. Boston: Houghton Mifflin, 1883.

Weigley, Russell F. *A Great Civil War: A Military and Political History, 1861–1865.* Bloomington: University of Indiana Press, 2000.

Wellman, Paul I. *The House Divides: The Age of Jackson and Lincoln, from the War of 1812 to the Civil War.* Garden City, New York: Doubleday, 1966.

Wilson, Douglas L. *Honor's Voice: The Transformation of Abraham Lincoln.* New York: Alfred A. Knopf, 1998.

_____. *Lincoln Before Washington: New Perspectives on the Illinois Years.* Urbana: University of Illinois Press, 1997.

_____, and Rodney O. Davis, editors. *Herndon's Informants: Letters, Interviews, and Statements about Abraham Lincoln.* Urbana, Illinois: University of Illinois Press, 1998.

Wilson, Rufus Rockwell. *Lincoln in Caricature.* New York: Horizon, 1953.

Winkle, Kenneth J. *The Young Eagle: The Rise of Abraham Lincoln.* Dallas: Taylor, 2001.

Woldman, Albert A. *Lawyer Lincoln.* New York: Carroll & Graf, 1994.

Index

225